Records Management

Tenth Edition

Judith Read

Adjunct Faculty
Computer Applications and Office Systems
Portland Community College
Portland, Oregon

Mary Lea Ginn, PhD

Director, International Learner Services and Institutional Review Board
Cincinnati, Ohio

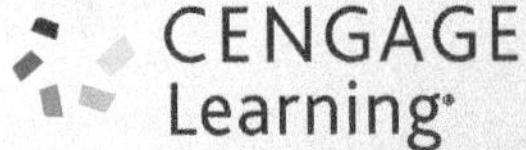

Australia • Brazil • Mexico • Singapore • United Kingdom • United States

Records Management, Tenth Edition
Judith Read, Mary Lea Ginn

Senior Vice President, GM Skills & Global Product: Dawn Gerrain

Product Manager: Paul Lamond

Senior Director, Development-Career and Computing: Marah Bellegarde

Senior Product Development Manager: Larry Main

Senior Content Developer: Anne Orgren

Senior Product Assistant: Diane Chrysler

Senior Marketing Manager: Eric La Scola

Senior Production Director: Wendy Troeger

Production Director: Andrew Crouth

Senior Content Project Manager: Betty Dickson

Managing Art Director: Jack Pendleton

Software Development Manager: Pavan Ethakota

Cover image(s): ©LeonART/Shutterstock.com, ©LeonART/Shutterstock.com, ©iStockPhoto.com/baranozdemir, ©iStockPhoto.com/mbortolino, ©iStockPhoto.com/PixHouse, ©iStockPhoto.com/youngvet

Library of Congress Control Number: 2014946856

ISBN: 978-1-305-11916-1

Cengage Learning
20 Channel Center Street
Boston, MA 02210
USA

Cengage Learning is a leading provider of customized learning solutions with office locations around the globe, including Singapore, the United Kingdom, Australia, Mexico, Brazil, and Japan. Locate your local office at: **www.cengage.com/global**

Cengage Learning products are represented in Canada by Nelson Education, Ltd.

To learn more about Cengage Learning, visit **www.cengage.com**

Purchase any of our products at your local college store or at our preferred online store **www.cengagebrain.com**

Printed in the United States of America
Print Number: 04 Print Year: 2017

PREFACE

***Records Management*, Tenth Edition,** is a strong introduction to the increasingly comprehensive field of records and information management. The following factors contribute to today's state of flux in records and information management:

- Continued growth of new information at a rapid rate
- The pace of technological changes
- New laws and regulations
- New risks with security breaches, data lost or misused, and legal e-discovery
- New records formats as business processes are amended and streamlined

This edition emphasizes principles and practices of effective records and information management for physical and electronic records systems. This approach offers practical information to students as well as to professionals at managerial, supervisory, and operating levels. Emphasis is placed on the need to understand the changes occurring with the volume of information, the need for compliance to government regulations, and advances in technology.

Records Management may be used for short courses or seminars emphasizing filing systems or for longer courses such as quarter or semester plans. Basic physical systems concepts and the concepts needed for understanding electronic records storage and retrieval methods are discussed and applied.

As a reference book, this latest edition of ***Records Management*** serves several purposes. It presents sound principles of records and information management that include the entire range of records—physical (paper), image, and electronic media used in computerized systems. Professionals who direct the operation of records systems will find this edition to be valuable because the rules in the textbook agree with the latest standard filing guidelines presented by ARMA International.

ORGANIZATION

Records Management is designed for easy reading and maximum retention. The text is organized in three parts:

Part I Records and Information Management

- Chapters 1 and 2 introduce the student to the expanding area of records and information management (RIM) as well as the environment in which RIM lives.
- Chapters 3–7 center on alphabetic storage and retrieval methods for physical and electronic systems and transferring records from active to inactive storage.
- Chapters 8–10 adapt the alphabetic storage and retrieval method to subject, numeric, and geographic storage methods.

Part II Electronic Records Management

- Chapter 11, formerly Chapter 5, introduces electronic records file management as well as classifying electronic files using metadata, taxonomies, and file plans. Database elements, how to find information in a database, and using databases in RIM and e-commerce are also discussed.
- Chapter 12 provides a thorough discussion of magnetic, optical, and solid state media through the phases of the records management life cycle. Using micrographics is discussed.
- Chapter 13 (new to this edition) introduces enterprise content management (ECM) describing how Microsoft® SharePoint® is used. Four business processes are described.

Part III RIM Program Administration

- Chapter 14, formerly Chapter 12, is reorganized with additional information on governance and social media sections. Details about the records and information manager's responsibilities are also included. In this chapter, students learn about enterprise content management, storing records in the cloud, SharePoint®, and how to determine whether a record is a record, a nonrecord, or a work in progress. Additionally, students will also learn about how three different businesses manage their records.

NEW TO THIS EDITION

- A **new chapter** has been added: Chapter 13, Electronic Records Management Tools and Processes. This chapter introduces enterprise content management and describes how Microsoft® SharePoint® is used.
- All chapters have been thoroughly updated to reflect changes in the field, including new discussions of metadata, managing information on mobile devices, and bring your own device (BYOD) policies. Additionally, the coverage of information governance, social media and social media policies, and the duties and responsibilities of a RIM manager has been expanded.
- Chapters have been reorganized, adding a unit structure and consolidating the electronic records management chapters.
- Chapter 1 is now separated into two shorter chapters: Records and Information Management and The RIM Environment.
- On The Job profiles have been updated, with seven new interviewees, including SharePoint and electronic recordkeeping expert Bruce Miller.

CHAPTER FEATURES

Learning Tools

- **Learning Objectives** highlight each chapter's major concepts.
- **Glossary terms** and definitions appear in the margin.
- **Margin notes** help students reflect on key content.

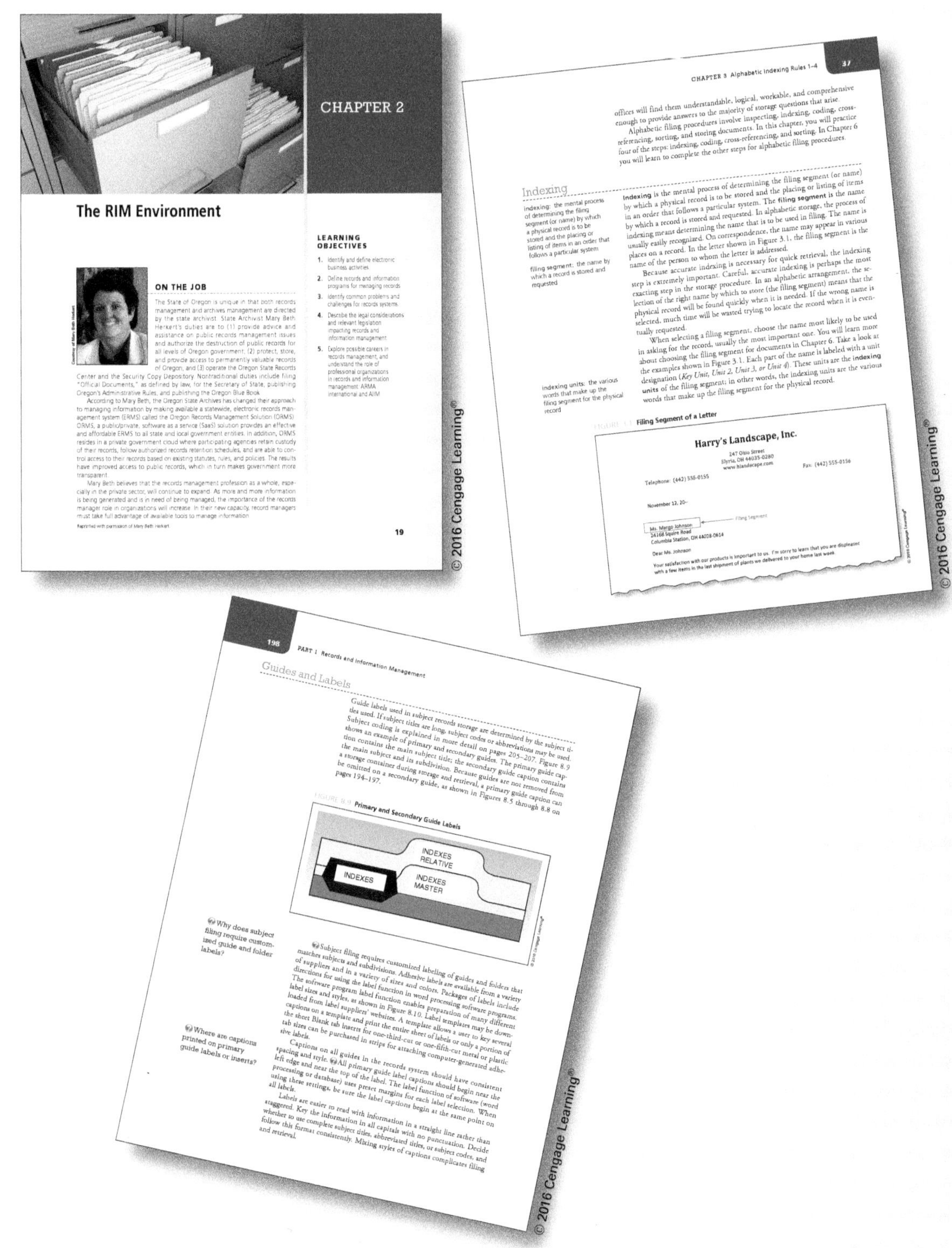

Special Sections

- **Career Corner** job descriptions of careers in records management give students a preview of potential career paths and requirements.
- **Records Management in Action** case studies give real-life examples of records management topics.
- **My Records** tips bring home chapter concepts with suggestions for managing personal records.
- **On the Job** interviews with professionals in the field add relevancy to the concepts.

Do not rely on memory to determine the subject under which a record should be stored. Consult the master or relative index to be sure that you have selected and coded the filing segment correctly.

Why would using subject codes save coding time?

Coding in an alphabetic subject filing system may include an entire subject title such as PURCHASING. However, abbreviations can simplify coding in a large, complex subject filing system because writing subjects on records, especially subjects of more than one word, can be done much quicker with abbreviated subject codes. Create an abbreviation with the first alphabetic character of the subject title followed by the next one or two consonants such as PRC for PURCHASING, or use the first character of each word in a multiple-word subject heading such as RRS for RECORDS RETENTION SCHEDULE. Because the codes may consist of as many as six characters, PRCH may be more easily remembered for PURCHASING than PRC. Consistency is essential when developing a subject code system in which two- to six-character abbreviations are used. Everyone using the system must understand the codes and how to develop new ones when necessary. If abbreviations are used, the master index should show codes as well as complete subject titles. Be sure to write subject letter codes on each record, and include them on individual folder label captions, along with the subject title.

CAREER CORNER

Human Resources Records Administrator

The following job description is an example of a career opportunity in a manufacturing company.

GENERAL INFORMATION

The records administrator manages employee-related files such as medical, vacation, discipline, and performance review records.

RESPONSIBILITIES

- Ensure that employee file requests have proper authorization.
- Implement and maintain standard employee folder organization.
- File and retrieve all employee-related records.
- Comply with the company's records retention schedule for human resources records.
- Produce periodic statistical reports of employee demographic information.

EXPERIENCE AND EDUCATION

- High school diploma or equivalent
- Two to three years' administrative experience
- Excellent verbal and written communication skills
- Ability to properly handle confidential and sensitive information
- Strong attention to detail and organization
- Strong database software and report writing experience

Electronic Records

electronic record: a record stored on electronic media that can be readily accessed or changed

An **electronic record** is a record stored on electronic media that can be readily accessed or changed. A piece of equipment is required to view and read or listen to electronic records. With the development and use of application software on personal computers, e-mall, letters, memos, and reports are created electronically; however, the original purpose of these systems was to facilitate the creation of physical records. As technology has advanced, true electronic records are in use today, that is, records created, distributed, used, and stored in electronic form. The contents of these records are accessible by machine or by querying a database.

The challenge for the records manager is to ensure that all records are what they appear to be. The ARMA Generally Accepted Recordkeeping Principles® introduced in Chapter 2 define parameters for records and information management. Increases in fraud and theft of electronic records have left records and information managers desperate to ensure the safety and security of the organization's valuable resources.

To that end, each person responsible for electronic records follows the records management storage and retrieval procedures set up for the organization. Consistently following procedures helps protect the company in legal actions. The same benefits of following proper records management procedures for physical records also apply to electronic records: the information is available at the right time to help make effective decisions.

RECORDS MANAGEMENT IN ACTION

E-Discovery Costs Can Damage Business Profitability

As businesses create more and more electronic records, the costs of identifying and retrieving relevant information due to a lawsuit can severely impact the profitability of the company. For example, when the roofs of three airplane hangars collapsed due to heavy snow and ice and crushed 18 private jets, the aviation company that owned the hangers had to retain 8,000 gigabytes of electronic documents. Approximately 2 million electronic documents might have contained information pertinent to the multiple lawsuits that were filed. These documents had to be sifted through for possible liability for the roof collapses. The estimated cost for attorneys to read and manually review the documents was $1.00 each.

Fortunately, the court gave permission for the company to use a computer program that uses *predictive coding* to sort through the documents for keywords or elements. As a result, the number of documents that had to be manually reviewed was reduced to about 10 percent of the original number.

This example illustrates that even with the assistance of computer programs, E-Discovery can still be a very expensive process for businesses that are subject to legal action. In addition, recent court rulings have sided with plaintiffs, agreeing that keywords used in searching for relevant documents may be disclosed. This ruling could lead to additional litigation and costs to the business if the initial search is determined to be inadequate.

Source: Joe Palazzolo. "Why Hire a Lawyer? Computers Are Cheaper," *The Wall Street Journal*, June 18, 2012; Ralph Losey, e-Discovery Team website, http://e-discoveryteam.com/2013/10/06/party-ordered-to-disclose-where-and-how-it-searched-for-esi-you-can-expect-this-kind-of-order-to-become-commonplace/, accessed October 23, 2013.

MY RECORDS

Do You Know Where Your Records Are?

Think quickly—where is your birth certificate? Where is the title of your car?

If you are like most people, you might not know exactly where your important records are. Do you know where you keep each of these records?		
• Birth certificate • Marriage license • Marriage certificate • Passport • Diploma • Auto loan documents • Auto insurance policy • Life insurance policy • Property deeds • Mortgage loan documents	• Tax returns for previous years • Will or trust documents • Automobile title • Renter's or homeowner's insurance policy • Rental or lease agreement • Divorce decree • Adoption or naturalization papers	• Military discharge papers • Vaccination records for all family members • Medical histories for all family members • Pay stubs from current and previous jobs • Stock purchases and other investment records
Each record listed above is either vital or important. What degree of protection have you provided for each record? Are your records in a fire-resistant container or in a safe deposit box? Follow these suggestions for keeping your vital and important records safe:		
• Identify a single location to store all vital papers and information related to your financial transactions. • Create copies of your vital records. Some of the copies may need to be certified as official copies. • Put important original documents in plastic sheet protectors to protect and easily identify them.	• Notify family members or friends not living with you where important information will be located if disaster strikes. • Inventory the records you and/or your financial institutions keep only on computers. Include account numbers and passwords on your inventory. Keep the inventory safe.	• Make backups of your computer records. If possible, store the backups at another location. • Once a month, update your stored information. Has anything changed? Make another backup.

By knowing the meaning and importance of each part of the entire records life cycle, you will be able to understand what is needed to manage all records—both physical and electronic.

RECORDS FORMATS

As you have learned from the examples at the beginning of the chapter, a record can be physical or electronic. The next section addresses the importance of physical or paper records. After physical records, electronic records formats are identified and discussed.

CHAPTER 3

Alphabetic Indexing Rules 1–4

LEARNING OBJECTIVES

1. Explain the need for indexing rules in alphabetic storage of records and the importance of following these rules consistently.
2. Index, code, and arrange personal and business names in indexing order of units.
3. Index, code, and arrange minor words and symbols in business names.
4. Index, code, and arrange names with punctuation and possessives.
5. Index, code, and arrange names with single letters and abbreviations.
6. Apply alphabetic filing procedures.
7. Prepare and arrange cross-references for personal and business names.
8. Sort personal and business names.
9. Find information in database records.

Photo © Judith Read

ON THE JOB

Andrew Penta is the Records Officer for Clark County in southwest Washington. Andrew is the county liaison with Washington State Archives for permanent and historic records and also serves as the Oregon ARMA president. Andrew is a certified records manager (CRM). Andrew's road to his current job included being in the right place at the right time; he liked working with records. His people skills, management skills, and RIM background, as well as his CRM credential, help him enjoy his career.

Currently, Andrew manages the centralized inactive records storage facility for Clark County. The facility holds over 20,000 cubic feet of law and justice, financial, and administrative records. Andrew is responsible for record maintenance, updating and applying a legally defensible retention schedule, and coordinating records disposition. In addition, Andrew supervises the microfilming and digital scanning within an imaging system that contains 4 million pages of records.

Andrew's advice to students is to give themselves a head start in the records management field through formal education. Andrew encourages all people, at any stage of their career—but especially students and younger workers—to pursue coursework, or at least independent study, for the strongest chance of success. He believes that the best part of obtaining a CRM credential is that you must continue your education to maintain it. This provides extra motivation to keep learning—and there is so much to study. To illustrate Andrew's dedication to the records management profession, he is studying to be become a certified document imaging architect. In general, students should complete business technology and record management courses as well as library or archival science courses. Computer science or IT courses are also useful for record managers.

Microsoft® Access Activities

- Microsoft® Access activities, included throughout the text and in the "**Records Management Simulation**", give students practice in using a database for records management. In the textbook, an Access Activity icon identifies applications that utilize Microsoft® Access.

Data Files

Data File

Students use data files (provided on the companion website for this book) to complete self-check activities in Chapters 3–5 and end-of-chapter applications in all chapters. Because an understanding of the hierarchy of our government is helpful when applying alphabetic indexing rules to government names, a file that provides an overview of government structures is also included. In the textbook, a data files icon identifies applications that require data files. Students will download, unzip, and use the data files in practical applications of electronic records management.

Self-Check Activities

Self-check activities throughout Chapters 3–5 offer students the opportunity to practice applying each filing rule immediately after reading about it in the text.

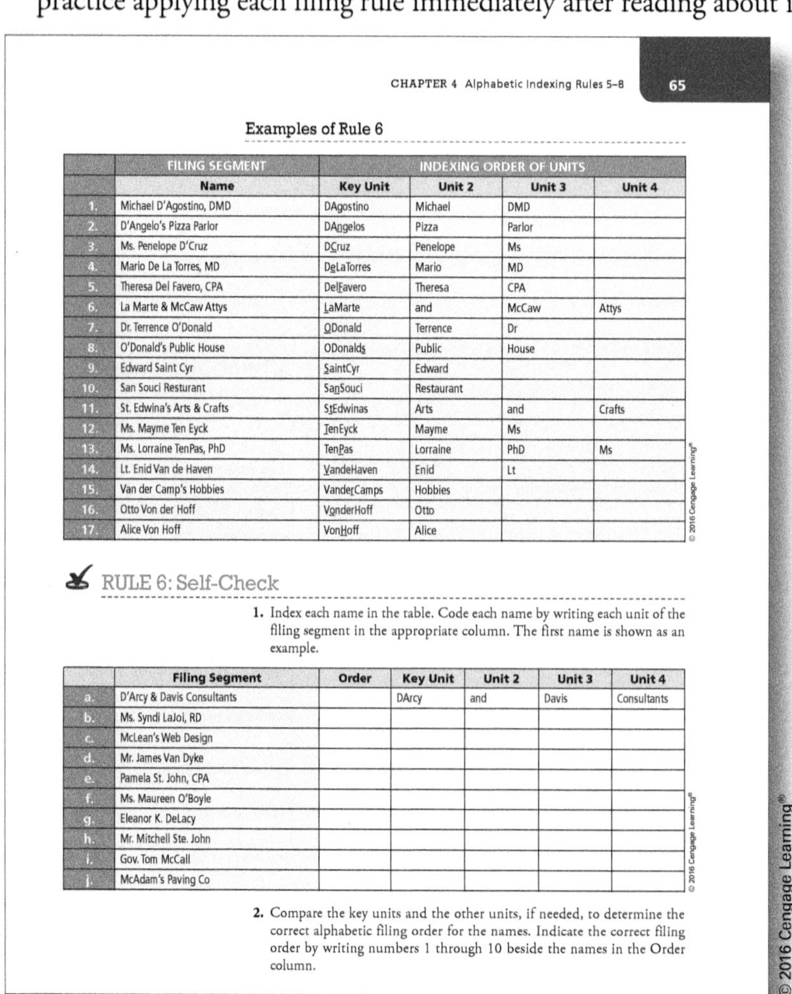

CHAPTER 4 Alphabetic Indexing Rules 5–8 65

Examples of Rule 6

	FILING SEGMENT	INDEXING ORDER OF UNITS			
	Name	Key Unit	Unit 2	Unit 3	Unit 4
1.	Michael D'Agostino, DMD	DAgostino	Michael	DMD	
2.	D'Angelo's Pizza Parlor	DAngelos	Pizza	Parlor	
3.	Ms. Penelope D'Cruz	DCruz	Penelope	Ms	
4.	Mario De La Torres, MD	DeLaTorres	Mario	MD	
5.	Theresa Del Favero, CPA	DelFavero	Theresa	CPA	
6.	La Marte & McCaw Attys	LaMarte	and	McCaw	Attys
7.	Dr. Terrence O'Donald	ODonald	Terrence	Dr	
8.	O'Donald's Public House	ODonalds	Public	House	
9.	Edward Saint Cyr	SaintCyr	Edward		
10.	San Souci Resturant	SanSouci	Restaurant		
11.	St. Edwina's Arts & Crafts	StEdwinas	Arts	and	Crafts
12.	Ms. Mayme Ten Eyck	TenEyck	Mayme	Ms	
13.	Ms. Lorraine TenPas, PhD	TenPas	Lorraine	PhD	Ms
14.	Lt. Enid Van de Haven	VandeHaven	Enid	Lt	
15.	Van der Camp's Hobbies	VanderCamps	Hobbies		
16.	Otto Von der Hoff	VonderHoff	Otto		
17.	Alice Von Hoff	VonHoff	Alice		

RULE 6: Self-Check

1. Index each name in the table. Code each name by writing each unit of the filing segment in the appropriate column. The first name is shown as an example.

	Filing Segment	Order	Key Unit	Unit 2	Unit 3	Unit 4
a.	D'Arcy & Davis Consultants		DArcy	and	Davis	Consultants
b.	Ms. Syndi LaJoi, RD					
c.	McLean's Web Design					
d.	Mr. James Van Dyke					
e.	Pamela St. John, CPA					
f.	Ms. Maureen O'Boyle					
g.	Eleanor K. DeLacy					
h.	Mr. Mitchell Ste. John					
i.	Gov. Tom McCall					
j.	McAdam's Paving Co					

2. Compare the key units and the other units, if needed, to determine the correct alphabetic filing order for the names. Indicate the correct filing order by writing numbers 1 through 10 beside the names in the Order column.

End-of-Chapter Review

- **Key Points** and **Terms** lists remind students of important chapter concepts and terminology.
- **Review and Discuss** questions and activities guide reflection on the learning objectives.
- **Applications** put chapter concepts to use in practical exercises.

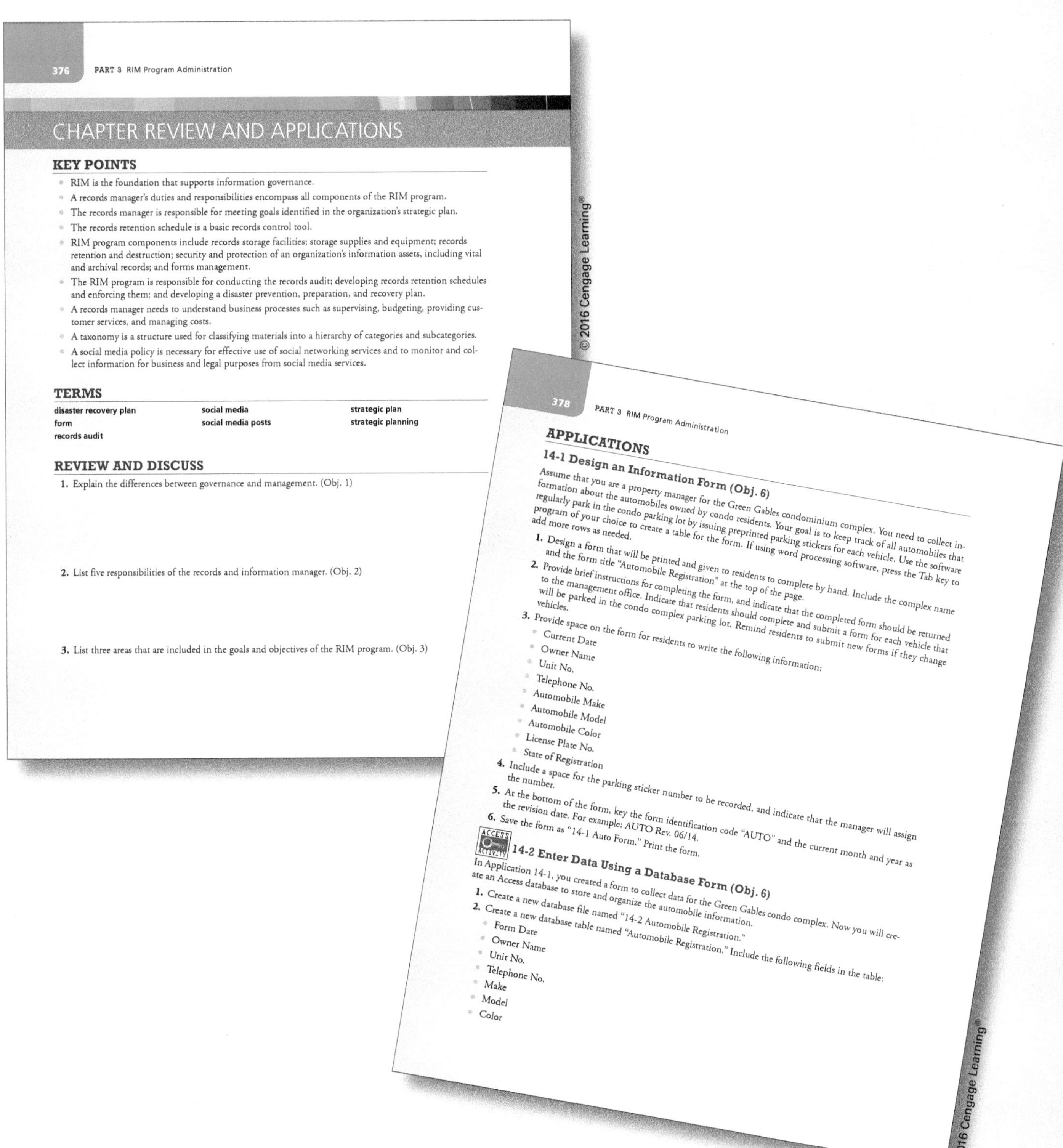

376 PART 3 RIM Program Administration

CHAPTER REVIEW AND APPLICATIONS

KEY POINTS

- RIM is the foundation that supports information governance.
- A records manager's duties and responsibilities encompass all components of the RIM program.
- The records manager is responsible for meeting goals identified in the organization's strategic plan.
- The records retention schedule is a basic records control tool.
- RIM program components include records storage facilities; storage supplies and equipment; records retention and destruction; security and protection of an organization's information assets, including vital and archival records; and forms management.
- The RIM program is responsible for conducting the records audit; developing records retention schedules and enforcing them; and developing a disaster prevention, preparation, and recovery plan.
- A records manager needs to understand business processes such as supervising, budgeting, providing customer services, and managing costs.
- A taxonomy is a structure used for classifying materials into a hierarchy of categories and subcategories.
- A social media policy is necessary for effective use of social networking services and to monitor and collect information for business and legal purposes from social media services.

TERMS

disaster recovery plan	social media	strategic plan
form	social media posts	strategic planning
records audit		

REVIEW AND DISCUSS

1. Explain the differences between governance and management. (Obj. 1)
2. List five responsibilities of the records and information manager. (Obj. 2)
3. List three areas that are included in the goals and objectives of the RIM program. (Obj. 3)

378 PART 3 RIM Program Administration

APPLICATIONS

14-1 Design an Information Form (Obj. 6)

Assume that you are a property manager for the Green Gables condominium complex. You need to collect information about the automobiles owned by condo residents. Your goal is to keep track of all automobiles that regularly park in the condo parking lot by issuing preprinted parking stickers for each vehicle. Use the software program of your choice to create a table for the form. If using word processing software, press the Tab key to add more rows as needed.

1. Design a form that will be printed and given to residents to complete by hand. Include the complex name and the form title "Automobile Registration" at the top of the page.
2. Provide brief instructions for completing the form, and indicate that the completed form should be returned to the management office. Indicate that residents should complete and submit a form for each vehicle that will be parked in the condo complex parking lot. Remind residents to submit new forms if they change vehicles.
3. Provide space on the form for residents to write the following information:
   - Current Date
   - Owner Name
   - Unit No.
   - Telephone No.
   - Automobile Make
   - Automobile Model
   - Automobile Color
   - License Plate No.
   - State of Registration
4. Include a space for the parking sticker number to be recorded, and indicate that the manager will assign the number.
5. At the bottom of the form, key the form identification code "AUTO" and the current month and year as the revision date. For example: AUTO Rev. 06/14.
6. Save the form as "14-1 Auto Form." Print the form.

ACCESS ACTIVITY **14-2 Enter Data Using a Database Form (Obj. 6)**

In Application 14-1, you created a form to collect data for the Green Gables condo complex. Now you will create an Access database to store and organize the automobile information.

1. Create a new database file named "14-2 Automobile Registration."
2. Create a new database table named "Automobile Registration." Include the following fields in the table:
   - Form Date
   - Owner Name
   - Unit No.
   - Telephone No.
   - Make
   - Model
   - Color

SUPPLEMENTAL RESOURCES

Free Companion Website

Records Management offers a free companion website for instructors and students, with data files, Access tutorials, web links, and instructor resources.

Instructor Resources

Instructor resources on the companion website include:

- The **Instructor's Manual** provides teaching suggestions for the course, schedules to supplement the course syllabus, chapter-specific teaching suggestions, and solutions to all self-checks and end-of-chapter activities. The Instructor's Manual also includes teaching suggestions, finding tests, and all solutions for the "**Records Management Simulation**".
- **Cengage Learning Testing Powered by Cognero**, a flexible, online system that allows instructors to accomplish the following:
  - Author, edit, and manage test bank content from multiple Cengage Learning solutions.
  - Create multiple test versions in an instant.
  - Deliver tests from the learning management system (LMS), the classroom, or wherever the instructor wants.
- **PowerPoint® lecture slides** distill key concepts for classroom presentation and discussion.
- **Solutions for self-check activities**
- **Filing and placement tests and solutions**
- **Supplemental activities and solutions**
- **Simulation finding tests, forms, and solutions**

Student Resources

Student resources found on the companion website include:

- Data files for the textbook and the simulation
- Microsoft® Access 2010 and 2013 tutorials
- Helpful web links

Simulation

"Records Management Simulation," available for separate purchase, provides realistic activities for filing and retrieval of both physical and electronic records in a business environment. Rules are compatible with ARMA International guidelines. This set of practical learning materials consists of 13 filing jobs in which students practice physical document filing in alphabetic, subject, consecutive numeric, terminal-digit numeric, and geographic filing systems, as well as requisition/charge-out and transfer procedures. A data CD includes report sheets that students fill out after they complete each job, finding test forms, simulated e-mail messages, and files for use with database applications. ISBN: 9781305119178.

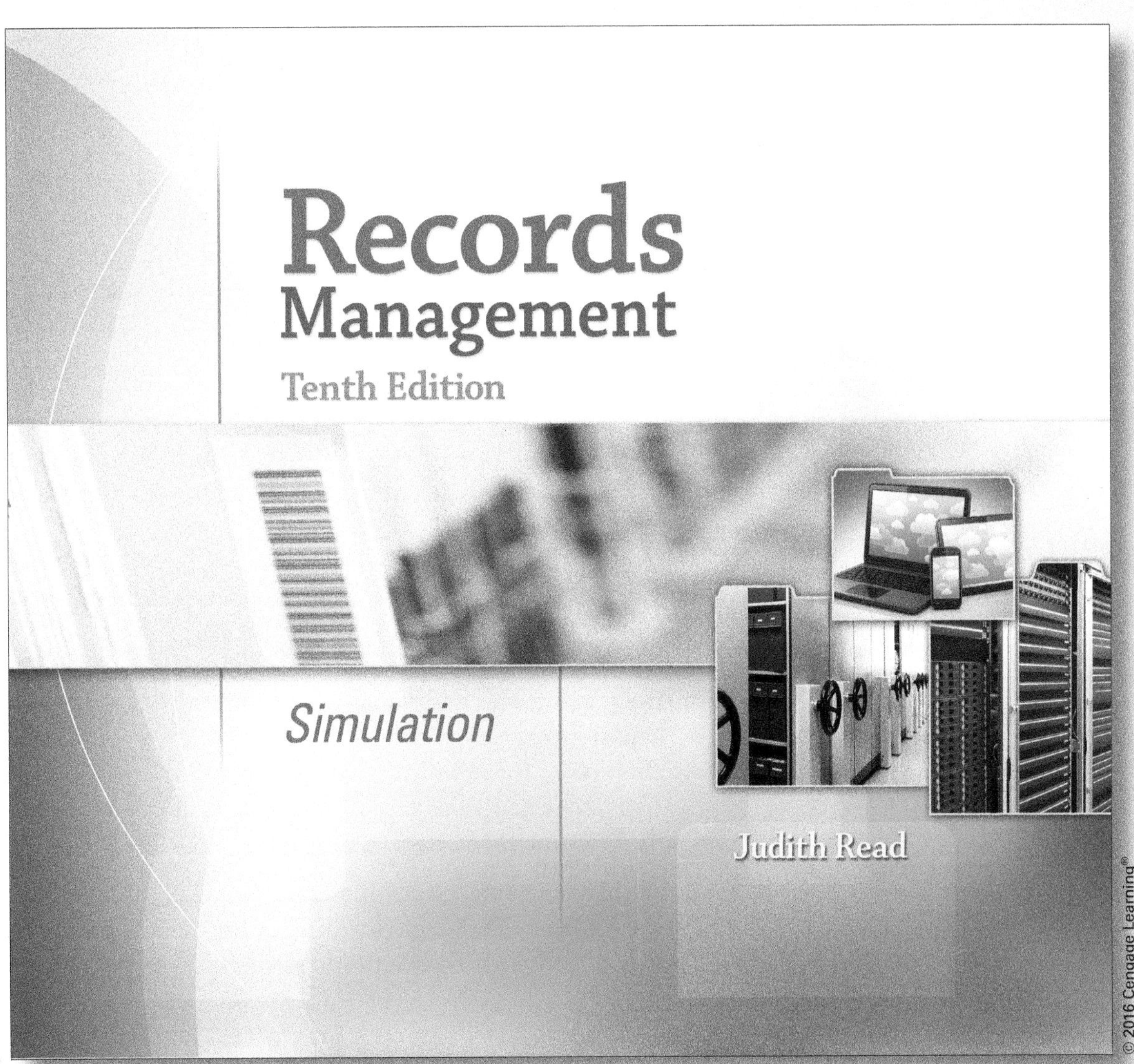

MindTap

MindTap Office Technology for Records Management, 10th edition, is the first of its kind in an entirely new category: the personal learning experience (PLE). This personalized program of digital products and services uses interactivity and customization to engage students, while offering instructors a wide range of choice in content, platforms, devices, and learning tools. MindTap is device agnostic, meaning that it will work with any platform or learning management system (LMS) and will be accessible anytime, anywhere: on desktops, laptops, tablets, mobile phones, and other Internet-enabled devices.

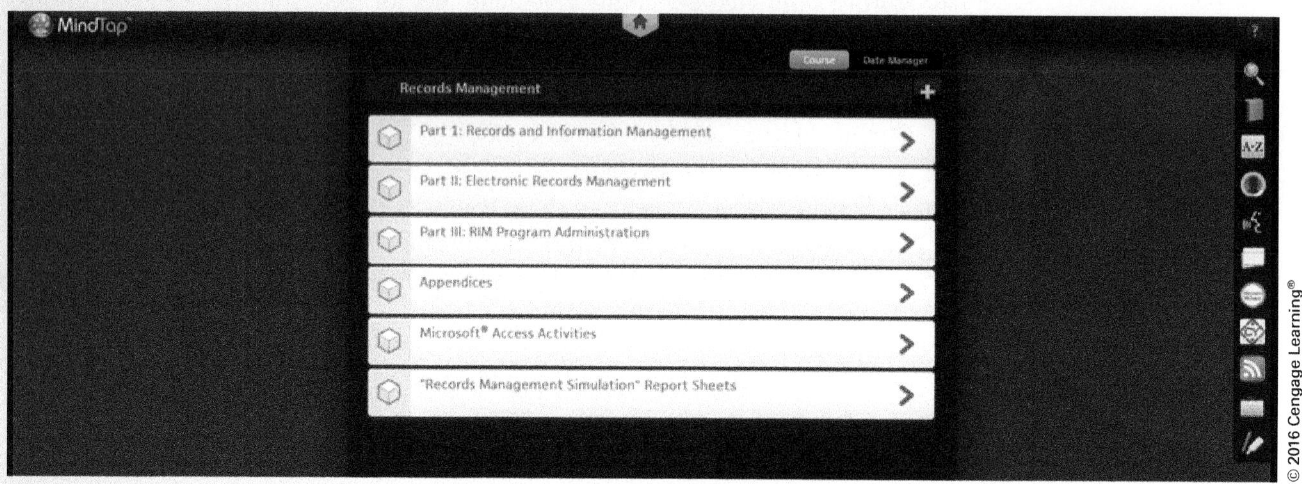

MindTap Office Technology for Records Management, 10th edition, includes the following:

- An interactive e-book with highlighting, note taking (integrated with Evernote), and more
- Flashcards for practicing chapter terms
- Computer-graded activities and exercises using the CengageNOW MindApp:
  - Self-check and application activities, integrated with the e-book
  - Study guide with additional computer-graded activities and exercises
  - Report forms for the simulation
  - Drop boxes for submitting instructor-graded exercises·
- Computer-graded Microsoft® Access activities provided via SAM (Skills Assessment Manager)

ISBN: 9781305119208 (electronic access code)/9781305119192 (printed access card)/9781305119239 (for integration with learning management systems (LMS) such as Blackboard, Moodlerooms, Desire2Learn, etc.)

ACKNOWLEDGMENTS

The authors are grateful to many companies and individuals who assisted in completing this revision of ***Records Management***. Further, we appreciate the help of the filing equipment and supplies manufacturers and vendors who gave time and information to the authors in their efforts to update this edition effectively.

In addition, special appreciation is extended to the instructors who provided valuable feedback by responding to our surveys, including Geoffrey J. Aguirre, UEI, Anaheim; Benay Berl, San Diego City College; Lyda Black, Shelton State Community College; Edna K. Boroski, PhD, Trident Technical College; Shirley Brooks, Holmes Community College; Cathy Combs, Tennessee College of Applied Technology Morristown; Janel C. Doyle, Southcentral Kentucky Community and Technical College; Juanita Fraley, Dine College; Laurie Gambrell, Copiah-Lincoln Community College; Winona Hatcher, USC Upstate; Brenda K. Heschke, DuBois Business College; Trisha Hopper, Southeastern Community College; Sharon Horne, Haskell Indian Nations University; Patricia Johnson, South Piedmont Community College; Deborah H. Littrell, Northwest Community College, Oxford Center; Kristy McAuliffe, San Jacinto College South; Cora Newcomb, Technical College of the Lowcountry; Dennis Newson-Craig, UEI College; Jessica Pace, Panola College; D. L. Presley, Los Angeles Harbor College; Carlton R. Raines, Lehigh Carbon Community College; Patricia A. Saccone, MA, RHIA, Waubonsee Community College; Angela Snelling, Madison Area Technical College; Linda Snider, Grossmont College; Elizabeth Wanielista, Valencia College; MaryLou Wilson, Piedmont Technical College; and Lisa Ann Winfrey, Bluegrass Community and Technical College.

We would like to thank each other and to express our appreciation to our families, friends, coworkers, project manager, and consulting editor, whose encouragement and direction have been invaluable in completing this revision. The result, we believe, is an easily understandable, instructive, up-to-date introduction to the field of records and information management.

I dedicate this edition to my husband, Rod.

Judy Read
Mary Lea Ginn

CONTENTS

PART 1
Records and Information Management

PART 2
Electronic Records Management

PART 3
RIM Program Administration

PART 1 Records and Information Management

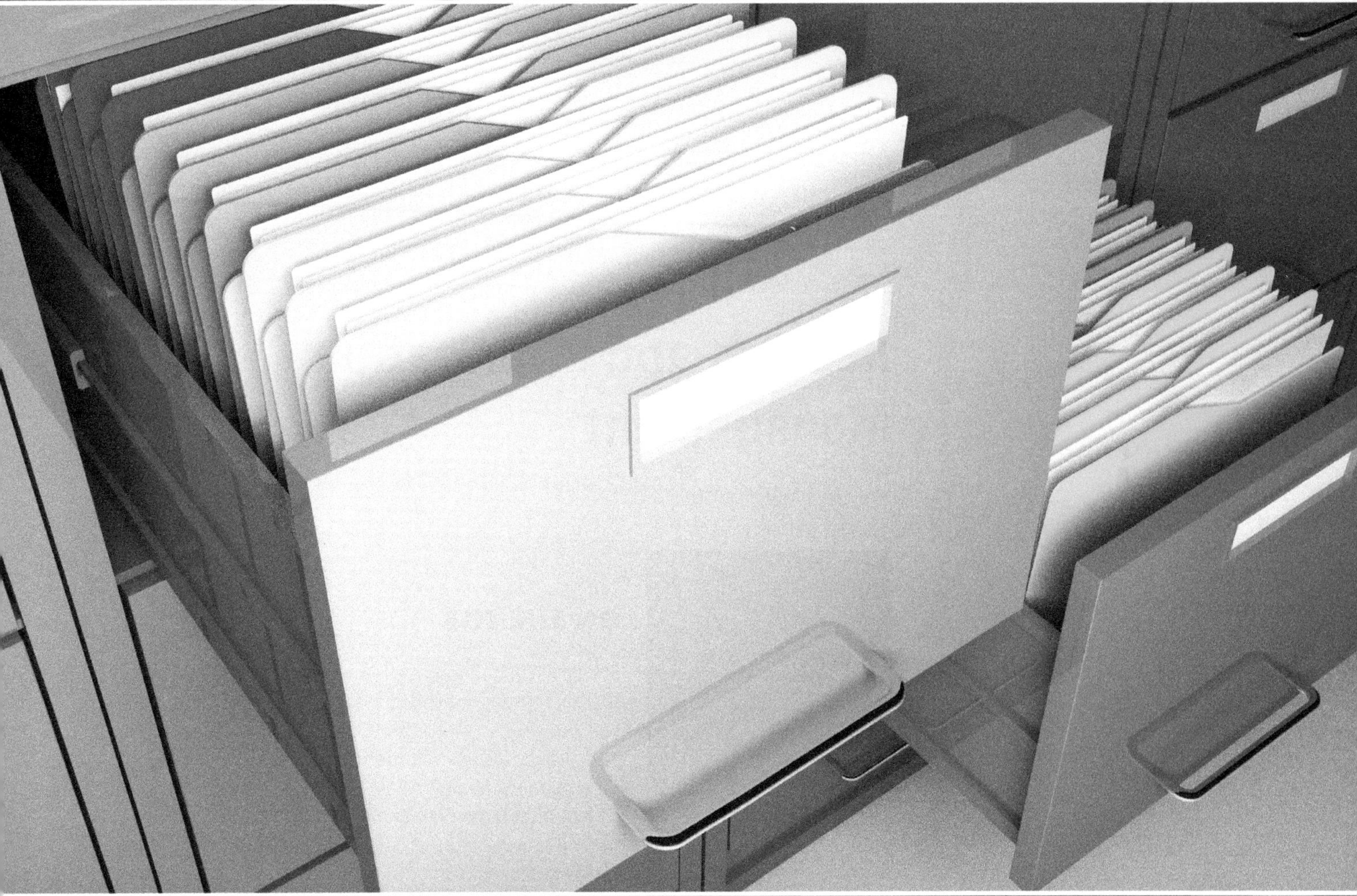

CHAPTER 1

Records and Information Management

LEARNING OBJECTIVES

1. Discuss the reasons that businesses and individuals need records and information.
2. Identify records, record types, and the value of the record for an organization.
3. Describe the life cycle of records and information.
4. Identify the various kinds of physical and electronic records formats.

Courtesy of Doug Allen

ON THE JOB

Effective management of land records and vital statistics records that reflect property ownership in the United States is largely unknown to many records and information management professionals. Tyler Technologies' Regional Sales Manager, Douglas Allen, certified records manager (CRM) and certified document imaging architect (CDIA+), has spent most of his career working with county clerks, county recorders, and county registers of deed in acquiring and implementing software that facilitates the reliable capture, storage, and retrieval of land records, and vital statistics records. He manages a team of eight (8) account executives spread across the United States.

Doug has been a member of ARMA International since 1977 and has been a CRM since 1982. As an ARMA member, Doug has served two "tours of duty" on the ARMA International Board of Directors and is a past president of the Association. Throughout his career, Doug has found his association membership and professional certifications to be valuable to his work, the training of his sales force, and the clients with whom he has worked. Both have also contributed to the longevity of his career.

The field of records and information management will continue to evolve. As our technologies continue to migrate to digital format and as organizations focus on information governance, the field will become both more rewarding and more challenging. Doug's advice for students studying for a career in the field is that they expand their learning horizons with significant exposure to IT systems and issues, risk management, and legal issues. Further, Doug recommends that students dedicate themselves to lifelong learning, to demonstrate their abilities by achieving and maintaining meaningful certifications, and to work within associations like ARMA to help build the networks that they will need to ensure long-term career success.

INFORMATION AND RECORDS ARE ESSENTIAL FOR BUSINESS

As a business customer, every time you buy a product or service, you are creating a record of that transaction. For instance, the last time you went to the movies, you paid in cash or by debit/credit card. You received a receipt as well as your ticket to enter the movie of your choice. The receipt is the record of your expenditure. The ticket is handed to the usher to prove that you have paid for the movie.

Business records are created in many different ways. For instance, what kinds of business records can be created when you pay your monthly cell phone bill?

- **Option 1:** You receive your paper bill in the mail. You check the bill for accuracy. You pay the bill by writing a paper check and mailing it with the remittance portion of the invoice to the phone company.
- **Option 2:** You receive your bill in an e-mail or text message on your cell phone. You check the bill for accuracy. You pay the bill by accessing your online bank checking account. The bank then electronically transfers the money from your checking account to the phone company.
- **Option 3:** You receive a bill via e-mail or text message on your phone. You check the bill for accuracy. You have set up an auto-pay authorization between the phone company and your credit card company. The amount due appears on the next credit card statement. You pay the credit card balance by accessing your online checking account to pay the bill electronically. You receive reward mileage for using your credit card.

Cell phone users carry out these options daily. Which option do you use?

The phone company creates transaction records each time a bill is sent by US mail, e-mail, or as a text message. When the phone company receives your payment, they update your payment record and credit your account.

The bank creates transaction records when your checking account is debited to make a payment to the phone company.

How many of your transactions are in electronic form?

The credit card company creates transaction records when they charge the phone billing to your account, when they receive your payment, and when they credit your rewards account.

Your bill is a record of your cell phone usage, data plans, and so on. This record becomes part of your contract agreement with the phone company.

As you can see from the previous examples, records and information are essential to conduct business for all who are involved in the transaction.

Records Keeping Meets Regulatory Compliance Requirements

The purchase of a new car provides another example of transaction records. You go to a dealer and agree to purchase a new auto. Let's say that you fill out the paper work to finance your new car. This application is sent to the financial institution that you would work with, and it is approved. Then, the dealer fills out the Department of Motor Vehicles (DMV) registration. Your name is on the title to the new vehicle, as is the name of the financial institution until you pay off the loan for the car.

Someone at the car dealership fills out the financial application, and that record becomes a legally binding contract. A copy of the financial application is sent to the financial institution as a promissory note. You are given a copy of the contract you have signed.

What is a record?

The Department of Motor Vehicles receives registration and title applications. Both these records become part of the database of registered vehicles in your state.

You must continue to provide the financial institution with evidence of insurance, as indicated on your vehicle registration.

Each document meets the legal and regulatory requirements for the purchase of your new car. Transaction records are vital to various government agencies in ensuring compliance with legal requirements.

Organizations and Individuals Need Records

Why do organizations need records?

As you can see from the previous examples, records serve as the memory of an organization or individual. Records also document the information needed for complying with regulations and the transactions of an organization. For example, management policies are developed and recorded to furnish broad guidelines for operating a business. Each department (for example, finance, marketing, accounting, and human resources) bases its entire method of operations upon records.

record: stored information, regardless of media or characteristics, made or received by an organization that is evidence of its operations and has value requiring its retention for a specific period of time

ARMA International: an association for information management professionals

The term **record** has a specific meaning in records and information management. **ARMA International** (an association for information management professionals) defines a record as stored information, regardless of media or characteristics, made or received by an organization that is evidence of its operations and has value requiring its retention for a specific period of time.

From a personal standpoint, why do you keep your diploma, birth certificate, the title of ownership to your car, or the promissory note that provided you with the money to attend college? The answer is simple: In today's complex world, people cannot get along without records. They need the information that records contain; information is needed for driver's licenses, job applications, credit card and mortgage applications, lease agreements, tax returns, voter registrations, and medical services.

records management: the systematic control of all records from their creation or receipt, through their processing, distribution, organization, storage, and retrieval, to their ultimate disposition

Business owners and managers have learned more about the importance and value of their records and have incorporated processes and procedures to preserve and protect them. Many businesses now follow guidelines and standards for maintaining their records for the lengths of time necessary for their business operations. Some of the more important standards are discussed next.

RECORDS MANAGEMENT

Records management is the systematic control of all records from their creation or receipt, through their processing, distribution, organization, storage, and retrieval, to their ultimate disposition. Because information is such an important resource to organizations, the records management function also includes information management. Therefore, records management is also known as *records and information management (RIM).*

ANSI and ISO Standards

ISO 15489: a standard for records management policies and procedures

The American National Standards Institute (ANSI), a voluntary group of private sector businesses and government agencies, is a member of the International Organization for Standardization (ISO). The ISO is a worldwide federation of national standards organizations. **ISO 15489** is a standard for records management policies and procedures. The purpose of this standard is to ensure that appropriate attention and protection apply to all records, and that the evidence and information records contain can be retrieved efficiently and effectively using standard practices and procedures. International standards help the records management function of an organization clarify its purpose and prove its value by managing important information.

Traditional records management is being transformed because of changes in technology and the proliferation of data generated. Records management is also affected by legislation related to how businesses must operate and keep records. This textbook deals with records in business organizations; however, the principles you learn should also help you understand how to use records efficiently in other types of organizations and in your personal life.

ISO 15489 defines a record as follows:[1]

> A record is information created, received, and maintained as evidence and information by an organization or person, in pursuance of legal obligations or in the transaction of business.

Records are not just any document an organization produces or receives. Some experts estimate that of all the documents that an organization creates, only 10 to 15 percent qualify as records. Records management procedures for each organization specify which documents or information become records, based on their types and value to the organization.

RECORDS TYPES AND VALUES

cloud: Internet or a network of servers

Common records, such as e-mails and their attachments, reports, forms, and books, can appear on paper, on remote servers in "the **cloud**," on optical or digital storage media, or on an organization's intranet pages. The cloud refers to the Internet (or a network of servers). Cloud computing refers to using these servers for data storage or to run computer programs and software applications such as e-mail. An organization may receive records through regular mail, electronic mail, facsimile machines (fax), special couriers, or by accessing computer networks, including the Internet and company intranets.

Other types of records to consider are video and oral records that capture the human voice and/or images that can be stored in the cloud, and other

---

[1]International Organization for Standardization, ISO 15489-1:2001, Information and Documentation—Records Management, Part 1: General (Geneva, Switzerland: ISO, 2001).

magnetic or digital media. Records are also stored on film, CDs, DVDs, videotapes, photographs, and microfilm. Records are valuable property, or resources, of an organization and, like all other resources, they must be managed properly.

external record: a record created for use outside of the organization. It may be created inside or outside of the organization

Records can be created for internal or external usage. An **external record** contains information for use outside of the organization. It may be created inside or outside of the organization. Examples are communications between a firm and its employees (payroll records, bulletins, newsletters, and government regulations).

internal record: a record that contains information needed to operate an organization

An **internal record** contains information needed to operate an organization. Such a record may be created inside or outside an organization. Many internal records are created through the use of e-commerce systems using databases and web server application. An example is the communications among an organization's departments (inventory control records, interoffice memos or e-mail, purchase requisitions, and reports).

transaction record: a document used in an organization's day-today operations

A **transaction record** is a document used in an organization's day-to-day operations. These documents consist primarily of business forms that can be created manually, electronically, or generated via e-commerce systems on the Internet. Examples are invoices, requisitions, purchase and sales orders, bank checks, statements, contracts, shipping documents, and personnel records such as employment applications, time sheets, and attendance reports.

reference record: a record that contains information needed to carry on the operations of an organization over long periods

A **reference record**, on the other hand, contains information needed to carry on the operations of an organization over long periods. These records are referenced for information about previous decisions, quotations on items to purchase, statements of administrative policy, and plans for running the organization. Examples of common reference documents include policy manuals, policy memos, sales performance, and financial reports. Other examples include catalogs, price lists, and brochures. Any of these reference documents can be accessed on an organization's website, intranet, or in the cloud.

Figure 1.1 shows the types of records and the contents of each record type. Regardless of their type, these records must be categorized based on their value to the organization, as illustrated in Figure 1.2.

FIGURE 1.1 **Records Types and Contents**

RECORD TYPE	CONTENTS
Internal	Contains information for operation of the organization
External	Contains information for use outside the organization
Transaction	Contains information used in day-to-day operations
Reference	Contains information needed for long-term operations

Categorizing the Value of Record(s)

Through review and analysis of the organization's records inventory, a determination is made as to the value of the records and to which category each record belongs. This evaluation is used to develop a records retention schedule specifying how long to keep the records in an organization. Developing a legally defensible retention schedule is of critical importance. You will learn more about this in Chapter 7: Storing, Retrieving, and Transferring Records.

What four categories are used to identify the value of a record?

Some records are so valuable to the organization that they require special measures of protection. Each record maintained by an organization falls into one of four categories that determine how the records should be retained and the level of protection they require. These categories are vital records, important records, useful records, and nonessential records, as shown in Figure 1.2.

FIGURE 1.2 **Records Categories**

CATEGORY	EXAMPLES
Vital Records	
• Necessary for the mission-critical business operations • Usually not replaceable: operations not possible without these records • Highest degree of protection necessary	Legal papers, articles of incorporation, titles of property, reports to shareholders, bookkeeping related to profit and loss Vital records can be classified as active or inactive, and they may only be vital for a portion of their life cycle.
Important Records	
• Necessary in performing business operations • Usually replaceable but at great cost • High degree of protection necessary	Personnel records, sales records, financial and tax records, policy manuals and memos, reports, and contracts
Useful Records	
• Helpful in conducting business operations • Usually replaceable at slight cost • Low to medium degree of protection	General e-mails, letters, memos
Nonessential Documents (Usually will not be classified as a record)	
• Documents that have no predictable value after their initial use • Lowest degree of protection	Announcements and bulletins to employees, acknowledgments and routine telephone/e-mail messages

Normally, records are used and retained because they have administrative, legal, or historical values to a firm. Policy manuals and handbooks have administrative value and provide guidance for employees who represent the business or organization while performing their job duties. Accounting records have administrative value. Contracts and deeds are documents that have legal value to a firm. Meeting minutes have historical value. All these records can be subject to Legal Discovery, which is discussed in Chapter 2. More examples of records and their values and usefulness to an organization are shown in Figure 1.3.

FIGURE 1.3 **Records Value Examples**

VALUE AND RECORDS TYPE	EXAMPLES
Administrative	
Records that help employees perform office operations Fiscal records used to document operating funds and other financial processes	• Policy and procedures manuals/documents/websites • Handbooks • Organizational charts • Tax returns • Records of financial transactions: purchase and sales orders, invoices, balance sheets, and income statements
Legal	
Records that provide evidence of business transactions	• Contracts • Financial agreements that are legally binding • Deeds to property owned • Articles of incorporation
Historical	
Records that document the organization's operations and major shifts of direction over the years	• Minutes of meetings • Corporate charter • Public relations documents • Information on corporate officers

RECORDS AND INFORMATION LIFE CYCLE

records and information life cycle: the life span of a record as expressed in the five phases of creation, distribution, use, maintenance, and final disposition

The **records and information life cycle** is the life span of a record as expressed in the five phases of creation, distribution, use, maintenance, and final disposition. The phases in the life cycle often overlap. Figure 1.4 shows how this cycle is carried out.

The previous examples of paying your cell phone bill and buying a new car show the records life cycle in action. When you pay your monthly cell phone bill, you create a record of the transaction. The distribution, maintenance, and retention phases would be completed in a year. After a year, these records are no longer needed and can be shredded.

Creation or Receipt

Whenever a letter is produced, an e-mail written, or a form completed either physically or electronically, a record may be created. Records can also be received by e-mail or other means from an outside source.

Distribution

This record is then distributed (sent) to the person responsible for its use. Records are commonly used in decision making, for documentation or reference, in answering inquiries, or in satisfying legal requirements.

Retention (Use and Maintenance)

When a decision is made to keep the record for use at a later date, it must be stored, retrieved, and protected—three key steps in the maintenance of physical

FIGURE 1.4 **Records and Information Cycle**

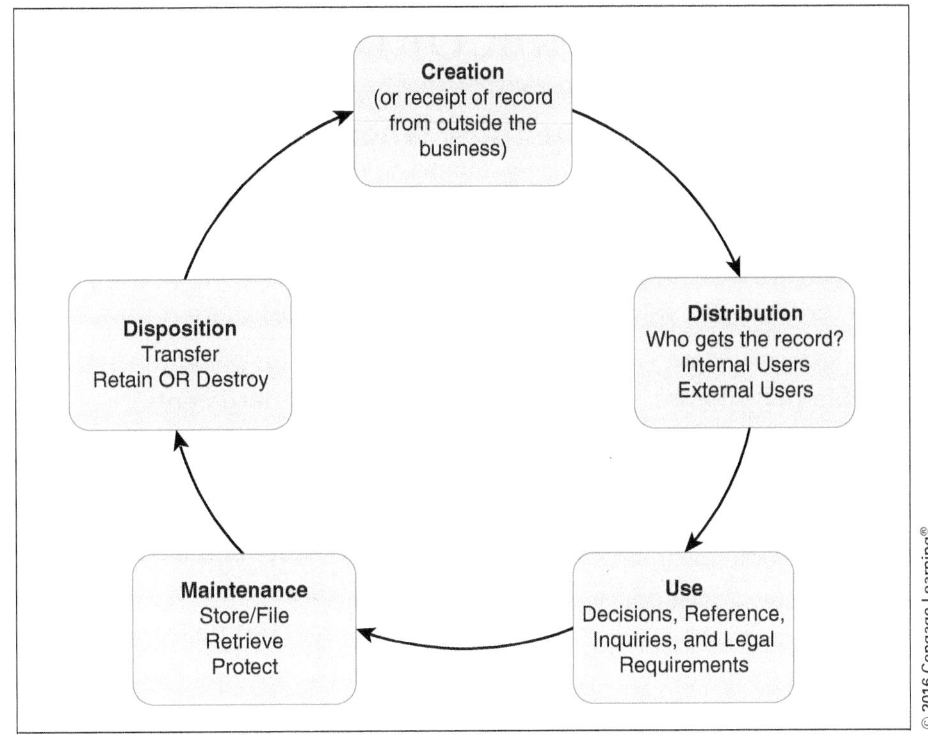

or electronic records. During this phase, the records must be stored (filed), which involves preparing and placing records into their proper storage place—a filing cabinet or a folder on a computer system. After a record is stored, a request may be made to retrieve it (find and remove a physical record from storage or open an electronic file and look up the information). When the retrieved record is no longer needed for active use, it may be re-stored and protected, using appropriate equipment, environmental, and human controls to ensure the record's security. Also involved in the maintenance phase are activities such as updating stored information and discarding obsolete physical or electronic records that are no longer useful or that have been replaced by more current ones.

Electronic records are usually stored or saved on the organization's servers or in the cloud and are backed up on a daily, weekly, or monthly basis. Vital and important electronic records can also be maintained as physical records.

Disposition

When are records sent to the archives?

The last phase in the records and information life cycle is disposition. After a predetermined period of time has elapsed, records to be kept are transferred to less-expensive storage sites within the firm or to an external records storage facility. At the end of the number of years indicated in the retention schedule, the records are disposed of, either by destruction or by transfer to a permanent storage place. Facilities where records of an organization are preserved because of their continuing or historical value are called archives. The records retention schedule is discussed in detail in Chapter 7.

The records and information life cycle is an important concept for you to understand. It shows, for example, that filing and/or storing is only one part of records and information management. Many interrelated parts must work together for an effective records and information management program.

MY RECORDS

Do You Know Where Your Records Are?

Think quickly—where is your birth certificate? Where is the title of your car?

If you are like most people, you might not know exactly where your important records are. Do you know where you keep each of these records?		
• Birth certificate • Marriage license • Marriage certificate • Passport • Diploma • Auto loan documents • Auto insurance policy • Life insurance policy • Property deeds • Mortgage loan documents	• Tax returns for previous years • Will or trust documents • Automobile title • Renter's or homeowner's insurance policy • Rental or lease agreement • Divorce decree • Adoption or naturalization papers	• Military discharge papers • Vaccination records for all family members • Medical histories for all family members • Pay stubs from current and previous jobs • Stock purchases and other investment records
Each record listed above is either vital or important. What degree of protection have you provided for each record? Are your records in a fire-resistant container or in a safe deposit box? Follow these suggestions for keeping your vital and important records safe:		
• Identify a single location to store all vital papers and information related to your financial transactions. • Create copies of your vital records. Some of the copies may need to be certified as official copies. • Put important original documents in plastic sheet protectors to protect and easily identify them.	• Notify family members or friends not living with you where important information will be located if disaster strikes. • Inventory the records you and/or your financial institutions keep only on computers. Include account numbers and passwords on your inventory. Keep the inventory safe.	• Make backups of your computer records. If possible, store the backups at another location. • Once a month, update your stored information. Has anything changed? Make another backup.

By knowing the meaning and importance of each part of the entire records life cycle, you will be able to understand what is needed to manage all records—both physical and electronic.

RECORDS FORMATS

As you have learned from the examples at the beginning of the chapter, a record can be physical or electronic. The next section addresses the importance of physical or paper records. After physical records, electronic records formats are identified and discussed.

Physical Records

Even though more businesses than ever are investing in new technologies, using physical records continues to be a fact of office life. The increased use of equipment that enables employees to create physical records from electronic media contributes to the use of physical records. Copiers, printers, and facsimile machines all have the ability to interface with office computer systems to produce large volumes of physical documents.

Why are physical records popular?

Physical records continue to be popular because they are more personal and individual: paper requires no additional equipment for viewing; people can write on and annotate physical documents; and paper is easily transportable.

People who have grown up reading from a screen are comfortable with that medium. Will this comfort of reading from a screen change the dependence on physical documents? This change in work and learning methods could help reduce the amount of physical records in the future. As a consequence of the current information explosion, records managers must deal with increasing numbers of records both physical and electronic.

CAREER CORNER

Document Management Specialist

The following job description is an example of a career opportunity in a pharmaceutical company.

DUTIES AND RESPONSIBILITIES

- Responsible for the preparation and scanning of time-sensitive departmental documentation for presentation to internal and external customers.
- Works in a team environment to ensure timely and accurate preparation of documents. Organization, distributing, or tracking of paperwork or mail according to departmental procedures.
- Works to ensure accurate preparation and scanning of time-sensitive documents.
- Records and tracks carrier and batch information into tracking software, and monitors scanner activity to ensure the appropriate proper carrier information is captured to facilitate accurate departmental workflow and client reporting.
- Prepares pharmacy invoices and EORs (explanation of review documents) for return to the customer, based on specific carrier requirements.
- Uses office machinery (scanning equipment, fax, copier, PC, etc.) appropriately to communicate, document, duplicate, print, verify, research, or forward pharmacy bill information to both internal and external customers.

Job Qualifications

Education

Required: Associate's degree or equivalent experience

Desired: Training in office automation

Work Experience

Required: 1+ year of office experience, to include the use of document management software and equipment (scanning equipment, FTP solutions). Intermediate Microsoft Excel® skills required.

Desired: Related work experience

Electronic Records

An electronic record is a record stored on electronic media that can be readily accessed or changed. A piece of equipment is required to view and read or listen to electronic records. With the development and use of application software on personal computers, e-mail, letters, memos, and reports are created electronically; however, the original purpose of these systems was to facilitate the creation of physical records. As technology has advanced, true electronic records are in use today, that is, records created, distributed, used, and stored in electronic form. The contents of these records are accessible by machine or by querying a database.

The challenge for the records manager is to ensure that all records are what they appear to be. The ARMA Generally Accepted Recordkeeping Principles® introduced in Chapter 2 define parameters for records and information management. Increases in fraud and theft of electronic records have left records and information managers desperate to ensure the safety and security of the organization's valuable resources.

To that end, each person responsible for electronic records follows the records management storage and retrieval procedures set up for the organization. Consistently following procedures helps protect the company in legal actions. The same benefits of following proper records management procedures for physical records also apply to electronic records: the information is available at the right time to help make effective decisions.

RECORDS MANAGEMENT IN ACTION

E-Discovery Costs Can Damage Business Profitability

As businesses create more and more electronic records, the costs of identifying and retrieving relevant information due to a lawsuit can severely impact the profitability of the company. For example, when the roofs of three airplane hangars collapsed due to heavy snow and ice and crushed 18 private jets, the aviation company that owned the hangers had to retain 8,000 gigabytes of electronic documents. Approximately 2 million electronic documents might have contained information pertinent to the multiple lawsuits that were filed. These documents had to be sifted through for possible liability for the roof collapses. The estimated cost for attorneys to read and manually review the documents was $1.00 each.

Fortunately, the court gave permission for the company to use a computer program that uses *predictive coding* to sort through the documents for keywords or elements. As a result, the number of documents that had to be manually reviewed was reduced to about 10 percent of the original number.

This example illustrates that even with the assistance of computer programs, E-Discovery can still be a very expensive process for businesses that are subject to legal action. In addition, recent court rulings have sided with plaintiffs, agreeing that keywords used in searching for relevant documents may be disclosed. This ruling could lead to additional litigation and costs to the business if the initial search is determined to be inadequate.

Source: Joe Palazzolo. "Why Hire a Lawyer? Computers Are Cheaper," *The Wall Street Journal*, June 18, 2012; Ralph Losey, e-Discovery Team website, http://e-discoveryteam.com/2013/10/06/party-ordered-to-disclose-where-and-how-it-searched-for-esi-you-can-expect-this-kind-of-order-to-become-commonplace/, accessed October 23, 2013.

Electronic Mail

electronic mail (e-mail): a system that enables users to compose, transmit, receive, and manage electronic documents and images across networks

Electronic mail (e-mail) is a system that enables users to compose, transmit, receive, and manage electronic documents and images across networks. A variety of electronic mail systems allow users to write and send messages via computers and software.

E-mail is now the primary mode of communication between employees in corporations and governmental agencies. The many advantages of using e-mail include its ease of use and short delivery time. The message sent and delivery process of e-mail is nearly instantaneous on some networks. Unfortunately, e-mail has a potential for abuse and disaster. Records and information managers have developed policies related to electronic records for their organizations. Employees must follow the policies developed for effective and efficient management of electronic records.

Many questions related to records management and e-mail must be addressed by records managers. E-mail communications can be used in a court of law. What procedures are in place to respond to a court order to produce e-mail records? How can the integrity of a record be maintained? Can it be kept confidential? How long should an electronic mail message be kept? Is sending personal e-mails over the company network acceptable? These questions are addressed in Chapter 11, Electronic Records File Management. Records and information managers work with information technology, business functions, and legal departments to determine the feasibility of storage. Many organizations are changing their archiving policies because the volume of e-mail grows exponentially.

Other Electronic Records

Wikis, blogs, podcasts, webinars, online forums, tweets, and social media sites such as Facebook® are some of the newer modes of electronic communication. Recorded information on these media can be official records; or they can also be unstructured and not considered to be records.

wiki: a page or collection of web pages that allows people who access the site to contribute or modify content

A **wiki** is a page or collection of web pages that allows people who access the site to contribute or modify content. Wikis allow users to work collaboratively, updating each other's entries or creating new entries. Wikis are used in business to provide product information or instructions for the firm's operation, gather feedback from product or service users, and communicate on other issues.

blog: a shared online journal

A **blog** (short for the term *web log*) is a shared online journal. The journal is hosted by a company, organization, or individual who makes regular entries called *posts*. The posts contain text comments on the blog topic. Some blogs also contain graphics or video. Entries are usually shown in reverse chronological order. The blog host may allow readers to post comments or replies to the blog entries. *Blog* can also be used as a verb, meaning "to post content to a blog." A *blogger* is a person who contributes to a blog.

podcast: a broadcast sent over the Internet to receivers who hear and/or view the information via computers or other electronic devices

A **podcast** is a broadcast sent over the Internet to receivers who hear and/or view the information via computers or other electronic devices. Early podcasts were often received using iPods, thus the name *podcast*. A *podcaster* is the organization or person who creates and broadcasts the content of a podcast. A podcast may be audio only, or it may contain video and audio. Many podcasts are free to receivers. For some podcasts, receivers have to pay a fee. Receivers may subscribe to an RRS feed to receive podcasts. RRS stands for "*really simple syndication*" and is the technology used in creating the feed. Updated information from the feed is automatically downloaded to the subscriber's computer and can be viewed at his or her convenience.

webinar: a video presentation given over the World Wide Web

A **webinar** (short for web seminar) is a video presentation given over the World Wide Web. Videoconferencing is used so that participants and the presenter can interact, asking and answering questions. Participants may be in a special room designed with cameras and other equipment for videoconferencing, or they may use a webcam and a personal computer to take part in the webinar.

Social media websites such as Facebook are used by businesses to promote and advertise their products and services. On Facebook, if a follower likes a business posting and shares it with his or her friends, the product or service receives further exposure and possibly more sales for the company. Many businesses now have social media coordinators who are tasked with ensuring that posts on these sites reflect positively on the company and promote the business.

tweet: a short message posted on the Twitter® social network website

A **tweet** is a short message posted on the Twitter® social network website. The messages can be posted or viewed on a computer or a mobile device. A tweet is similar to a blog post or an e-mail, but shorter—usually limited to 140 characters. Businesses can use tweets to announce sales and promote their products and services. Businesses can post links to their website from tweets. Images, blogs, and videos can also be linked to tweets. Individuals or other organizations can follow businesses on Twitter for the ongoing updates.

Imaged Documents

document imaging: an automated system for scanning, storing, retrieving, and managing images of physical records in an electronic format

Document imaging is an automated system for scanning, storing, retrieving, and managing images of physical records in an electronic format. A physical document is scanned into a computer file, thus creating an electronic image of the document. Scanned files are usually large; consequently, optical or digital disk storage (discussed in Chapter 12) is recommended.

Textual data can be converted electronically using optical character recognition (OCR) software. Lists of keywords are created for each scanned file. An image and text database is developed, enabling a search by keywords to find a document in a matter of seconds. Once found, the document can be sent to the requester by fax, computer-to-computer communication, or a physical copy. Chapter 12 includes a discussion of this technology.

In summary, you can see the tremendous amount of records and information that is being generated daily with these technologies. As new technologies evolve, new modes of communication are created, and more information is generated.

Adapted from a 2012 report by Royal Pingdom.com,[2] the following information is sent or posted yearly or daily:

---

[2] http://royal.pingdom.com/2013/01/16/internet-2012-in-numbers/, accessed June 2014.

- 2.4 billion Internet users worldwide
- 2.2 billion e-mail users worldwide
- 144 billion e-mail messages sent daily
- More than 191 million visitors to Google® daily
- 1.2 trillion Google searches conducted in 2012
- 1 billion active Facebook users passed in October 2012
- 200 million monthly active Twitter users
- 2.7 billion "likes" on Facebook every day
- 51 million new websites created in 2012
- 5 billion mobile phone users worldwide in 2012

You will learn about the records and information management environment, professional organizations, and possible careers in Chapter 2, The RIM Environment.

CHAPTER REVIEW AND APPLICATIONS

KEY POINTS

- Records and information management is essential for businesses and individuals.
- Records are used to document information needed for complying with regulations, documenting transactions of an organization, and serve as the memory of an organization.
- Records are created for internal and external usage and as reference or transaction documents.
- Records have different values to an organization and exist in physical and electronic formats.
- Managing the records life cycle is the systematic control of all records from creation to disposition.

TERMS

ARMA International
blog
cloud
document imaging
electronic mail (e-mail)
external record
important records
internal record
ISO 15489
nonessential documents
podcast
record
records and information life cycle
records management
reference records
transaction records
tweet
useful records
vital records
webinar
wiki

REVIEW AND DISCUSS

1. Give three reasons that businesses need records. (Obj. 1)

2. From a personal standpoint, why do you need records? (Obj. 1)

3. What is a *record* as defined by ARMA? (Obj. 2)

4. Name the four records types and the kind of information each would contain. (Obj. 2)

5. What four categories are used to classify the value of a record to an organization? Give examples for each category. (Obj. 2)

6. What phases, if any, do you eliminate in your own personal records cycle? Why? (Obj. 3)

7. Physical records are available in which formats? (Obj. 4)

8. List at least four electronic record formats and how businesses and organizations would use each to promote their products and services. (Obj. 4)

9. Why do physical records remain popular, even though businesses have invested in new electronic technologies? (Obj. 4)

APPLICATIONS

1-1 Records Management Website Discovery

The publisher of this textbook maintains a website where you can access data files, and links to other sites you need to visit as you complete applications. You will explore this site in this application. (If you are using MindTap in addition to the print text, please note that you will not need to follow the steps outlined below. Instead, you will want to complete Application 1-1 in the MindTap, which is an exploration of the MindTap for this book.)

1. Access the Internet and go to http://www.cengagebrain.com. Search for ISBN 9781305119161 to find materials relating to this textbook.
2. Add this site to your Favorites or Bookmarks list. Use the Favorites or Bookmarks link for quick access to this site in later activities.
3. Browse the site to become familiar with it. Locate the links to related sites.
4. Locate and download the data files you will use with this book:
   - Double-click Data Files under Book Resources in the navigation area on the left.
   - Double-click on the link to the .zip file that is posted. Navigate to the drive and folder where you want to store the data files. Click **Save**.
   - When the download is complete, a file (such as *Datafiles.zip*) that contains the data files in compressed format will be saved on your computer. You will need to decompress (extract) the files, using a program such as Windows Explorer®.
5. Exit the website.

1-2 Classifying Records (Obj. 2)

Data File

1. Open the Microsoft Word® file *1-2 Classification* from the data files.

2. Working with your teammates, decide how each record should be classified primarily for external or internal usage. Key an "X" in the correct column. Next, determine whether the record is a transactional or reference document. Key an "X" in the correct column.
3. The records are listed again in the second chart in the data file. Working with your teammates, decide how each record should be classified—vital, important, useful, or nonessential. Key an X in the appropriate column on the chart for each record.
4. Compare your charts with another team in the class. Discuss the reasons for any differences in the way you classified the records.

1-3 Using Technology (Obj. 1)

1. Access a search engine on the Internet, and key in www.arma.org.
2. From the home page, read and summarize an article from the "Current News" list.
3. Send an e-mail that contains a summary of your findings to your instructor.

USING COMPUTERS TO SORT DATA

See Appendix A of this textbook for more information about using computers to sort data, including tips on using Microsoft® Word and Microsoft® Excel to sort data and some key differences between manual sorting and computer sorting.

MICROSOFT® ACCESS BASICS

As you complete later chapters of this textbook and the related simulation, you will use Microsoft Access® database software for electronic records management. Before completing these activities, you should complete the Microsoft® Access tutorial (found on the website for this textbook and in the MindTap for this textbook). This tutorial will allow you to review or learn the basics of using Microsoft® Access. The tutorial is provided in PDF files. You will need a program that can read PDF files, such as Adobe Acrobat Reader, to view or print the tutorial.

Microsoft® Access data files for use in completing the tutorial and other applications are provided on the website for this textbook and in the MindTap for this textbook. To use a Microsoft® Access data file, you should download the student data files from the website to a working folder on a hard drive or a removable storage device. Directions for copying files using Microsoft Windows Explorer® are provided in the Access tutorial.

To download the Microsoft® Access lessons and the Microsoft® Access data files from the website for this textbook, follow these steps:

1. Using a computer with Microsoft® Access and an Internet connection, go to the website www.cengagebrain.com, and locate the companion website for this text by typing ISBN 9781305119161 in the search field.
2. Once you have found the text, click on the **Free Materials** tab and choose either **Access Now** or **Save to MyHome** to access the companion website.
3. Click **Access Data Files, Access Lessons,** or **Access Tutorial**. (You will need to click on each item by itself.)
4. You will see a downloading box. Choose **Save**.
5. Navigate to the drive and folder where you want to save the files. Click **Save**.
6. When the download is complete, a file in compressed format will be saved onto your computer. You will need to decompress (extract) the files, using a program such as WinZip.

If you are an experienced Microsoft® Access user, read the tutorial to review Microsoft® Access concepts. Follow the instructions provided to learn to use any Microsoft® Access features with which you are not familiar. If you have little or no experience using Microsoft® Access, read and complete each lesson carefully to learn to use the basic features of Microsoft® Access.

ADDITIONAL RESOURCES

For data files, Microsoft® Access tutorials and more, go to www.cengagebrain.com.

CHAPTER 2

The RIM Environment

LEARNING OBJECTIVES

1. Identify and define electronic business activities.
2. Define records and information programs for managing records.
3. Identify common problems and challenges for records systems.
4. Describe the legal considerations and relevant legislation impacting records and information management.
5. Explore possible careers in records management, and understand the role of professional organizations in records and information management: ARMA International and AIIM.

Courtesy of Mary Beth Herkert

ON THE JOB

The State of Oregon is unique in that both records management and archives management are directed by the state archivist. State Archivist Mary Beth Herkert's duties are to (1) provide advice and assistance on public records management issues and authorize the destruction of public records for all levels of Oregon government; (2) protect, store, and provide access to permanently valuable records of Oregon; and (3) operate the Oregon State Records Center and the Security Copy Depository. Nontraditional duties include filing "Official Documents," as defined by law, for the Secretary of State; publishing Oregon's Administrative Rules; and publishing the Oregon Blue Book.

According to Mary Beth, the Oregon State Archives has changed their approach to managing information by making available a statewide, electronic records management system (ERMS) called the Oregon Records Management Solution (ORMS). ORMS, a public/private, software as a service (SaaS) solution provides an effective and affordable ERMS to all state and local government entities. In addition, ORMS resides in a private government cloud where participating agencies retain custody of their records, follow authorized records retention schedules, and are able to control access to their records based on existing statutes, rules, and policies. The results have improved access to public records, which in turn makes government more transparent.

Mary Beth believes that the records management profession as a whole, especially in the private sector, will continue to expand. As more and more information is being generated and is in need of being managed, the importance of the records manager role in organizations will increase. In their new capacity, record managers must take full advantage of available tools to manage information.

Reprinted with permission of Mary Beth Herkert.

This chapter is about the record management environment and the challenges faced by records and information managers. New technology has expanded the ways in which individuals communicate and e-commerce records are created or modified. This chapter addresses legal issues that can arise for individuals, businesses, and organizations due to this expansion. The role of records management professional organizations is examined, as well as possible career paths for records managers.

ELECTRONIC BUSINESS ACTIVITIES

Internet: a worldwide network of computers that allows public access to send, store, and receive electronic information over public networks

The **Internet** is a worldwide network of computers that allows public access to send, store, and receive electronic information over public networks. The multimedia center of the Internet, the World Wide Web (www), is a worldwide hypermedia system (a network of computers that can read documents containing hyperlinks) that allows browsing, or "surfing," on a variety of organizations sites. Companies, organizations, and individuals create locations, called websites, that can be accessed by anyone who has an Internet connection.

E-Commerce

e-commerce: an electronic method to communicate and to transact business over networks and through computers

Have you used e-commerce?

Companies use these sites to share information about themselves and their products. They also conduct business using these sites. A broad definition of **e-commerce** is an electronic method to communicate and to transact business over networks and through computers. In other words, e-commerce is the buying and selling of goods and services using the Internet and other digital communications such as electronic funds transfer, smart cards, and digital cash.

Complex, sophisticated e-commerce systems use a combination of technology: the organization's databases, server applications, and browser software to display the transaction. For example, when you decide to buy something from an e-commerce site, you create an account. Your account information is entered into a database—you, as the user, are creating a record for the company. The record is stored in the company's database until the next time you look at the company's website. Companies utilize "cookies," which are embedded information stored on your computer. When you visit the company site again, the cookie sends information about you to the site so that you can add purchases or edit your account.

What are cookies?

As you buy more products, the company tracks your particular taste in products. If you have not purchased anything for a while, an e-mail may be automatically generated to let you know of new products that match your previous purchases. The company is able to generate new business based on previous business. This process is called niche marketing, and it is available in an all-electronic format. Amazon.com is an example of a sophisticated e-commerce system with which you may be familiar.

Management of e-commerce bridges the gap between information technology, records and information management, and the company's legal departments. Cooperation among these departments ensures a smooth flow of customer service, sales, and evidence of the transactions.

Electronic File Transfer and Data Interchange

The business processes of electronic file transfer and data interchange are another way organizations use digital communications.

electronic fund transfer (EFT): electronic payments and collections

Electronic fund transfer (EFT) provides for electronic payments and collections. It is safe, secure, efficient, and less expensive than paper check payments and collections. Many organizations deposit their employees' pay by using EFT.

electronic data interchange (EDI): a communication procedure between two companies that allows the exchange of standardized documents (most commonly invoices or purchase orders) through computers

Electronic data interchange (EDI) is a communication procedure between two companies that allows the exchange of standardized documents (most commonly invoices or purchase orders) through computers. If the two companies have compatible systems, the computers talk to each other through a connection. Walmart® is an example of a retailer that communicates with suppliers using EDI. For example, suppose you buy a pair of jeans at a local retailer, such as Walmart. The item is scanned, and the inventory of these jeans is updated. If more jeans are needed, the retailer sends a purchase order to the apparel company by EDI. When the apparel company ships the order, an invoice is created and sent to the retailer, again through EDI. The retailer can then pay the apparel company by electronic funds transfer. Thus, no physical records are exchanged. Records and information managers should ensure that the records transmitted in this business process are authentic, correct, and usable.

The next section addresses the procedures and processes that organizations are implementing as a way to enhance the effectiveness of records creation, distribution, storage, and retrieval.

PROGRAMS FOR MANAGING RECORDS

Records management is not new; it has been taking place in organizations for over 50 years. In recent years, terrorist attacks on the United States and the well-known corporate scandals have affected the profession of records and information management. These events have forced senior managers in corporate America and the government to reconsider how information and records management processes should be updated and improved.

Information Governance

information governance (IG): the overarching framework within which the records and information management (RIM) program resides

Is information governance broader in scope than RIM?

Information governance (IG) is the overarching framework within which the records and information management (RIM) program resides. Information governance is broader than RIM and provides a structure for which all business transactions and reference information within an organization are managed.

Under information governance, measures or standards are used to ensure compliance in the creation, use, retention, and disposition of organizational information regardless of its origin. Standards are set for managing all records, including records generated through social media or mobile devices, records stored on shared drivers, or records residing in the cloud.

Ideally, information governance policies, procedures, and compliance standards are developed through the efforts of a cross-functional steering committee made up of business, legal, RIM, and information technology (IT). The records and information management program must then conform to IG policies, procedures, and compliance standards.

The Generally Accepted Recordkeeping Principles® ("The Principles")

ARMA's Generally Accepted Recordkeeping Principles® ("The Principles"): form the foundation for which an effective information governance program can be built.

ARMA's Generally Accepted Recordkeeping Principles® ("The Principles") form the foundation for which an effective Information Governance Program can be built. The Principles were developed and published through ARMA International (www.arma.org).

ARMA is a not-for-profit professional association and the authority on information governance programs. According to their website, "ARMA has approximately 27,000+ members include records and information managers, information governance professionals, archivists, corporate librarians, imaging specialists, legal professionals, IT managers, consultants, and educators, all of whom work in a wide variety of industries, including government, legal, healthcare, financial services, and petroleum in the United States, Canada, and more than 30 other countries around the globe."

What is the purpose of ARMA's Generally Accepted Recordkeeping Principles® ("The Principles")?

As set forth in the executive summary preamble to the Principles,[1] ARMA states:

> ARMA International developed and published the Principles to foster general awareness of information governance standards and principles and to assist organizations in developing information management systems that comply with them.
>
> The Principles are comprehensive in scope, but general in nature. They are not addressed to a specific situation, industry, country, or organization, nor are they intended to set forth a legal rule for compliance that every organization must strictly adhere to in every circumstance.
>
> They are intended to set forth the characteristics of an effective information governance program, while allowing flexibility based upon the unique circumstances of an organization's size, sophistication, legal environment, and resources.
>
> Thoughtful consideration of the Principles, combined with a reasonable approach when applying them, will yield sound results for any organization: a responsive, effective, and legally compliant information governance program and recordkeeping system.

More information about the Principles can be found at www.arma.org/principles. The Principles are listed in Figure 2.1.

Records Program Management Guidelines

In summary, a records and information program must be in place to manage all phases in the records life cycle. Records and information management programs should have these common features:

- Adherence to the ARMA Principles for guidance and assessment of the program.
- A legally defensible retention schedule to reduce risk and legal liability. (You will be introduced to legal considerations later in this chapter).

[1] http://www.arma.org/r2/generally-accepted-br-recordkeeping-principles, accessed November 4, 2013. Used with permission.

FIGURE 2.1 **ARMA International's Generally Accepted Recordkeeping Principles®**

PRINCIPLE	SUMMARY
Accountability	A senior executive (or a person of comparable authority) shall oversee the information governance program and delegate responsibility for records and information management to appropriate individuals. The organization adopts policies and procedures to guide personnel and ensure that the program can be audited.
Integrity	An information governance program shall be constructed so the information generated by or managed for the organization has a reasonable and suitable guarantee of authenticity and reliability.
Protection	An information governance program shall be constructed to ensure a reasonable level of protection for records and information that are private, confidential, privileged, secret, classified, or essential to business continuity or that otherwise require protection.
Compliance	An information governance program shall be constructed to comply with applicable laws and other binding authorities, as well as with the organization's policies.
Availability	An organization shall maintain records and information in a manner that ensures timely, efficient, and accurate retrieval of needed information.
Retention	An organization shall maintain its records and information for an appropriate time, taking into account its legal, regulatory, fiscal, operational, and historical requirements.
Disposition	An organization shall provide secure and appropriate disposition for records and information that are no longer required to be maintained by applicable laws and the organization's policies.
Transparency	An organization's business processes and activities, including its information governance program, shall be documented in an open and verifiable manner, and that documentation shall be available to all personnel and appropriate interested parties.

Source: Adapted from www.arma.org/principles. Used with permission.

- Efficient procedures in place for managing each of the five stages in the records life cycle. (See Figure 1.4 in Chapter 1. You will study these procedures in detail in Chapters 7 and 12.)
- A well-trained staff. (See the "Careers in Records Management" section later in this chapter.)

Sometimes, the RIM system is centralized (records are physically located and controlled in one area); in other cases, it is decentralized (records are physically located in the departments where they are created and used). Each plan offers advantages and disadvantages that managers should consider carefully before deciding on an organizational plan. In large firms where work can be specialized, computers and other information systems play a major role in records and information management.

Electronic Record Management Tools

AIIM (Association for Information and Image Management): a global, non-profit organization that provides independent research, education and certification programs to information professionals

Many terms can be used to describe a broad process, policies, and procedures to manage electronic records such as enterprise content management (ECM) or electronic document records management systems (EDRMS).

AIIM (Association for Information and Image Management) is a global, non-profit organization that provides independent research, education, and certification programs to information professionals.[2]

[2]http://www.aiim.org/About, accessed November 6, 2013.

RECORDS MANAGEMENT IN ACTION

Student Records Stolen

Confidential electronic records stored on PCs or laptop computers can be extremely vulnerable to theft. Businesses and organizations need to have policies and procedures in place to ensure that unauthorized disclosure does not occur. On October 5, 2012, the records of more than 2,000 students from over 100 schools in Calgary, Alberta, Canada, were stolen. The report card records involved kindergarten through high school students. The theft occurred when a laptop containing the information was left unattended in a car.

Besides grades, the stolen information included names, student numbers, and photos of kindergarten through ninth-grade students. In addition, the high school student records included home addresses and phone numbers.

In an effort to reduce the impact of the lost records, school employees were tasked with attempting to contact all parents and/or students affected by the theft. This 11-day effort entailed a significant cost in time and money.

As a result of this data breach, the Calgary Board of Education approved spending in excess of $1 million to encrypt its computers to better safeguard sensitive, confidential electronic records.

Source: Richard Cuthbertson, "Report card data stolen," "CBE Spending $1M to bolster data protection," *Calgary Herald*, October 17–18, 2012.

enterprise content management (ECM): the strategies, methods, and tools used to capture, manage, store, preserve, and deliver content and documents related to organizational processes

Enterprise Content Management (ECM) is the strategies, methods, and tools used to capture, manage, store, preserve, and deliver content and documents related to organizational processes. ECM tools and strategies allow the management of an organization's unstructured information, wherever that information exists.[3]

An enterprise is a business venture or company. Systems have long been in place for electronic document management (EDM) and electronic document and records management systems (EDRMS). The broader term of enterprise content management (ECM) is an attempt to deal with the complex world of information technology where one technology can become outdated and is replaced with several new ones.

The value of ECM and EDRMS is not only in technology but also in the activities that involve people and processes. Organizations need a solution that enables their users to share documents and provides collaborative features (such as discussion threads, calendar items, team-managed documents, and additional project information) in a secure manner.

How much information is unstructured?

As with all records, electronic management tools acknowledge that not all documents are created equally. The records have business, operation, legal, and/or regulatory value, as discussed in Chapter 1. These tools also address unstructured information that exists outside the confines of databases and other electronic storage systems. The vast majority of information in most organizations comes from e-mail, word processing documents, digital images, and PDF (portable document format) files. Industry experts place unstructured information at 80 percent of all information created for a company.

---

[3]http://www.aiim.org/What-is-ECM-Enterprise-Content-Management, accessed November 6, 2013.

COMMON RECORD SYSTEM PROBLEMS AND CHALLENGES

records system: a group of interrelated resources—people, equipment and supplies, space, procedures, and information—acting together according to a plan to accomplish the goals of the records and information management program

What are common problems in records systems?

The programs for managing records discussed earlier achieve their goals through the operation of an organization's records system. A **records system** is a group of interrelated resources—people, equipment and supplies, space, procedures, and information—acting together according to a plan to accomplish the goals of the records and information management program. In this sense, anything that interferes with the operation of one or more resources creates a problem in the records system and therefore hinders the effectiveness of the records and information management program. Common problems in records systems and typical symptoms of such problems are listed in Figure 2.2.

As discussed earlier, ECM or EDRMS have gained popularity in organizations. A thorough discussion of these systems is detailed in Chapter 13.

RIM Systems Problems

As new technologies are developed, providing new ways for individuals and organizations to communicate, more and more documents are created that may or may not be records. As stated earlier, under ISO 15489 a record is

FIGURE 2.2 **Common Problems in Records Systems**

PROBLEM	SYMPTOMS
Management	• Lowest level for the assessment of the Principles • No overall plan for managing records problems • No plan for retaining or destroying records • No standards for evaluating workers
Human problems	• Lack of concern about the importance of records • Inaccurate classification of records as they are created and revised • Hoarding of records • Assuming that people know how to use the files for storage and retrieval of records
Insufficient filing procedures	• Computer files not organized into folders • Not using the built-in features of the records management software • Overloaded and poorly labeled drawers and folders • Failure to protect records • Misfiles resulting in lost records or slow retrieval • Records removed from and placed into files without proper authorization
Poor use of equipment	• No equipment standards • No use of fire-resistant equipment • Improper type of storage containers for records • Lack of or improper use of automated systems
Inefficient use of space	• Crowded working conditions • Poor layout of storage area • Resistance to the use of magnetic and/or digital media
Excessive records costs	• Inefficiency due to the above problems

defined as "information created, received, and maintained as evidence and information by an organization or person, in pursuance of legal obligations or in the transaction of business." RIM professionals must keep this definition in mind as they manage information being generated from the new and expanding technologies.

What are the RIM challenges facing records managers?

As a result, privacy, security concerns, and legal risks give rise to new laws and regulations. Therefore, records managers must be continually willing to adapt to and meet these challenges, as shown in Figure 2.3.

FIGURE 2.3 **Major RIM Challenges**

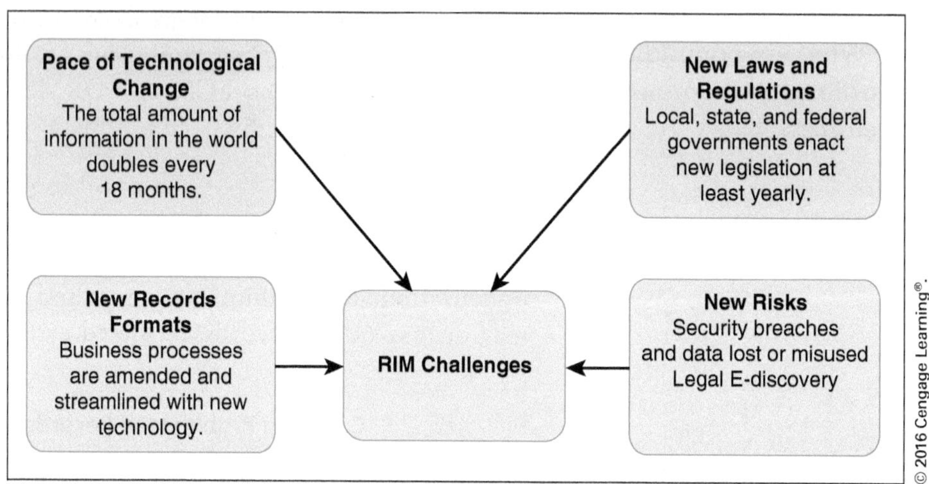

LEGAL CONSIDERATIONS FOR RECORDS MANAGEMENT

What three rights are addressed by legislation?

As the number of records increases dramatically, legislation to balance and protect an individual's right to privacy, the public's right to access information, and the quest for national security also increases. When individuals' rights to privacy have been violated, the public's access to information denied, or the national security has been breached, steps must be taken to protect these three important rights in a democratic society. These three rights are kept in balance by legislation.

How does the Privacy Act impact you?

Figure 2.4 contains a summary of key legislation related to the field of records and information management. Records and information managers are responsible for implementing phases of these laws.

As companies rely increasingly on information stored on a variety of media, records managers must be certain that their companies' recordkeeping systems are legally acceptable to governmental agencies and courts of law. Compliance issues are a concern to many organizations. Records management professionals are working together in organizations such as ARMA International and Association for Information and Image Management (AIIM) to optimize the effectiveness of records and information management to their organizations.

When a company is subject to litigation or a lawsuit, all information, records, and other evidence that are relevant to the case must be identified

FIGURE 2.4 **Legislation Related to Records and Information Management**

LEGISLATION AND AMENDMENTS	OUTCOME AND/OR INTENDED SOLUTION
General Services Administration records (GSA) 1947	Improve government practices and control in management
Freedom of Information Act, 1966 Privacy Act, 1974, 1994	Individuals have a right to see information about themselves. Imposes strict rules on the government's use of records collected about individuals, requiring government agencies to permit individuals to: • Control disclosure of information in their records. • Retain records of information that is disclosed. • Review and have a copy of information in their records. • Request amendment of information in their records.
Copyright Act, 1976 Intellectual Property Protection and Court Amendments of 2004	Provides copyright protection for many forms of physical and media works
Right to Financial Privacy Act, 1978	• Prevents financial institutions from requiring customers to authorize the release of financial records as a condition of doing business • States that customers have a right to access a record of all disclosures
Paperwork Reduction Act, 1980, 1995	To have federal agencies become more responsible and publicly accountable for reducing the burden of federal paperwork on the public and for other purposes
Video Privacy Protection Act, 1988	A criminal law that prohibits disclosure about videotapes individuals have rented without the informed, written consent of the individual
Computer Matching and Privacy Protection Act, 1988	• Establishes procedural requirements for government agencies to follow when engaging in computer matching activities • Provides matching subjects with opportunities to receive notice and to refute adverse information before having a benefit denied or terminated • Requires that agencies engaged in matching activities establish data protection boards to oversee those activities
Uniform Electronic Transaction Act, 1999	• First federal effort to provide uniform rules to govern electronic commerce and transactions in every state • Gives electronic signatures and records the same validity and enforceability as natural signatures and paper-based transactions
Electronics Signature in Global and National Commerce Act (E-SIGN), 2000	Eliminates legal barriers to the use of electronic technology to form and sign contracts, collect and store documents, and send and receive notices and disclosures
Fair Credit Reporting Act	• Designed to promote accuracy and ensure the privacy of the information used in consumer reports • Allows controlled access to credit bureau files
Health Insurance Portability and Accountability Act (HIPAA), Privacy Rule, 2001	• Creates national standards to protect individuals' medical records and other personal health information • Gives patients more control over their health information • Sets boundaries on the use and release of health records • Establishes appropriate safeguards that health care providers and others must achieve to protect the privacy of health information
Patriot Act, 2001 (in response to the terrorist attacks on September 11, 2001)	• Allows investigators to use the tools already available to investigate possible terrorist activities • Facilitates information sharing and cooperation among government agencies • Updates the law to reflect new technologies and new threats

continues on next page

FIGURE 2.4 *(continued)*

LEGISLATION AND AMENDMENTS	OUTCOME AND/OR INTENDED SOLUTION
Sarbanes-Oxley (SOX) Act, 2002	Passed in response to a number of major corporate and accounting scandals, this law: • Enhances standards for all US public company boards, management, and public accounting firms • Strengthens corporate governance
Amendments to the Federal Rules of Civil Procedures, 2006	All electronically stored information is discoverable. Parties must pay early attention to electronic information in the discovery process to control scope and expense.

discovery: When a company is subject to litigation or a lawsuit, all information, records, and other evidence that are relevant to the case must be identified and retrieved. These procedures are called the discovery process

e-discovery: the process of identifying and providing all electronically stored information and records relevant to the case

and retrieved. These procedures are called the **discovery** process. **E-discovery** is the process of identifying and providing all electronically stored information and records relevant to the case. Some electronic records that could be subject to e-discovery include internal memos, e-mails, employer postings on Twitter and/or Facebook, blogs, spreadsheets, and even webinar content.

Companies need to have policies and procedures for control and distribution of electronic records, as well as a legally defensible retention schedule. These measures are necessary as the cost of e-discovery can be very expensive for the company.

The role of records in recent business scandals affects the business climate. Searching for remedies, Congress has enacted legislation that affects the management of records. Compliance with the new rules and new auditing standards is now part of doing business in the United States. Records managers carry out these complex responsibilities in cooperation with the information technology and legal departments in an organization.

CAREERS IN RECORDS MANAGEMENT

What opportunities for work exist in records management?

Opportunities to work with records exist in every type and size of office. In a small office with one administrative assistant and an owner/manager, working with physical records occupies much of the time of both people. In this setting, opportunities for records work are unlimited. The classified ads section of newspapers, temporary employment websites, and job search websites list many general positions in small offices.

As illustrated earlier in Chapter 1, small business owners are using the many electronic tools available for keeping track of their business records. Someone who understands the business processes of electronic recordkeeping could find job opportunities in this setting.

Another potential career connected to records and information management is the marketing of physical records supplies and storage equipment. Offices need the paper, folders, file cabinets, shelves, and other supplies and equipment that are necessary for records storage and retrieval. Office supply vendors are an important resource to a records and information management department. A career as a marketing service representative for an office supplies company offers growth opportunities.

Many electronic software vendors offer solutions for managing electronic records. A customer service representative for a vendor is another avenue for employment in the RIM field.

In times of economic downsizing, many organizations are outsourcing portions of their records and information management services such as inactive records storage. Because inactive records may be kept for a long period of time but may not be referenced often, records storage facilities are usually located offsite in lower rent districts. Many companies offer storage and retrieval services for several types of businesses. Career opportunities exist in these records and information management service businesses.

Larger firms with more specialized staff often employ records supervisors who direct the work of several records clerks. In major corporations or other large administrative headquarters, you can find levels of records workers as described below.

1. **Operating level**—includes those workers responsible for routine filing and retrieving tasks, assisting with vital records, and records retention work. A records technician can work with imaging/microfilm, or data entry/indexing and quality control. Electronic records are usually created outside the records and information management departments. Because the operating level of work is emphasized in this textbook, you will concentrate on the basic principles involved in physically and electronically storing and retrieving records.
2. **Advanced operating level**—includes records analysts for active, inactive, retention, and vital records.
3. **Supervisory level**—includes specialists responsible for operating the records center, supervising the design and use of business forms, and directing the creation and use of physical and electronic records.
4. **Managerial/executive level**—the top position is the chief information officer or records director who is responsible for directing the entire RIM program.

Companies that place a high value on their information resources have created a new position to oversee all information-related departments, including records and information management. These new positions are variously titled chief information officer (CIO) or chief technology officer (CTO). Because of the potential liability due to the unlawful disclosure of confidential records, some government agencies have created an information security program manager position.

ARMA International has published Job Descriptions for Records and Information Management. The chart in Figure 2.5 shows possible job titles at each level.

ARMA International has published Records and Information Management Core Competencies.[4] The Level 1 assumptions are that entry-level practitioners have the basic skills of computation, legible writing, keyboarding, reading comprehension, and the ability to follow directions and procedures. Each level of the ARMA Core Competencies has a total of six domains: Business Functions, RIM Practices, Risk Management, Communication and Marketing, Information Technology, and Leadership.

As technology changes, students must not only understand but also use the available technology. The chapters in this textbook incorporate both physical and electronic RIM practices.

---

[4]Records and Information Management Core Competencies, 2007, by ARMA International, p. 4.

FIGURE 2.5 **Job Descriptions**

OPERATING LEVEL		
Records Clerk • Active and inactive records and vital records operations	**Records Technician** • Includes imaging/ microfilm/ digitizing, data entry/indexing, and quality-control technicians	**Senior Records Clerk** • Active, inactive, and vital records senior records clerk
ANALYST OPERATING LEVEL		
Records Analyst • Active, inactive, retention, and vital records analyst	**Senior Records Analyst** • Active, inactive, retention, and vital records senior records analyst	**Records Coordinator/ Records Specialist**
SUPERVISORY/MANAGERIAL LEVEL		
ERM Administrator/ ERM Architect	**RIM Supervisor** • Active, inactive, retention, and vital records supervisor	**RIM Manager**
MANAGERIAL/EXECUTIVE LEVEL		
RIM Director	**Executive Officer** • Chief information officer (CIO) • Chief technology officer (CTO) • Compliance officer/general counsel chief records officer	

Source: Job Descriptions for Records and Information Management, May 2008, by ARMA International, pp. 8, 29, 54, and 89. Used with permission.

Career Resources and Professional Organizations

Certificate Programs

Many experienced records and information management professionals have become certified records managers (CRMs) by taking and passing a multipart test administered by members of the Institute of Certified Records Managers (ICRM). This certification represents a standard by which persons involved in records and information management can be measured, accredited, and recognized according to criteria of experience and capability established by their peers. Each individual is experienced in active and inactive records systems and related areas such as archives, computer technology, micrographics, and optical disk technology. The CRM designation is earned by meeting both educational and work experience requirements and by passing the required examinations.[5]

What is ARMA International?

You can easily locate information on the records and information management profession by checking the publications and websites of the various professional associations specializing in the records and information management profession. ARMA International is an important professional group interested in improving educational programs in schools and industry and providing on-the-job knowledge about records and information management. ARMA members receive subscriptions to *Information Management* magazine and other features when accessing the website. Learn more about ARMA International at the organization's website.

Information on records management jobs can be found in the *Occupational Outlook Handbook.* This handbook is published by US Bureau of Labor Statistics and is available online. O*NET, the Occupational Information

[5] http://www.icrm.org, accessed October 24, 2013.

Network, is a comprehensive database of worker attributes and job characteristics. O*NET is the primary source of occupational information in the United States, which may also be accessed online. You can find links to these two sites at the website for this textbook.

What is AIIM?

As mentioned earlier in the chapter, AIIM is the international authority on enterprise content management, the tools and technologies that capture, manage, store, preserve, and deliver content in support of business processes. AIIM provides case studies, industry watch, and white paper publications, and a variety of electronic publications such as webinars, podcasts, blogs, and industry-specific forums. Learn more about AIIM at their website. You can find a link to this site at the website for this textbook.

AHIMA (American Health Information Management Association) is specifically for health and related industry records and information managers. AHIMA provides members' subscriptions to the *Journal of AHIMA*, as well as information about careers, schools, and online courses. Learn more about AHIMA at the organization's website. You can find a link to this site at the website for this textbook. Records and information management is universal in its concepts; however, medical records procedures are unique. This text does not cover managing medical records.

The physical records system is a place to begin a study of records management. Good records and information management principles are universal. They can and should be applied to electronic records systems as well. Additionally, the tangible nature of physical records, the fact that physical records are familiar to most people, and that such records can be located easily make the study of physical records the logical introduction to the records and information management field.

From such study, you need to understand alphabetic storage and retrieval systems, discussed in Chapters 3–7, along with subject, numeric, and geographic storage and retrieval systems, explained in Chapters 8–10. Chapters 11–13 focus on electronic records management. Chapter 14 describes the role and responsibilities of the records manager.

CHAPTER REVIEW AND APPLICATIONS

KEY POINTS

- The number of electronic processes that organizations use has greatly increased in recent years.
- The Generally Accepted Recordkeeping Principles (the Principles) should be used to establish an effective information governance program.
- Records managers must be willing to meet the challenges created by new technology, new laws, new business forms, and new risks.
- Legislation balances and protects an individual's right to privacy, the public's access to information, and the quest for national security.
- Career opportunities in records and information management are available in small, medium, and large offices.

TERMS

AIIM
ARMA International's Generally Accepted Recordkeeping Principles®
discovery
e-commerce
e-discovery
electronic data interchange (EDI)
electronic fund transfer (EFT)
enterprise content management (ECM)
information governance (IG)
Internet
records system

REVIEW AND DISCUSS

1. Have you ever used the electronic fund transfer process? Were you satisfied with the result? (Obj. 1)
2. Have you ever used the Internet to buy a product? Describe the process you used to complete your purchase. (Obj. 1)
3. What is information governance? (Obj. 2)
4. What is ARMA International, and what is the intent of the Generally Accepted Recordkeeping Principles (the Principles)? (Obj. 2)
5. What are some common problems found in records systems? (Obj. 3)
6. As new technologies are developed, what are the challenges for records and information management? (Obj. 3)

7. Records management legislation balances and protects what three rights? (Obj. 4)

8. What is e-discovery? (Obj. 4)

9. What is the intended outcome of the Sarbanes-Oxley Act? (Obj. 4)

10. How can you best prepare for work and advancement in records and information management positions? (Obj. 5)

11. Describe two benefits available for members of ARMA International. (Obj. 5)

12. What is the biggest difference between ARMA International and AIIM professional organizations? (Obj. 5)

APPLICATIONS

2-1 AIIM History

1. Access a search engine on the Internet, key in www.aiim.org.
2. From the home page, click "About AIIM."
3. In an e-mail to your instructor, summarize the history of AIIM.

2-2 ARMA International Certificates

1. Access a search engine on the Internet, key in www.arma.org.
2. From the home page, click "Professional Development."
3. Click "Certificate Programs."
4. In an e-mail to your instructor, summarize one of the certificate offerings.

2-3 ARMA Core Competencies, Level 1

Working with a group of students, read through the ARMA International Core Competencies Assumptions shown below:

> The RIM Core Competencies were developed with the following assumptions in business operational skills.[6]
>
> Level 1 practitioners can demonstrate:
> 1. Basic computational skills
> 2. Basic legible writing skills
> 3. Basic keyboarding skills
> 4. Reading comprehension
> 5. The ability to follow directions and procedures.

Discuss with your group what competencies you have, what competencies need more work, and what competencies you don't have.

Be prepared to report your answers to your instructor.

ADDITIONAL RESOURCES

For data files, Microsoft® Access tutorials and more, go to www.cengagebrain.com.

[6] Records and Information Management Core Competencies, p. 4, ARMA International, 2007. Used with permission.

CHAPTER 3

Alphabetic Indexing Rules 1–4

LEARNING OBJECTIVES

1. Explain the need for indexing rules in alphabetic storage of records and the importance of following these rules consistently.
2. Index, code, and arrange personal and business names in indexing order of units.
3. Index, code, and arrange minor words and symbols in business names.
4. Index, code, and arrange names with punctuation and possessives.
5. Index, code, and arrange names with single letters and abbreviations.
6. Apply alphabetic filing procedures.
7. Prepare and arrange cross-references for personal and business names.
8. Sort personal and business names.
9. Find information in database records.

Photo © Judith Read

ON THE JOB

Andrew Penta is the Records Officer for Clark County in southwest Washington. Andrew is the county liaison with Washington State Archives for permanent and historic records and also serves as the Oregon ARMA president. Andrew is a certified records manager (CRM). Andrew's road to his current job included being in the right place at the right time; he liked working with records. His people skills, management skills, and RIM background, as well as his CRM credential, help him enjoy his career.

Currently, Andrew manages the centralized inactive records storage facility for Clark County. The facility holds over 20,000 cubic feet of law and justice, financial, and administrative records. Andrew is responsible for record maintenance, updating and applying a legally defensible retention schedule, and coordinating records disposition. In addition, Andrew supervises the microfilming and digital scanning within an imaging system that contains 4 million pages of records.

Andrew's advice to students is to give themselves a head start in the records management field through formal education. Andrew encourages all people, at any stage of their career—but especially students and younger workers—to pursue coursework, or at least independent study, for the strongest chance of success. He believes that the best part of obtaining a CRM credential is that you must continue your education to maintain it. This provides extra motivation to keep learning—and there is so much to study. To illustrate Andrew's dedication to the records management profession, he is studying to be become a certified document imaging architect. In general, students should complete business technology and record management courses as well as library or archival science courses. Computer science or IT courses are also useful for record managers.

Reprinted with permission of Andrew Penta.

NEED FOR ALPHABETIC ORDER

How do business records help decision makers?

filing method: the way in which records are stored in a container, such as a filing cabinet or a folder on a hard disk, on a removable storage device, or in the cloud

As you learned in Chapters 1 and 2, records serve as the memory of an organization. Records also help an organization conduct business. Business records help provide decision makers with the right information when it is needed. To store records in an efficient way, some type of filing or storing method must be used. A **filing method**, sometimes called a *storage method*, describes the way in which records are stored in a container, such as a filing cabinet or a folder on a hard disk, on a removable storage device, or in the cloud. This text presents alphabetic, subject, numeric, and geographic methods of storage. Alphabetic storage is discussed in Chapters 3 to 7, subject storage in Chapter 8, numeric storage in Chapter 9, and geographic storage in Chapter 10. The most common filing method is alphabetic. Chapters 11, 12, and 13 look at electronic records and information management. Chapter 14 summarizes the responsibilities and duties of records managers.

The alphabetic filing method is a method of storing records arranged according to the letters of the alphabet. Sounds simple, right? Everyone knows the alphabet. However, consistently accurate alphabetic filing is not that simple.

Filing Rules

The most important filing concept to remember is that all filing is done to facilitate retrieving information when it is needed. To retrieve information efficiently, a set of rules must be followed. You will learn in Chapters 11, 12, and 13 about electronic records classification and storage. Different businesses have different needs for information retrieval.

ARMA International has published *Establishing Alphabetic, Numeric, and Subject Filing Systems,*[1] containing standard rules for storing records alphabetically. By using ARMA International's alphabetic indexing rules, businesses have a place to start when setting up an efficient alphabetic storage system. The rules in this textbook are written to agree with the standard filing rules presented in *Establishing Alphabetic, Numeric, and Subject Filing Systems,* published by ARMA International. See Appendix B for these guidelines for alphabetic filing.

Procedures for storing records alphabetically vary among organizations and among departments within organizations. Therefore, the filing procedures to be used in any *one* office must be determined, recorded, approved, and followed with no deviation. Without written rules for storing records in any filing method or format, procedures will vary with time, changes in personnel, and oral explanations. Unless those who maintain the records are consistent in following storage procedures, locating records will be difficult. The real test of an efficient records storage system is being able to find records quickly once they have been stored. This is true for electronic records as well.

Why are written rules needed for filing?

If you thoroughly understand the rules in this textbook, you will be able to adjust to any exceptions encountered in the specific office where you may work. Records and information managers who adopt these rules for their

[1]ARMA International, *Establishing Alphabetic, Numeric and Subject Filing Systems,* Lenexa, KS: ARMA International, 2005, pp. 17–22.

offices will find them understandable, logical, workable, and comprehensive enough to provide answers to the majority of storage questions that arise.

Alphabetic filing procedures involve inspecting, indexing, coding, cross-referencing, sorting, and storing documents. In this chapter, you will practice four of the steps: indexing, coding, cross-referencing, and sorting. In Chapter 6 you will learn to complete the other steps for alphabetic filing procedures.

Indexing

indexing: the mental process of determining the filing segment (or name) by which a physical record is to be stored and the placing or listing of items in an order that follows a particular system

filing segment: the name by which a record is stored and requested

indexing units: the various words that make up the filing segment for the physical record

Indexing is the mental process of determining the filing segment (or name) by which a physical record is to be stored and the placing or listing of items in an order that follows a particular system. The **filing segment** is the name by which a record is stored and requested. In alphabetic storage, the process of indexing means determining the name that is to be used in filing. The name is usually easily recognized. On correspondence, the name may appear in various places on a record. In the letter shown in Figure 3.1, the filing segment is the name of the person to whom the letter is addressed.

Because accurate indexing is necessary for quick retrieval, the indexing step is extremely important. Careful, accurate indexing is perhaps the most exacting step in the storage procedure. In an alphabetic arrangement, the selection of the right name by which to store (the filing segment) means that the physical record will be found quickly when it is needed. If the wrong name is selected, much time will be wasted trying to locate the record when it is eventually requested.

When selecting a filing segment, choose the name most likely to be used in asking for the record, usually the most important one. You will learn more about choosing the filing segment for documents in Chapter 6. Take a look at the examples shown in Figure 3.1. Each part of the name is labeled with a unit designation (*Key Unit, Unit 2, Unit 3, or Unit 4*). These units are the **indexing units** of the filing segment; in other words, the indexing units are the various words that make up the filing segment for the physical record.

FIGURE 3.1 **Filing Segment of a Letter**

Harry's Landscape, Inc.

247 Ohio Street
Elyria, OH 44035-0280
www.hlandscape.com

Telephone: (442) 555-0155 Fax: (442) 555-0156

November 12, 20--

Ms. Margo Johnson
24168 Squire Road
Columbia Station, OH 44028-0614

Dear Ms. Johnson

Your satisfaction with our products is important to us. I'm sorry to learn that you are displeased with a few items in the last shipment of plants we delivered to your home last week.

key unit: the first unit of a filing segment

indexing order: the order in which units of the filing segment are considered

The **key unit** is the first unit of a filing segment. It is the part of the segment considered first when determining where the record will be stored. Units 2, 3, 4, and so on are the next units by which the placement of the record is further determined. The order in which units of the filing segment are considered is called the **indexing order**. Identifying the key and succeeding units makes a complex process simpler and easier to handle. Marking these units is the next step in the process.

Coding

coding: the act of assigning a file designation to records as they are classified

indexing rules: written procedures that describe how the filing segments are ordered

Coding is the act of assigning a file designation to records as they are classified. For paper records, coding is physically marking a record to indicate the filing segment (name, number, or subject) by which it is to be stored and indicating the indexing units. Coding for a list of names may also be accomplished by placing the units of the filing segment in separate columns of a table. Coding is a physical act, as contrasted with indexing, which is a mental determination.

Coding procedures for paper records are to place diagonals (/) between the parts of the filing segment, underline the key unit, and then number each succeeding unit (i.e., 2, 3, 4), which you have mentally identified in the indexing process. The filing segments shown in Figure 3.2 are coded in this manner.

To code properly, a set of rules for alphabetic storage must be faithfully followed. **Indexing rules** are the written procedures that describe how the filing segments are ordered. The indexing rules that follow give you a good start in following appropriate alphabetic storage procedures.

FIGURE 3.2 **Coded Filing Segments for Personal and Business Names**

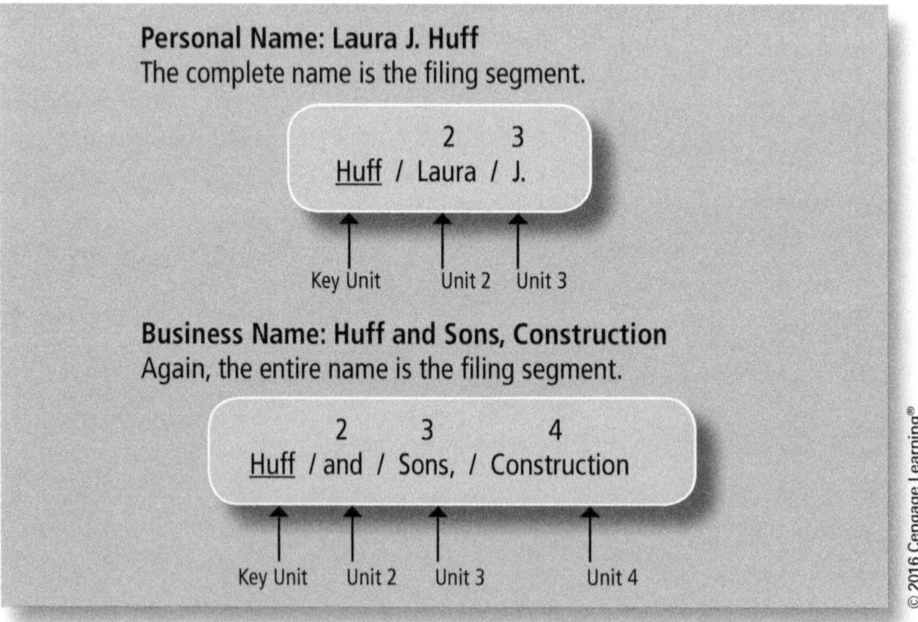

ALPHABETIC INDEXING RULES

In this section, rules for alphabetic storage are presented with examples to help you understand how to apply the rules. Study each rule and the examples of its application carefully; above all, be sure you understand the rule.

RECORDS MANAGEMENT IN ACTION

Banking: It Isn't What It Used To Be

The days of driving to your local bank branch with your paper paycheck, filling out a deposit slip, endorsing the check, and handing all of the documents to a teller are fading fast.

Electronic transfers with direct deposits into your bank account(s) are becoming the norm. Online banking via computers and mobile devices now prevail. According to an August 2013 Pew Research Center report, 51 percent of US adults and 61 percent of Internet users now bank online. The report also indicated that the percentage of cell phone owners conducting mobile banking has nearly doubled, from 18 percent to 35 percent since 2011.

As more and more customers go online or use their mobile devices to bank, financial institutions are finding that keeping some small branches open can be too costly. Those expenses include personnel costs, space leasing, property taxes, heating, lighting, and all of the other costs associated with maintaining a bank space. This leaves branches in small rural communities, with fewer customers, vulnerable to closures. According to SNL Financial, US banks closed 2,267 branches in 2012. The trend toward closing branches in sparse population areas is expected to continue into the near future. AlixPartners, a New York consulting firm, predicts that the number of US branches will drop from 93,000 to 80,000 over the next decade.

Source: Robin Sidel, "After Years of Growth, Banks are Pruning Their Branches," *Wall Street Journal*, March 31, 2013; and Pete Rizzo, "Pew: Mobile Banking Growth Outpaces Online Banking," PYMNTS.com, August 26, 2013, http://www.pymnts.com/briefing-room/consumer-engagement/consumer-behavior/2013/pew-mobile-banking-growth-outpaces-online-banking/(accessed November 26, 2013)

Follow these guidelines to study the indexing rules effectively:

- Read the rule carefully. Make sure you understand the meaning of the words used to state the rule.
- Look at the examples. Note that the complete filing segment (the name and other words, such as a title) is given at the left. Then the filing segment is separated into indexing units at the right, according to the rule you are studying.
- Be sure you understand why the filing segment has been separated as it has.

What is an effective way to study alphabetic indexing rules?

In determining alphabetic order, compare the units in the filing segments for differences. If the key units are alike, move to the second units, the third units, and succeeding units until a difference occurs. The point of difference determines the correct alphabetic order, as shown here. Compare the three filing segments shown in the units, and note the correct order.

FILING SEGMENT	KEY UNIT	UNIT 2	UNIT 3
Diane Ruhl	Ruhl	Diane	
Diane M. Ruhl	Ruhl	Diane	M
Dianne Ruhl	Ruhl	Dianne	

In an office, filing records goes much more quickly when filers are able to determine the proper indexing order of personal and business names on the physical records. Filing records based on incorrect indexing order can result in lost records or additional time required when users want to retrieve records.

When working with paper documents, the next step in the filing process is sorting. Sorting is arranging records in the sequence in which they are to be stored (placed in filing cabinets or folders on storage media.) In this chapter, you will practice sorting coded names.

Examples are provided for each alphabetic indexing rule. In the examples, you will find an underscore in one of the indexing units for each filing segment except the first one. This underscore indicates the letter of the unit that determines alphabetic order. Examples are numbered for ease in referring to them. Indexing units are shown in mixed case. Marks that appear over or under some letters in different languages are disregarded (such as Señora, Marçal, René, Valhallavägen). Be sure you understand each rule before going to the next.

RULE 1: INDEXING ORDER OF UNITS

A. Personal Names

A personal name is indexed in this manner: (1) the surname (last name) is the key unit, (2) the given name (first name) or initial is the second unit, and (3) the middle name or initial is the third unit. If determining the surname is difficult, consider the last name written as the surname. (You will learn how to handle titles that appear with names in a later rule.)

What does "nothing before something" mean?

A unit consisting of just an initial precedes a unit that consists of a complete name beginning with the same letter—*nothing before something.* Punctuation is omitted. Remember, the underscored letter in the example shows the correct order. For instance, 1 and 2 in the examples table have the same key unit (*Sample*). The underscored "D" in *Darin* shows the alphabetic difference between the two names.

Examples of Rule 1A

	FILING SEGMENT	INDEXING ORDER OF UNITS		
	Name	**Key Unit**	**Unit 2**	**Unit 3**
1.	Charlene Sample	Sample	Charlene	
2.	Darin Sample	Sample	Darin	
3.	Darlene A. Samples	Samples	Darlene	A
4.	Jeff Simmons	Simmons	Jeff	
5.	Neil S. Simon	Simon	Neil	S
6.	Paula Simon	Simon	Paula	
7.	Neil S. Simone	Simone	Neil	S
8.	Michelle Skrzynski	Skrzynski	Michelle	
9.	Robert Sunderland	Sunderland	Robert	
10.	Roberta Sunderland	Sunderland	Roberta	
11.	Andrew Taylor	Taylor	Andrew	
12.	Andy Taylor	Taylor	Andy	
13.	Anne M. Taylor	Taylor	Anne	M
14.	Armand R. Taylor	Taylor	Armand	R
15.	Joyce Utterbock	Utterbock	Joyce	

B. Business Names

Business names are indexed as written using letterheads or trademarks as guides. Each word in a business name is a separate unit. Business names containing personal names are indexed as written.

Examples of Rule 1B

	FILING SEGMENT	INDEXING ORDER OF UNITS		
	Name	Key Unit	Unit 2	Unit 3
1.	Samantha Seger Designs	Samantha	Seger	Designs
2.	Secure Design	Secure	Design	
3.	Secure Digital Networks	Secure	Digital	Networks
4.	Sester Farms, Inc.	Sester	Farms	Inc
5.	Settlement Professionals, Inc.	Settlement	Professionals	Inc
6.	Shelly Sherman Photography	Shelly	Sherman	Photography
7.	Sherman Auto Sales	Sherman	Auto	Sales
8.	Silver Pizza Co.	Silver	Pizza	Co
9.	Silverwood Apartments	Silverwood	Apartments	
10.	Silvin Painting, Inc.	Silvin	Painting	Inc

RULE 1: Self-Check

1. Index each name in the table. Code each name by writing each unit of the filing segment in the appropriate column. The first name is shown as an example.
2. Compare the key units and the other units, if needed, to determine the correct alphabetic filing order for the names. Indicate the correct filing order by writing numbers 1 through 10 beside the names in the Order column.

	Filing Segment	Order	Key Unit	Unit 2	Unit 3	Unit 4
a.	Thi Dien Personnel, Inc.		Thi	Dien	Personnel	Inc
b.	Latasha Gregory					
c.	Edward Simmons					
d.	Greg Simmons Car Company					
e.	Albert Brown Suit Shop					
f.	Elbert Albert					
g.	Thi Dien					
h.	T. F. Simmons					
i.	Dien Dry Cleaners					
j.	Anna C. Dien					

3. Are the two names in each of the following pairs in correct alphabetic order? If the order is correct, write Yes in the blank below the names. If the order is not correct, write No in the blank.

   a. Dahlin Clothing Store
   Charlotte Dahling
   ____

   b. Rose Andrews
   Rose Garden Nursery
   ____

c. Rayburn Law Office
Rayborn Electrical Co.

____

d. Little Pond Productions
Lyle A. Little

____

e. David Allen
Allen Furniture Company

____

f. Rosalie Simmons
Rod Simmons

____

g. Kent Wade
Wade Eves Designs

____

h. Red Robin Restaurant
Red Robin Bait Shop

____

i. Tewksbury Ornamental Plants
Olivia Tewksbury

____

j. Gerald Minton
G. L. Minton

____

4. Are the names in each group listed in correct order? If the names are in correct order, write Correct in the blank beside the names. If the names are not in correct order, indicate the correct order of the names by writing their numbers in the blank. For example, 3, 1, 2.

_____ **a.** 1. Mark Joackims
2. Vicky Jolly
3. Ardis Johnson

_____ **b.** 1. Zelda Bruss
2. Bruss Flower Arranging
3. Ryan T. Bruss

_____ **c.** 1. Linda Podany
2. Daniel Potter
3. Maria Ponzi

_____ **d.** 1. Miranda Moore
2. Miranda's Hobbies
3. Miranda A. Moore

_____ **e.** 1. Richard Pope
2. Popeye's Deli
3. Theresa Pope

_____ **f.** 1. Carroll Guest
2. Edgar Guest
3. Ella May Guest

Data File

5. Answers to this exercise are shown in the Word file *3 Check Answers*, found in the data files. Compare them with your answers.

RULE 2: MINOR WORDS AND SYMBOLS IN BUSINESS NAMES

Articles, prepositions, conjunctions, and symbols are considered separate indexing units. Symbols are considered as spelled in full. When the word *The* appears as the first word of a business name, it is considered the last unit.

How are symbols indexed?

Articles:	a, an, the
Conjunctions:	and, but, or, nor
Prepositions:	at, in, out, on, off, by, to, with, for, of, over
Symbols:	&, ¢, $, #, % (and, cent or cents, dollar or dollars, number or pound, percent)

Examples of Rule 2

	FILING SEGMENT	INDEXING ORDER OF UNITS			
	Name	**Key Unit**	**Unit 2**	**Unit 3**	**Unit 4**
1.	A & A Drilling	A	and	A	Drilling
2.	A Clean House	A	Clean	House	
3.	The An Dong Market	An	Dong	Market	The
4.	Dollar Drug Store	Dollar	Drug	Store	
5.	The $ Shop	Dollar	Shop	The	
6.	Golf By The Mountain	Golf	By	The	Mountain
7.	Gone But Not Forgotten	Gone	But	Not	Forgotten
8.	Gone To The Dogs	Gone	To	The	Dogs
9.	Granger & Graves Yachts	Granger	and	Graves	Yachts
10.	# One Copy Store	Number	One	Copy	Store

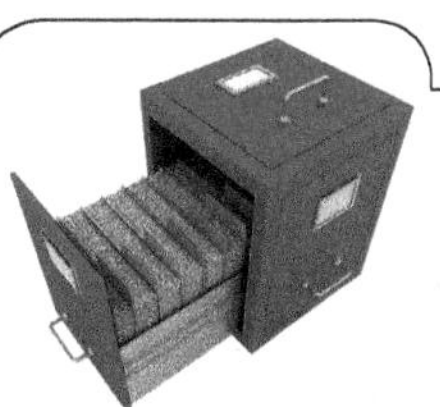

MY RECORDS

Protect Yourself from Identity Theft

Identity theft is a serious problem. What can you do to reduce the chances that you will be a victim?

Although no one can guarantee that you are safe from identity theft, you can reduce your risks by following these guidelines.

- Do not carry your Social Security card, passport, or birth certificate on your person.
- Do not give out personal information on the phone, through the mail, or online unless you know the site is safe, and you initiated the call or transaction.
- Create passwords and/or personal identification numbers (PINs) to protect your credit card, bank, and phone accounts. (Avoid using your mother's maiden name, your birth date, the last four digits of your Social Security number, your phone number, or a series of consecutive numbers.)
- Change passwords often, and include upper- and lowercase letters, numbers, and symbols.
- Check your debit and credit account activity every few days, and keep an eye out for any unfamiliar transactions. If you find any, notify your bank or credit card company immediately.
- Secure personal information at home in a locked, fire-resistant box.
- Shred charge receipts, credit records, checks, bank statements, and unwanted credit card offers before throwing them away.
- Update your computer's virus and spyware protection software regularly.
- Review a copy of your credit report each year to make sure no new credit cards or other accounts have been issued in your name without your authorization.
- Remove incoming mail daily from your mailbox and request that your mail be held at the post office until you return from a vacation or other absence from home.
- Mail letters or documents that contain personal data (such as tax forms or checks) at the post office or in an official postal service mailbox.
- React quickly if a creditor or merchant calls about charges you did not make.
- Show only your name and address on printed checks and deposit slips.
- Watch out for "shoulder surfers." Use your free hand to shield the keypad when using ATMs or pay phones.
- Pay attention to your billing cycles. If bills or financial statements are late, contact the sender.

RULE 2: Self-Check

1. Index each name in the table. Code each name by writing each unit of the filing segment in the appropriate column.
2. Compare the key units and the other units, if needed, to determine the correct alphabetic filing order for the names. Indicate the correct filing order by writing numbers 1 through 10 beside the names in the Order column.

	Filing Segment	Order	Key Unit	Unit 2	Unit 3	Unit 4
a.	The Chimney Sweepers					
b.	The Crazy Fox					
c.	A Shop of Wonders					
d.	An Honorable Store					
e.	C & R Offerings					
f.	Camp By the Sea					
g.	C & R Company					
h.	The Clip Joint					
i.	$ Saver Cleaners					
j.	Cybersurf By the Hour					

Data File

3. Answers to this exercise are shown in the Word file *3 Check Answers* found in the data files. Compare them with your answers.

RULE 3: PUNCTUATION AND POSSESSIVES

What do you do with punctuation marks when indexing?

All punctuation is disregarded when indexing personal and business names. Commas, periods, hyphens, apostrophes, dashes, exclamation points, question marks, quotation marks, underscores, and diagonals (/) are disregarded, and names are indexed as written.

Examples of Rule 3

FILING SEGMENT		INDEXING ORDER OF UNITS			
	Name	Key Unit	Unit 2	Unit 3	Unit 4
1.	Grant & Reardon Sales	Grant	and	Reardon	Sales
2.	Grant's Barber Shop, Inc.	Grants	Barber	Shop	Inc
3.	Grant's Homestyle Eatery	Grants	Homestyle	Eatery	
4.	I Do Windows!	I	Do	Windows	
5.	I_can_do_it.com	Icandoitcom			
6.	Ike & Sons Realty	Ike	and	Sons	Realty
7.	Inter-Asia Services	InterAsia	Services		
8.	Iron Mountain	Iron	Mountain		
9.	Iron Mountain Mining Co.	Iron	Mountain	Mining	Co
10.	Julia Jones-Zeta	JonesZeta	Julia		

RULE 3: Self-Check

1. Index each name in the table. Code each name by writing each unit of the filing segment in the appropriate column.
2. Compare the key units and the other units to determine the correct alphabetic filing order for the names. Indicate the correct filing order by writing numbers 1 through 10 beside the names in the Order column.

	Filing Segment	Order	Key Unit	Unit 2	Unit 3	Unit 4
a.	In-and-Out Car Wash					
b.	Imelda Irving-Brown					
c.	The Flying Cow Dairy					
d.	Inside/Outside Games, Inc.					
e.	#s Away Diet Center					
f.	The Ink-a-Do Stamp Store					
g.	$ Saver Store					
h.	In-Town Couriers					
i.	Allison Love-Jarvis					
j.	Lovely & Ripley Clothing					

3. Are the two names in each of the following pairs in correct alphabetic order? If the order is correct, write "Yes" in the blank below the names. If the order is not correct, write "No" in the blank.

   a. Yolanda's $ Saver
   Yolanda Doolittle
   ____

   b. Rod-N-Reel Store
   Rodney Associates, Inc.
   ____

   c. Do-Rite Pharmacy
   Do-Rite Builders
   ____

   d. Rob & Son Electric
   Rob & Sons Alignment
   ____

   e. Colt-Western Company
   Colt Industries
   ____

   f. Temp-A-Cure Company
   Temp-Control Mechanics
   ____

   g. Nor-West Growing Company
   Nor' Wester Novelties
   ____

   h. Ezekiel M. Swanson
   The Swan Dive Shop
   ____

   i. Heckman Law Firm
   Dennis Heckman
   ____

   j. Chi Kuo
   Ching-yu Kuo
   ____

Data File

4. Answers to this exercise are shown in the Word file *3 Check Answers* found in the data files. Compare them with your answers.

RULE 4: SINGLE LETTERS AND ABBREVIATIONS

A. Personal Names

How do you index abbreviated personal names?

Initials in personal names are considered separate indexing units. Abbreviations of personal names (Wm., Jos., Thos.) and nicknames (Liz, Bill) are indexed as they are written.

B. Business Names

If the first name for a business is "The," which unit is used?

How do you index single letters in business names?

Single letters in business and organization names are indexed as written. If single letters are separated by spaces, index each letter as a separate unit. An acronym (a word formed from the first, or first few, letters of several words, such as NASDAQ and ARCO) is indexed as one unit regardless of punctuation or spacing. Abbreviated words (Mfg., Corp., Inc.) and names (IBM, GE) are indexed as one unit regardless of punctuation or spacing. Radio and television station call letters (KDKA, WNBC) are indexed as one unit.

Examples of Rule 4

	FILING SEGMENT	INDEX ORDER OF UNITS			
	Name	Key Unit	Unit 2	Unit 3	Unit 4
1.	A C T Realty	A	C	T	Realty
2.	Ace Smile Dental Lab	Ace	Smile	Dental	Lab
3.	Ackerson & Day Mfgs.	Ackerson	and	Day	Mfgs
4.	KKRS Radio Station	KKRS	Radio	Station	
5.	K-Nine Security	KNine	Security		
6.	KOGO Television	KOGO	Television		
7.	M A C Construction	M	A	C	Construction
8.	MAC, Inc.	MAC	Inc		
9.	U & I Nursery	U	and	I	Nursery
10.	Ulys. A. Udey	Udey	Ulys	A	

RULE 4: Self-Check

1. Index each name in the table. Code each name by writing each unit of the filing segment in the appropriate column.
2. Compare the key units and the other units, if needed, to determine the correct alphabetic filing order for the names. Indicate the correct filing order by writing numbers 1 through 10 beside the names in the Order column.

	Filing Segment	Order	Key Unit	Unit 2	Unit 3	Unit 4
a.	IDEA Corporate Services					
b.	I-Can-Fix-It Auto Body					
c.	I C A Corp.					
d.	I Dig It Services					
e.	I Am Woman, Inc.					
f.	I C Clearly Vision					
g.	I Buy Antiques					
h.	ICAP, Inc.					
i.	ID Booth, Inc.					
j.	IBT Associates					

Data File

3. Answers to this exercise are shown in the Word file *3 Check Answers*, found in the data files. Compare them with your answers.

CAREER CORNER

Job Description for Law Firm Records Clerk

The following job description is an example of a career opportunity in a law firm.

DUTIES AND RESPONSIBILITIES

- Assist attorneys, paralegals, and assistants with extended file searches
- Manage Autonomy Records Manager (ARM) and generate labels for client file materials
- Manage file room and records, including updating and re-filing client files
- Process files for off-site storage, including but not limited to verification of the box content printouts
- Assist with the assembly of records and files responsive to the client's request
- Print reports, update files, deliver files, and other duties as assigned

QUALIFICATIONS

- Must have a working knowledge of Word and Outlook and be able to type 45+ wpm
- Knowledge of Autonomy Records Manager (ARM), FileSurf, or LegalKey a plus
- Aptitude for clerical work related to accurate alphabetical filing
- Must have excellent interpersonal skills and ability to work effectively in time-sensitive and fast-paced situations
- Must have ability to remain focused on tasks at hand in spite of interruptions

CROSS-REFERENCING

Why are cross-references needed?

cross-reference: shows the name in a form other than that used on the original record, and it indicates the storage location of the original record

Some records of persons and businesses may be requested by names that are different from the ones by which they were stored. This is particularly true if the key unit is difficult to determine. When a record is likely to be requested by more than one name, an aid called a cross-reference is prepared. A **cross-reference** shows the name in a form other than that used on the original record, and it indicates the storage location of the original record. The filer can then find requested records regardless of the name used in the request for those records.

Both the filing segment used to determine the storage location for the record and the cross-reference notation are coded on the document, as shown in Figure 3.3. A copy of the document may be stored in the cross-reference location, or a cross-reference sheet may be prepared. Cross-reference sheets used with correspondence records are discussed in Chapter 6.

Cross-referencing must be done with discretion. Too many cross-references crowd the files and may hinder retrieval, rather than help. Each cross-reference requires valuable time to prepare, creates at least one additional sheet to be stored, and therefore requires additional space in a file.

Cross-references for data stored in an electronic database are often not needed. Because the search features of database software are extensive,

FIGURE 3.3 **Letter with Filing Segment and Cross-Reference Coded**

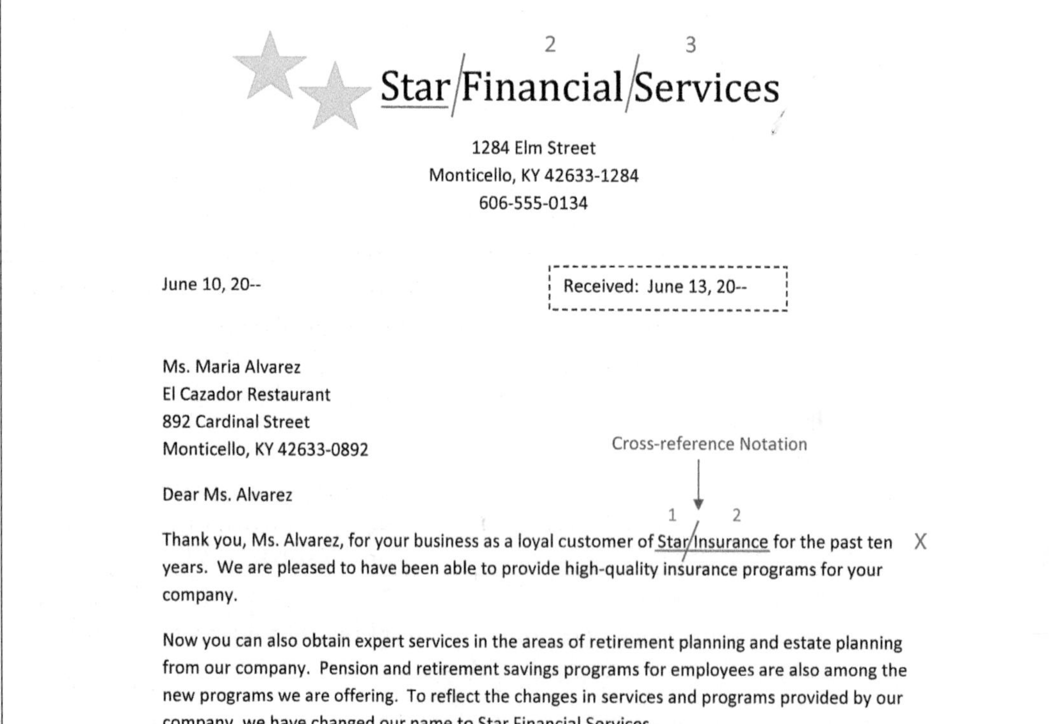

2 3
Star/Financial/Services

1284 Elm Street
Monticello, KY 42633-1284
606-555-0134

June 10, 20--

Received: June 13, 20--

Ms. Maria Alvarez
El Cazador Restaurant
892 Cardinal Street
Monticello, KY 42633-0892

Dear Ms. Alvarez

Thank you, Ms. Alvarez, for your business as a loyal customer of Star/Insurance for the past ten years. We are pleased to have been able to provide high-quality insurance programs for your company. X

Now you can also obtain expert services in the areas of retirement planning and estate planning from our company. Pension and retirement savings programs for employees are also among the new programs we are offering. To reflect the changes in services and programs provided by our company, we have changed our name to Star Financial Services.

a record can usually be found easily using any part of the filing segment. Also, entire records are often visible when a search result shows on the screen. In some instances, however, a cross-reference is needed under an entirely different name. In these instances a cross-reference database record can be created.

Four types of personal names should be cross-referenced:

1. Unusual names
2. Hyphenated surnames
3. Alternate names
4. Similar names

Also, nine types of business names should be cross-referenced. Two will be presented in this chapter; the remainder, in Chapters 4 and 5.

1. Compound names
2. Names with abbreviations and acronyms

An explanation of the procedure to be followed in cross-referencing each of these kinds of names follows. To practice coding and cross-referencing records in these early chapters, you will work with names that might appear on paper documents. Later, in Chapter 6, you will code and file actual business documents. Database entries have a primary field that is a unique identifier for the record. See Appendix A for more information about databases.

Personal Names

Cross-references should be prepared for the following types of personal names.

1. **Unusual (easily confused) names.** When determining the surname is difficult, use the last name written as the key unit on the original record. Prepare a cross-reference with the first name written as the key unit. On the original correspondence for Charles David, *David* (last name) is the key unit, and *Charles* (first name) is the second unit. However, a request might be made for *David Charles*. In a correspondence file, the cross-reference sheet would show *Charles* as the key unit and *David* as the second unit. Someone looking under *C* for *Charles* would find the cross-reference directing the filer to look under *D* for *David*. Study the following examples.

CODED FILING SEGMENT	CROSS-REFERENCE
2 Charles / David	2 Charles / David SEE David Charles
2 Gee-Hong / Cheung	2 Gee-Hong / Cheung SEE Cheung GeeHong
2 Keooudon / Sayasene	2 Keooudon / Sayasene SEE Sayasene Keooudon

How do you cross-reference a hyphenated surname?

2. **Hyphenated surnames.** Married women often use hyphenated surnames. With hyphenated surnames, a request for records could be in either of the two surnames. A cross-reference enables retrieval in either case. An example is *Wendy Reardon-Bruss*, shown below.

Many men use hyphenated surnames that are their family names, and they are known only by their hyphenated surnames. A cross-reference is not necessary. Some men choose to adopt a hyphenated surname when they marry and may, in that case, be known by more than one name. A cross-reference is needed for accurate retrieval of records when a man changes his surname to a hyphenated surname. See *Douglas Edwards-Read*, shown below. You will be told when a cross-reference is needed for a man's name; otherwise, a cross-reference is not required.

CODED FILING SEGMENT	CROSS-REFERENCE
2 Wendy / Reardon-Bruss	2 3 Bruss / Wendy / Reardon SEE ReardonBruss Wendy
2 Douglas / Edwards-Read	2 3 Read / Douglas / Edwards SEE EdwardsRead Douglas

3. **Alternate names.** When a person is known by more than one name, you need to make cross-references. Two examples are *Michelle Starkinsky* doing business as *Michelle Star* and *Faith Moran*, who is also known as *Faith Moran-Ripley*, *Mrs. Michael Ripley*, and *Mrs. Faith Ripley*. Note that three cross-references are required for Faith Moran.

CODED FILING SEGMENT	CROSS-REFERENCE
2 Michelle / Star	2 Starkinsky / Michelle SEE Star Michelle
2 Faith / Moran	2 MoranRipley / Faith SEE Moran Faith --- 2 3 Ripley / Michael / Mrs SEE Moran Faith --- 2 3 Ripley / Faith / Mrs SEE Moran Faith

4. **Similar names.** A variety of spellings exist for some names like *Brown* and *Johnson.* A SEE ALSO cross-reference is prepared for all likely spellings. If the name is not found under one spelling, the filer checks the SEE ALSO sheet for other possible spellings. In a correspondence file, there would likely be a permanent cross-reference (could be a guide) to show the different spellings for common names. Cross-reference guides are discussed in Chapter 6. SEE ALSO cross-references are not need in electronic databases. Other information helps determine the correct record, such as a birth date or another unique identifier.

CODED FILING SEGMENT	CROSS-REFERENCE
Brown SEE ALSO Browne, Braun, Brawn	Browne SEE ALSO Brown, Braun, Brawn --- Braun SEE ALSO Brown, Brawn, Browne --- Brawn SEE ALSO Brown, Browne, Braun
Johnson SEE ALSO Johnsen, Johnston, Jonson	Johnsen SEE ALSO Johnson, Johnston, Jonson --- Johnston SEE ALSO Johnson, Jonson, Johnsen --- Jonson SEE ALSO Johnson, Johnsen, Johnston

Business Names

Cross-references should be prepared for the following types of business names. The original name is the name appearing on the letterhead.

How many cross-references are needed for a business that includes three surnames?

1. **Compound names.** When a business name includes two or more individual surnames, prepare a cross-reference for each surname other than the first.

CODED FILING SEGMENT	CROSS-REFERENCE
Jarvis, (1) / Rasmussen, (2) / and (3) / Sheraden (4) / Antiques (5)	Rasmussen (1) / Sheraden (2) / and (3) / Jarvis (4) / Antiques (5) SEE Jarvis Rasmussen and Sheraden Antiques --- Sheraden (1) / Jarvis (2) / and (3) / Rasmussen (4) / Antiques (5) SEE Jarvis Rasmussen and Sheraden Antiques

2. **Abbreviations and acronyms.** When a business is commonly known by an abbreviation or an acronym, a cross-reference is prepared for the full name. Examples are *MADD* (Mothers Against Drunk Driving) and *EZ Electronics* (Ewen and Zucker Electronics), shown below.

CODED FILING SEGMENT	CROSS-REFERENCE
MADD	Mothers (1) / Against (2) / Drunk (3) / Driving (4) SEE MADD
EZ (1) / Electronics (2) (Ewen and Zucker Electronics)	Ewen (1) / and (2) / Zucker (3) / Electronics (4) SEE EZ Electronics --- Zucker (1) / and (2) / Ewen (3) / Electronics (4) SEE EZ Electronics

CROSS-REFERENCING: Self-Check

1. Identify the units in the filing segments (names). Code the names by underlining the key unit, numbering the other units, and placing diagonal lines between the units.
2. Write cross-references for the names that require them. See the example below.

2 3 4 Lundry / and / Masur / Meats	2 3 4 Masur / and / Lundry / Meats SEE Lundry and Masur Meats

	CODED FILING SEGMENT	CROSS-REFERENCE (IF NEEDED)
a.	WKKP Radio Station	
b.	IBM (International Business Machines)	
c.	Sideras and Shadduck Company	
d.	Platika and Miller Investment Firm	
e.	Joan Childress-Edwards	
f.	The Riverside Terrace	
g.	Akeo Saga	
h.	Mauruka's Diner	
i.	Smith, Childers, & Jones, Inc.	
j.	BBCC (Big Bend Community College)	

Data File

3. Answers to this exercise are shown in the Word file *3 Check Answers* found in the data files. Compare them with your answers.

RULES 1–4: Self-Check

1. Index each name in the table. Code each name by writing each unit of the filing segment in the appropriate column.
2. Compare the key units and the other units, if needed, to determine the correct alphabetic filing order for the names. Indicate the correct filing order by writing numbers 1 through 10 beside the names in the Order column.

	Filing Segment	Order	Key Unit	Unit 2	Unit 3	Unit 4
a.	Carolyn's Autos for Less					
b.	Janet Crawford					
c.	Crow's Nest Pass Inn					
d.	Andrew Carstairs					
e.	Crawford Law Firm					
f.	Deseree Campbell					
g.	George M. Caldwell					
h.	Cross-Town Transit					
i.	Linda E. Craft					
j.	Cyrus Campbell					

Data File

3. Answers to this exercise are shown in the Word file *3 Check Answers*, found in the data files. Compare them with your answers.

CHAPTER REVIEW AND APPLICATIONS

KEY POINTS

- A set of written rules helps make filing consistent.
- Indexing is the mental process of determining the filing segment (or name) by which the record is to be stored.
- Coding is the physical process of marking the filing segment into indexing units on paper records.
- Personal names are indexed by the surname, the given name, and then middle name or initial.
- Business names are indexed as written.
- Minor words and symbols in business names are indexed as written and are considered separate indexing units.
- Symbols in business names are spelled out.
- When the word "The" is the first word in a business name, it is considered the last indexing unit.
- Ignore all punctuation marks when indexing personal and business names.
- Single letters and abbreviations are indexed as written for both personal and business names. When single letters in a business name are separated by spaces, each letter is considered a separate indexing unit.

- Cross-reference personal names that are unusual, hyphenated surnames, alternate names, and similarly spelled names.
- Cross-reference business names that are abbreviations and acronyms and those that contain more than one surname.
- Sorting is the process of arranging records in the sequence in which they are to be stored.

TERMS

coding	**filing segment**	**indexing rules**
cross-reference	**indexing**	**indexing units**
filing or storage method	**indexing order**	**key unit**

REVIEW AND DISCUSS

1. Why is consistency in filing important? (Obj. 1)
2. Why are indexing rules important when filing names alphabetically? (Obj. 1)
3. In personal names, what is the key unit? (Obj. 2)
4. How is the key unit of a business name determined? (Obj. 2)
5. Index and code the following names by underlining the key unit, numbering the other units, and placing diagonal lines between the units. Sort the names in alphabetic order for filing. Indicate the order for the names in the blank provided. (Objs. 2 and 4)
   a. Randolph Thornton
   b. Randy's Painting Company
   c. Rachelle Thornton
   d. Randall Printing Company
   Order: ______________________
6. Index, code, and sort the following names as instructed in question 5. (Objs. 2 and 3)
   a. Gardner & House Produce
   b. The Garden Deli & Restaurant
   c. G/T Delivery
   d. The $ Off Store
   Order: ______________________

7. Index, code, and sort the following names. (Objs. 2, 3, and 4)
   a. Lindsey Morris-Hatfield
   b. Moore's Mercantile
   c. Lindsey's Copies, Inc.
   d. Morris and Moore Hardware Store
   Order: ____________________

8. Index, code, and sort the following names. (Objs. 2 and 5)
   a. MLG, Inc.
   b. M L G Associates
   c. Will Jones
   d. Wm. S. Jones
   Order: ____________________

9. Index, code, and sort the following names. (Objs. 2, 4, and 5)
   a. Janet Owens
   b. Owen's Mower Repair
   c. Lisa Ovey
   d. O T H Consulting
   Order: ____________________

10. Can you have too many cross-references? Explain. (Obj. 7)

11. Give two examples of types of personal names that should be cross-referenced. (Obj. 7)

12. Give two examples of types of business names that should be cross-referenced. (Obj. 7)

APPLICATIONS

3-1 Index, Code, and Sort Records (Objs. 2–8)

1. Practice using alphabetic indexing rules 1-4. Index each name in the table on page 56. Code each name by writing each unit of the filing segment in the appropriate column.
2. Determine which names should be cross-referenced. Then complete the cross-reference blanks, numbering each card with its original number plus X. See example.
3. Add the names to the table. Then alphabetize all the names by numbering them in the Order column.

	2 3
4X	Anderson / Jane / Carter
	SEE CarterAnderson Jane

	Filing Segment	Order	Key Unit	Unit 2	Unit 3	Unit 4	Unit 5
1.	Lydia Cavanaugh						
2.	Maria Christina Castro						
3.	Vagif Agayev						
4.	Jane Carter-Anderson						
5.	Chia Cha						
6.	Best-Lock Gate Company						
7.	C & R, Inc.						
8.	Allison's Salon of Beauty						
9.	Julie Anderson						
10.	C A B Services						
11.	Bio-Logic Resources						
12.	Abbott, Brady, & Craig Attorneys						
13.	Anderson Hardware Store						
14.	Anderson and Carter Associates						
15.	Abbott Furniture Store						
16.	C/K Corporation						
17.	Anne Carter Brokerage						
18.	BioGems, Inc.						
19.	Be-U-Ti-Ful Salon						
20.	"Build-It" Construction Co.						

Cross-Reference

Cross-Reference

Cross-Reference

Cross-Reference

Cross-Reference

Cross-Reference

3-2 Index, Code, and Sort Records (Objs. 2–8)

In this activity, you will practice using alphabetic indexing rules 1–4 to index, code, and sort names such as those that would be found on paper documents.

1. Index each name in the table. Code each name by writing each unit of the filing segment in the appropriate column.
2. Determine which names should be cross-referenced. Then complete the cross-reference blanks, numbering each card with its original number plus X. See example.
3. Add the names to the table. Then alphabetize all the names by numbering them in the Order column.

	2	3	4
5X	Travis /	and /	Wilson / Consulting
	SEE Wilson and Travis Consulting		

	Filing Segment	Order	Key Unit	Unit 2	Unit 3	Unit 4
1.	WRAP Television Station					
2.	TUT Games & Video (Taylor, Underwood, and Travis)					
3.	John Vanguard					
4.	U-Nique Business Solutions					
5.	Wilson and Travis Consulting					
6.	Watson's Electronics					
7.	Tots-R-Us Pre-School					
8.	Williams Business College					
9.	Will's Construction Company					
10.	The # One Printer					
11.	U-n-I Delivery Service					
12.	U-R-Healthy Natural Foods					
13.	Mary Underwood-Watson					
14.	Wanda Wells Bakery					
15.	Ultra-Bright Skin Care					
16.	Trent Taylor					
17.	Upper/Lower Deliveries, Ltd.					
18.	San-li Truong					
19.	WORK Radio Station					
20.	Tall/Big Clothing Store					
21.	Watch Repair					
22.	Lucinda Watson					
23.	Jos. H. Warner					
24.	Ralph Ventura					
25.	Laura Wilson					

Cross-Reference	Cross-Reference
Cross-Reference	Cross-Reference
Cross-Reference	Cross-Reference
Cross-Reference	Cross-Reference

3-3 Find Information in Database Records (Obj. 9)

Data File

Locate the Access file *3-3 Customers* in the data files. Download the data files to a computer that has Microsoft® Access. If you are working on more than one computer, you can use a removable storage device to move the data files from one computer to another. Open the file. This file includes contact data for customers as well as the indexing units used to file physical records for the customer. If a physical record is requested by number, this database can be used to find the customer name and how the physical records should be coded for filing in the alphabetic filing system. This facilitates finding the records quickly. The database can also be used to find other information about the customers.

Open the Customer Form database form. Use the Find feature to find the answers to the following questions.

1. How many people or businesses are located in Illinois?

2. Where is the Sterling Investments, Inc., located?

3. Which record number contains data for Donna Saba?

4. A record with data for a storage company is included in the database. What is the exact name of this company?

5. How many beauty salons have records in the database? Give the name(s) of the beauty salons.

6. Are any of the people or businesses in the database from Alaska? If yes, list the record number(s).

7. One of the people listed in the database is from Hartford, Connecticut. What is the name of the person who lives there?

8. One record in the database is for an agency. What is the name of the agency?

9. In which city is the Satin-N-Lace Boutique located?

10. What is the Postal Code for the Sav-On Oil Company?

3-4 Research Identity Theft

1. Access a search engine on the Internet. Search using the keywords *identity theft*. You are interested in learning about what identity theft is, not how to prevent it.

2. Follow at least three links in the search results list. Read and summarize the article or other information you find at each of the three sites. Be sure to list each site as a reference.

3. Send an e-mail containing the summary of your findings to your instructor.

SIMULATION

Job 1 Alphabetic Filing Rules 1–4

A simulation titled "Records Management Simulation", Tenth Edition, is available for use with this textbook. If you have been instructed to complete this simulation, you should begin to do so now.

Welcome to Auric Systems, Inc., a company that sells cell phones and high-speed Internet access to individuals, companies, and government agencies. Read the Overview and examine the organization chart; then complete Job 1. All supplies necessary for completing Job 1 and all other jobs in "Records Management Simulation", Tenth Edition, are contained in the simulation packet.

ADDITIONAL RESOURCES

For data files, Microsoft® Access tutorials and more, go to www.cengagebrain.com.

CHAPTER 4

Alphabetic Indexing Rules 5–8

LEARNING OBJECTIVES

1. Index, code, and arrange personal and business names with titles and suffixes.
2. Index, code, and arrange personal and business names with articles and particles.
3. Index, code, and arrange business names with numbers.
4. Index, code, and arrange the names of organizations and institutions.
5. Apply alphabetic filing procedures.
6. Prepare and arrange cross-references for business names.
7. Sort personal, business, organization, and institution names.
8. Create and find information in a database table.

Courtesy of Tyrene Bada

ON THE JOB

Tyrene Bada is a Record Management Specialist with the City of Beaverton, Oregon. She holds a Master's of Library Science (MLS) degree and is a certified records manager (CRM). She is also a past president of the Oregon ARMA Chapter.

Tyrene spoke of her life experiences that eventually led to her current position. "Like many in our profession, I did not choose to be working in the field of information governance. Perhaps it chose me, as evidenced by the people I have encountered along the way. I displayed signs at an early age that I was destined to govern data. When I was young, I remember making an inventory of my Halloween candy and sorting the list by the level of 'tastiness.'"

Later, Tyrene worked in the Department of Music at Portland State University (PSU), where she saw how students register for classes and how their information is used by the faculty members. That experience served her well, as her next two jobs were also at places of higher education. At University of California, San Diego, Tyrene continued to work with student records, and at Portland Community College (PCC) she had the rare opportunity to build the college's first records management program. While at PCC, she finally realized that records management was what she wanted to do when she "grew up."

According to Tyrene, ARMA has inspired her to learn more. This resulted in her MLS degree with a Certificate in Archival Studies. When she became chapter president, Tyrene felt she needed to know whether she could truly consider herself a professional in this field. Therefore, Tyrene went on to earn the CRM credential to prove that she could "walk the walk" and not just "talk the talk."

Tyrene is proud to be an information governance and records management professional and a member of ARMA. Her hope is to inspire and encourage others who want to be successful in this profession.

ALPHABETIC INDEXING RULES

In this chapter, you will continue your study of alphabetic filing rules. Remember to follow these guidelines to study the indexing rules effectively:

- Read each rule carefully. Make sure you understand the meaning of the words used to state the rule.
- Look at the examples. Note that the complete filing segment (the name and other words such as the title) is given at the left. Then the filing segment is separated into indexing units at the right, according to the rule you are studying.
- Be sure you understand why the filing segment has been separated as it has.

RULE 5: TITLES AND SUFFIXES

A. Personal Names

What are some suffixes for personal names?

A title before a name (Dr., Miss, Mr., Mrs., Ms., Professor, Sir, Sister), a seniority suffix (II, III, Jr., Sr.), or a professional suffix (CRM, DDS, Mayor, MD, PhD, Senator) after a name is the last indexing unit. Numeric suffixes (II, III) are filed before alphabetic suffixes (Jr., Mayor, Senator, Sr.). If a name contains a title and a suffix (Ms. Lucy Wheeler, DVM), the title *Ms.* is the last unit.

Royal and religious titles followed by either a given name or a surname only (Princess Anne, Father Leo) are indexed and filed as written.

Examples of Rule 5A

	FILING SEGMENT	INDEXING ORDER OF UNITS			
	Name	**Key Unit**	**Unit 2**	**Unit 3**	**Unit 4**
1.	Father Paul	Father	Paul		
2.	Ms. Noreen Forrest, CPA	Forrest	Noreen	CPA	Ms
3.	Dr. Noreen Forrest	Forrest	Noreen	Dr	
4.	Mr. Huyen Huong	Huong	Huyen	Mr	
5.	Bishop Barnard Hyatt	Hyatt	Barnard	Bishop	
6.	Benjamin D. Hyatt	Hyatt	Benjamin	D	
7.	Benjamin D. Hyatt II	Hyatt	Benjamin	D	II
8.	Benjamin D. Hyatt III	Hyatt	Benjamin	D	III
9.	Benjamin Hyatt, Jr.	Hyatt	Benjamin	Jr	
10.	Benjamin Hyatt, Sr.	Hyatt	Benjamin	Sr	
11.	King Olaf	King	Olaf		
12.	Ms. Naomi Luu, CRM	Luu	Naomi	CRM	Ms
13.	Miss Naomi Luu	Luu	Naomi	Miss	
14.	Mrs. Naomi Luu	Luu	Naomi	Mrs	
15.	Sister Joy Miller	Miller	Joy	Sister	

B. Business Names

How are titles in business names indexed?

Titles in business names (Capt. Hook's Bait Shop) are indexed as written. Remember, the word *The* is considered the last indexing unit when it appears as the first word of a business name.

Examples of Rule 5B

	FILING SEGMENT	INDEXING ORDER OF UNITS			
	Name	**Key Unit**	**Unit 2**	**Unit 3**	**Unit 4**
1.	Capt. Hook's Bait Shop	Capt	Hooks	Bait	Shop
2.	Dr. Pane's Windows	Dr	Panes	Windows	
3.	Grandma's Cookie Shop	Grandmas	Cookie	Shop	
4.	Mister Hulk's Gym	Mister	Hulks	Gym	
5.	Mr. Mom's Day Care	Mr	Moms	Day	Care
6.	Ms. Salon of Beauty	Ms	Salon	of	Beauty
7.	Professor Little's Bookstore	Professor	Littles	Bookstore	
8.	The Prof's Tutorial Service	Profs	Tutorial	Service	The

RULE 5: Self-Check

1. Index each name in the table. Code each name by writing each unit of the filing segment in the appropriate column. The first name is shown as an example.

	Filing Segment	Order	Key Unit	Unit 2	Unit 3	Unit 4
a.	Father Tom		Father	Tom		
b.	Ms. Rosalie Torres, CRM					
c.	Mrs. Darlene Talbot, DVM					
d.	Doctor Dee's Delivery					
e.	Governor Talbot's Construction Co.					
f.	Father Steven Gerzinski					
g.	Grandfather Ben's Recycling					
h.	Queen Anne II					
i.	Mom's TLC Services					
j.	Ms. Karen Farthing, PhD					

2. Compare the key units and the other units, if needed, to determine the correct alphabetic filing order for the names. Indicate the correct filing order by writing numbers 1 through 10 beside the names in the Order column.
3. Are the two names in each of the following pairs in correct alphabetic order? If the order is correct, write "Yes" in the blank beside the names. If the order is not correct, write "No" in the blank.

_____ **a.** The Magic Shop
Maggie's $ Save

_____ **b.** Robert Norberg, Sr.
Robert Norberg, Jr.

_____ **c.** Mrs. Carmen Libby
Lady Liberty Realty

_____ **d.** ABC Rentals, Inc.
Allied Chemical Co.

_____ **e.** MVP Pizza Shop
Mrs. Marvis Miller

_____ **f.** Red Hot Tamales
Red Hat Shop

_____ **g.** LMNO Shipping Co.
L & N Appliance Repair

_____ **h.** Sharon's "Of Course"
Miss Sharon Oest

_____ **i.** The Office King
The Office Doctor

_____ **j.** I-Net, Inc.
I-Freenet Company

4. Are the names in each group listed in correct order? If the names are in correct order, write "Correct" in the blank beside the names. If the names are not in correct order, indicate the correct order of the names by writing their numbers in the blank, for example, "3, 1, 2."

____________ **a.** 1. Closets by Elizabeth
2. Dr. Claudia Carter
3. Admiral Tristan Chandler

____________ **b.** 1. Senator Alex Hatfield
2. Hatfield's Department Store
3. Ms. Margaret Hayes

____________ **c.** 1. Ms. Linda Podany, CRM
2. Mr. Daniel Potter, CPA
3. Maria Podany, DDS

____________ **d.** 1. Mayor Miranda A. Moore
2. Miranda's Hobbies
3. Miranda A. Moore, MD

____________ **e.** 1. Richard Pope, Sr.
2. Theresa Pope
3. Richard Pope, Jr.

____________ **f.** 1. Sen. Carroll Guest
2. Rep. Carroll Guest
3. Ms. Carol Guest

Data File

5. Answers to this exercise are shown in the Word file *4 Check Answers*, found in the data files. Compare them with your answers.

RULE 6: PREFIXES, ARTICLES, AND PARTICLES

A foreign article or particle in a personal or business name is combined with the part of the name following it to form a single indexing unit. The indexing order is not affected by a space between a prefix and the rest of the name (Alexander La Guardia), and the space is disregarded when indexing.

What are some examples of names with foreign articles and particles?

Examples of articles and particles are: a la, D', Da, De, Del, De La, Della, Den, Des, Di, Dos, Du, E', El, Fitz, Il, L', La, Las, Le, Les, Lo, Los, M', Mac, Mc, O', Per, Saint, San, Santa, Santo, St., Ste., Te, Ten, Ter, Van, Van de, Van der, Von, Von der.

Examples of Rule 6

	FILING SEGMENT	INDEXING ORDER OF UNITS			
	Name	Key Unit	Unit 2	Unit 3	Unit 4
1.	Michael D'Agostino, DMD	DAgostino	Michael	DMD	
2.	D'Angelo's Pizza Parlor	DAngelos	Pizza	Parlor	
3.	Ms. Penelope D'Cruz	DCruz	Penelope	Ms	
4.	Mario De La Torres, MD	DeLaTorres	Mario	MD	
5.	Theresa Del Favero, CPA	DelFavero	Theresa	CPA	
6.	La Marte & McCaw Attys	LaMarte	and	McCaw	Attys
7.	Dr. Terrence O'Donald	ODonald	Terrence	Dr	
8.	O'Donald's Public House	ODonalds	Public	House	
9.	Edward Saint Cyr	SaintCyr	Edward		
10.	San Souci Resturant	SanSouci	Restaurant		
11.	St. Edwina's Arts & Crafts	StEdwinas	Arts	and	Crafts
12.	Ms. Mayme Ten Eyck	TenEyck	Mayme	Ms	
13.	Ms. Lorraine TenPas, PhD	TenPas	Lorraine	PhD	Ms
14.	Lt. Enid Van de Haven	VandeHaven	Enid	Lt	
15.	Van der Camp's Hobbies	VanderCamps	Hobbies		
16.	Otto Von der Hoff	VonderHoff	Otto		
17.	Alice Von Hoff	VonHoff	Alice		

RULE 6: Self-Check

1. Index each name in the table. Code each name by writing each unit of the filing segment in the appropriate column. The first name is shown as an example.

	Filing Segment	Order	Key Unit	Unit 2	Unit 3	Unit 4
a.	D'Arcy & Davis Consultants		DArcy	and	Davis	Consultants
b.	Ms. Syndi LaJoi, RD					
c.	McLean's Web Design					
d.	Mr. James Van Dyke					
e.	Pamela St. John, CPA					
f.	Ms. Maureen O'Boyle					
g.	Eleanor K. DeLacy					
h.	Mr. Mitchell Ste. John					
i.	Gov. Tom McCall					
j.	McAdam's Paving Co					

2. Compare the key units and the other units, if needed, to determine the correct alphabetic filing order for the names. Indicate the correct filing order by writing numbers 1 through 10 beside the names in the Order column.

Data File

3. Answers to this exercise are shown in the Word file 4 *Check Answers*, found in the data files. Compare them with your answers.

MY RECORDS

Recovering from Identity Theft

Has your personal information or identity been stolen? What's the next step?

If your personal information has been stolen or if you become a victim of identity theft, you must act quickly to minimize the damage that may result from this theft of your records.

Follow these four steps.

1. Notify the fraud units of the three credit reporting companies: Equifax, Experian (formerly known as TRW), and TransUnion.
   - Ask to be placed on a fraud alert on a person's account on your credit report. This alert tells creditors to contact you before opening any new accounts or making any changes to your existing accounts.
   - Ask for a free copy of your credit report. Scrutinize the report. Report any errors by writing to the credit bureaus.
   - Read the online publication, "Take Charge: What To Do If Your Identity Is Stolen," available on the Federal Trade Commission (FTC) website.
2. Close the accounts that you know or believe have been fraudulently opened.
   - Notify the security or fraud department of each company.
   - Follow up in writing, and include copies of supporting documents.
   - Keep a log of phone calls and letters you send and receive.
3. Report the identity theft to your local police or sheriff's department.
   - Document the theft.
   - Make sure the police report lists the fraud accounts.
   - Obtain a copy of the police report, which is called an *identity theft report*.
4. Report the crime to the Federal Trade Commission.
   - Include your police report number.
   - Call the FTC's Identity Theft Hotline (877-438-4338).
   - Use the FTC's online identity theft complaint form.

Following the above guidelines will help you recover from identity theft. The best way to beat identity theft is to do all you can to prevent it. (Links to the websites mentioned are available on the website for this textbook.)

RULE 7: NUMBERS IN BUSINESS NAMES

Numbers in business names have unique rules.

- Numbers spelled out (Seven Lakes Nursery) in business names are filed alphabetically.
- Numbers written in digits are filed before alphabetic letters or words (B4 Photographers comes before Beleau Building and Loan).
- Names with numbers written in digits in the first units are filed in ascending order (lowest to highest number) before alphabetic names (229 Club, 534 Shop, First National Bank of Chicago).

FIGURE 4.1 **Table of Roman Numerals**

I	1	XX	20
II	2	XXX	30
III	3	XL	40
IV	4	L	50
V	5	LX	60
VI	6	LXX	70
VII	7	LXXX	80
VIII	8	XC	90
IX	9	C	100
X	10	D	500
		M	1000

- Arabic numerals are filed before Roman numerals (2 Brothers Deli, 5 Cities Transit, XII Knights Inn).
- Names containing Roman numerals are filed in ascending order according to their Arabic number equivalents. VIII-Ball Club, XL Days & XL Nights Motel, C-Note Lounge (8, 40, 100); Lucky VII Casino, Lucky X Car Wash, Lucky LX Drive-In (7, 10, 60). A chart of Roman numerals is shown in Figure 4.1.
- Names with inclusive numbers (20–39 Singles Club) are arranged by the first digit(s) only (20).
- When hyphens separate three or more numbers written as digits, remove the hyphens as you would when hyphens separate words. (1-2-3 Market would be coded as 123/Market.)
- Names with numbers appearing in other than the first position (Pier 36 Cafe) are filed alphabetically and immediately before a similar name without a number (Pier 36 Cafe comes before Pier and Port Cafe).
- When indexing names with numbers written in digit form that contain *st, d,* and *th* (1st Mortgage Co., 2d Avenue Cinemas, 3d Street Pest Control), ignore the letter endings and consider only the digits (1, 2, 3).
- When indexing names with a number (in figures or words) linked by a hyphen to a letter or word (A-1 Laundry, Fifty-Eight Auto Body, 10-Minute Photo), ignore the hyphen and treat it as a single unit (10Minute, A1, FiftyEight).
- When indexing a name with a number plus a symbol (55Ĺ Social Center), treat it as a single unit (55Plus).

Examples of Rule 7

	FILING SEGMENT	INDEXING ORDER OF UNITS			
	Name	**Key Unit**	**Unit 2**	**Unit 3**	**Unit 4**
1.	7 Days Market	7	Days	Market	
2.	17th Avenue Fashions	17	Avenue	Fashions	
3.	21 Club, Inc.	21	Club	Inc	
4.	50% Discounters	50Percent	Discounters		
5.	65+ Retirement Village	65Plus	Retirement	Village	
6.	405 Auto Body	405	Auto	Body	
7.	500–510 Princess Court	500	Princess	Court	
8.	The 500 Princess Shop	500	Princess	Shop	The
9.	XXI Club	XXI	Club		
10.	Fourth Dimension Printing	Fourth	Dimension	Printing	
11.	Highway 18 Café	Highway	18	Cafe	
12.	I-90 Road Services	I90	Road	Services	
13.	#1 Pet Grooming	Number1	Pet	Grooming	
14.	One Main Place	One	Main	Place	
15.	Pier 99 Imports	Pier	99	Imports	
16.	Tea for Two	Tea	for	Two	
17.	Three Sisters Wilderness	Three	Sisters	Wilderness	
18.	Two Wheels Only	Two	Wheels	Only	

RULE 7: Self-Check

1. Are the names in each group listed in correct order? If the names are in correct order, write "Correct" in the blank below the names. If the names are not in correct order, indicate the correct order of the names by writing their numbers in the blank, for example, "3, 1, 2."

a. 1. Lady Bug Enterprises
2. Denise J. LaMonte
3. LaMonte Beauty Shop

____

b. 1. 50% Discount Shop
2. V Roman Way
3. 21st Century & Beyond Shop

____

c. 1. Labels 4 All, Inc.
2. Lawrence LaBerge, DVM
3. Patricia La Belle

____

d. 1. Marsha Mc Beth
2. Marsha McBath
3. 10 Minute Lube Shop

____

e. 1. Mackenzie M. Minten
2. McKenzie 500 Realty
3. McKenzie and Eft Realty

____

f. 1. Ralph DaCosta, Sr.
2. 10 Minute Delivery
3. Ralph DaCosta, Jr.

____

g. 1. #1 Delivery Express
2. A-1 Auto Sales
3. 10# Line Shop

____

h. 1. One Dollar Store
2. #1 Sports Gear
3. 5-7-9 Petites 2 Go

____

i. 1. Daniel Van de Bos
2. Venture Tours, Inc.
3. Matthew Van der Sluys

____

j. 1. 4-5-6 Nursery
2. Four Corners Bistro
3. 4 Movers & A Truck

____

Data File

2. Answers to this exercise are shown in the Word file *4 Check Answers*, found in the data files. Compare them with your answers.

RECORDS MANAGEMENT IN ACTION

Microchips Everywhere—The Future of Computing and Records Creation?

According to Steve Johnson of the *San Jose Mercury News*, in an article titled, "'The Internet of Things' Seen as Tech Industry's Next Big Driver":

> Billions of ordinary things—from farm cows and factory gear to pollution monitors and prescription-drug bottles—are being outfitted with microchips and linked by online networks in a technological transformation that some experts predict will be as profound as the Industrial Revolution. . . .

[With the placement of] billions of connected gadgets, experts foresee a world in which:

- More elderly people survive once-life-threatening accidents, because doctors and emergency responders will be alerted the moment their patients fall;
- Fewer planes will crash, because every part on every aircraft will be electronically monitored so that they can be quickly replaced at the slightest sign of failure;
- Wines will get better, as vineyard operators will know precisely when their grapes have the perfect sugar concentrations for picking. . . .
- Insurance companies are using data gathered by automobile sensors to identify high-risk motorists and adjust their rates accordingly. . . .
- In addition, cows in England are being connected to the Internet to track their movements. And thousands of smart trash cans in use at the University of California-San Diego and other places let waste-management officials check online to see how much garbage has piled up in each container."

These types of tech companies should profit from the increased demand for these smart gadgets:

1. Microchip producers
2. Makers of computer networking gear such as the routers, switches, and other equipment
3. Software companies also are expected to benefit, because their coded instructions are essential for telling computerized gadgets what to do and making sense of the data generated.

Source: San Jose Mercury News, Steve Johnson "The Internet of Things" Seen as Techs Next Big Driver — January 8, 2014. http://www.arcamax.com/business/businessnews/s-1452205?fs. Accessed January 9, 2014.

RULE 8: ORGANIZATIONS AND INSTITUTIONS

How are names of organizations and other institutions indexed?

Banks and other financial institutions, clubs, colleges, hospitals, hotels, lodges, magazines, motels, museums, newspapers, religious institutions, schools, unions, universities, and other organizations and institutions are indexed and filed according to the names written on their letterheads.

Examples of Rule 8

	FILING SEGMENT	INDEXING ORDER OF UNITS			
	Name	**Key Unit**	**Unit 2**	**Unit 3**	**Unit 4**
1.	1st National Bank	1	National	Bank	
2.	American Quilters Museum	American	Quilters	Museum	
3.	Associated Auctioneers	Associated	Auctioneers		
4.	Bank of the West	Bank	of	the	West
5.	Billings Community College	Billings	Community	College	
6.	De Long Seaside Motel	DeLong	Seaside	Motel	
7.	Disabled American Veterans	Disabled	American	Veterans	
8.	Findley Creek Lodge	Findley	Creek	Lodge	
9.	First United Methodist Church	First	United	Methodist	Church
10.	Freeport Daily News	Freeport	Daily	News	
11.	Jewish Historical Society	Jewish	Historical	Society	
12.	JFK High School	JFK	High	School	
13.	Journal of Photography	Journal	of	Photography	
14.	Public Employees Union	Public	Employees	Union	
15.	Rotary Club of Denver	Rotary	Club	of	Denver
16.	St. Vincent's Medical Center	StVincents	Medical	Center	
17.	Temple Beth Israel	Temple	Beth	Israel	
18.	University of Michigan	University	of	Michigan	
19.	Valley Community Center	Valley	Community	Center	
20.	Volunteers of America	Volunteers	of	America	
21.	Winston State College	Winston	State	College	
22.	Young Voters of Salem	Young	Voters	of	Salem

RULE 8: Self-Check

1. Index each name in the table. Code each name by writing each unit of the filing segment in the appropriate column.

	Filing Segment	Order	Key Unit	Unit 2	Unit 3	Unit 4
a.	National Business Education Association					
b.	Immaculate Heart Catholic Church					
c.	Church of Religious Science					
d.	St. Paul's Episcopal Church					
e.	St. Thomas's Lutheran Church					
f.	Temple Sinai					
g.	Quran Foundation					
h.	ARMA International					
i.	University of Utah Hospital					
j.	New Mexico State University					

2. Compare the key units and the other units, if needed, to determine the correct alphabetic filing order for the names. Indicate the correct filing order by writing numbers 1 through 10 beside the names in the Order column.
3. Are the two names in each of the following pairs in correct alphabetic order? If the order is correct, write "Yes" in the blank below the names. If the order is not correct, write "No" in the blank.
   a. International Webmasters Association
      International Association of Organ Donation
      ____
   b. United Cerebral Palsy
      United Four Wheel Drive Associations
      ____
   c. Association of American Publishers
      American Society for Training & Development
      ____
   d. World Federation of United Nations Associations
      World Federation of Personnel Management Association
      ____
   e. Union of Needletrades, Textiles and Industrial Employees
      United Food and Commercial Workers International Union
      ____

Data File

4. Answers to this exercise are shown in the Word file *4 Check Answers*, found in the data files. Compare them with your answers.

RULES 5–8: Self-Check

1. Index each name in the table. Code each name by writing each unit of the filing segment in the appropriate column.

	Filing Segment	Order	Key Unit	Unit 2	Unit 3	Unit 4
a.	1st Methodist Church					
b.	First National Bank					
c.	First Baptist Church					
d.	The St. Paul Chronicle					
e.	The Savannah Union Tribune					
f.	The New York Times					
g.	Sisters of Charity					
h.	The Seattle Post-Intelligencer					
i.	Fountain of Youth Spa					
j.	1 Stop Dry Cleaners					

2. Compare the key units and the other units, if needed, to determine the correct alphabetic filing order for the names. Indicate the correct filing order by writing numbers 1 through 10 beside the names in the Order column.

3. Are the two names in each of the following pairs in correct alphabetic order? If the order is correct, write "Yes" in the blank below the names. If the order is not correct, write "No" in the blank.

____________ **a.** St. John's Academy
St. John's Church

____________ **b.** 21st Century Gallery
The 21 Club

____________ **c.** Astor Elementary School
Astoria Community College

____________ **d.** Bai Tong Thai Cuisine
Berbati Restaurant

____________ **e.** Center-Line Curtains
Center Pointe Mill Works

____________ **f.** Dr. June DeSimone
Design-A-Weld Inc.

____________ **g.** Green Acres Kennels
Ms. Towanda Greco

____________ **h.** School of Arts and Crafts
School of the Arts

____________ **i.** San Carlos Apartments
Mr. Tatsumi Sanada

____________ **j.** Grisvold McEwen, LLP
Dr. Kevin M. McEvoy

Data File

4. Answers to this exercise are shown in the Word file *4 Check Answers*, found in the data files. Compare them with your answers.

CROSS-REFERENCING BUSINESS NAMES

In Chapter 3, you prepared cross-references for two of the nine types of business names that should be cross-referenced:

- Compound names
- Names that are abbreviations and acronyms

In this chapter, you will learn to prepare cross-references for the following types of business names:

- Popular and coined names
- Hyphenated names

- Divisions and subsidiaries
- Changed names
- Similar names

An explanation of the procedure to be followed in cross-referencing each of these types of names follows. The original record is stored in one place, according to the alphabetic rules being used. A cross-reference is made, if necessary, for any of the reasons discussed here and in Chapter 3.

CAREER CORNER

Job Description for Records Technician

The following job description is an example of a career opportunity with an athletic shoe and gear manufacturer, wholesaler, and distributor.

DUTIES AND RESPONSIBILITIES

Provide records/archive related services to the company in accordance with established policies and procedures, and analyze and prioritize customer requests for records. Access the records database, and using variable search parameters, determine which records will fulfill the requests for records and the informational needs of clients.

Complete documentation paperwork for each request handled; verify the accuracy of the box contents; place cartons on shelving; assign location codes on the form; verify the originating department, and determine the appropriate retention code for the carton contents; enter the information into the Access database; and affix the generated bar code labels to the cartons. Update the checkout documentation, and return the records to their respective locations. Drive the departmental van to pick up records cartons, and hand deliver original records. Destroy confidential materials through use of the industrial shredder/baler.

Qualifications

Requirements for the position include:

High school diploma or GED

6 months' experience in a customer service environment

Basic knowledge of Microsoft® Word, Excel, and Outlook

Ability to maintain confidentiality

A valid driving license

Ability to lift 50-pound boxes repetitively, carry boxes up and down stairs, and push a hand truck loaded with up to twenty 40-pound boxes

Previous experience using Microsoft® Access is a plus.

Popular and Coined Names

How is a company's popular name cross-referenced?

Often a business is known by its popular and/or coined name. A cross-reference will assist in retrieval. For example, the official name is shown as the coded filing segment. The popular or coined name is the name usually mentioned when retrieving anything for this business; therefore, a cross-reference with the popular name is helpful for retrieving. In the following examples, *Fred Meyer One-Stop Shopping* is commonly known as *Freddy's,* and *Smiths Homestyle Eatery* is commonly known as *Smitty's. Dixie Lee's Homestyle Restaurant* is commonly known as *Dixie's.*

CODED FILING SEGMENT	CROSS-REFERENCE
2 3 4 5 Fred / Meyer / One / Stop / Shopping	Freddys SEE Fred Meyer One Stop Shopping
2 3 Smiths / Homestyle / Eatery	Smittys SEE Smiths Homestyle Eatery
2 3 4 Dixie / Lee's / Homestyle / Restaurant	Dixies SEE Dixie Lees Homestyle Restaurant

Hyphenated Names

Many business names include hyphenated surnames. Like hyphenated personal names, business surnames with hyphens must be cross-referenced for each surname combination. Three examples follow.

CODED FILING SEGMENT	CROSS-REFERENCE
2 3 Jolly-Reardon / Consulting / Co.	2 3 ReardonJolly / Consulting / Co. SEE JollyReardon Consulting Co.
2 3 Heckman-O'Connor / Tour / Guides	2 3 OConnorHeckman / Tour / Guides SEE HeckmanOConnor Tour Guides
2 3 Bruss-Podany-Moore / Law / Firm	2 3 PodanyMooreBruss / Law / Firm SEE BrussPodanyMoore Law Firm 2 3 MooreBrussPodany / Law / Firm SEE BrussPodanyMoore Law Firm

Divisions and Subsidiaries

How is a cross-reference for a division of a company prepared?

When one company is a subsidiary or a division or branch of another company, the name appearing on the letterhead of the branch or subsidiary is the one indexed on the original record. A cross-reference is made under the name of the parent company. Two examples follow. Ricoh Business Systems is a division of Ricoh USA, and Micro-Weld Operations is a subsidiary of Kintech Corporation.

CODED FILING SEGMENT	CROSS-REFERENCE
2 3 Ricoh / Business / Systems (a div. of Ricoh USA)	2 Ricoh / USA SEE Ricoh Business Systems
2 Micro-Weld / Operations (a subsidiary of Kintech Corporation)	2 Kintech / Corporation SEE MicroWeld Operations

Changed Names

If an organization changes its name, how is the cross-reference prepared?

A company may change its name. Records must then be changed to indicate the name change and to ensure that the new name will be used for storage purposes. If only a few records are already in storage, they are usually refiled under the new name, and the former name is marked as a cross-reference. If many records are filed under the former name, a permanent cross-reference is placed at the beginning of the records for the former name. Any new records are placed under the new name. In the examples, *AT&T Wireless* changed its name to *Cingular Wireless,* and *Hershey Foods Corporation* changed its name to *The Hershey Co.*

CODED FILING SEGMENT	CROSS-REFERENCE
2 Cingular / Wireless	2 ATandT / Wireless SEE Cingular Wireless
3 2 The / Hershey / Co.	2 3 Hershey / Foods / Corporation SEE Hershey Co The

Similar Names

When is a SEE ALSO cross-reference used?

A SEE ALSO cross-reference is used to alert the filer to check other possible spellings for a business name. A SEE ALSO cross-reference is usually not needed in an electronic database. The complete business name is not cross-referenced—only the similar name. Similar names for a business include examples like *Northwest* and *North West, Southeast* and *South East, Goodwill* and *Good Will,* and *All State* and *Allstate.* If a name could be considered either as one unit or as two units, it is a good candidate for a cross-reference. Two examples follow.

CODED FILING SEGMENT	CROSS-REFERENCE
2 3 Allstate / Insurance / Co.	2 All / State SEE ALSO Allstate
2 3 4 South / East / Distribution / Co.	Southeast SEE ALSO South East

CROSS-REFERENCING: Self-Check

1. Identify the units in the filing segments (names). Code the names by underlining the key unit, numbering the other units, and placing diagonal lines between the units.
2. Write cross-references for the names that require them. See the following example.

2 3 4 Lundry / and / Masur / Meats	2 3 4 Masur / and / Lundry / Meats SEE Lundry and Masur Meats

	CODED FILING SEGMENT	CROSS-REFERENCE (IF NEEDED)
a.	Napen-Crawford Fishing Gear	
b.	Lettson-Ridgeway Antique Cars	
c.	St. Peter's Episcopal Church	
d.	Woody's Dog and Cat Grooming	
e.	Tech-N-Go Co. (a division of Systems Solutions Corp.)	
f.	Northwest Computer Systems	
g.	Anchorage Daily News	
h.	Westpark Aquarium	
i.	All State Supply Co.	
j.	Thao Huong Distributing Company (changed its name to Huong Distribution, Inc.)	

Data File

3. Answers to this exercise are shown in the *Word* file *4 Check Answers*, found in the data files. Compare them with your answers.

CHAPTER REVIEW AND APPLICATIONS

KEY POINTS

- A title before a personal name or a professional suffix after a personal name becomes the last indexing unit.
- Business names with titles are indexed as written.
- A foreign article or particle in a personal or business name is combined with the part of the name following it to form a single indexing unit.
- Numbers spelled out in business names are filed alphabetically.
- Numbers written in digits are filed before alphabetic letters or words.
- Numbers written as digits are filed in ascending order.
- The name of an organization or institution is indexed and filed according to how its name is shown on its letterhead.
- Cross-reference business names that are popular and/or coined, hyphenated, divisions and subsidiaries, changed names, or similar names.

REVIEW AND DISCUSS

1. Index and code the following names by underlining the key unit, numbering the other units, and placing diagonal lines between the units. Sort the names in alphabetic order for filing. Indicate the order for the names in the blank provided. (Obj. 1)

a. Mr. Paul Childers, Jr.
b. Ms. Paula Childers
c. Mrs. Paul Childers, CRM
d. Mr. Paul Childers, Sr.
e. Father Paul Childers
Order: ____________________

2. Index, code, and sort the following names as instructed in question 1. (Obj. 1)

a. Sister Ellen
b. Sister Ellen McSorley
c. Sister Elena
d. Sisters of Mercy
e. Ms. Ellen Mc Sorley
Order: ____________________

3. Index, code, and sort the following names as instructed in question 1. (Obj. 2)

a. Frank LaBarre
b. L-A-B Supply Service
c. Frank S. LaBarre
d. Joanna LaBarge
e. LaBar's Web Design
Order: ____________________

4. Index, code, and sort the following names as instructed in question 1. (Objs. 1 and 2)
   a. Ms. Colleen McHenry, CRM
   b. Mr. Colin McHenry
   c. Mrs. Colin Mac Henry
   d. Colleen McHenry, MD
   e. Dean Colleen Mac Henry
   Order: ______________________

5. Index, code, and sort the following names as instructed in question 1. (Obj. 3)
   a. 3 Rs Study Service
   b. 7 Gnomes Mining Co.
   c. 5 Star Hotels Association
   d. 205 Interstate Inn
   e. 1-Stop Shopping
   Order: ______________________

6. Index, code, and sort the following names as instructed in question 1. (Objs. 1–3)
   a. 1-2-3 Go Store!
   b. 2 B-True Memories, Inc.
   c. 30 McNamara Suites
   d. Cardinal Joseph O'Neill
   e. One-Stop Repair Mart
   Order: ______________________

7. Index, code, and sort the following names as instructed in question 1. (Obj. 4)
   a. St. Peter's Orthodox Church
   b. St. Paul First National Bank
   c. The St. Paul Times
   d. St. Peter's Children's Home
   e. Abbot Paul's Chapel
   Order: ______________________

8. Index, code, and sort the following names. (Objs. 1 and 4)
   a. 4 Seasons Hotel
   b. 4-Fold Way, Inc.
   c. Mr. Russell Forrett, CPA
   d. 444 Fountain Court Apts.
   e. Four Rivers Stadium
   Order: ______________________

9. Review the names and prepare the necessary cross-references. (Obj. 6)

	FILING SEGMENT	CROSS-REFERENCE
a.	Carter-Watters Real Estate	
b.	E'Lan Construction (changed its name to Buildings by E'Lan)	
c.	Southwest Computer Institute	
d.	Modular Housing (a subsidiary of St. Cyr Construction Company, Inc.)	
e.	PJs (a popular name of Pat Jennings Gourmet Bakery)	

10. What is the difference between a regular cross-reference and a SEE ALSO cross-reference? (Obj. 6)

APPLICATIONS

4-1 Index, Code, and Sort Records (Objs. 1–7)

In this activity, you will practice using alphabetic indexing rules 5–8.

1. Index each name in the table. Code each name by writing each unit of the filing segment in the appropriate column.

	Filing Segment	Order	Key Unit	Unit 2	Unit 3	Unit 4	Unit 5
1.	9 to 5 Uniform Shop						
2.	Albany Baptist Church						
3.	All State Packing Co.						
4.	Mr. Elmer Darby, Jr.						
5.	Big Rock Candies (a division of Heavenly Sweets, Inc.)						
6.	2 B-True Pet Supply						
7.	Akron Foundation for the Blind						
8.	DBB Inc. (DeHart, Brady, & Baldwin, Inc.)						
9.	Abraham Lincoln Museum						
10.	The Astoria Times						
11.	21st Avenue Bistro						
12.	Belleville Hospital						
13.	Elmer Darby, PhD						
14.	The Badger Times						
15.	Mr. Louis DeBois						
16.	Beauty on Broadway						
17.	Albany Brotherhood of Iron Workers						
18.	Ms. Andrea Adams, CRM						
19.	Abbot & Anderson Law Firm						
20.	All State Shopping, Inc.						

2. Determine which names should be cross-referenced. Then complete the cross-reference blanks, numbering each card with its original number plus X. See the example. Note that three cross-references are needed for DBB, Inc. (DeHart, Brady, & Baldwin, Inc.).

3. Add the names to the table. Then alphabetize all the names by numbering them in the Order column.

	2 3
4X	Anderson / Jane / Carter
	SEE CarterAnderson Jane

Cross-Reference

Cross-Reference

Cross-Reference

Cross-Reference

Cross-Reference

Cross-Reference

4-2 Index, Code, and Sort Records (Objs. 1–7)

In this activity, you will practice using alphabetic indexing rules 5–8.

1. Index each name in the table. Code each name by writing each unit of the filing segment in the appropriate column.

	Filing Segment	Order	Key Unit	Unit 2	Unit 3	Unit 4
1.	St. Theresa Lutheran Church					
2.	TTW Trucking (Travis, Trent, and Wilson Trucking)					
3.	Ms. Julia Van der Hay, CRM					
4.	Union Workers Federation					
5.	Simon & Travis Consulting					
6.	Clara St. Ambach, CRM					
7.	Teddy Roosevelt Prep School					
8.	The St. Joseph Foundation					
9.	Ms. Angela Stamp- VandeCamp					
10.	1-Stop Shopping					
11.	#1 Print Shop					
12.	3 Square Meals, Inc.					
13.	100 Points of Light Co.					
14.	Walla Walla Hospital					
15.	5000 King's Court Suites					
16.	Tours, Inc. (a division of Travel America)					
17.	1-2-3 Lawn Care Co.					
18.	Southwest Airlines					
19.	Salem General Hospital					
20.	The Temple Institute					
21.	James Ten Eyck, DVM					
22.	Daniel L. Smith Commercial Diving					
23.	St. Genistus Village for Children					
24.	Sam the Clown					
25.	Ms. Wilma Tescher, CPA					

2. Determine which names should be cross-referenced. Then complete the cross-reference blanks, numbering each card with its original number plus X. See the example.
3. Add the names to the table. Then alphabetize all the names by numbering them in the Order column.

	2	3
4X	Anderson / Jane / Carter	
	SEE CarterAnderson Jane	

Cross-Reference	Cross-Reference

Cross-Reference	Cross-Reference

Cross-Reference	Cross-Reference

4-3 Index, Code, and Sort Records (Objs. 1–7)

In this activity, you will practice using alphabetic indexing rules 1–8 to index, code, and sort names such as those that would be found on paper documents.

1. Index each name in the table. Code each name by writing each unit of the filing segment in the appropriate column.

	Filing Segment	Order	Key Unit	Unit 2	Unit 3	Unit 4
1.	L. M. Kale, CPA					
2.	Sister Doreen Mellman					
3.	Arun Lakra, MD					
4.	Keene Baptist Church					
5.	9 to 5 Uniforms					
6.	LaBelle Beauty Shop					
7.	Mr. Santos Mejia, CRM					
8.	Life-Time Gate Company					
9.	Layla's Salon of Beauty					
10.	Leadoff Investment Co.					
11.	The Kelso Times					
12.	Memo (a div. of Mason Office Products)					
13.	Lace-N-Satin Boutique					
14.	Lawson & Mason Attys.					
15.	Lynda Kemper Brokerage					
16.	57 Street Club					
17.	Ms. Colleen McNamara, CPS					
18.	Keene Brotherhood of Iron-Workers					
19.	LaBelle Origins, Inc.					
20.	Richard LaBelle, DVM					

2. Determine which names should be cross-referenced. Then complete the cross-reference blanks, numbering each card with its original number plus X. See the example.
3. Add the names to the table. Then alphabetize all the names by numbering them in the Order column.

	2 3
4X	Anderson / Jane / Carter
	SEE CarterAnderson Jane

Cross-Reference	Cross-Reference

Cross-Reference	Cross-Reference

Cross-Reference	Cross-Reference

4-4 Enter Names into a Database (Objs. 1–7)

In Application 4-2, you practiced using alphabetic indexing rules 5–8 to file names that would appear on physical documents. In this application, you will use the same names in an electronic database. To compare the results of the two methods, you will enter the names as written (the filing segment) and by filing units.

1. Create a new Access database file named *4-4 Customers.*
2. Create a table in the database named Customers. Create these fields in the table: ID Number, Filing Segment, Key Unit, Unit 2, Unit 3, Unit 4, Unit 5. Select AutoNumber for the field type for the ID Number field. Select Text or Short Text for the field type for all other fields. Set the ID Number field as the primary key.
3. Enter the names from Application 4-2 in the Customer table. In the Filing Segment field, enter the complete name as written. In the other fields, enter the data in all capitals and follow the alphabetic indexing rules 5–8 presented in this chapter. (Do not enter information shown in parentheses after a company name in the Units fields.)
4. Sort the records in the Customer table in ascending order by the Key Unit field. Does the order of the records in the sorted table match the order of the records you sorted manually in Application 4-2? If not, how does the order differ?

4-5 Find Information in Database Records (Obj. 8)

When filing paper documents, cross-references are created to help users find names that might be requested in different ways. In a Microsoft® Access database, the Find feature can be used to locate records using any part of a name. This eliminates the need for some types of cross-references. You will practice using the Find feature in this application.

Open the Microsoft® Access database file *4-4 Customers* that you created in Application 4-4. Select the Customers table but do not open it. Create an autoform based on the Customers table. Use the Find feature to answer the questions that follow. Close the form without saving it, after answering the questions.

Hint: When searching, look in the Filing Segment field, and match any part of the record.

1. What is the name of the hospital in Salem that is included in this database?

2. What is the name of the consulting company that is included in this database?

3. What is the full name and title of the CRM whose last name is St. Ambach?

4. What is the complete name of the business whose name begins with 1-2-3?

5. What is the name of the church in the database?

4-6 Research Identity Theft Prevention

1. Access a search engine on the Internet. Search using the key words *preventing identity theft.*
2. Follow at least three links in the search results list. Read and summarize the article or other information you find at each of the three sites. Be sure to list each site as a reference.
3. Work as a team with two other students to compile a list of strategies for preventing identity theft. Share your findings as your instructor directs.

SIMULATION

Job 2 Alphabetic Filing Rules 5–8

Continue working with Auric Systems, Inc.

Complete Job 2.

ADDITIONAL RESOURCES

For data files, Microsoft® Access tutorials and more, go to www.cengagebrain.com.

CHAPTER 5

Alphabetic Indexing Rules 9 and 10

LEARNING OBJECTIVES

1. Index, code, and arrange personal and business names that are identical.
2. Index, code, and arrange government names.
3. Apply alphabetic filing procedures.
4. Prepare and arrange cross-references for foreign business and government names.
5. Sort personal, business, and government names.
6. Select appropriate subject categories to be used within an alphabetic arrangement.
7. Create, sort, and query a database.

Courtesy of Judith Read

ON THE JOB

MinhHang Tran is the Records and Information Management Supervisor of 14 employees for Portland General Electric (PGE) in Portland, Oregon. PGE is a large utility company with approximately 2700 employees working in 204 departments. The Records and Information Management (RIM) Department's mission is "to develop and maintain a comprehensive records management program" and "to promote sound records management principles and provide a variety of application and services for the efficient creation, management and disposition of records meeting the legal, regulatory, and operating requirements of PGE."

As supervisor, MinhHang must ensure that records management policies and procedures are consistently applied to a wide variety of records such as human resources, finance, employee training, vendor contracts, customer, and outage records The records managed under her supervision are captured in PGE Corporate Records Information System (CRIS). CRIS is a web-based index of the company's official records. CRIS provides a uniform filing system for identifying and managing all types of records, from creation to their ultimate disposition.

MinhHang continues her long and distinguished career of over 36 years with PGE. Having entered the United States as a Vietnamese refugee in 1975, MinhHang remains grateful and passionate about her work. Her advice to students interested in the records management field is to learn basic records management skills and obtain knowledge of information technology (IT). A successful worker, according to MinhHang, is detail oriented, has a "detective" mind, and is willing to ask "why."

Reprinted with permission of MinhHang Tran.

ALPHABETIC INDEXING RULES

In this chapter, you continue your study of alphabetic storage rules. Follow these guidelines to study the indexing rules effectively:

- Read each rule carefully. Make sure that you understand the meaning of the words used to state the rule.
- Look at the examples. Note that the complete filing segment is given at the left. Then the filing segment is separated into indexing units at the right according to the rule that you are studying. Be sure you that understand why the filing segment is separated as it is.

RULE 9: IDENTICAL NAMES

Retrieving the correct record when there are identical names of people or businesses is easy when using a computer database. A records management database typically contains a unique field with information specific to a particular person or business name—often a phone number, a special identification number, or an assigned number generated by the database software. Because each person or business has a unique identifier, you do not need to look for other information to determine which person is the correct one.

In physical document files, determining which person or business is the correct one when other identical names are in the files can be a challenge. When personal names and names of businesses, institutions, and organizations are identical (including titles as explained in Rule 5), the filing order is determined by the addresses. Compare addresses in the following order:

When names are identical, which indexing units are compared next?

1. City names
2. State or province names spelled in full—not abbreviated (if city names are identical)
3. Street names, including *Avenue, Boulevard, Drive*, and *Street* (if city and state names are identical)
   a. When the first units of street names are written in digits (18th Street), the names are considered in ascending numeric order (1, 2, 3) and placed together before alphabetic street names (18th Street, 24th Avenue, Academy Circle).
   b. Street names written as digits are filed before street names written as words (22nd Street, 34th Avenue, First Street, Second Avenue).
   c. Street names with compass directions (North, South, East, and West) are considered as written (SE Park Avenue, South Park Avenue).
   d. Street names with numbers written as digits after compass directions are considered before alphabetic names (East 8th Street, East Main Street, Sandusky Drive, South Eighth Avenue).
4. House or building numbers (if city, state, and street names are identical)
   a. House and building numbers written as digits are considered in ascending numeric order (8 Riverside Terrace, 912 Riverside Terrace) and placed together before spelled-out building names (The Riverside Terrace).

b. House and building numbers written as words are filed after house and building numbers written as digits (11 Park Avenue South, One Park Avenue).

c. If a street address and a building name are included in an address, disregard the building name.

Are ZIP codes considered in determining filing order?

ZIP Codes are not considered in determining filing order.

Examples of Rule 9

Names of Cities and States Used to Determine Filing Order

	FILING SEGMENT	INDEXING ORDER OF UNITS			
	Name	Key Unit	Unit 2	Unit 3	Unit 4
1.	Seaside Inn Oceanside, California	Seaside	Inn	Oceanside	California
2.	Seaside Inn Oceanside, New Jersey	Seaside	Inn	Oceanside	New Jersey
3.	Seaside Inn Oceanside, Washington	Seaside	Inn	Oceanside	Washington
4.	Seaside Inn Ventura, California	Seaside	Inn	Ventura	California
5.	Seaside Inn Walnut, California	Seaside	Inn	Walnut	California
6.	Seaside Inn Westwood, California	Seaside	Inn	Westwood	California

Examples of Rule 9

Names of States and Provinces Used to Determine Filing Order

	FILING SEGMENT	INDEXING ORDER OF UNITS				
	Name	Key Unit	Unit 2	Unit 3	Unit 4	Unit 5
1.	Sam's Restaurant Monticello, Iowa	Sams	Restaurant	Monticello	Iowa	
2.	Sam's Restaurant Monticello, Kentucky	Sams	Restaurant	Monticello	Kentucky	
3.	Anita J. Spencer Fenwick, Ontario	Spencer	Anita	J	Fenwick	Ontario
4.	Anita J. Spencer Fenwick, West Virginia	Spencer	Anita	J	Fenwick	West Virginia
5.	Topper's Restaurant Clifton, Arizona	Toppers	Restaurant	Clifton	Arizona	
6.	Topper's Restaurant Clifton, Tennessee	Toppers	Restaurant	Clifton	Tennessee	
7.	Topper's Restaurant Clifton, Texas	Toppers	Restaurant	Clifton	Texas	
8.	Topper's Restaurant Clifton, Wisconsin	Toppers	Restaurant	Clifton	Wisconsin	

Examples of Rule 9

Names of Streets and Building Numbers Used to Determine Filing Order

	FILING SEGMENT	INDEXING ORDER OF UNITS					
	Name	Key Unit	Unit 2	Unit 3	Unit 4	Unit 5	Unit 6
1.	Subs-2-Go 6570 8th St. Houston, Texas	Subs2Go	Houston	Texas	8	St	
2.	Subs-2-Go 4560 48th St. Houston, Texas	Subs2Go	Houston	Texas	48	St	
3.	Subs-2-Go 16450 Carter Ave. Houston, Texas	Subs2Go	Houston	Texas	Carter	Ave	
4.	Subs-2-Go 12800 Carter St. Houston, Texas	Subs2Go	Houston	Texas	Carter	St	12800
5.	Subs-2-Go 18800 Carter St. Houston, Texas	Subs2Go	Houston	Texas	Carter	St	18800
6.	Subs-2-Go 255 SW 15th St. Houston, Texas	Subs2Go	Houston	Texas	SW	15	St
7.	Subs-2-Go 576 SW Eighth St. Houston, Texas	Subs2Go	Houston	Texas	SW	Eighth	St
8.	Subs-2-Go 6224 SW Pecan Dr. Houston, Texas	Subs2Go	Houston	Texas	SW	Pecan	Dr
9.	Subs-2-Go 17 Tyler Way Houston, Texas	Subs2Go	Houston	Texas	Tyler	Way	17
10.	Subs-2-Go 296 Tyler Way Houston, Texas	Subs2Go	Houston	Texas	Tyler	Way	296
11.	Subs-2-Go 11815 Westheimer Rd. Houston, Texas	Subs2Go	Houston	Texas	Westheimer	Rd	11815
12.	Subs-2-Go 13805 Westheimer Rd. Houston, Texas	Subs2Go	Houston	Texas	Westheimer	Rd	13805
13.	Subs-2-Go 467 Wyoming Ave. Houston, Texas	Subs2Go	Houston	Texas	Wyoming	Ave	

RULE 9: Self-Check

1. Are the two names in each of the following pairs in correct alphabetic order? If the order is correct, write "Yes" in the blank by the names. If the order is not correct, write "No" in the blank.

_____________ **a.** 1. United Methodist Church
1250 SE Concord
Salisbury, Massachusetts
2. United Methodist Church
2725 N 48th Street
Salisbury, Vermont

_____________ **b.** 1. Ms. Andrea Moore
4550 SE Flavel St.
Salem, Oregon
2. Ms. Andrea Moore
975 Cedar Street
Salem, Massachusetts

_____________ **c.** 1. The Granite Times
One Martin Street
Granite, Oklahoma
2. The Granite Times
371 Martin Street
Granite, Oklahoma

_____________ **d.** 1. The Burger Barn
1015 17th Street
Pittsburgh, Pennsylvania
2. The Burger Barn
11500 8th Street
Pittsburgh, Pennsylvania

_____________ **e.** 1. Mr. Daniel L. Gerson
8th and Grand Streets
Melbourne, Florida
2. Mr. Daniel L. Gerson
16875 Carnation Way
Madeira Beach, Florida

_____________ **f.** 1. Key West Bank
210 N Elgin Blvd.
St. Louis, Missouri
2. Key West Bank
150 S Elgin Ave.
St. Louis, Missouri

Data File

2. Answers to this exercise are shown in the Word file *5 Check Answers*, found in the data files. Compare them with your answers.

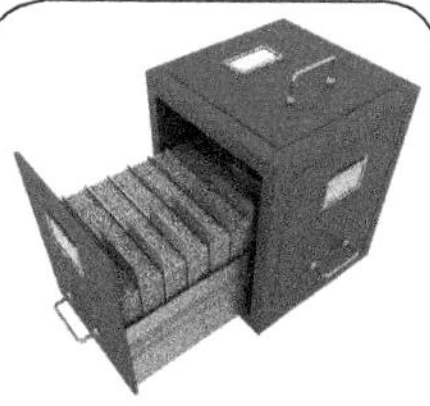

MY RECORDS

Backing Up Data

What backup operations are needed for your computer records?
Do you know how to restore data on the computer system?

Storage disk failure is a matter of *when* rather than *if*. The software loaded onto your computer can be reinstalled if the hard drive fails; thus, backing up the software applications is usually not necessary. Three types of backup operations are needed on your personal computer (PC).

WINDOWS SYSTEM RESTORE

The purpose of this utility is to allow you to undo harmful changes to your computer. For example, suppose you loaded some software that is not as compatible with your system as you thought it would be. Restoring the system through Microsoft Windows allows you to go back to an earlier time (called a restore point) and restore the settings in effect at that time. *Windows* automatically sets restore points. You can also create a restore point before you install a new hardware device or a new program. Make sure the Windows System Restore is turned on.

SPECIFIC PROGRAM AND DATA BACKUP

Some financial programs such as Microsoft Money® or Quicken® allow users to create a backup of the data used in the program. For example, Quicken requests a backup when you close the program. Quicken stores your data in its own folder on your hard drive and provides instructions to make a backup on another drive or folder. Make the backup copy on removable storage such as a rewritable compact disk or a flash drive. This type of backup ensures that the data is safe even if the hard drive on the computer fails. For these types of programs, plan and schedule backups at least once a week. Store the backup copy in another location, so it will be safe from fire or other disasters that may occur at your office.

HARD DRIVE DATA BACKUP

Regularly schedule and back up data on your hard drive in the cloud. For example, suppose you are in college and are completing homework assignments, using software on your computer. Make a backup copy of the homework assignments on removable storage devices. When the hard drive fails, you will be able to read your data from removable storage or the cloud.

RULE 10: GOVERNMENT NAMES

As a citizen of a democratic society, you have rights and responsibilities. Governmental rules and regulations define the rights and responsibilities individuals and organizations enjoy. Documents from government entities are often vital records such as your birth certificate, Social Security card, or a marriage certificate. These documents should be organized and retained permanently. You also receive documents asking for payment of taxes or other obligations to the government. These documents should be kept for varying lengths of time. You will learn about records retention in Chapter 7.

Records that an organization may receive from various governmental agencies uphold the rights and responsibilities of an individual or a business. For example, an electronics company doing business with the city of

Philadelphia and the state of Pennsylvania interacts with city, county, state, and federal agencies by:

- Obtaining a business name and/or incorporating.
- Obtaining permits to do business within the city.
- Paying property taxes.
- Paying employer taxes.
- Complying with transportation regulations when shipping products.
- Complying with employment eligibility verification for employees.
- Complying with regulations regarding workers' compensation.
- Complying with other regulations while operating a business.

Data File

An understanding of our government's hierarchy may be helpful when applying alphabetic indexing rules to government names. Open the Word file *5 Government*, found in the data files, to review the structure of the US government and learn how organizations interact with government agencies. You can also find links to federal governmental sites on the website for this textbook.

Government names are indexed first by the name of the governmental unit—city, county, state, or country. Next, index the distinctive name of the department, bureau, office, or board. A discussion of local and regional, state, federal, and foreign government names is provided in this chapter.

A. Local and Regional Government Names

How are city government names indexed?

The first indexing unit is the name of the county, city, town, township, or village. *Charlotte Sanitation Department* is an example. *Charlotte* (a city) would be the first indexing unit. Next, index the most distinctive name of the department, board, bureau, office, or government/political division. In this case, *Sanitation* would be the most distinctive name of the department. The words *County of, City of, Department of, Office of,* etc., are retained for clarity and are considered separate indexing units. If *of* is not a part of the official name as written, it is not added as an indexing unit.

Examples of Rule 10A

	FILING SEGMENT	INDEXING ORDER OF UNITS				
	Name	Key Unit	Unit 2	Unit 3	Unit 4	Unit 5
1.	County of Alameda Aquatic Center	Alameda	County	of	Aquatic	Center
2.	City of Arlington Public Library	Arlington	City	of	Public	Library
3.	City of Arlington Senior Center	Arlington	City	of	Senior	Center
4.	Ashley County Department of Elections	Ashley	County	Elections	Department	of
5.	Augusta City Water Works	Augusta	City	Water	Works	
6.	Baker County Bureau of Licenses	Baker	County	Licenses	Bureau	of
7.	City of Banks Water Department	Banks	City	of	Water	Department
8.	Barstow Municipal Court	Barstow	Municipal	Court		
9.	Benton City Hall Benton, Georgia	Benton	City	Hall	Benton	Georgia
10.	Benton City Hall Benton, Tennessee	Benton	City	Hall	Benton	Tennessee
11.	Benton City Police Department	Benton	City	Police	Department	

RULE 10A: Self-Check

1. Index each name in the table. Code each name by writing each unit of the filing segment in the appropriate column. The first name is shown as an example.

	Filing Segment	Order	Key Unit	Unit 2	Unit 3	Unit 4	Unit 5
Ex.	Warren County Department Sheriff's		Warren	County	Sheriffs	Department	
a.	Douglas City Library						
b.	City of Douglas, Water Bureau						
c.	Douglas County Emergency Services						
d.	Douglas City, Human Resources Department						
e.	City of Douglas, Public Library						
f.	Douglas County, Public Works Department						
g.	Douglas City Hall						
h.	Douglas County Circuit Court						
i.	Douglas County, Youth Services Agency						
j.	Douglas County, Welfare Department						

2. Compare the key units and the other units, if needed, to determine the correct alphabetic filing order for the names. Indicate the correct filing order by writing numbers 1 through 10 beside the names in the Order column. (Do not include the example name in the order.)

Data File

3. Answers to this exercise are shown in the Word file *5 Check Answers*, found in the data files. Compare them with your answers.

B. State Government Names

How are state government names indexed?

Similar to local and regional political/governmental agencies, the first indexing unit is the name of the state or province. Then index the most distinctive name of the department, board, bureau, office, or government/political division. The words *State of, Province of, Department of,* and so on, are retained for clarity and are considered separate indexing units. If *of* is not a part of the official name as written, it is not added as an indexing unit.

Examples of Rule 10B

	FILING SEGMENT	INDEXING ORDER OF UNITS				
	Name	Key Unit	Unit 2	Unit 3	Unit 4	Unit 5
1.	Michigan Office of Attorney General	Michigan	Attorney	General	Office	of
2.	Michigan Department of Civil Service	Michigan	Civil	Service	Department	of
3.	Michigan Department of Community Health	Michigan	Community	Health	Department	of
4.	Michigan Department of Education	Michigan	Education	Department	of	
5.	Michigan Department of Environmental Quality	Michigan	Environmental	Quality	Department	of
6.	Michigan Lottery Commissioner	Michigan	Lottery	Commissioner		
7.	Michigan Department of Natural Resources	Michigan	Natural	Resources	Department	of
8.	Michigan Superintendent of Public Instruction	Michigan	Public	Instruction	Superintendent	of
9.	Michigan Department of State	Michigan	State	Department	of	
10.	Michigan State Police	Michigan	State	Police		

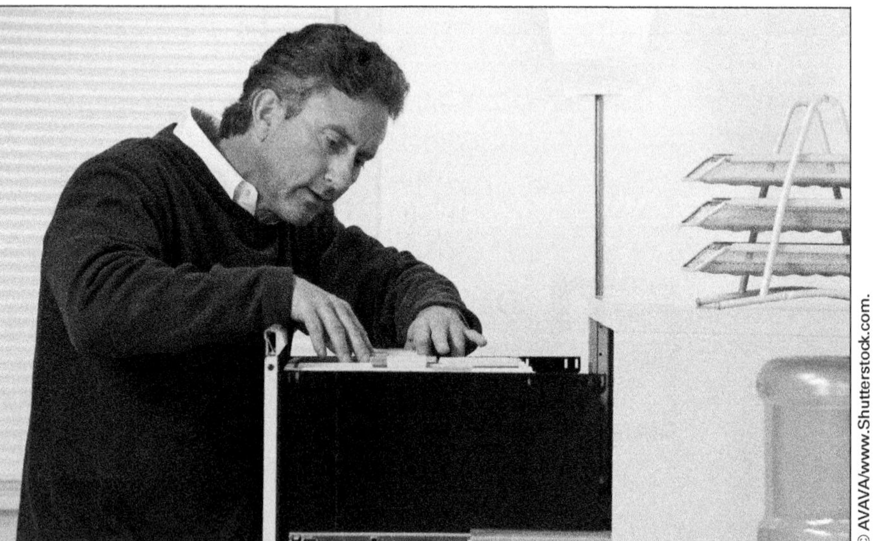

In records for states or provinces, the first indexing unit is the name of the state or province.

RULE 10B: Self-Check

1. Index each name in the table. Code the names by writing the units of the filing segment in the appropriate columns. (Note that units 5 and 6 are combined due to space limitations.)

	Filing Segment	Order	Key Unit	Unit 2	Unit 3	Unit 4	Units 5 and 6
a.	State of Hawaii, Department of Health						
b.	Washington State Department of Transportation						
c.	Washington State, Division of Child Support						
d.	Washington State, Office of the Governor						
e.	Washington State Penitentiary						
f.	Washington State Patrol						
g.	Washington State Senate, Judiciary Committee						
h.	Washington State, Department of Veterans' Affairs						
i.	Washington Secretary of State						
j.	State of Hawaii, Human Services Department						
k.	Hawaii State Public Library						
l.	Washington State History Museum						
m.	Washington State Law Library						
n.	Washington State, Office of Attorney General						
o.	Washington State Fire Marshal's Office						

2. Compare the units to determine the correct alphabetic filing order for the names. Indicate the correct filing order by writing numbers 1 through 15 beside the names in the Order column.

Data File

3. Answers to this exercise are shown in the Word file *5 Check Answers*, found in the data files. Compare them with your answers.

C. Federal Government Names

How are federal government names indexed?

Use three indexing "levels" (rather than units) for the United States federal government. Consider *United States Government* as the first level. The second level is the name of a department or top-level agency that is rearranged to show the most distinctive part first; for example, *Agriculture Department (of)*. Level three is the next most distinctive name; for example, *Forest Service*. The words *of* and *of the* are extraneous and should not be considered when indexing. These words are shown in parentheses for reference only. In the following examples, note that *United States Government* is the first level in all cases.

Examples of Rule 10C

	FILING SEGMENT		
		LEVEL 1 UNITED STATES GOVERNMENT	
	Name	Level 2	Level 3
1.	National Weather Service, Department of Commerce	Commerce Department (of)	National Weather Service
2.	Office of Civil Rights, Department of Education	Education Department (of)	Civil Rights Office (of)
3.	Department of Health and Human Services	Health and Human Services Department (of)	
4.	Office of Energy Assurance, Department of Homeland Security	Homeland Security Department (of)	Energy Assurance Office (of)
5.	Bureau of Reclamation, Department of the Interior	Interior Department (of the)	Reclamation Bureau (of)
6.	Federal Bureau of Investigation, Department of Justice	Justice Department (of)	Investigation Federal Bureau (of)
7.	Federal Bureau of Prisons, Department of Justice	Justice Department (of)	Prisons Federal Bureau (of)
8.	Global Affairs, Department of State	State Department (of)	Global Affairs
9.	Federal Aviation Administration, Department of Transportation	Transportation Department (of)	Federal Aviation Administration
10.	Internal Revenue Service, Department of the Treasury	Treasury Department (of the)	Internal Revenue Service
11.	Bureau of Public Debt, Department of the Treasury	Treasury Department (of the)	Public Debt Bureau (of)
12.	National Cemetery Administration, Department of Veterans Affairs	Veterans Affairs Department (of)	National Cemetery Administration
13.	Veterans Benefits Administration, Department of Veterans Affairs	Veterans Affairs Department (of)	Veterans Benefits Administration
14.	Veterans Health Administration, Department of Veterans Affairs	Veterans Affairs Department (of)	Veterans Health Administration

What sources could you use to find information about the local government where you live?

Resources are available to help you find the correct department, bureau, division, or office of your local, state, or federal government. Several resources are listed here.

- Many cities and states have websites with government information. The city of Pittsburgh and the Commonwealth of Pennsylvania are two examples.
- Telephone directories list local, state, and federal government offices.

The *United States Government Manual* (USGM) provides the correct hierarchical order of the departments, bureaus, offices, and so on, within the government. You can find the link to the main page of the *United States Government Manual* at the website for this textbook.

RULE 10C: Self-Check

1. Index each name in the table. The first level of each name is United States Government. Code each name by writing the remaining levels of the filing segment in the appropriate column. The first name is shown as an example.

	FILING SEGMENT			
			LEVEL 1 UNITED STATES GOVERNMENT	
	Name	Order	Level 2	Level 3
Ex.	National Cemetery Administration, Department of Veterans Affairs		Veterans Affairs Department (of)	National Cemetery Administration
a.	National Park Service Department of the Interior			
b.	Marshals Service, Department of Justice			
c.	National Nuclear Security Administration, Department of Energy			
d.	Fish & Wildlife Service, Department of the Interior			
e.	Bureau of Land Management, Department of the Interior			
f.	Federal Bureau of Prisons, Department of Justice			
g.	Southwestern Power Administration, Department of Energy			
h.	Drug Enforcement Administration, Department of Justice			
i.	Bureau of Alcohol, Tobacco, Firearms, and Explosives, Department of Justice			
j.	Office of Fossil Energy, Department of Energy			

2. Compare the levels to determine the correct alphabetic filing order for the names. Indicate the correct filing order by writing numbers 1 through 10 beside the names. Do not include the example name in the order.

Data File

3. Answers to this exercise are shown in the Word file *5 Check Answers*, found in the data files. Compare them with your answers.

D. Foreign Government Names

How are foreign government names indexed?

The name of a foreign government and its agencies is often written in a foreign language. When indexing foreign names, begin by writing the English translation of the government name on the document. The English name is the first indexing unit. Then index the balance of the formal name of the government, if needed, or if it is in the official name (China Republic of ——). Branches, departments, and divisions follow in order by their distinctive names. States, colonies, provinces, cities, and other divisions of foreign governments are followed by their distinctive or official names as spelled in English.

Examples of Rule 10D

	FOREIGN GOVERNMENT NAME	ENGLISH TRANSLATION IN INDEXED ORDER			
	Name	Unit 1	Unit 2	Unit 3	Unit 4
1.	Principat Andorra	Andorra	Principality	of	
2.	Republik of Österreich	Austria	Republic	of	
3.	Druk-yul	Bhutan	Kingdom	of	
4.	Bundesrepublik Deutschland	Germany	Federal	Republic	of
5.	Jamhuri ya Kenya	Kenya	Republic	of	
6.	Al-Joumhouriya al-Lubnaniya	Lebanese	Republic		
7.	Fuerstentum Liechtenstein	Liechtenstein	Principality	of	
8.	Republica Moldova	Moldova	Republic	of	
9.	Mongol Uls	Mongolia			
10.	Koninkrijk der Nederlanden	Netherlands			
11.	Republica de Nicaragua	Nicaragua	Republic	of	
12.	Republika ng Pilipinas	Philippines	Republic	of	
13.	Dawlat Qatar	Qatar	State	of	
14.	Al Jumhuriyah at Tunisiyah	Tunisian	Republic		

What source will help you find the English spelling of a foreign country?

The *World Almanac and Book of Facts,* updated annually, includes facts and statistics on many foreign nations, and is helpful as a source for the English spellings of many foreign names. The Central Intelligence Agency (CIA) maintains an online World FactBook. The World Factbook provides information on the history, people, government, economy, geography, communications, transportation, military, and transnational issues for 266 world entities. Maps of the major world regions as well as flags of the world, a physical map of the world, a political map of the world, and a standard time zones of the world map are provided on the site.[1] A link to this site is provided at the website for this textbook.

Rule 10D: Self-Check

1. Index the English translation of each name in the table. Code each name by writing the units in the appropriate columns.

	Foreign Government Name	English Translation	Order	Key Unit	Unit 2	Unit 3
a.	République de Guinée	Republic of Guinea				
b.	Lietuvos Respublika	Republic of Lithuania				
c.	Republika Hrvatska	Republic of Croatia				
d.	República del Ecudor	Republic of Ecuador				
e.	Nippon	Japan				
f.	Azarbaycan Respublikasi	Republic of Azerbaijan				

[1] "The World Factbook," Central Intelligence Agency, https://www.cia.gov/library/publications/the-world-factbook/index.html, accessed July 14, 2014

2. Compare the key units and the other units, if needed, to determine the correct alphabetic filing order for the names. Indicate the correct filing order by writing numbers 1 through 6 beside the names.

Data File

3. Answers to this exercise are shown in the Word file *5 Check Answers*, found in the data files. Compare them with your answers.

CROSS-REFERENCING BUSINESS NAMES

In Chapters 3 and 4, you prepared cross-references for seven of the nine types of business names that should be cross-referenced:

1. Compound names
2. Names that are abbreviations and acronyms
3. Popular and coined names
4. Hyphenated names
5. Divisions and subsidiaries
6. Changed names
7. Similar names

In this chapter, you learn to prepare cross-references for the last two of the nine types of business names:

8. Foreign business names
9. Foreign government names

An explanation of the procedure to be followed in cross-referencing each of these types of names follows. The original record is stored in one place, according to the alphabetic rules being used. A cross-reference is also made, if necessary, for any of the reasons discussed in Chapters 3 and 4.

As discussed earlier, a copy of the document may be stored in the cross-reference location or a cross-reference sheet may be prepared. Cross-reference sheets used with physical document records are discussed in Chapter 6.

Foreign Business Names

The original spelling of a foreign business or organization name is often written in the foreign language, which is then translated into English for coding. For example, Universiteit van Amsterdam is translated to University of Amsterdam. When working with foreign business names, take special note of the correct spellings and markings because they may differ greatly from the English form.

CAREER CORNER

Job Description for Records Management Support Specialist

The following job description is an example of a career opportunity with a security company.

PRINCIPAL JOB DUTIES

1. Assist with general office duties including photocopying, faxing, packing, data entry, and mailing documents.
2. Demonstrate customer service skills.
3. Must have database data entry skills.
4. Create and maintain files, ensuring documents and correspondence are appropriately stored.
5. Ability to work independently on assigned tasks and time-management skills.
6. Must be able to reach over your head and bend in order to retrieve files.
7. Other duties as assigned.

BASIC QUALIFICATIONS

- Must be a US citizen;
- Must be at least 18 years of age;
- Must have high school diploma /GED; Bachelor's degree preferred;
- Must possess the ability to conduct and interpret database checks;
- Must have proficiency with Microsoft Office (Word, Excel, PowerPoint, Project, Visio), Internet, e-mail.)

LEVEL II POSITION—MUST MEET ALL BASIC QUALIFICATIONS AND:

1. Bachelor's degree and one (1) year of experience or two (2) years of related experience.
2. Must have experience processing personnel records as they relate to background investigations and working knowledge of ICD 704 and E.O. 12968 guidelines.

LEVEL III POSITION—MUST MEET ALL BASIC QUALIFICATIONS AND:

- Bachelor's degree and five (5) years of experience or eight (8) years of related experience.

OTHER REQUIREMENTS:

1. Must be able to pass pre-employment testing;
2. Must be able to successfully complete a security screening interview;
3. Must pass criminal and credit history record checks;
4. Must be able to obtain a US government security clearance and polygraph;
5. Must meet client suitability.

In what language is the original record of a foreign business name filed?

Write the English translation of the foreign business name on the document to be stored, and store the document under the English spelling. Prepare a cross-reference sheet with the foreign spelling as written in its native language, using the first word as the key unit. When a request for a record is written in the native language, the filer will find that a cross-reference sheet bearing the original spelling is an aid in finding the record. Two examples follow.

CODED FILING SEGMENT	CROSS-REFERENCE
2 Humboldt / University	Humboldt-Universitat SEE Humboldt University
2 Venezuelan / Line	2 3 Venezolana / de / Navegacion SEE Venezuelan Line

Foreign Government Names

In what language is a cross-reference prepared for a foreign government name?

The name of a foreign government and its agencies, like the name of a foreign business, is often written in a foreign language. Write the English translation of the government name on each document to be stored. Store all documents under the English spelling. Prepare a cross-reference sheet using the foreign spelling as written in its native language, using the first word as the key unit. Two examples follow.

CODED VFILING SEGMENT	CROSS-REFERENCE
2 3 4 Federal / Republic / of / Brazil	2 3 4 Republica / Federativa / do / Brasil SEE Brazil Federal Republic of
2 3 Kingdom / of / Bhutan	Druk-yul SEE Bhutan Kingdom of

CROSS-REFERENCING: Self-Check

1. Identify the units in the filing segments (names). Code the English translation of the names by underlining the key unit, numbering the other units, and placing diagonal lines between the units.

	Foreign Name	English Translation	Cross-Reference
a.	Hotel Vier Jahreszeiten	Four Seasons Hotel	
b.	Repubblika ta' Malta	Republic of Malta	
c.	Socitété Européene des Satellite	European Society of Satellites	
d.	Republica Bolivariana de Venezuela	Bolivarian Republic of Venezuela	
e.	Ristorante do Leoni	The Two Lions Restaurant	
f.	Kongeriket Norge	Kingdom of Norway	

2. Write cross-references for the names that require them.

Data File

3. Answers to this exercise are shown in the Word file *5 Check Answers*, found in the data files. Compare them with your answers.

RECORDS MANAGEMENT IN ACTION

Dealing with Data Breaches for Organizations

During the Christmas shopping season of 2013, Target Inc., experienced a massive data breach in which debit card and personal identification numbers (PINs), names, addresses, e-mail addresses, and phone numbers of approximately 70 million customers were stolen. With the severity of such data breaches, companies and organizations need to develop action plans to prevent and reduce the amount of damage that might occur. IDExperts® has identified three principles to follow for organizations when developing data breach action plans that are discussed next.

BE PREPARED

A well-thought-out, cross-functional, detailed data breach incident response plan takes the uncertainty out of responding to a privacy incident. Have a plan and make sure that it is current.

RESPOND QUICKLY

Your customers will not understand or appreciate any delays in being notified about your data breach. Increasingly, regulatory and enforcement authorities are also taking a hard-line position of rapid notification. Lax response times can and will lead to investigations, fines, and penalties.

ADDRESS CUSTOMER CONCERNS

Amazingly, many organizations treat a data breach response as primarily a legal exercise. Yet the manner in which you choose to care for your customers will determine whether they decide to "fire" you as their provider of products or services. The most important thing you can do is to provide them with a real, live, knowledgeable person to talk with about the situation and their issues."

Source: IDExperts®: "10 Actions To Take When a Data Breach Strikes: Your Path to Recovery," http://www2.idexpertscorp.com/resources/BestPracticesChecklists/data-breach-response-guide/?gclid=CKixx62N77sCFUpBQgodECwADw, accessed January 8, 2014.

SUBJECTS WITHIN AN ALPHABETIC ARRANGEMENT

In what situation would you find records grouped by subject in an alphabetic file?

Within an alphabetic arrangement, records may sometimes be stored and retrieved more conveniently by a subject title than by a specific name. Beware, however, of using so many subjects that the arrangement becomes primarily a subject arrangement with alphabetic names as subdivisions. Here are a few typical examples of acceptable subjects to use within an otherwise alphabetic name arrangement:

- **Applications.** All records pertaining to job openings are kept together under the job title. The job for which individuals are applying is more important than are the names of the applicants.
- **Bids or projects.** All records pertaining to the same bid or the same project are kept together under the project or bid title.
- **Special promotions or celebrations.** All records relating to a specific event are grouped together by subject.

The filing procedure for the subject storage method is explained in detail in Chapter 8. Its application in this chapter consists of writing the subject title on the record if it does not already appear there.

When coding a record, the main subject is the key unit. Subdivisions of the main subject are considered as successive units. The name of the correspondent (individual or company name) is considered last. For example, on all records pertaining to applications, the word *Applications* is written as the key unit. The specific job title is a subdivision of that main subject and is the next unit (*Assistant*, for example). The applicant's name is coded last.

Examples of Subject Within an Alphabetic Arrangement

INDEXING ORDER OF UNITS					
	Key Unit	Unit 2	Unit 3	Unit 4	Unit 5
1.	Applications	Assistant	Bianchi	Jason	
2.	Applications	Assistant	Fung	Brenda	
3.	Applications	Cashier	Corbett	Lucy	
4.	Applications	Cashier	Jennings	Kenneth	
5.	Applications	Data	Entry	Neally	Joyce
6.	Applications	Data	Entry	Rodrigez	Luis
7.	Applications	Records	Clerk	Adamson	Cody
8.	Applications	Records	Clerk	Osuna	Jamella
9.	Applications	Records	Clerk	Tisio	Angelo
10.	Applications	Records	Supervisor	Kakazu	Nancy
11.	Applications	Records	Supervisor	Wasserman	Robert
12.	Applications	Records	Supervisor	Wu	Vivian
13.	Applications	Sales	Representative	Fusilli	Brian
14.	Applications	Sales	Representative	Gagliardo	Carmella
15.	Applications	Sales	Representative	Gains	Sara

CHAPTER REVIEW AND APPLICATIONS

KEY POINTS

- When filing identical names of persons, businesses, and organizations, filing is determined by the city names, state or province names, street names, and house or building numbers.
- Index local and regional governments first by the name of the government unit; then index the most distinctive name of the department, board, bureau, or office.
- Index state or province government names first by the name of the state or province. Next, index the descriptive name of the department, division, or office.
- Use three indexing levels for US federal government names. The first level of indexing is *United States Government.* The second level is the department name; and the third level is the name of the bureau, service, administration, or office.
- Index the distinctive English name for foreign government names. Next, index the balance of the formal name of the government.
- Index the English translation of a foreign business name.
- Cross-reference foreign business or government names.
- Within an alphabetic file, subject files are appropriate for applications, bids or projects, and special promotions or celebrations.

REVIEW AND DISCUSS

1. Index and code the following names by underlining the key unit, numbering the other units, and placing diagonal lines between the units. Sort the names in alphabetic order for filing. Indicate the order for the names in the blank provided. (Obj. 1)

a. The Longview Times, Longview, Minnesota
b. The Longview Times, Longview, Texas
c. The Longview Times, Longview, Illinois
d. The Longview Times, Longview, North Carolina
Order: ____________________

2. Index, code, and sort the following names as instructed in question 1. (Obj. 1)

a. Chad Davis, CRM, Ludlow, South Dakota
b. Dr. Chad Davis, Ludlow, South Dakota
c. Mr. Chad Davis, Ludlow, California
d. Chad Davis, CPA, Ludlow, Vermont
Order: ____________________

3. Index, code, and sort the following names as instructed in question 1. (Obj. 1)

a. John Miller, 425 Mayberry Street, Independence, Oregon
b. John Miller, 145 Lakeshore Dr., Independence, Missouri
c. John Miller, 375 E. Washington Street, Independence, Kentucky
d. John Miller, 2650 Cedar Street, Independence, Missouri
Order: ____________________

4. When arranging city, county, province, or state government names, what are the key units? (Obj. 2)
5. Index, code, and sort the following names as instructed in question 1. (Obj. 2)
   a. City of Rice, City Manager, Rice, Texas
   b. City of Rice, Police Department, Rice, Virginia
   c. City of Rice, Fire Department, Rice, Minnesota
   d. City of Rice, Mayor's Office, Rice, Washington

   Order: ____________________
6. Index each name in the table. Code each name by writing each level of the filing segment in the appropriate column. Then indicate the correct filing order. Level 1 is the same for all names and has been recorded at the top of the table. (Obj. 2)

			LEVEL 1 UNITED STATES GOVERNMENT	
	Name	**Order**	**Level 2**	**Level 3**
a.	Animal and Plant Health Inspection Service, Department of Agriculture			
b.	Oakland Operations Office, Environmental Protection Agency			
c.	Coast Guard, Department of Homeland Security			
d.	Export Administration, Department of Commerce			
e.	Maritime Administration, Department of Transportation			
f.	Bureau of Engraving and Printing, Department of the Treasury			
g.	Bureau of Public Affairs, Department of State			
h.	Department of the Navy, Department of Defense			
i.	Research, Education, and Economics Office, Department of Agriculture			
j.	Office of Vocational and Adult Education, Department of Education			

7. Index, code, and sort the following names as instructed in question 1. (Obj. 2)
   a. Board of Commissioners, Beaver County
   b. Information Technology Department, Beaver County
   c. Department of Emergency Services, Beaver County
   d. Community Services Department, Beaver County

   Order: ____________________
8. Index, code, and sort the following names as instructed in question 1. (Obj. 2)
   a. Illinois Department on Aging
   b. Office of Management and Budget, State of Illinois
   c. Illinois General Assembly
   d. Department of Labor, State of Illinois

   Order: ____________________

9. Code the English translation and prepare the necessary cross-references for the names below. (Obj. 4)

	Filing Segment	Cross-Reference
a.	Filing Respublika Byelarus (Republic of Belarus)	
b.	Slovenska Republika (Slovak Republic)	
c.	Latvijas Republika (Republic of Latvia)	
d.	Preahreacheanacha Kampuchea (Kingdom of Cambodia)	

10. Why are subject categories sometimes used in an alphabetically arranged name file? Give two examples of subjects that might be found in an alphabetic file. (Obj. 6)

APPLICATIONS

5-1 Index, Code, and Sort Records (Objs. 1–5)

In this activity, you will practice using alphabetic indexing rules 9 and 10.

1. Index each name in the table. Code each name by writing each unit of the filing segment in the appropriate column.

	Filing Segment	Order	Key Unit or Level 1	Unit 2 or Level 2	Unit 3 or Level 3	Unit 4	Unit 5
1.	Royaume de Belgique (French) Koninkrijk Belgie (Dutch) Kingdom of Belgium						
2.	Minority Business Development Agency, Department of Commerce (federal government)						
3.	Emergency Services Department, Allegany County						
4.	Ashland City Hall, Ashland, Wisconsin						
5.	Colorado Commissioner of Education						
6.	Rural Utilities Service, Department of Agriculture (federal government)						
7.	Colorado Community College System						
8.	Ashland City Hall, Ashland, Oregon						

continues on next page

9.	Patent & Trademark Office, Department of Commerce (federal government)						
10.	Board of Commissioners, Allegany County						
11.	Colorado Office of Information Technology						
12.	Ashland City Hall, Ashland, Maine						
13.	Zhonghua Renmin Gongheguo (People's Republic of China)						
14.	Ashland City Hall, Ashland, Nebraska						
15.	Colorado Department of Revenue						
16.	Environmental Management, Department of Energy (federal government)						
17.	Fiscal Services, Allegany County						
18.	Colorado State Parks						
19.	Ashland City Hall, Ashland, Kentucky						
20.	Centers for Disease Control and Prevention, Department of Health & Human Services (federal government)						

2. Determine which names should be cross-referenced. Then complete the cross-reference blanks, numbering each card with its original number plus X. See the example.
3. Add the names to the table. Then alphabetize all the names by numbering them in the Order column.

53X	2 3 Zhonghua / Renmin / Gongheguo SEE China Peoples Republic of

Cross-Reference

Cross-Reference

Cross-Reference

Cross-Reference

5-2 Index, Code, and Sort Records (Objs. 1–5)

In this activity, you will practice using alphabetic indexing rules 9 and 10.

1. Index each name in the table. Code each name by writing each unit or level of the filing segment in the appropriate column. If a sixth unit exists, write it to the right of the unit 5 column.

	Filing Segment	Order	Key Unit or Level 1	Unit 2 or Level 2	Unit 3 or Level 3	Unit 4	Unit 5
1.	Al Mamlakah al Arabiyah as Suudiyah (Kingdom of Saudi Arabia)						
2.	Texas Department of Criminal Justice						
3.	Shelby Fire Department, Shelby, Alabama						
4.	Records Clerk Applications, Heather Zane						
5.	Board of Supervisors, Washington County						
6.	Office of Disability Employment Policy, Department of Labor (federal government)						
7.	Records Clerk Applications, Tom Snell						
8.	Shelby Fire Department, Shelby, North Carolina						
9.	Texas Courts of Appeals						
10.	Department of Elections, Washington County						
11.	Konungariket Sverige (Kingdom of Sweden)						
12.	Political Affairs, Department of State (federal government)						
13.	Records Clerk Applications, Angela Berg						
14.	Shelby Fire Department, Shelby, Indiana						
15.	Office of the Governor, Texas						
16.	Emergency Services, Washington County						

continues on next page

17.	Records Clerk Applications, Elias Boljuncic						
18.	Texas Educator Certification						
19.	Bureau of Public Debt, Department of the Treasury (federal government)						
20.	Records Clerk Applications, Pei-Fang Hung						
21.	Shelby Fire Department, Shelby, Mississippi						
22.	Research & Innovative Technology Administration, Department of Transportation (federal government)						
23.	Records Clerk Applications, Leslie Strickland						
24.	Community Development Program, Department of Agriculture (federal government)						
25.	Shelby Police Department, Shelby, Ohio						

2. Determine which names should have cross-references. Using the cross-reference blanks, write the number of the original name plus an X. Then write the cross-reference.

Cross-Reference	Cross-Reference

Cross-Reference	Cross-Reference

3. Add the names you prepared as cross-references to the bottom of the table with the other names. Code the cross-reference names by writing each unit/level in the appropriate column.
4. Compare the key units/levels and the other units/levels, if needed, to determine the correct alphabetic filing order for the names, including the cross-references. Indicate the correct filing order by writing numbers beside the names in the Order column.

5-3 Index and Sort Records For Rule 10 (Obj. 2)

In this exercise, foreign government names are followed by the English translations in parentheses. Are the names in each of the pairs in correct alphabetic order according to the English translation? If the order is correct, write "Yes" in the blank by the names. If the order is not correct, write "No" in the blank.

________ **1.** a. Reino de Espana
(Kingdom of Spain)
b. Confederation Suisse
(Swiss Confederation)

________ **2.** a. Qazaqstan Respublikasy
(Republic of Kazakhstan)
b. Ozbekiston Respublikasi
(Republic of Uzbekistan)

________ **3.** a. Konungariket Sverige
(Kingdom of Sweden)
b. Repubblica Italiana
(Italian Republic)

________ **4.** a. Suomen Tasavalta
(Republic of Finland)
b. Republica del Paraguay
(Republic of Paraguay)

________ **5.** a. Magyar Koztarsasag
(Republic of Hungary)
b. Republica de Chile
(Republic of Chile)

________ **6.** a. Republica de Guatemala
(Republic of Guatemala)
b. Jumhuriyat al-Iraq
(Republic of Iraq)

5-4 Index, Code, and Sort Records for Rules 1–10 (Objs. 1–5)

In this activity, you will practice using alphabetic indexing rules 1–10 to index, code, and sort names such as individual and business names that would be found on physical documents.

1. Index each name in the table. Code each name by writing each unit of the filing segment in the appropriate column.

	Filing Segment	Order	Key Unit or Level 1	Unit 2 or Level 2	Unit 3 or Level 3	Unit 4	Unit 5
1.	Mr. Bruce Unger Springfield, Oregon						
2.	Rev. Charles Rodgers						
3.	Quisenberry's Department Store						
4.	St. John Police Department						
5.	Tunes 2 Go						
6.	1 Stop Quik-Lube						
7.	Department of Homeland Security (federal government)						
8.	Tennessee Supreme Court						
9.	Resource One, Inc. Pembroke, Maine						
10.	Southwest Christian Church						
11.	Ms. Shannon Quezada San Carlos						
12.	Mr. Bruce Unger Springfield, Illinois						
13.	Mr. Albert Tunno, CRM						
14.	Dr. Charles Rogers						
15.	Stewart & Tunno Insurance Agency						
16.	Queen Noor						
17.	Department of Agriculture Forest Service (federal government)						
18.	Tennessee State University						
19.	Ms. Shannon SanCarlos, CPA						
20.	Resource One, Inc. Pembroke, Kentucky						
21.	Xiao-Guang Qi						
22.	South Carolina State Police						
23.	State of Tennessee, Governor						
24.	Department of the Interior Bureau of Indian Affairs (federal government)						
25.	Rogers Machinery, Inc.						

2. Determine which names should have cross-references. Using the cross-reference blanks, write the number of the original name plus an X. Then write the cross-reference.

Cross-Reference	Cross-Reference

Cross-Reference	Cross-Reference

3. Add the names that you prepared as cross-references to the bottom of the table with the other names. Code the cross-reference names by writing each unit/level in the appropriate column.
4. Compare the key units/levels and the other units/levels, if needed, to determine the correct alphabetic filing order for the names, including the cross-references. Indicate the correct filing order by writing numbers beside the names in the Order column.

5-5 Create and Query a Database (Objs. 6–7)

You have been hired as the records clerk for a new Catchy Containers store scheduled for opening in the spring. The store owner has asked you to create a database table to keep track of all applicants for store jobs.

1. Open Access and create a new database named *5-5 Applicants.*
2. Create a table named Applicants with the following fields: Date, Position, First Name, Last Name, Phone. Select Date as the field type for the Date field. Select Short Text or Text as the field type for the other fields. Select the Phone field as the primary key.

3. Enter the following information into the table. Enter the current year in the dates (instead of 20--).

Date	Position	First Name	Last Name	Phone
1/3/20--	Cashier	Jennifer	Smith	541-555-0101
1/4/20--	Stocker	Forrest	Bayly	541-555-0122
1/4/20--	Cashier	Susan	Mcintyre	541-555-0131
1/5/20--	Manager	Barry	Gamble	541-555-0125
1/5/20--	Cashier	Joshua	Neslund	541-555-0030
1/6/20--	Stocker	Erin	Gonzales	541-555-0127
1/6/20--	Manager	Laura	Reynolds	541-555-0129
1/7/20--	Cashier	Amy	Pederson	541-555-0124
1/7/20--	Cashier	Serena	Worcester	541-555-0126
1/7/20--	Stocker	Philip	Raymond	541-555-0133
1/8/20--	Cashier	Bryan	Crider	541-555-0108
1/8/20--	Manager	Sara	Reyes	541-555-0115
1/8/20--	Stocker	Lauren	Hurst	541-555-0128
1/9/20--	Manager	Jennifer	Smith	541-555-0154
1/9/20--	Stocker	Tom	Reitz	541-555-0114
1/9/20--	Cashier	Kelly	Tumpane	541-555-0111

4. Even when a database contains identical names, retrieving the correct record is easy when a unique field is used to identify records. In this database, the Phone field is the unique field/primary key. The store owner said to you, "I need to return a call from an applicant, but the message has only her first name and phone number: 541-555-0154. What is the applicant's full name and for what position did she apply?" Use the Find feature with the Applicants table to find this information.
5. The owner has asked you to create a list of applicants sorted in ascending order first by the position and then by the last name. Create a query based on the Applicants table. In the query results, display all fields, and sort the data as requested. Save the query as "Position Sort Query." Run the query and print the results table.

5-6 Research the Federal Executive Branch

Earlier in this chapter, you reviewed the Word file *5 Government*, found in the data files. You learned that the three branches of state and federal government are Executive, Legislative, and Judicial. In this activity, you will research one aspect of the executive branch of the federal government.

1. Access the Internet and go to the website for this textbook. Find the links for this chapter. Follow the link to the Federal Executive Branch site.
2. Work as a team with another student to answer the following questions:
   a. What is one of the principal purposes of the President's Cabinet?
   b. How many members does the current Cabinet include?

c. What are the names of the executive departments within the Cabinet? What are the names of the current secretaries of those departments?
d. What is the primary responsibility of the Secretary of Defense? Of the Secretary of Transportation?
3. Share your findings as your instructor directs.

SIMULATION

Job 3 Alphabetic Filing Rules 9-10

Job 4 Alphabetic Filing Rules 1-10

Continue working with Auric Systems, Inc. Complete Jobs 3 and 4.

ADDITIONAL RESOURCES

For data files, Microsoft® Access tutorials and more, go to www.cengagebrain.com.

CHAPTER 6

Alphabetic Records Management, Equipment, and Procedures

LEARNING OBJECTIVES

1. Explain terms used in physical document records management systems.
2. Identify the basic types of equipment and supplies for physical document records storage.
3. Explain considerations for selecting storage equipment and supplies.
4. Discuss the advantages and disadvantages of the alphabetic method of records storage.
5. Describe types of information that should be determined before selection and design of an alphabetic records system.
6. Explain how color can be used in physical document records storage.
7. Apply procedures for storing physical documents.

Courtesy of Lee Nemchek

ON THE JOB

As Vice President of Enterprise Records Governance at Oaktree Capital Management, L.P., a global alternative investment management firm, Lee R. Nemchek, MLS, CRM, information governance professional (IGP), developed and manages all aspects of its information governance (IG) program, including traditional records management activities (active and inactive RIM, retention, disposition and archival preservation for business records in all formats). In addition, she works in close collaboration with Information Technology, Change Services, Legal, Compliance, Human Resources, and business unit stakeholders on information access, security and privacy initiatives, regulatory compliance, automation projects, disaster preparedness and business continuity planning, and information risk analysis and mitigation.

Over the next few years, Ms. Nemchek expects that associations, vendors, and practitioners in the RIM arena will further develop the information governance brand, thereby creating great opportunities for experienced RIM professionals to re-invent themselves in the workplace. She also anticipates that sector-specific groups (e.g., legal records managers, financial services records managers) will lead the way in developing IG program standards and best practices for their industries. Business and information science schools will offer new courses and/or degree programs to prepare students for information governance careers.

For students interested in entering the RIM or IG fields in the future, marketability is the single most important factor in career planning. Students should acquire the educational credentials and experience necessary to position themselves as viable candidates for the majority of available positions and distinguish themselves from others applying for the same positions.

PHYSICAL DOCUMENT RECORDS STORAGE

What are examples of physical business documents?

You learned in earlier chapters of this textbook how to index, code, and cross-reference names and addresses. Beginning with this chapter, you will learn other considerations for working with documents—the types of records found in all kinds of businesses. Business letters, forms, reports, e-mail messages, and memorandums (memos) are all part of daily documents that businesses create and receive.

Business offices continue to use paper (physical) records in addition to a variety of electronic records. Therefore, the discussion in this chapter focuses on the use of equipment and supplies for paper/physical records. Chapters 11, 12, and 13 discuss electronic systems used in records management.

As you complete this chapter, you will apply the 10 alphabetic indexing rules learned from Chapters 3, 4, and 5 to indexing, coding, and cross-referencing business documents. In addition, you will learn three other steps in alphabetic storage procedures: inspecting, sorting, and storing.

Information requirements make systematic storage and retrieval of records increasingly important. Businesses use records to complete transactions, to communicate with customers or clients, and to document compliance with laws and regulations. You have discovered that a set of written rules for alphabetic indexing provides consistency for storing and retrieving records. Consistent application of the alphabetic indexing rules is only one part of an efficient records management program. Using effective, appropriate equipment and supplies is another. In this chapter, you learn about a variety of available records storage equipment and supplies and the criteria for selecting them.

The following terms and definitions will help you understand the information in this chapter:

- Records management is the systematic control of all records from their creation, or receipt, through their processing, distribution, organization, storage, and retrieval, to their ultimate disposition. The goal of records management is to get the right record to the right person at the right time and at the lowest possible cost.
- **Storage**, or storing, is the placement of records onto a shelf or into a file drawer, according to a plan. Storage can also be saving a record to an electronic medium that is readable by a computer. The term *filing* may be used to mean storage, but filing is usually associated with paper records only.
- A **storage method** is a systematic way of storing records according to an alphabetic, subject, numeric, geographic, or chronologic plan. A specific system for organizing and arranging records can be referred to as a records management system or filing system. Often these terms are used synonymously.
- **Alphabetic records management** is a method of storing and arranging records according to the letters of the alphabet.
- Storage procedures are a series of steps for the orderly arrangement of records as required by a specific storage method or records management system.

storage: The placement of records, according to a plan, on a shelf or in a file drawer or saving an electronic record.

storage method: a systematic way of storing records according to an alphabetic, subject, numeric, geographic, or chronologic plan

alphabetic records management: a method of storing and arranging records according to the letters of the alphabet

The storage method or system discussed here and in previous chapters is alphabetic. Subject and geographic methods are not considered separate methods because the subjects and geographic names are filed alphabetically.

How many storage methods are used to file records?

In this text, alphabetic, subject, numeric, and geographic are considered as four RIM methods. With the exception of chronologic storage, each of these methods uses alphabetic concepts in its operation. Subject, numeric, and geographic records are described in detail in Chapters 8, 9, and 10.

RECORDS STORAGE EQUIPMENT AND SUPPLIES

Records managers are responsible for identifying and evaluating the need for storage equipment and supplies, based on the types of records, records formats, records locations, levels of importance of the records, and the records retention schedule. Based on these determinations, the records manager will identify vendors and suppliers for the required storage equipment and filing supplies. Storage equipment will vary among records formats and their levels of importance to the organization.

Storage Equipment

Types of storage equipment commonly used for physical/paper records are (1) vertical file cabinets, (2) lateral file cabinets, (3) shelf files, and (4) mobile shelving. Other types of storage equipment and their special uses for RIM are discussed in later chapters.

Vertical File Cabinets

A vertical file cabinet is storage equipment that is deeper than it is wide. Generally, the arrangement of folders in the file drawers is from front to back. A folder is a container used to hold and protect the contents of a file together and separate them from other files. Vertical file cabinets are the conventional storage cabinets in one- to five-drawer designs, as shown in Figure 6.1.

FIGURE 6.1 **Vertical File Cabinets Are the Conventional Storage Cabinets in One- to Five-Drawer Designs**

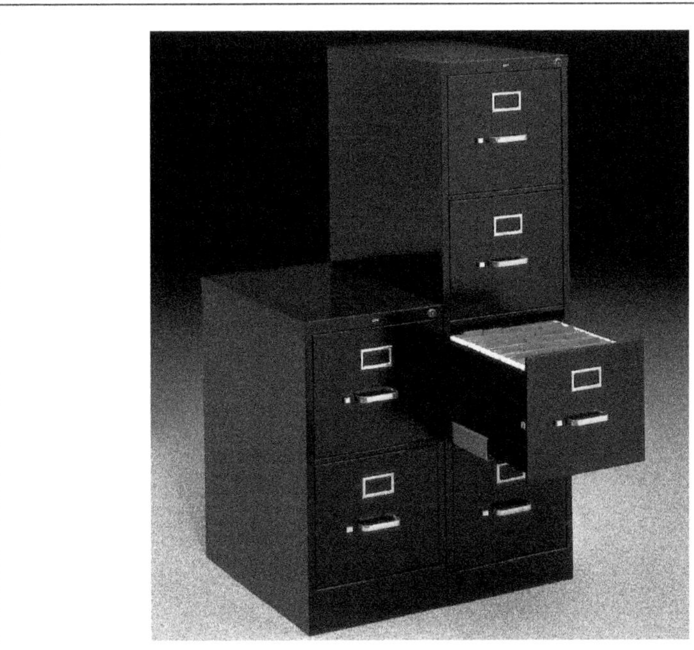

The HON Company

Two rows of vertical file cabinets may be placed back to back in a large central storage area with aisle space on either side. The type and volume of records to be stored determines the width, depth, number, and size of drawers. The two-drawer file is desk height and sometimes used beside a desk for additional workspace as well as for ready access to frequently used records. The most common widths of vertical file cabinet drawers are appropriate for letters or legal-size documents.

Lateral File Cabinets

How do vertical and lateral file cabinets differ?

A lateral file cabinet is storage equipment that is wider than it is deep—records are accessed from the side (horizontally). Records can be arranged in the drawers from front to back or side to side. Because the long (narrow) side opens, lateral file cabinets are particularly well suited to narrow aisle spaces. They are available in a variety of sizes, depending on the number and depth of the drawers. Figure 6.2 shows a lateral file cabinet with roll-back drawer fronts and one with pull-out drawers.

Shelf Files

A shelf file is open-shelving equipment in which records are accessed horizontally from the open side, as shown in Figure 6.3. Shelf files may be an open style or have roll-back or roll-down fronts. They may be stationary shelves or have shelves arranged in rotary form. Rotary shelf files have a rotating bank of shelves so that records can be stored and accessed from both sides of the shelves.

Mobile Shelving

Areas with limited space may use mobile banks of shelves that can be moved as needed for storage and retrieval. Mobile shelving is a series of shelving units

FIGURE 6.2 **A Lateral File Cabinet Is Wider than It Is Deep**

The HON Company

FIGURE 6.3 **A Shelf File Provides Easy Access to Records**

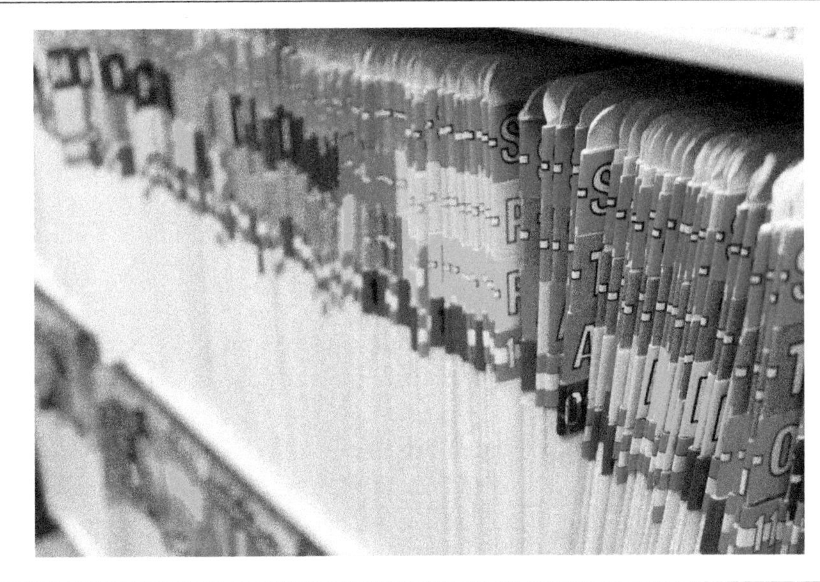

©val lawless/Shutterstock.com

that move on tracks attached to the floor for access to files. In some movable shelving equipment, the shelves slide from side to side. Records on shelves behind the moved shelves are then exposed for use. The units may operate with electric power, or they may be moved manually by the operator. Because aisle space is not constantly maintained between each unit, mobile shelving can approximately double the storage capacity of an area.

How does a motorized rotary storage unit operate?

Motorized rotary storage is a unit that rotates shelves in the unit around a central hub to bring the files to the operator. Such systems may have an automated keypad-driven retrieval system. This system uses overhead storage, with the rotation of the files moving horizontally around a central core to bring files to the operator, and it provides access at a height that can accommodate persons with a disability who require a wheelchair. A rotary shelf file is shown in Figure 6.4.

FIGURE 6.4 **This Rotary Shelf File Has a System of No-Walk Carousels with Banks of Vertical Shelves Rotating for Access by an Operator**

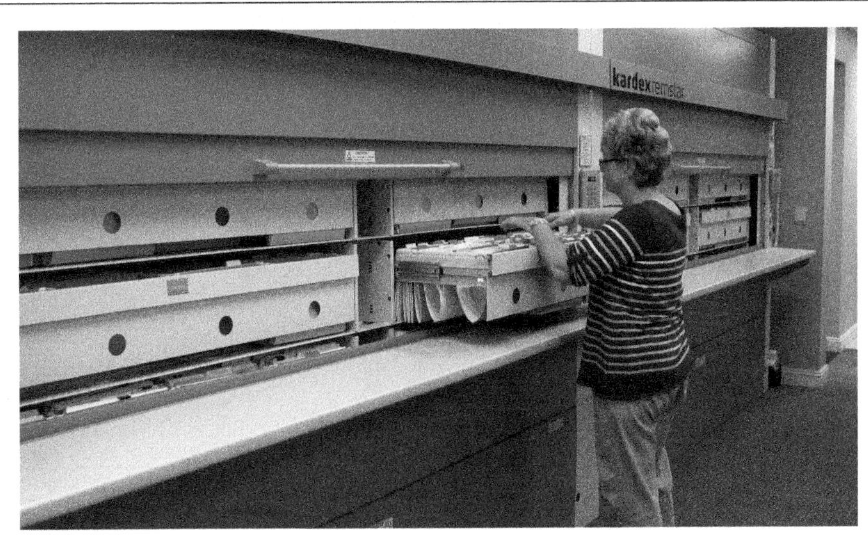

Courtesy of Kardex Remster

File Capacity and Space Requirements

When choosing storage cabinets or shelves, a comparison of file capacity and floor space requirements helps determine cost effectiveness. An estimated capacity for a standard four-drawer file cabinet is about 10,000 records (calculated at about 100 sheets per linear inch, including guides and folders). Three to four inches of space should be left as working space at the end of a file drawer or shelf section to allow easy removal and replacement of file folders. A letter-size vertical cabinet drawer measures 15 by 28 inches and therefore holds about 25 linear inches of records. A lateral file drawer is 18 by 36 inches, with a file capacity of 33 linear inches. Pull-out drawer space for vertical files requires about two feet; lateral file drawers use approximately one foot of pull-out space. Sufficient aisle space must be available for multiple filers to be able to walk between file cabinet drawers that are extended to their full length. Shelf files require less aisle space because they need no drawer-pull space, are not as deep as file cabinets, and hold records that can be readily accessed up to seven shelves high. Figure 6.5 illustrates the capacity and floor space requirements for these three types of storage equipment.

Which type of cabinet requires the least amount of aisle space?

Shelf files save filer time as well as floor space because records can be accessed without having to open drawers; however, open-shelf filing for confidential or vital records must be placed into a records vault for security. File drawers and closed-front cabinets can be purchased with locks. Fire protection is a safety consideration. Vital records can be duplicated and kept in off-site storage. Fireproof storage cabinets, which are heavier and cost more than standard file cabinets, can be purchased for important records.

Storage Supplies

Efficient storage and retrieval requires the use of the right equipment and the right supplies. The principal supplies used in manual storage of paper records are discussed briefly in this section.

FIGURE 6.5 **File Cabinets Are Available in Several Sizes**

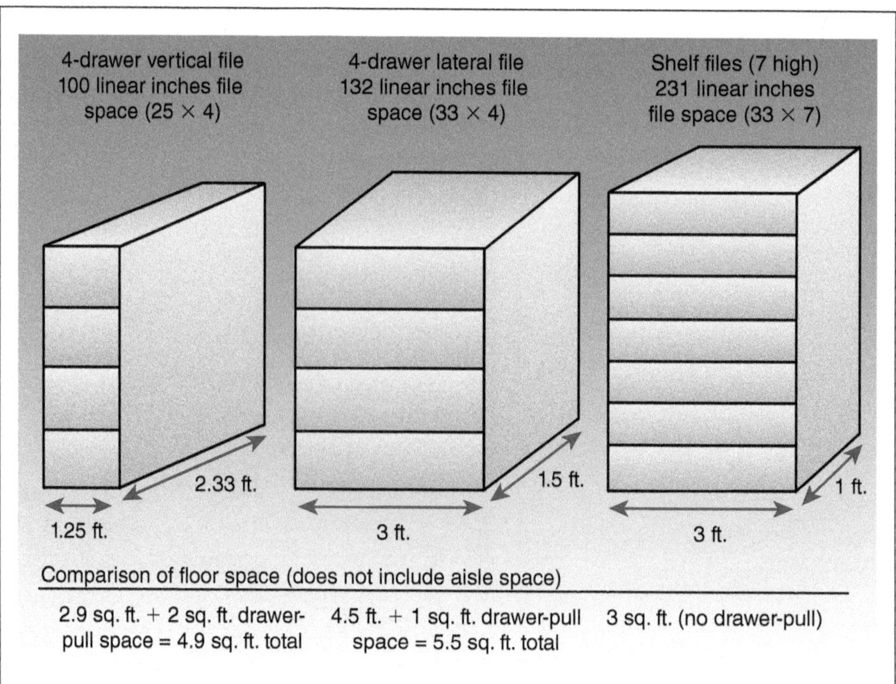

Guides

guide: a rigid divider used to identify a section in a file and to facilitate reference to a particular record location

tab: a projection for a caption on a folder or guide that extends above the regular height or beyond the regular width of the folder or guide

A **guide** is a rigid divider used to identify a section in a file and to facilitate reference to a particular record location. Guides are made of heavy material, such as pressboard, manila, or plastic, and serve as guideposts that speed location of records. A **tab** is a projection for a caption on a folder or guide that extends above the regular height or beyond the regular width of the folder or guide. Some guides have reinforced tabs of metal or acetate to give added strength for long wear. Tabs and tab cuts are discussed in detail later in this chapter.

Proper placement of guides eliminates the need to spend time searching through similar names to find the part of the alphabet needed. The same set of guides may be used year after year with no change, or the guides may be added to or changed as the quantity of records increases. Because of their thickness and sturdy construction, guides also serve to keep the contents of a container (drawer, shelf, or box) upright. Keeping contents upright promotes efficient storage and retrieval. With too few guides, filers spend unnecessary time looking for the correct place to store or find a record. Too many guides that are unevenly distributed throughout the files can slow storage and retrieval because the filer must look at so many tabs to find the right storage section. Using about 20 guides for each file drawer or for each 28 linear inches of stored records will facilitate efficient storage and retrieval in a typical system.

Primary Guides

primary guide: a divider that identifies a main division or section of a file and always precedes all other material in a section

A **primary guide** is a divider that identifies a main division or section of a file and always precedes all other material in a section. In Figure 6.6, the NAMES WITH NUMBERS, A, and B guides in first position (at the left) are primary guides. Remember Rule 7 about business names beginning with numbers? Numbers are filed before letters of the alphabet; the NAMES WITH NUMBERS guide and NAMES WITH NUMBERS folder are filed before the A guide.

A small volume of stored business documents with many individuals or firms requires only primary guides to indicate the alphabetic sections. Systems that use color extensively may use only primary guides with the letters of the alphabet because blocks of colored folders act as a visual guide to a section of the alphabet.

Guide sets that divide the alphabet into many different segments are available from manufacturers of filing supplies. The simplest set is a 23- or 25-division set, the latter having a tab for each letter from *A* to *W*, a tab labeled *Mc,* and a last tab with the combination *XYZ.* Figure 6.7 compares an 80-division and a 120-division breakdown of guides printed by manufacturers.

The number of alphabetic guides furnished by different manufacturers can vary, even though each plan may divide the alphabet into 40 subdivisions. Manufacturers may elect to omit *Mc*, subdivide letters differently, or combine different letters. Before purchasing a set of guides, the records manager should examine the manufacturer's alphabetic subdivisions to see whether the subdivisions fit specific office requirements. Alphabetic guides can be purchased with preprinted tabs or tabs with slotted holders for the labels. Records managers can also create their own subdivisions using guides with blank tabs. Plain or color-coded labels can be applied to the guide tabs.

FIGURE 6.6 **One Section of an Alphabetic Arrangement**

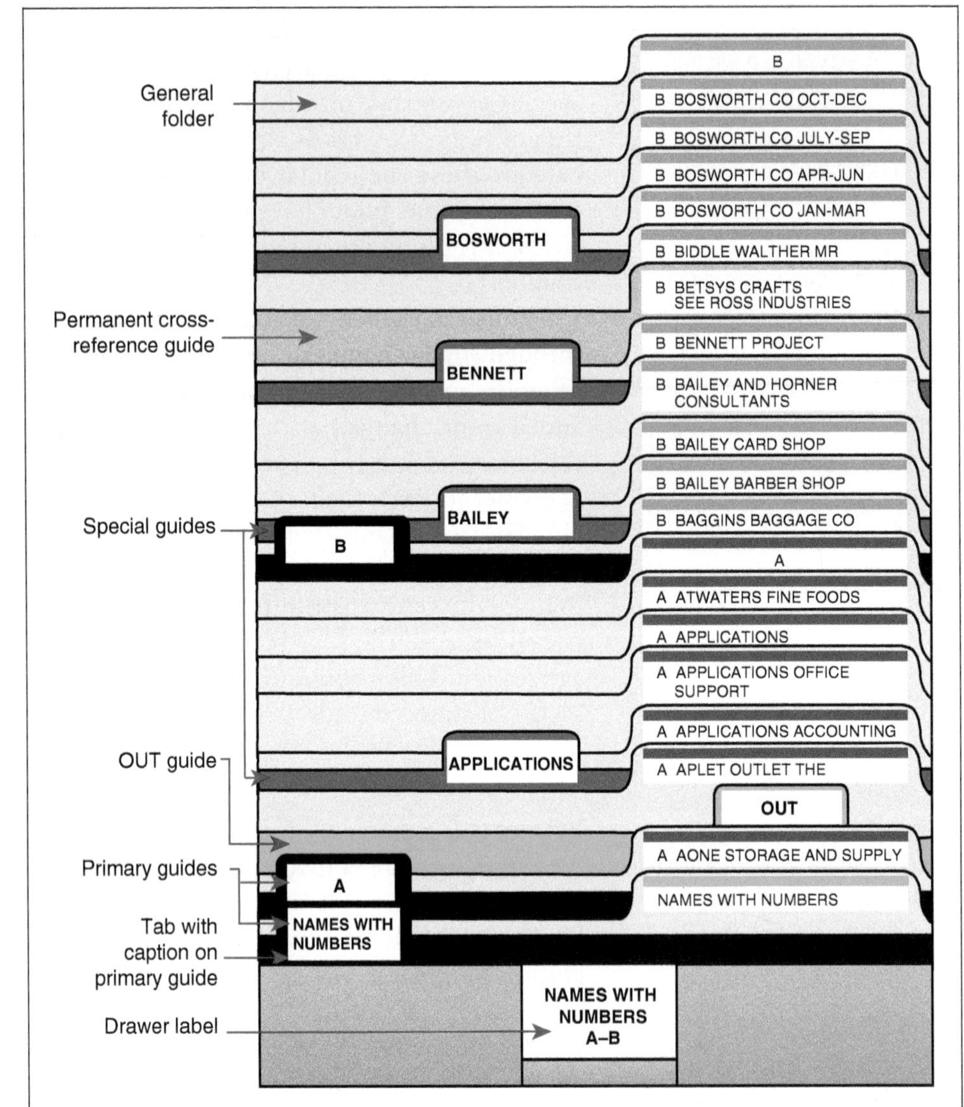

Special Guides

special (auxiliary) guide: a divider used to lead the eye quickly to a specific place in a file

A **special (auxiliary) guide** is a divider used to lead the eye quickly to a specific place in a file. Use special guides to:

1. Indicate the location of an individual or a company folder with a high volume of physical documents. In Figure 6.6, the guides labeled *BAILEY, BENNETT,* and *BOSWORTH* are special (auxiliary) name guides.
2. Introduce a special section of subjects such as Applications, Bids, Conferences, Exhibits, Projects, or Speeches. Figure 6.6 shows a special subject guide, APPLICATIONS, placed in alphabetic order in the A section. Applications for positions in accounting and office support and associated documents are stored behind APPLICATIONS, in properly labeled folders.
3. Identify a section reserved for names with the same first indexing unit. In Figure 6.6, the BAILEY special name guide leads the filer to the section with numerous folders labeled with BAILEY as the first indexing unit.

FIGURE 6.7 **Comparison of Guide Sets for A to Z Indexes**

80 Div. A to Z				120 Div. A to Z					
A	1	L	41	A	1	Gr	41	Pe	81
An	2	Le	42	Al	2	H	42	Pi	82
B	3	Li	43	An	3	Han	43	Pl	83
Be	4	Lo	44	As	4	Has	44	Pr	84
Bi	5	M	45	B	5	He	45	Pu	85
Bo	6	Map	46	Bar	6	Hen	46	Q	86
Br	7	McA	47	Bas	7	Hi	47	R	87
Bro	8	McH	48	Be	8	Ho	48	Re	88
Bu	9	McN	49	Ber	9	Hon	49	Ri	89
C	10	Me	50	Bi	10	Hu	50	Ro	90
Ce	11	Mi	51	Bo	11	I	51	Rog	91
Co	12	Mo	52	Br	12	J	52	Ru	92
Coo	13	N	53	Bre	13	Jo	53	S	93
Cr	14	O	54	Bro	14	K	54	Sch	94
D	15	P	55	Bu	15	Ke	55	Scho	95
De	16	PL	56	C	16	Ki	56	Se	96
Do	17	Q	57	Car	17	Kl	57	Sh	97
Dr	18	R	58	Ce	18	Kr	58	Shi	98
E	19	Re	59	Ci	19	L	59	Si	99
En	20	Ro	60	Co	20	Lar	60	Sm	100
F	21	S	61	Corn	21	Le	61	Sn	101
Fi	22	Sch	62	Cop	22	Len	62	Sp	102
Fo	23	Se	63	Cr	23	Li	63	St	103
G	24	Sh	64	Cu	24	Lo	64	Sti	104
Ge	25	Si	65	D	25	M	65	Su	105
Gi	26	Sm	66	De	26	Map	66	T	106
Gr	27	St	67	Di	27	McA	67	Th	107
H	28	Sti	68	Do	28	McD	68	Tr	108
Har	29	Su	69	Du	29	McH	69	U	109
Has	30	T	70	E	30	McN	70	V	110
He	31	To	71	El	31	Me	71	W	111
Her	32	U	72	Er	32	Mi	72	Wam	112
Hi	33	V	73	F	33	Mo	73	We	113
Ho	34	W	74	Fi	34	Mu	74	Wh	114
Hu	35	We	75	Fo	35	N	75	Wi	115
I	36	Wh	76	Fr	36	Ne	76	Wil	116
J	37	Wi	77	G	37	No	77	Wim	117
K	38	Wo	78	Ge	38	O	78	Wo	118
Ki	39	X–Y	79	Gi	39	On	79	X–Y	119
Kr	40	Z	80	Go	40	P	80	Z	120

The tabs on guides for open-shelf equipment are at the side, as shown in Figure 6.8. Because materials stored in open-shelf equipment are visible at one edge instead of across the top (as is true in drawer files), the alphabetic or other divisions must extend from the side of the guide so that they can be seen easily. Printing on these side-guide tabs may be read from either side.

FIGURE 6.8 **Guides Used in Cabinets and Open-Shelf Files**

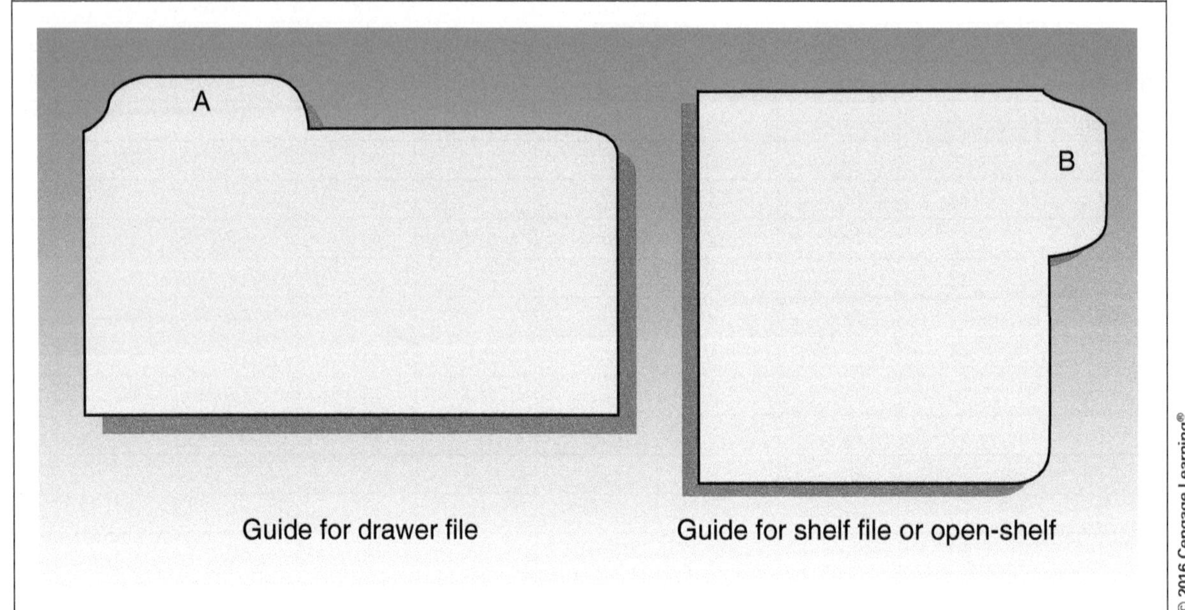

Folders

Folders are containers used to hold and protect the records in a file. Folders are usually made of heavy material such as manila, plastic, or pressboard and can have either top or side tabs in varying sizes.

Folder and guide tabs are available in different sizes or cuts. A tab cut is the length of the tab expressed as a proportion of the width or height of the folder or guide. A straight cut tab extends across the complete width of a folder. A one-third-cut tab extends only one-third the width of a folder and may be in any of three positions, as shown in Figure 6.9.

position: the location of the tab across the top or down one side of a guide or folder

Position refers to the location of the tab across the top or down one side of a guide or folder. First position means the tab is at the left; second position means the tab is second from the left; and so on. Straight-line arrangement is a system that aligns folder tabs in one position; for example, all folder tabs are third position (see Figure 6.9).

Guide and folder tabs may be arranged in different ways. In a staggered arrangement, tabs are placed in a series of positions from left to right, according to a set pattern. Straight-line position is preferred because of ease in reading label captions; the filer can read label captions faster in a straight line than when looking back and forth from left to right. The most efficient position for folders is third, with third-cut tabs; the most efficient position for guides is either first or second, with fifth-cut tabs, as shown in Figure 6.6.

FIGURE 6.9 **Folder Cuts and Tab Positions**

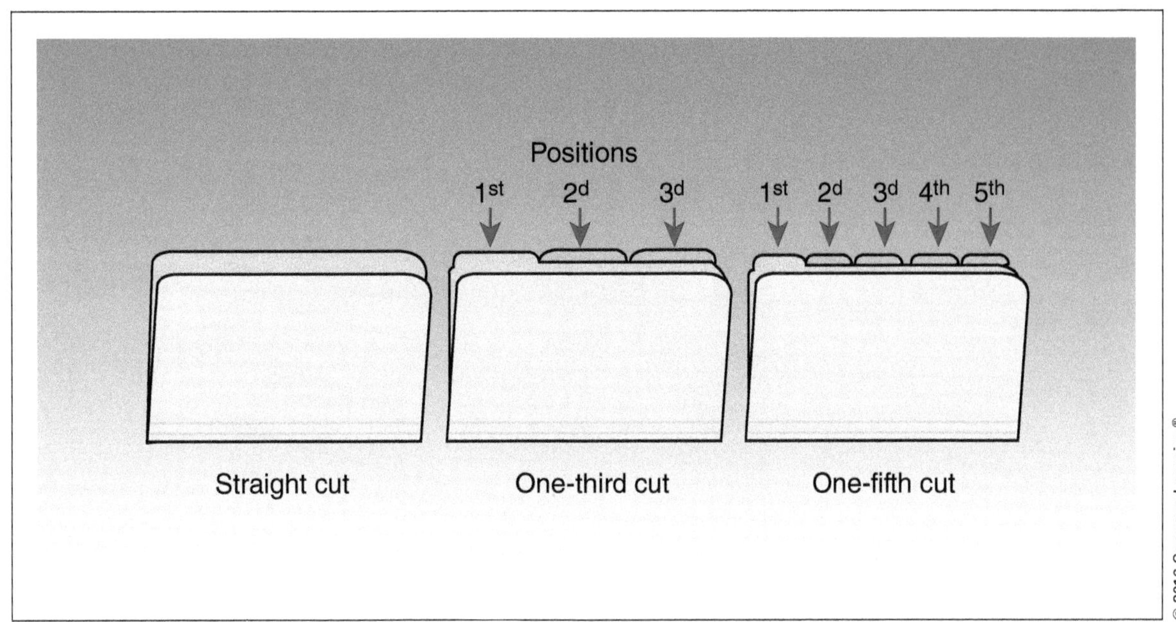

Tabs on folders for open-shelf equipment are on the side edge (Figure 6.10) in various positions according to the manufacturer's system or the customer's preference.

Folders behind every guide are used to keep like records together. The three main types of folders used in alphabetic storage are general folders, individual folders, and special folders.

FIGURE 6.10 **Folder Cuts and Positions for Open-Shelf Files**

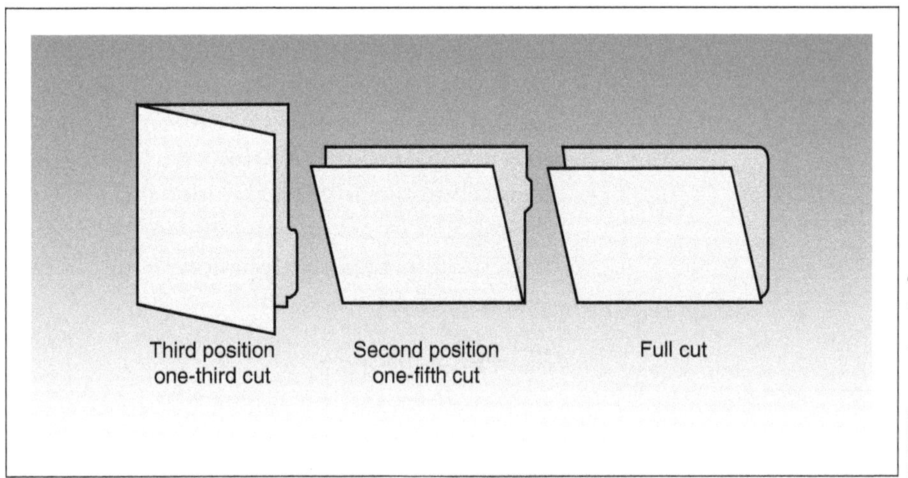

General Folders

general folder: a folder for records to and from correspondents, which has a small volume of records that does not require an individual folder

Every primary guide has a corresponding general folder bearing the same caption as is on the guide. A **general folder** is a folder for records to and from correspondents, with a small volume of records that does not require an individual folder or folders. In Figure 6.6, the *A* folder is a general folder and is the last folder in that section. General folders often are color coded for greater visibility.

Records are arranged inside a general folder alphabetically by the correspondents' names. Then, the most recently dated record is placed on top within each correspondent's records, as shown in Figure 6.11.

FIGURE 6.11 **Arrangement of Records in a General Folder**

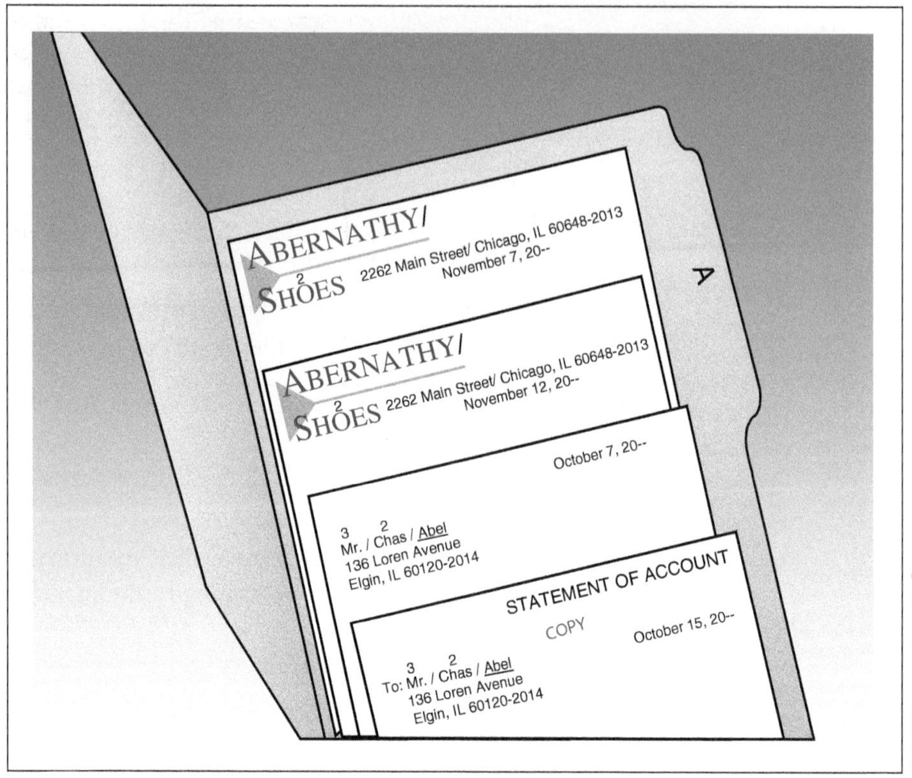

Individual Folders

individual folder: a folder used to store the records of an individual correspondent, with enough records to warrant a separate folder

An **individual folder** is a folder used to store the records of an individual correspondent with enough records to warrant a separate folder. Records are arranged chronologically within an individual folder, with the most recently dated record on top. In Figure 6.6, all individual folders are one-third cut, third position. Records pertaining to one correspondent are removed from the general folder and placed into an individual folder when the number of records accumulates to a predetermined number. Individual folders are placed in alphabetic order between the primary guide and its general folder.

Special Folders

special folder: a folder that follows a special guide in an alphabetic arrangement

A **special folder** is a folder that follows a special guide in an alphabetic arrangement. In Figure 6.6, three special folders are shown: two behind APPLICATIONS and one behind BENNETT. Within the APPLICATIONS ACCOUNTING folder, all records pertaining to accounting positions are arranged first by the names of the applicants. If an applicant has more than one record in the folder, those records are arranged by date, with the most recent date on top. Within the BENNETT PROJECT folder, records are arranged by date, the most recent one on top.

Care of Folders

Proper care of folders will help make stored records readily accessible. When records start to "ride up" in any folder, too many papers are in the folder.

The number of records that will fit into one folder obviously depends on the thickness of the papers. Records should never protrude from the folder edges and should always be inserted with their tops to the left. The most useful folders have score marks. Score marks are indented or raised lines or series of marks along the bottom edge of a folder to allow for expansion (Figure 6.12). As a folder is filled, it is refolded along a score mark and expanded to give it a flat base on which to rest. Most folders can be expanded from 3/4 to 1 inch. Refolding a folder at the score marks reduces the danger of folders bending and sliding under others, avoids curling papers, and results in a neater file.

Why do file folders have score marks?

FIGURE 6.12 **Flat Folder and Expanded Folder**

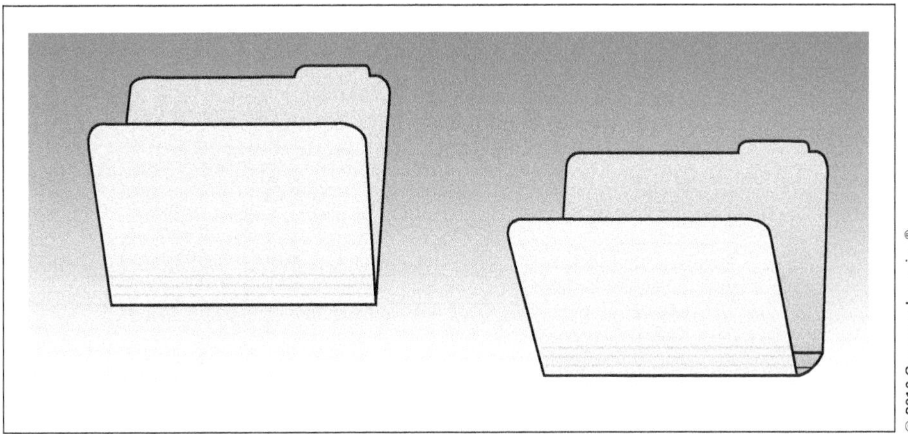

A folder lasts longer and is easier to use if it is not stuffed beyond its capacity. If too many papers are in an individual folder, prepare a second folder for that correspondent. Then label the folders to show that the records are arranged chronologically in them (see the four BOSWORTH CO folders in Figure 6.6). Sometimes papers in a folder are redistributed by adding subject folders instead of subdividing by dates, as is the case with APPLICATIONS in Figure 6.6.

When are new folders needed?

New folders may be needed because:

- A new group of names is to be added to a file.
- Older folders have become full, and additional ones must be added to handle the overload.
- Enough records have accumulated for certain correspondents so that their records can be removed from the general folders and put into individual folders.
- Folders have worn out from heavy use and must be replaced.
- The scheduled time has arrived for replacing folders and transferring infrequently used folders to inactive storage. Records transfer procedures are discussed in detail in Chapter 7.

Types of Folders

Other folders frequently used in offices are a suspension, or hanging, folder; a bellows folder; and a pocket folder. These folder types can be useful for particular types of records within a RIM system.

suspension (hanging) folder: a folder with built-in hooks on each side that hang from parallel metal rails on each side of a file drawer or other storage equipment

A **suspension (hanging) folder** is a folder with built-in hooks on each side that hang from parallel metal rails on each side of a file drawer or other

FIGURE 6.13 **Hanging Folders Are Convenient for Storing Records**

storage equipment, as shown in Figure 6.13. The main advantage of hanging folders over conventional folders is their added support for holding records in a neat, upright position due to support of both the front and back of the folder by the hooks on the drawer rails. If your file cabinet does not have built-in rails for hanging folders, you can purchase drawer frames with rails that adjust for letter- or legal-size files. Hanging folders have up to 10 slots across the upper edge for inserting plastic tabs and can hold several interior folders to subdivide a file.

Generally, hanging folders should not be removed from a file drawer. Placing the contents of these folders into interior conventional-type folders or interior folders that are shorter than traditional file folders provides records protection and facilitates removal or placement of records. In addition, some hanging folders have a pocket for small items like computer disks, notes, or receipts.

How is a bellows folder different from a pocket folder?

A bellows (expansion) folder has a top flap and sides to enclose records in a case with creases along its bottom and sides that allow it to expand. These folders usually come with dividers inside for subdividing the records and are used when the volume of stored records is small. In Figure 6.14, the bellows folder is on the left.

A pocket folder has partially enclosed sides and more expansion at the bottom than an ordinary folder. A pocket folder (Figure 6.14) is useful for transporting as well as for storing records. Also, these folders can be used to store records such as bound reports or other records media with more bulk than can be easily fitted into a traditional file folder.

Follower Blocks or Compressors

Failing to use proper means to hold drawer contents upright causes folders to bend and slide under one another. The proper number of guides and correct use of a follower block behind the guides and folders keeps folders upright.

FIGURE 6.14 **Special Folders for Storing Physical Records**

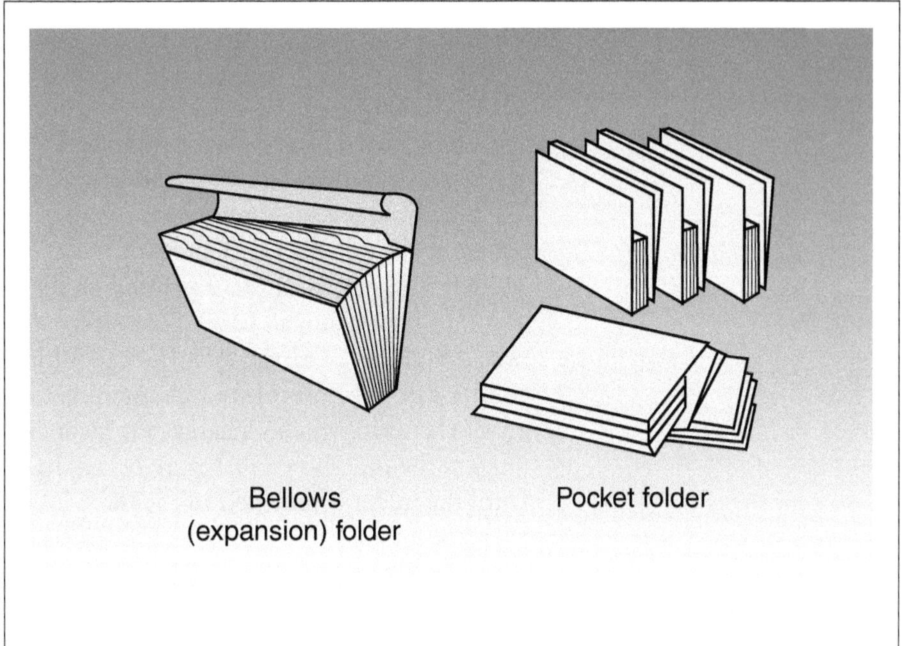

follower block (compressor): a device at the back of a file drawer that can be moved to allow contraction or expansion of the drawer contents

OUT indicator: a control device, such as a guide, sheet, or folder, that shows the location of borrowed records

A **follower block (compressor)** is a device at the back of a file drawer that can be moved to allow contraction or expansion of the drawer contents, as shown in Figure 6.15. A follower block that is too loose will allow the drawer contents to sag; one that is too tight will make filing and retrieving difficult. In an over-compressed drawer, as in an overcrowded drawer, locating and removing a single sheet of paper is difficult. Instead of follower blocks, some file drawers have slim steel upright dividers placed permanently throughout the file drawer to keep the contents vertical. Also, shelf files use a series of metal upright dividers to hold records upright. A lateral or vertical file with metal rails and hanging folders does not require the use of a follower block; the suspension of each folder on the drawer rack holds records upright.

FIGURE 6.15 **A Follower Block (Compressor) Helps Keep Files Upright in a File Drawer**

OUT Indicators

An **OUT indicator** is a control device, such as a guide, sheet, or folder, which shows the location of borrowed records. These indicators contain a form for recording the name of the person borrowing the record, the date it was borrowed, a brief statement of the contents of the record, and the due date for return to storage. When a borrowed record is returned to storage, the OUT indicator is removed, to be reused, recycled, or saved and later used to check the activity at the files or to determine which records are active or inactive. Commonly used indicators are OUT guides, OUT folders, and OUT sheets.

OUT Guides

An OUT guide is a special guide used to replace any record that has been removed from storage and to indicate what was taken and by whom. When the borrowed record is returned, the filer can quickly find the exact place to refile the record. An OUT guide is made of the same sturdy material as other guides, with the word *OUT* printed on its tab in large letters and a distinctive color. In Figure 6.6, an OUT guide is located between the AONE STORAGE AND SUPPLY and the APLET OUTLET THE individual folders. OUT guides can have preprinted charge-out forms on both sides or have a plastic pocket into which a charge-out form can be inserted. Some OUT guides, such as the one shown in Figure 6.16a, have a pocket for holding documents until the folder is returned to the file.

OUT Folders

An OUT folder, as shown in Figure 6.16b, is a special folder used to replace a complete folder that has been removed from storage. This folder has a pocket or slot for a small card bearing information concerning who took the folder, the date it was taken, its contents, and the date the folder should be returned to storage. The OUT folder remains in the file as a temporary storage place for records that will be transferred to the permanent folder when it is returned to storage.

OUT Sheets

An OUT sheet is a form that is inserted in place of a record removed from a folder. An OUT sheet is often the same size and color as an OUT guide, but its thickness is that of a sheet of paper. An OUT sheet remains in the file folder until replaced with the returned record.

FIGURE 6.16a and b **An OUT Guide or Folder Indicates the Location of Records That Have Been Removed from the Files**

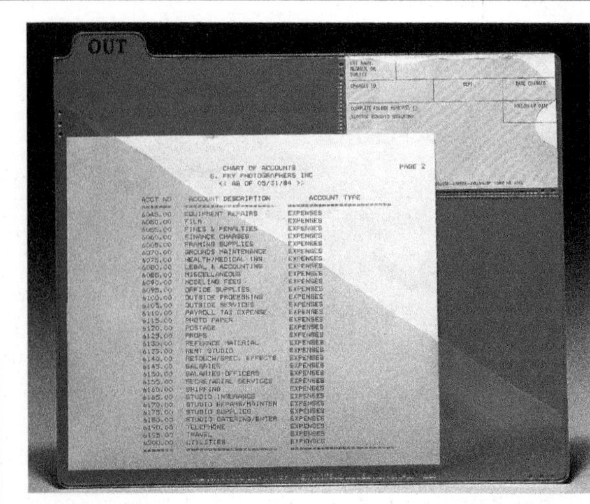

a. OUT guide

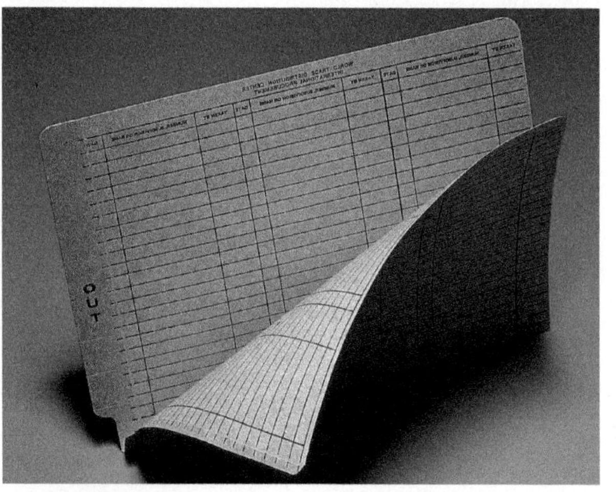

b. OUT folder

Courtesy of TAB Products Co., LLC

Labels

label: a device that contains the name of the subject or number assigned to the file folder or section contents

caption: a title, heading, short explanation, or description of a document or records

Containers, guides, and folders that help filers store records efficiently must be labeled to guide the filer to the appropriate storage location. A **label** is a device that contains the name of the subject or number assigned to the file folder or section contents. It may have other pertinent information, be color coded to denote its place in an overall filing system, or have a bar code. A **caption** is a title, heading, short explanation, or description of a document or records.

Container Labels

Labels on drawers, shelf files, or other storage containers should be clearly but briefly worded and inclusive enough to represent the contents. Storage containers usually have holders on the outside, where card stock labels can be inserted. Various colors are available on perforated card stock sheets. ARMA International guidelines recommend centering information for the container label in all caps with no punctuation. The caption on the drawer illustrated in Figure 6.6 reads *NAMES WITH NUMBERS A–B*, indicating that records of correspondents whose names are within the A and B sections of the alphabet are stored in that drawer. Names in which the key units are numbers written as digits are filed before all alphabetic names. For example, *123 Builders* comes before *Albany Builders*.

Guide Labels

Guide labels consist of words, letters, or numbers (or some combination of these items). In Figure 6.6, the guides have window tabs into which keyed captions have been inserted (NAMES WITH NUMBERS, A, APPLICATIONS, B, BAILEY, BENNETT, BOSWORTH). Some guides (alphabetic or numeric guides) are available with preprinted information. ARMA International guidelines recommend placing guide captions near the left margin of the label and as near as possible to the top. Print captions in all capital letters with no punctuation. Single letters of the alphabet may be centered on guide labels if preferred.

FIGURE 6.17 **Color-Coded Labels Are Available in a Variety of Styles**

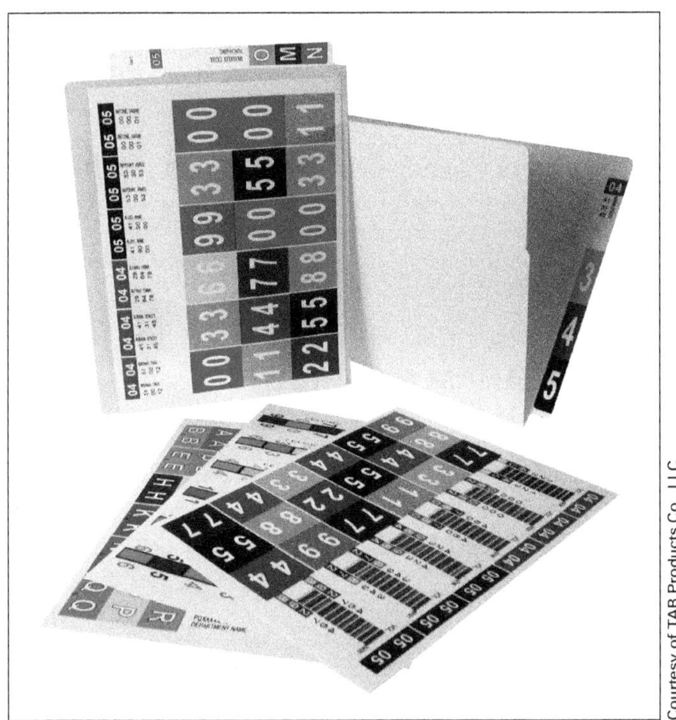

Courtesy of TAB Products Co., LLC

Folder Labels

Folder labels are available as pressure-sensitive adhesive labels in continuous folded strips or on sheets that can be prepared with computer software and affixed to folders. Sheets of labels for computer generation usually have columns of labels across an 8½- by 11-inch sheet, as shown in Figure 6.17. Most word processing software has settings for different label sizes that match common label product numbers. Also, label packaging often contains instructions for required software settings. Some vendors may generate custom-printed or laminated labels for their customers.

How do bar codes on labels aid in locating records?

Bar codes can be computer generated along with a name on a label. A bar code tracking system keeps a record of a file location at all times. When a file is checked out, a scanner reads the bar code. Information about the file and who checked it out is then updated and recorded in a computer program. Sometimes another label strip is generated for OUT indicators. Use of a bar code tracking system can greatly improve retrieval rates. Refer to Chapter 7 for more on bar code tracking.

What format should be used for folder labels?

Place folder labels near the left edge and as near the top of the label or the bottom of the color bar (if used) as possible. Wrap-around side-tab labels for open-sided lateral file cabinets or shelf filing are placed both above and below the color bar separator so that the information is readable from both sides of the folder. Word processing software with automatic label settings places information in the proper location on the label. For alphabetic filing, the letter of the alphabet is keyed first, followed by about one-half inch of blank space and then the filing segment. In all cases, the label is keyed in capital letters with no punctuation, as shown in Figure 6.18.

Label placement and caption format should be the same on new folders as on other folders already in use. Placement and label format consistency helps achieve faster folder retrieval. One way to achieve uniform placement of labels is as follows: When a new box of folders is opened, remove all the folders, hold them tightly together, and stand them upright on a flat surface. Place a ruler or stiff card over the tab edges at the spot where labels are to be affixed. Make a pencil mark across the top edge of all the tabs that will serve as a guide for attaching labels.

Sorters

How do filers use a sorter?

A sorter is a device used to arrange records into alphabetic or numeric categories and to hold records temporarily prior to storage. Records to be filed are organized alphabetically (or numerically for a numeric system) in the order in which they will be filed, to improve the speed and accuracy of filing in the records system. The type of sorter used depends on the volume of records in

FIGURE 6.18 **Labels for Shelf Files Have a Caption on Both Sides of the Label**

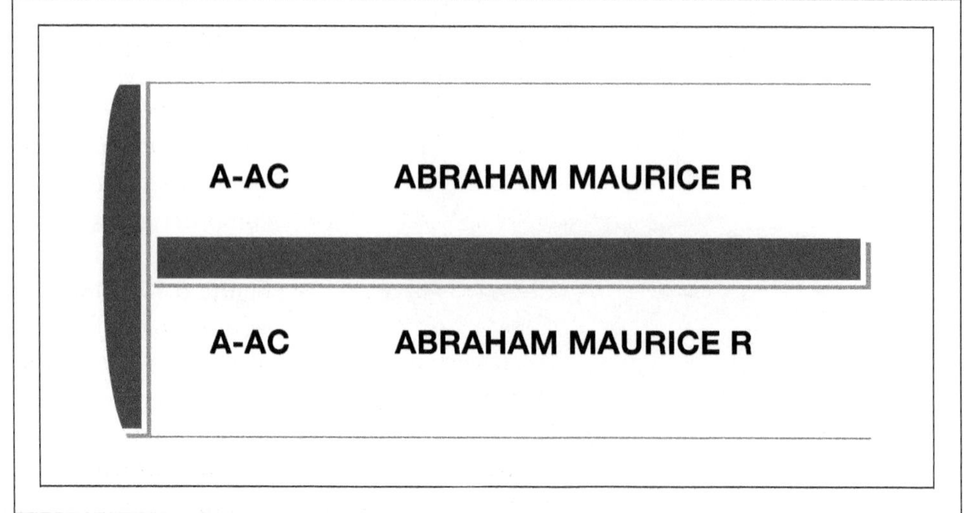

FIGURE 6.19 **A Sorter Is Used to Arrange Files in Preparation for Storage**

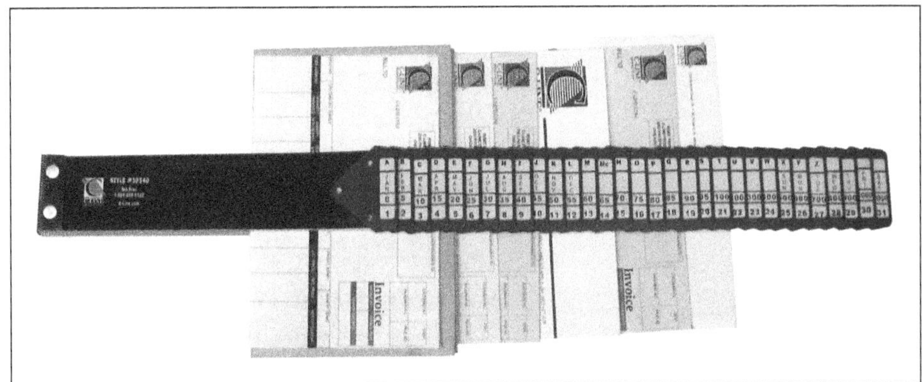

C-Line Products, Inc.

the office. The sorter shown in Figure 6.19 accommodates records such as checks, sales slips, time cards, and business documents. Placing documents into a sorter prior to storing them makes finding a document easy if a document is called for before it is stored.

Other specialized supplies are discussed in later chapters of the text as their use becomes necessary. The supplies just explained and illustrated are basic ones and applicable to all storage methods.

Selection of Storage Equipment and Supplies

What are the benefits of using the right type and quality of storage equipment and supplies?

Every office has its own RIM system; and the right equipment, supplies, and filing accessories can improve document-handling efficiency. Proper selection of equipment can result in saving space and time, both factors that can reduce operating costs. Records and information managers should keep updated on new and improved products by reading business periodicals and trade magazines; viewing vendor catalogs, brochures, and websites; attending business shows; and participating in professional RIM association meetings.

What factors need to be considered when choosing a storage system?

Appropriate selection of storage equipment and supplies requires consideration of the following factors:

1. *Type and volume of records to be stored and retrieved.* An inventory of what is to be stored is a basic step in making the best choice of storage equipment and supplies. Records in different formats or media, such as papers, cards, books, computer disks, microfilm, videos, or architectural drawings, have special storage needs. A records inventory also shows the current volume of stored records. Future volume and needs must be forecast. The records inventory will also reveal the volume of active and inactive records. Chapter 7 presents more detailed information about the records inventory.
2. *Degree of required protection of records.* Confidential or classified records require equipment with locks or location in a records vault. Records vital to the operation of the business need fireproof or fire-resistant storage equipment.
3. *Efficiency and ease of use of equipment and systems.* The ease with which records can be found is a major consideration. The simpler the system is to understand, the easier it is to use. Also, less training of new employees

is required when the system is a simple one. Time saved by personnel who store and retrieve records means dollars saved. The ease of expansion or modification of a system or the addition of compatible equipment will be important to meet the changing needs of an organization.

4. *Space considerations.* Floor-weight restrictions, use of space to the ceiling (air space), or the advisability of counter-type equipment or something in between, and the possibility of transferring some records to off-site storage facilities affect space, which, in an office, is costly. Lateral, shelf, or rotary equipment can house more square feet of records than can conventional drawer file cabinets in the same square footage of floor space. The effect of new equipment on present layout and workflow should also be considered.
5. *Cost.* After all other criteria have been examined, cost and the company budget may be the final determinants as to which equipment and supplies may be acquired. The astute records manager realizes that the least expensive equipment and supplies may not provide the most economical records storage. Quality in construction and materials is important. Inferior materials or lightweight stock may need frequent and costly replacement. In determining costs, keep in mind the points given in Figure 6.20.

Special needs of your organization could add other factors to your list of considerations. Also, consult users of equipment under consideration for purchase to learn about benefits, problems, or special considerations associated with the equipment.

PHYSICAL DOCUMENT STORAGE PROCEDURES

This last section of the chapter looks at the advantages and disadvantages of alphabetic records management, some criteria for selecting an alphabetic storage system, and procedures for storing documents alphabetically.

FIGURE 6.20 **Cost Considerations for Selecting Equipment**

Cost Considerations
Cost of personnel needed to work with the records
Compatibility of supplies and equipment
Benefits of using the right type and quality of storage equipment and supplies
Cost of new storage equipment and supplies that must be purchased
Advisability of using local vendors rather than purchasing from out-of-town vendors
Possibility of discounts for quantity purchases
Feasibility of choosing used rather than new equipment
Volume of records that can be stored within the equipment
Credit terms available from the vendor
Cost of assembling equipment
Cost of delivery for equipment and supplies

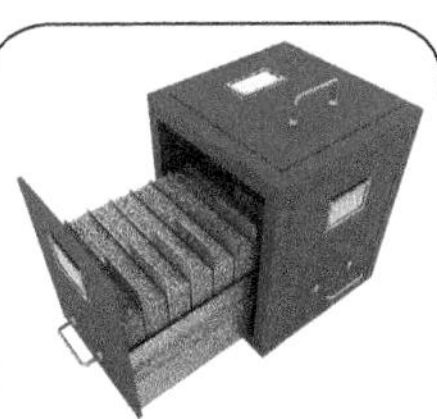

MY RECORDS

Storing Records

How and where should you store your records? What types of storage containers are needed for storing your records?

VITAL RECORDS

Vital records are usually not replaceable and require the highest degree of protection. Property deeds and wills are examples of vital records. Follow these guidelines for storing vital records:

- Store vital records in a bank safe deposit box.
- Keep the safe deposit key in a safe place accessible to you and your closest family members.
- Store copies of vital records at home in a fireproof box. Generally, the more hours that records will remain below the flash point (which is 450 degrees Fahrenheit [F] for paper documents) in the container, the more the container will cost. Fireproof boxes are tested at 1700°F for one, two, or three hours. The inside temperature cannot rise above 350°F to be considered fireproof. Look for a box that meets these standards.

IMPORTANT RECORDS

Important records are usually replaceable but at considerable cost. They require a high degree of protection. Bills and receipts are examples of important records. Follow these guidelines for storing important records:

- Use a secure location near where you pay your bills to store unpaid bills. When you pay the bills, write the date and amount that you paid on your copy of the bill. Store this copy with other copies of paid bills and receipts in an alphabetic file.
- Create folders for your major bills, such as rent or mortgage, car, utilities, and so on, and store them in a small file cabinet or a banker's storage box. Store copies of paid bills and receipts in this container.
- Store tax deductible receipts in a separate folder by date, with the most recent at the front. When you complete your tax return, you can find the receipts for deductions in this folder.
- Use the tax deduction portion of the money management software. Create backup copies of your data at least once a month, and store the backups in a secure container.
- Consider using a bellows file to store all information used to file your tax return, including a copy of the return itself. Date the outside of the file, and retain this container and records until the time to dispose of the records.

USEFUL RECORDS

Useful records are usually replaceable at slight cost and require a low degree of protection. Product manuals, warranties, and routine correspondence are examples of useful records. Follow these guidelines for storing useful records:

- Create separate folders to store records such as product manuals, warranties, and routine correspondence.
- Store the folders in a readily accessible safe place.
- Remove product manuals for items that you discarded and replaced from the storage container, and replace them with the manuals for the new products.
- Review warranties and note their expiration dates, periodically. Remove expired warranties and destroy them or place them into a folder marked "Expired Warranties."

Advantages and Disadvantages of Alphabetic Records Management

direct access: a method of accessing records by going directly to the file without first referring to an index or a list of names to find a document or folder

The advantages of using alphabetic records management are as follows:

- Alphabetic storage does not require an index and is therefore a direct access storage method. **Direct access** is a method of accessing records by going directly to the file without first referring to an index or a list of names to find a document or folder.
- All records for correspondent names that begin with numbers written as digits are filed before all alphabetic names, according to alphabetic indexing Rule 7. Knowing this rule facilitates storage and retrieval.
- The alphabetic dictionary (A to Z) order of arrangement is simple to understand.
- Storage is easy if standard procedures are followed.
- Misfiles are easily checked by examining alphabetic sequence.
- The direct access feature can save time and reduce operating costs.
- Related records from one name, either a company or an individual, are grouped together.

The disadvantages of alphabetic records management are as follows:

- Misfiling is prevalent if rules for alphabetic storage are not established and followed.
- Similar names may cause confusion, especially when spellings are not precise.
- Transposition of some letters of the alphabet is easy, causing filing sequence to be out of order.
- Filing under the wrong name can result in lost records.
- Security can be breached because names on folders are seen instantly by anyone who happens to glance at an open storage container. Consequently, confidential or classified records are not secure.
- Related records with different correspondent names are filed in more than one place.

Selection and Design of an Alphabetic Records Management System

In preparation for opening a new office, managers must decide the kind of storage system to be selected or designed. For established offices, the system in use may no longer serve the needs of filers or end users. If records are requested by names of individuals, businesses, and organizations with few subjects, then an alphabetic system is best for that office.

Selecting or designing a records and information storage method requires careful planning because that method will likely be used for a very long time. To select an alphabetic system, or to redesign one, the records manager should know:

What information does a records manager need to know before talking to a storage system vendor?

- The total volume of records to be stored.
- The number of records in each alphabetic section and which letters of the alphabet contain a large number of records.

- The expected activity in the files—an estimate of how many times records may be requested.
- The length of time that records are to be kept.
- The efficiency of filing personnel.
- The time and resources available for training personnel.

In some cases, the person in charge of the records may seek the help of a RIM consultant or a representative of a filing system manufacturer to determine the best records storage system. The consultant will study the information needs of the office, consult with the person in charge of the records, and make recommendations.

The records and information manager must know the current storage needs and be aware of expected or potential increases in the volume of records in the future. The ultimate test of any successful storage system (alphabetic or any other) is whether records that have been stored within the system can be found quickly when needed.

Examples of Records Storage Systems

A variety of manufacturers provide records and information storage supplies and systems. These systems often include the storage equipment as well as the supplies for storing records and information in the equipment. The use of color-coded supplies—folders and labels—enhances the effectiveness of a records storage system. Color coding improves retrieval times, eliminates misfiles, and reduces the risk of lost files. In one system, for instance, all key units beginning with *A* are stored in white folders with red labels. Filers can quickly find a misfiled folder when they see a yellow folder among the white folders.

How is color used in storage systems?

color coding: is using color as an identifying aid in a filing system to divide the alphabetic sections in the storage system

color accenting: the consistent use of different colors for different supplies in the storage system-one color for guides, various colors for folders, one color for OUT indicators, and specific colors of labels or stripes on labels

The use of color has two meanings: color coding and color accenting. **Color coding** is using color as an identifying aid in a filing system (for example, different colors might be used to divide the alphabetic sections in the storage system). **Color accenting** is the consistent use of different colors for different supplies in the storage system—one color for guides, various colors for folders, one color for OUT indicators, and specific colors of labels or stripes on labels. Color coding is used in the system illustrated in Figure 6.3 on page 121. Blocks of colored folders act as a visual guide to lead filers quickly to a section of the alphabet. Using a contrasting color for special folders for key customers, current projects, or unpaid bills makes them easy to locate.

For an alphabetic system, color bars can correspond to the first letters of the correspondent's name to create blocks of colors. Another use of color shows the same first color for alphabetic letter guides and a different second color on the label for secondary guides.

Some manufacturers produce trade-named alphabetic systems that use color extensively. The trade-named alphabetic systems discussed here—TAB Products and Smead Manufacturing Company—are representative of other available systems. You will search the websites for these two companies in Activity 6-4 at the end of this chapter.

TAB Products provides equipment, supplies, software, and services for filing systems using color coding and color accenting in a variety of records systems. Filers can produce labels to color code file folders and other items such as backup tapes, videos, books, and binders. Filers can track document location through the use of bar codes and bar code readers. Bar code readers enable filers to check items in or out or transfer them to a new location without manual data entry.

Smead Manufacturing Company's color-coded top-tab or end-tab folders have a large wrap-around color bar printed on the top or end tab of each folder. Smead software can be used for creating labels that include file headings, color-coded indexing, bar codes, text, images, and graphics.

Smead Manufacturing Company offers an online labeling system that allows users to print color labels without the expense of purchasing labeling software. Users simply access the website where they can design and print labels using the onscreen instructions and illustrations. The service is available for an annual subscription fee. You will learn more about the online labeling system in Application 6-4 at the end of the chapter.

Procedures for Storing Physical Records

Records and information storage filing procedures are the same for centralized or decentralized records facilities. Each record must be (1) inspected, (2) indexed, (3) coded, (4) cross-referenced if necessary, (5) sorted, and (6) stored. Filers must enjoy detailed work, be dexterous, have a good memory, be willing to follow procedures consistently, be interested in developing new and better procedures, and realize the importance of correctly storing all records so that they may be found immediately when needed. The following sections give details about each of these steps; Figures 6.21 and 6.22 illustrate these steps on an example letter and its associated cross-reference sheet.

Inspecting

inspecting: checking a record to determine whether it is ready to be filed

Checking a record to determine whether it is ready to be filed is known as **inspecting.** A business record must not be stored until someone with authority marks it to be released for filing. All required actions must be taken or noted in a reminder system prior to storage. Notation in a reminder system ensures that the record will be brought to the attention of the proper person at a future date. Storing records before their contents are noted and before appropriate action has been taken can sometimes cause embarrassment to a business and can directly or indirectly result in financial loss or loss of goodwill.

The copy of an outgoing letter or other communication would appear ready to be stored when it is received by the filer for storage. However, in most offices, every original (or incoming) record to be stored must bear a release mark. A **release mark** is an agreed-upon mark such as initials or a symbol placed onto a record to show that the record is ready for storage (see "JJ" on Figure 6.21). The person who prepared the reply or otherwise handled the matter usually puts this release mark on the letter.

release mark: an agreed-upon mark such as initials or a symbol placed onto a record to show that the record is ready for storage

Types of marks used are initials, a code or check mark, a punched symbol, a stamped notation, or some other agreed-upon mark. A missing mark is a signal to the filer to inquire about the release mark. A date/time stamp

FIGURE 6.21 **Letter Released and Coded for Filing**

Investment / 2 Strategies, / 3 Inc.

150 Salmon Ave.
Portland, OR 97202-0015
(503) 555-0192
(503) 555-0191 FAX

October 21, 20--

Oct. 23, 20-- 10:30 A.M.

Ms. Joan Jensen, Manager
1040 Tax Express
1500 SW Cedar Ave.
Portland, OR 97204-1500

JJ

Dear Ms. Jensen

Thank you for your interest in offering investment advice to your customers. We are happy you have asked us to work with you on this new program.

We have hired the 1 Trotter/ 2 Poll/ 3 Company to conduct a survey to help us gather information about your customers. In the near future, Trotter Poll Company will send to each of your customers a questionnaire that will provide spaces for the listing of annual income, approximate annual expenses, amount available for saving and investment, financial objectives, and other pertinent information. X

We will analyze the data received from all those who return the questionnaire and then make recommendations for types of investments your customers should consider.

Sincerely yours

James Washington

James Washington
Investment Counselor

psm

(see Oct 23, 20– 10:30 AM in Figure 6.21) is not a release mark. The person who opens mail often stamps the correspondence for reference purposes with a date/time stamp showing the date and time received. All filers must observe the following cardinal rule: Be sure the record to be stored has been released for storage.

Indexing

You learned how to index filing segments in applications for Chapters 3, 4, and 5, and you know that indexing is a mental process. On business letters, the name (filing segment) may appear in various places. As you know, the selection of the right or most important name by which to store the record means that the record can be found quickly when it is needed. If the wrong name is selected, filers will waste time trying to locate the record when it is requested.

How do you index incoming and outgoing documents?

Keep these rules in mind when indexing incoming documents:

- Use the name in the letterhead (usually) for storage purposes on incoming documents.
- Use the writer's name or the writer's business connection if a letterhead has no relationship with the contents of the letter. The letterhead name is disregarded for filing purposes if, for example, a letter is written on hotel stationery by a person who is out of town on a business trip.
- Use the name in the signature line on incoming documents on plain paper (paper without a letterhead—usually personal).
- Use the company name when both the company name and the name of the writer seem to be equally important.

Keep these rules in mind when indexing outgoing correspondence:

- Use the name in the letter address on the file copy of an outgoing letter.
- Use the company name when both the company name and the name of an individual are contained in the letter address of the file copy of an outgoing letter, unless the letter is personal or unless a name in the letter is the correct name to index.
- Use the writer's name on a copy of a personal letter.

How are special subjects used in an alphabetic storage arrangement?

If a special subject is used in an alphabetic arrangement (such as "Applications"), the subject is given precedence over both company and individual names appearing in the document. Often, the subject name is written on the document at the top right.

Sometimes two names seem equally important. One name is selected as the name by which the record is to be stored, and the other name is cross-referenced according to the rules learned in Chapters 3, 4, and 5. If you are unsure about the most important name, request clarification from the records supervisor or the department that created the document. Consult a RIM manual if one is in use in the office. See Chapter 14 for more on the RIM manual.

Coding

What are the advantages to coding records?

Filers are often responsible for coding records before filing them. The filing segment can be coded in any one of several ways. Figure 6.21 shows diagonals placed between the units, the key unit underlined, and the remaining units numbered. In some offices, a colored pencil is used for coding to make the code more obvious. In other offices, coding is done with a pencil to keep distracting marks on documents at a minimum. Coding saves time when refiling is necessary. An uncoded record removed from storage and returned at a later date must be indexed and coded before it is refiled.

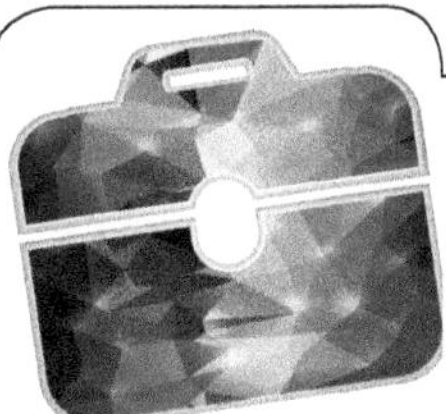

CAREER CORNER

Records Manager

The following job description is an example of a career opportunity in records management at a small architectural firm.

GENERAL INFORMATION

The manager's role is to supervise records-related tasks. The manager is expected to establish guidelines for and to document records processes and procedures in a records and information management manual to manage records throughout their life cycle.

RESPONSIBILITIES

- Conduct initial and periodic records inventories.
- Evaluate bids and select vendors for RIM supplies and equipment.
- Mentor, train, and develop employees in the RIM department and throughout the firm.
- Supervise periodic records destruction in compliance with the records retention schedule.
- Manage the in-house records center.

EXPERIENCE AND EDUCATION

- Bachelor's degree with five years' prior records management supervisory experience
- Strong leadership and organizational skills
- Extensive office suite software experience, especially in database software
- Knowledge of applicable state and federal regulations regarding records retention, tax documentation, and legal holds

Cross-Referencing

The same cross-reference rules that you learned in Chapters 3, 4, and 5 also apply for storing business letters. For example, assume that the letter shown in Figure 6.21 on page 141 comes to the filer for storage. The record is indexed and coded for Investment Strategies, Inc., by placing diagonals between the units, underlining the key unit, and numbering the other units. The letter is then coded for cross-referencing because some end users may request it by Trotter Poll Company. A line is drawn under Trotter Poll Company; diagonals are placed between the units; all units are numbered; and an X is written in the margin.

A separate cross-reference sheet, as shown in Figure 6.22, may be prepared for an alternative name, or a photocopy of the original record can be coded for cross-reference purposes. Note that the name at the top of the cross-reference sheet is coded for storage in exactly the same way as for any record—diagonals are placed between the units, the key unit is underlined, and succeeding units are numbered. The date of the record and a brief statement regarding the contents of the record should be recorded on the cross-reference sheet. The name or subject of the original record is recorded in the SEE section in as-written order. Entering the date the record is filed and your name completes the cross-reference sheet.

What is a permanent cross-reference?

At times, a permanent cross-reference is used instead of an individual folder to direct the filer to the correct storage place. A permanent cross-reference is a guide with a tab in the same position as the tabs on the individual

FIGURE 6.22 **Cross-Reference for Letter Shown in Figure 6.21**

CROSS-REFERENCE SHEET

Name or Subject

2 3
Trotter / Poll / Company

Date of Record

October 21, 20--

Regarding

Survey of customers regarding investment objectives

SEE

Name or Subject

Investment Strategies, Inc.

Date Filed 10/23/20-- By J. Phelps

folders and is placed in a location that is frequently assumed to be the location of that folder. The caption on the tab of the permanent cross-reference consists of the name by which the cross-reference is filed, the word *SEE*, and the name by which the alphabetic folder containing the original document may be found. In Figure 6.6 on page 124, a permanent cross-reference guide (BETSYS CRAFTS SEE ROSS INDUSTRIES) appears in proper alphabetic sequence in the file drawer.

A permanent cross-reference can be used, for instance, when a company changes its name. The company's folder is removed from the file, the name is changed on the folder, and the folder is refiled under the new name. A permanent cross-reference guide is prepared under the original name and is placed into the position of the original folder in the file. For example, assume that *Emory and Phillips* changes its name to *Riverside Distribution Co.* The EMORY AND

RECORDS MANAGEMENT IN ACTION

Social Services Agency Gains Control of Client Records with Hosted Service

Child Care Information Services (CCIS-North) in Philadelphia, Pennsylvania, provides child care information services to the public and, under contract from the state, administers child care subsidies for eligible families. The agency maintains information on local child care facilities and community resources to assist families in making informed child care choices. When Charles S. Carr assumed the directorship of CCIS-North, he quickly focused on increasing worker productivity, containing costs, and securing client information. He saw that records administration was an area in which automation could accomplish all three goals.

Manual filing practices were wasting labor, allowing creation of duplicate files, and making monitoring compliance of the State of Pennsylvania regulations impossible.

Sahid Khan, IT manager for CCIS-North selected FileTrail, a physical records management software and RFID-based file tracking technology, to solve the agency's manual filing problems, primarily because of its ease of use, ability to configure formal practices, and the availability of a hosted service with a low up-front cost.

Prior to using FileTrail, a great deal of time was spent finding files. When a file was needed, staff would walk to the file room. If the file wasn't there, a desk-to-desk search would begin, often ending with an e-mail blast to the entire office. When no file could be found, a new one was often created, which resulted in many duplicate files.

The FileTrail software helped CCIS-North to implement formal practices. Structured processes and tools guide staff through efficient handling processes step by step. Now, all staff have access to search and locate files through FileTrail without leaving their desks. Manual searches for files have been eliminated, and a great deal of time is saved.

Source: FileTrail.com, Case Study, accessed January 14, 2014. http://filetrail.com/uploads/documents/document_37.pdf.

PHILLIPS folder is removed from the file, the name on the folder is changed to RIVERSIDE DISTRIBUTION CO., and the folder is filed under the new name. A permanent cross-reference guide is made and filed in the E section of the file: EMORY AND PHILLIPS SEE RIVERSIDE DISTRIBUTION CO.

Sorting

sorting: arranging records in the sequence in which they are to be filed or stored

Sorting is arranging records in the sequence in which they are to be filed or stored. In most instances, a sorting step precedes the storing. Sorting should be done as soon as possible after coding and cross-referencing, especially if storage must be delayed. Sometimes coding and rough sorting are done in sequence. Rough sorting is arranging records in approximately the same order as the filing system in which they will be placed. After each record has been coded, it should be rough sorted into a pile of like pieces—all As, Bs, Cs are together; all Ds, Es, Fs are together; and so on. Records having filing segments that are numbers written as digits are rough sorted into 100s, 200s, and so on. Coordination of inspecting, indexing, coding, and sorting means handling each record only once. If a record is needed before it has been filed, it can be found with less delay if records have been rough sorted instead of being put into a stack on a desk or into a "to-be-filed" basket. Sorting can be done on a desk or table top, with the records placed in separate piles. Use of a desktop sorter that has holders or pockets for various sections of the alphabet makes sorting easier.

What is the difference between rough sorting and fine sorting?

After rough sorting the records according to alphabetic sections, the filer removes them section by section, alphabetizes them properly within each section, and replaces them in order in the sorter for temporary storage. This step is often called *fine sorting*. Fine sorting is arranging records in the exact order of the filing system in which they will be placed. Alphabetizing records in all sections prepares them for storage. Fine sorting records with numeric key units arranges them in numeric order prior to storing. Then the records are removed in sequence from all divisions of the sorter and taken to the files for storage.

Storing

storing: placing records into storage containers

Storing is placing records into storage containers. Storing records correctly is very important. A misfiled record is often a lost record; and a lost record means loss of time, money, and peace of mind while searching for the record.

What determines the time that records will be put into storage containers?

The workload during the day determines the time that filers will put records into storage containers. In some offices, storing is completed first in the morning, in the early afternoon, or it is the last task performed each day. In other offices, storing is done when records are ready to be filed, a stack of records to be filed has accumulated, or when a lull in other work occurs. In a centralized filing department, storage takes place routinely throughout the day every day—along with retrieving, and re-storing.

What steps should be taken before placing the record into its storage location?

Prior to storing records, the filer must remember to:

1. Remove paper clips from records to be stored.
2. Staple records together (if they belong together) in the upper right corner so that other records kept in the folder will not be inserted between them by mistake.
3. Mend torn records with tape.
4. Unfold folded records to conserve storage space unless the folded records fit the container better than when unfolded.

Before placing the record into its storage location, the filer should:

1. Glance quickly at the container label to locate the place to begin storage.
2. Scan the guides until the proper file section is located.
3. Pull the guides forward with one hand while searching for the correct folder.
4. Check for an individual or a special folder for the filing segment. If no special folders are in the file, locate the general folder.
5. Slightly raise the folder into which the record is to be placed. Avoid pulling the folder up by its tab, however, as continual pulling will separate the tab from its folder. Raising the folder ensures that the record will be inserted into the folder and not in front of or behind it.
6. Determine the correct placement of the document in the folder, because all records in the folder will bear the same coded name.
7. Place each record into the folder with its top to the left. When the folder is removed from storage and placed onto a desk to be used, the folder is opened like a book, with the tab edge to the right. All records in it are then in proper reading position.

8. Jog the folder to straighten any uneven records before replacing the folder into the storage container.

Special points to remember include:

- Avoid opening more than one drawer in a cabinet at a time. Unless file cabinets are attached to a wall or otherwise secured, a cabinet can fall forward when overbalanced by having two or three loaded drawers open.
- Place the most recently dated record in an individual folder at the front, and it will be on top when the folder is opened. The record bearing the oldest date is at the back of the folder.
- Place records that are removed from a folder and later refiled into their correct chronologic sequence, not on top of the contents of the folder.
- Arrange records within a general folder alphabetically by correspondents' names and then by date within each correspondent's records.
  The most recently dated record is, therefore, on top of each group (see Figure 6.11 on page 128).

Using a Tickler File

tickler file: a date-sequenced file by which matters pending are flagged for attention on the proper date

A **tickler file** is a date-sequenced file by which matters pending are flagged for attention on the proper date. This chronologic arrangement of information "tickles" the memory and serves as a reminder that specific action must be taken on a specific date. Other names sometimes used to describe such a file are *suspense file* and *pending file*. The basic arrangement of a tickler file is always the same: chronologic by current month and day. A manual arrangement usually takes the form of a series of 12 guides with the names of the months of the year printed on their tabs. One set of guides or folders with tabs printed with numbers 1 through 31 for the days of the month is also used. A computer tickler file is usually in the form of entries in a calendar or database, with a reminder list showing on the screen or printed in sort order by action date. Figure 6.23 shows a list of due dates for OUT files from a database. An example of a manual tickler file would be one for holding documents that require specific action to be taken before being placed into the alphabetic document file.

Many office workers use a tickler system to remind them of events that happen yearly, such as birthdays and anniversaries; membership expiration dates and dues payments; insurance premium payments; weekly, monthly, or annual meetings; subscription expiration dates; and the dates on which certificates of deposit or bonds are due. In records and information management, tickler files can be used to keep track of due dates for records that are borrowed or to keep track of records that do not have a release mark.

How might a tickler file be used in a records and information management system?

On the last day of each month, the person in charge of the tickler file checks through the date cards/folders to be certain that nothing has been inadvertently overlooked during the month. Then, all documents from behind the next month's guide are removed and redistributed behind the daily guides (numbered 1 through 31). At the end of October, for instance, the spaces behind all the daily guides would be checked; the October guide would be moved to the back of the file; and the November guide would be put into the front. All reminders filed behind November would then be redistributed behind the daily guides according to the dates on the reminders.

FIGURE 6.23 **Tickler Database OUT Log**

OUT Log Tickle File: Table

Request ID	Date Due	Requested By	Phone Ext	Department	Record Type	Correspondent Name	Record Date
1	10/6/2016	Thomas Logan	8966	Administration	Record	Miles Law Office	1/30/2015
2	10/9/2016	Margarita Shelby	9912	Advertising	Record	WAXI Radio	5/15/2016
3	10/10/2016	Mary Neismith	8999	Accounting	Folder	Martin Auto Parts	
4	10/12/2016	David Smelson	8875	Marketing	Record	Margaret Jackson	3/17/2013
5	10/12/2016	Juan Carlos	9986	Advertising	Record	ADVO Systems	7/18/2013
6	10/13/2016	Sue Bell	3264	Accounting	Record	Mid-Atlantic Boxes Inc.	5/16/2014
7	10/17/2016	Mary Jane Hilton	7792	Purchasing	Record	Jones Supply Co.	9/16/2016
8	10/19/2016	Jack Kline	8865	Marketing	Folder	Ikohoto Trade Center	
9	10/19/2016	Wanda Adams	8921	Training	Record	Misty Waters	2/17/2014
10	10/22/2016	John Frymire	8632	Purchasing	Record	J.P. Smith	1/10/2016

The tickler file must be the first item checked each day by the person in charge of it. Information on the notes found in the tickler file serves as a reminder to act or follow through on specific instructions.

Misfiled and Lost Records

A lost or misplaced record can delay or affect the work of employees. If storage is done haphazardly or without following consistent procedures, lost records will be numerous. Lack of attention to spelling, careless insertion of records into the storage equipment, and distractions often cause records to be misfiled and therefore "lost."

What techniques are used to locate lost or misfiled records?

Experienced filers use the following techniques in trying to find missing records:

- Look in the folders immediately in front of and behind the correct folder.
- Look between folders and under all folders in the drawer or shelf.
- Look completely through the correct folder, because alphabetic or other order of sequence may have been neglected due to carelessness or haste.
- Look in the general folder in addition to searching in the individual folder.
- Check for transposition of names (DAVID MILLER instead of MILLER DAVID) and alternate spellings (JON, JOHN).
- Look for the second, third, or succeeding units of a filing segment rather than for the key unit.
- Check for transposition of numbers (35 instead of 53).
- Look in the year preceding or following the one in question.
- Look in a related subject if the subject filing method is used.
- Look in the sorter or other places that have records en route to storage.
- Ask employees who might logically have the record to look for it in their desks or folders.

If every search fails to produce the missing record, some records managers try to reconstruct the record from memory, rekeying as much as is known. This information is placed into a folder labeled LOST, along with the name on the original folder. This new folder is stored in its correct place as a constant reminder to the filer to be on the alert for the missing record.

Electronic records can also be difficult to locate if they are not stored according to proper procedures. For example, an application for a job might be stored under the applicant's name in a general folder rather than in an Applications folder. Mistakes in keying a file name can also make a file difficult to find.

To locate electronic records, use the Search feature of your computer's operating system. You can search in one or more folders by entering all or part of a file name. Indicating a date of file creation and the author will further refine the search.

Efficient business records storage is the result of:

- Good planning to choose the right equipment, supplies, and system.
- Proper training of personnel who recognize the value of the release mark, know and consistently apply the rules for alphabetic indexing, code papers carefully, prepare cross-references skillfully, invariably sort papers before storing, and carefully store records in their proper location.
- Constant concerned supervision by records managers or others responsible for the storage and retrieval functions.

CHAPTER REVIEW AND APPLICATIONS

KEY POINTS

- The volume of recorded information is rapidly increasing. More electronic records are being created, but paper records still make up a significant portion of all records.
- The four most common types of filing equipment are vertical files, lateral files, shelf files, and mobile shelf files.
- Types of supplies used for physical document storage include guides, folders, labels, and OUT indicators.
- When selecting filing equipment and supplies, consider the type and volume of records to be stored, degree of protection required, efficiency and ease of use of equipment, space requirements, and cost.
- Alphabetic records management is appropriate for business document files with a low to moderate volume of records when records are requested by names of individuals, businesses, and organizations.
- Color can be used to visually separate sections of the file or to call attention to special folders.
- Filing procedures for storing correspondence records include inspecting, indexing, coding, cross-referencing, sorting, and storing.
- Tickler files can be manual or computer-based, and they are used as a reminder for tasks to be done daily.
- Systematic search strategies should be used for finding lost or misfiled records.

TERMS

alphabetic records management
caption
color accenting
color coding
direct access
follower block (compressor)
general folder
guide
individual folder
inspecting
label
OUT indicator
position
primary guide
release mark
sorting
special (auxiliary) guide
special folder
storage (storing)
storage method
suspension (hanging) folder
tab
tickler file

REVIEW AND DISCUSS

1. Compare and contrast the terms *storage, filing, storage method,* and *records management.* (Obj. 1)

2. List and briefly describe four kinds of commonly used storage equipment for physical records. (Obj. 2)

3. List and briefly describe five important supplies used in records storage. (Obj. 2)

4. Why is the straight-line arrangement of tabs on folders and guides easier to use than the staggered arrangement? (Obj. 2)

5. What five criteria should be considered when choosing storage equipment and supplies? (Obj. 3)

6. Discuss the advantages and disadvantages of the alphabetic storage method. (Obj. 4)

7. What types of information should be gathered before selecting and designing an alphabetic storage system? (Obj. 5)

8. Explain how color can be used in physical records storage. (Obj. 6)

9. List and briefly describe (in order) the six steps required to store a record properly. (Obj. 7)

10. What kinds of release marks might you find on records ready to be stored? (Obj. 7)

11. List at least five procedures to try to locate a "lost" or a "misfiled" record. (Obj. 7)

12. What is a tickler file, and how is one arranged? (Obj. 7)

APPLICATIONS

6-1 Code Business Documents (Obj. 7)

Correctly index and code the names and addresses for outgoing letters, shown below, to be filed in an alphabetic system. Place a diagonal between units in the filing segment. Underline the key unit, and number other units in the filing segment.

Dr. Joyce Phosgene, President
Callous Records Equipment, Inc.
Coney Towers #47
Dallas, TX 75202-1847

1-2-3 Tailor-made Publications
87 West Second Street
Sacramento, CA 95801-9985

Jaymire Communications Systems
1812 Roswell Avenue
Albuquerque, NM 87201-1254

Oney Jasmine
205 First Street, NE
Brenham, TX 77833-5415

J. C. Wilshire, Advertising Director
Johnson Office Supplies
100 Black Street
Yuma, AZ 88364-6943

6-2 Changing Storage Equipment (Obj. 2, 3, and 5)

You and one or two of your classmates have formed a records and information management consulting company. The Wilson Charter Co. has asked your company for a consultation about their storage equipment. You and your team visited the Wilson office and noted the following:

- Business documents are stored alphabetically in traditional four-drawer vertical file cabinets.
- Everyone in the office has access to the file cabinets.
- Ten to 20 stored records are retrieved daily, one paper at a time.

1. Along with your team members, analyze the Wilson Charter Co.'s current equipment, and determine whether anything should be changed. Would open-shelf files work better? Why do you think so? What factors would contribute to your decision? What other resources are available to help your team assemble the facts needed to propose a solution for Wilson Charter Co.?
2. Create a proposal for the Wilson Charter Co. giving your team's recommendations for changing the company's filing equipment or procedures.

6-3 Prepare Folder Labels (Obj. 7)

In this application, you will use Microsoft® Access to create folder labels for records to be filed in the J section of an alphabetic file.

1. Create a new Microsoft® Access database file named *6-4 Labels.*
2. Create a table named **Folder Labels**. Create these fields in the table: Record ID, Name as Written, Caption. Select **AutoNumber** for the field type for the Record ID field. Select **Text** or **Short Text** for the field type for all other fields. Set the Record ID Number field as the primary key.
3. Enter the names shown below into the Folder Labels table. In the Name as Written field, enter the complete name as written. In the Caption field, key the letter J followed by two spaces and the name in indexing order. Follow the alphabetic indexing rules studied earlier. In the Caption field, enter the data in all capitals with no punctuation.
4. Create a report for folder labels using the Labels wizard. Choose the **Folder Labels** table as the object the data comes from. Select **Avery Index Maker 3** for the label type (or a label of similar size, about 1 × 3 inches). Select **Arial 12** for the font. Include only the Caption field on the label and sort the labels. Name the report **Folder Labels Report.**
5. Print the labels (or print on plain paper if labels are not available).

Junk by Judy
Julie's Design Studio
Charles S. Jungworth
Christina A. Jensen
Jolly Roger Fish 'n Chips
Vernon L. Jensen, CPA
John's Jewelry Shop
Jill's Wishing Well
Jottings by Jolene
Jon Jungworth Law Firm

6-4 Research Storage Equipment and Supplies (Obj. 2)

1. Go to www.tab.com. Click "Filing Equipment & Supplies." Click "Color-Coding and Labels."
2. What is the name of the TAB Products' file labeling software?
3. List the filing methods for which labels are available from TAB.
4. Click "TAB Records Management and File Labeling Software." What is the name of this software?
5. Go to www.smead.com. Click "Products." Click "Product Categories." Click "Labeling/Software." Click "ColorBar© Labeling System." Labels created with this system are used on which type of folders and which type of storage container?

SIMULATION

Job 5 Correspondence Filing—Rules 1–5
Job 6 Correspondence Filing—Rules 6–10
Job 7 Correspondence Filing—Rules 1–10 and Tickler File Usage
Continue working with Auric Systems, Inc.
Complete Jobs 5, 6, and 7

ADDITIONAL RESOURCES

For data files, Microsoft® Access tutorials and more, go to www.cengagebrain.com.

CHAPTER 7

Storing, Retrieving, and Transferring Records

LEARNING OBJECTIVES

1. Explain the importance of developing and implementing a records retention program.
2. List the four values of records, describe each, and provide an example of each value.
3. Discuss the records inventory, including what it is, why it is done, and what it includes.
4. Describe a records retention schedule and explain its purpose.
5. Discuss manual and automated retrieval procedures.
6. List reasons for transferring records.
7. List capabilities of typical records center software.
8. Discuss types of records center control files.

Courtesy of Wendy Shade

ON THE JOB

A 33-year tenure at Iron Mountain Incorporated has provided Wendy Shade, Fellow of ARMA International (FAI), with the opportunity to experience the evolution of the records management industry and the myriad ways that the company has effectively responded to those changes. As the current program manager for the product management team, Wendy focuses on providing the tools and thoughtful leadership that will enable customers to meet the increasing demands that their organizations face with the explosion of information.

Ms. Shade likens ARMA's shift in focus to information governance to a paradigm shift from individual sports to team sports. In this model, the records management professional no longer bears the sole burden. In the future, organizations will become more and more aware that they will not succeed in this current era of explosive information without bringing to the table representation from legal, risk and compliance, privacy and security, IT, business partners, and records management when making decisions on the management of information. Now is a great time to be in this industry.

Ms. Shade advises students studying for a career in records management to be sure to learn about change management and to strengthen their analytical skills! The ability to be agile, strategic, and forward thinking is going to be critical to success. Although the fundamental tenants of the management of information will not change radically, the applications of those fundamentals will be stretched to the limit in the future. Too many professionals believe that their potential success is based on industry knowledge. Ms. Shade suggests that strong analytical skills, the ability to influence others, the ability to think strategically (see the big picture), and confidence in one's convictions are the bases of success.

RECORDS STORAGE

Phases of the records life cycle include creation, distribution, use, maintenance, and disposition. The last two phases—*maintenance* (i.e., storing, retrieving, and protecting records) and *disposition* (i.e., transferring, retaining, or destroying records)—are discussed in this chapter.

Why is a records retention program important?

records retention program: a program established and maintained to provide retention periods for records in an organization

records retention schedule (RRS): a comprehensive list of records series titles, indicating for each the length of time it is to be maintained

An effective records and information management (RIM) program adheres to best practices to ensure that records that continue to have value to the organization are stored and retained (kept). A **records retention program** consists of policies and procedures relating to *what* documents to keep, *where* and in what type of environment the documents are kept, and *how long* these documents are to be kept. Ideally, the time that a record should be retained is known when the record is created because the records series is listed on a **records retention schedule (RRS)**—a comprehensive list of records indicating the length of time that a records series is to be maintained.

Retention policies also allow destruction of records that no longer have value to the organization. Storing records no longer needed is costly because more floor space is used; more storage supplies and equipment are purchased (needed); and more labor is required.

The Value of Records

Records serve as the memory of an organization, and their purpose may be administrative, fiscal, legal, or historical. Classifying records by their value to an organization is useful for making retention decisions, as shown in Figure 7.1.

Once a record is stored, it may not be stored forever. One critical step in creating a records retention schedule is estimating the value of a record to an organization and determining how long the record is useful. Understanding the four categories of records values—nonessential, useful, important, and vital—is helpful when determining which records should be retained (and for how long) and which records should be destroyed. Before preparing a records retention schedule, an inventory of all records stored in an organization—in individual offices or departments, in central files areas, or in off-site storage locations—must be conducted.

Records Inventory

records inventory: a detailed listing that could include the types, locations, dates, volume, equipment, classification systems, and usage date of an organization's records

A **records inventory** is a detailed listing that could include the types, locations, dates, volumes, equipment, classification systems, and usage data of an organization's records. It usually involves a survey conducted by each department, with a member of each department assigned the task of inventorying its records and documenting important information about those records. Some organizations may also conduct an electronic records inventory or a vital records inventory, depending on the volume of records in those categories. Survey information from all departments is incorporated into an organization-wide records retention schedule. Some organizations use bar code and radio frequency identification (RFID) technology to speed

FIGURE 7.1 **Records Values**

RECORDS VALUES

Nonessential Records
- Not worth keeping
  - Bulk mail
  - Routine telephone messages
  - Bulletin board announcements
  - E-mail and fax message after action is taken

Useful Records
- Short-term storage—up to 3 years
- Helpful in conducting business operations
- May be replaced at small cost
- Active files of:
  - Business letters
  - Memos
  - Reports
  - Bank statements

Important Records
- Long-term storage—7 to 10 years
- Contain pertinent information
- Need to be recreated or replaced if lost
  - Financial data
  - Sales data
  - Credit histories
  - Statistical records

Vital Records
- Permanent storage
- Essential for the continuation or survival of organization
- Necessary for recreating organization's legal and financial status
  - Business ownership records
  - Customer profiles
  - Student transcripts

the records inventory process. A bar code (as shown in Figure 7.2) is a coding system consisting of vertical lines or bars set in a predetermined pattern that, when read by an optical reader, can be converted into machine-readable language. In records and information management, bar codes are used for tracking locations of documents, folders, or boxes of records. Bar code labels may be placed on individual documents or on folder and box labels. The use of bar code technology brings improvements in data accuracy over keyboard data entry. Bar code technology is used extensively for applications such as cataloging of books and files by libraries and archives.

radio frequency identification (RFID): a technology that incorporates the use of an electromagnetic or electrostatic radio frequency to identify an object, animal, or person

Radio frequency identification (RFID) is a technology that incorporates the use of an electromagnetic or electrostatic radio frequency to identify an object, animal, or person. RFID is increasingly used as an alternative to bar codes. The advantage of using RFID is that it does not require direct contact or line-of-sight scanning. An RFID system consists of three components: an antenna, a transceiver/reader, and a transponder (the tag or chip, as shown in Figure 7.3). Using microchips to transmit encoded information wirelessly through antennae, RFID tags are activated when placed in the transmission

FIGURE 7.2 **In Records and Information Management, Bar Codes Are Used for Tracking Locations of Documents, Folders, or Boxes of Records**

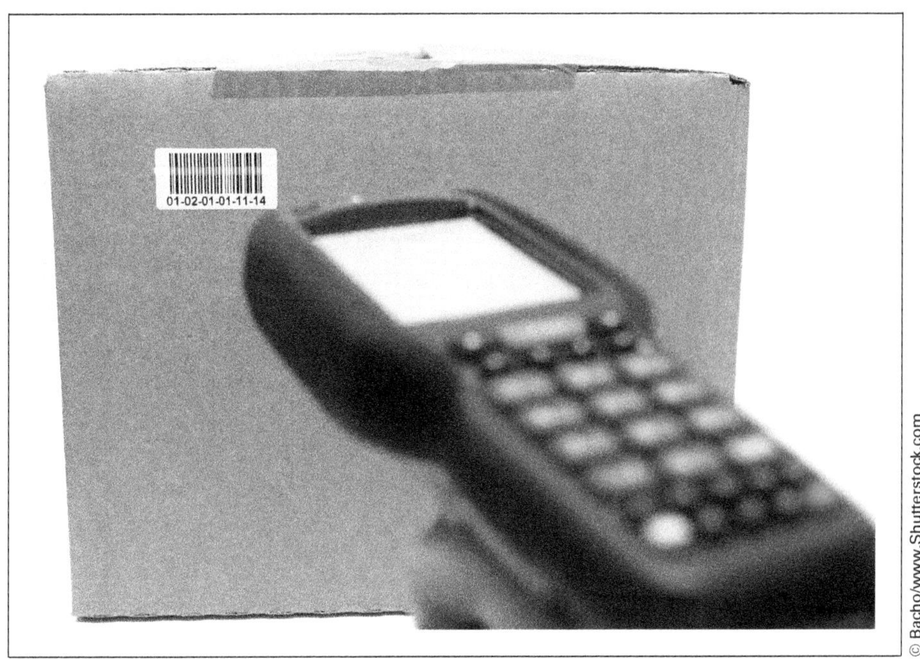

© Bacho/www.Shutterstock.com

FIGURE 7.3 **RFID Tags Convey Encoded Information Wirelessly and Do Not Require Line-of-Sight Scanning**

© hbas/www.Shutterstock.com

field of a reader. These tags convey encoded information that identifies documents, folders, or boxes. Because information is transmitted automatically beyond line-of-sight, boxes do not need to be unpacked to scan individual bar code labels on folders and/or documents. The result is reduced labor costs and improved accuracy.

When conducting a records inventory, a portable RFID reader can scan up to hundreds of folders in a matter of minutes. The RFID tags are read as the portable handheld reader passes within inches of the folders (see Figure 7.4).

FIGURE 7.4 **A Portable RFID Reader Can Scan up to Hundreds of Folders in a Matter of Minutes**

3M™ Digital Libaray Assistant, photo courtesy of 3M

Depending on the size of the file room, complete file room inventories can often be done in a matter of hours.

Information collected during a records inventory includes types of records (official, record copy, or nonrecord) and their media—paper, electronic, or image. An **official record** is a significant, vital, or important record of continuing value to be protected, managed, and retained according to established retention schedules. The official record is often, but not necessarily, an original. Another name for an official record is **record copy**, or the official copy of a record that is retained for legal, operational, or historical purposes. The record copy is sometimes the original. For example, a document printed from an electronic file is often considered the official record, rather than the electronic file, because the print copy can be read easily. It is durable, and it is easy to use.

The electronic file must still be retained for a week or two. However, the printed document may be saved for two or three years, depending on the content. The **office of record** is an office designated to maintain the *record* or *official copy* of a particular record in an organization.

A **nonrecord** is an item not usually included within the scope of official records such as a convenience file, a day file, reference materials such as dictionaries, and drafts. Nonrecords should not be retained past their usefulness. Typically, nonrecords are created, modified, and destroyed without formal RIM procedures and are not included in a records retention program.

Figure 7.5 shows a sample records inventory worksheet that would be prepared for each records series retained by each department in an organization. A **records series** is a group of related records that normally are used and filed as a unit and can be evaluated as a unit to determine the records retention period. For example, purchase orders for July are a records series. Bank statements retained for a year or longer are also a records series. Some organizations may identify physical and electronic records series for retention purposes that will be retained according to the records stored on electronic media. (See Chapter 11 for more information about electronic media storage.) The **retention period** is the time that records must be kept according to operational, legal, regulatory, and fiscal requirements.

A records inventory is also a valuable tool for helping managers decide which filing method (alphabetic, subject, numeric, or geographic) to use. Information obtained from a records survey and inventory usually includes the following:

- Name and dates of records series
- Records location by department or office, then building, floor, and room, if necessary
- Equipment in which records are stored—cabinets, shelves, or vaults
- Number of cabinets, shelves, or other storage containers

official record: a significant, vital, or important record of continuing value to be protected, managed, and retained according to established retention schedules

record copy: the official copy of a record that is retained for legal, operational, or historical purposes

office of record: an office designated to maintain the *record* or *official copy* of a particular record

nonrecord: an item that is not usually included within the scope of official records such as a day file, reference materials, and drafts

records series: a group of related records filed and used together as a unit and evaluated as a unit for retention purposes

retention period: the time that records must be kept according to operational, legal, regulatory, and fiscal requirements

FIGURE 7.5 **Records Inventory Worksheet**

RECORDS INVENTORY WORKSHEET

(Complete one form for each records series.)

Department	Person Taking Inventory	Date of Inventory
Legal	Ed Gregory	01/15/2014
Department Contact Person and Title	**Telephone / Ext.**	**E-mail**
Shunda Barkley, Records Coordinator	1153	Shunda.Barkley@rmg.com
Records Series Title	**Dates of Records Series**	**No. of Storage Containers**
Townsend v Hopkins LLC	From Jan 1, 2012 To Jan 1, 2013	6

Description of Records Series (Contents; Purpose; Form Numbers, etc. Continue on reverse side if needed.)
Closed case files, investigation reports, forensic reports, depositions, court records

Records Format/Media
☒ Physical ☒ Letter ☐ Legal
☐ Microform (Specify) ________
☐ Electronic (Specify) ________
☐ Optical (Specify) ________
☐ Publications/Books
☐ Maps, Drawings
☐ Printout
☐ Binders
☐ Video/Audio Tape
☐ Other ________

File Arrangement
☐ Alphabetic ☐ Geographic
☐ Numeric ☐ Chronologic
☐ Alphanumeric ☒ Calendar Year
☐ Subject ☐ Fiscal Year
☐ Other (Specify) ________

Volume of Records
Filing Inches ________
Cubic Feet 6
Annual Accumulation Rate
Filing Inches ________
Cubic Feet ________

Records Value
☐ Nonessential
☐ Useful
☒ Important
☐ Vital

Reference Rate
☐ Daily
☐ Weekly
☐ Monthly
☒ Less Than Once a Month
☐ Annually

Storage Equipment
☐ Cabinet ☒ Box
☐ Roll ☐ Shelf
☐ Flat ☐ Vault
☐ Other (Specify) ________

Current Retention Period
Active (in Office) 3 years
Inactive (in Storage) 5 years
Total 8 years

Required Retention Period—Schedule
Active Until case closed
Inactive 10 years
Total 20 years
Destruction Date Jan 1, 2043

Form 203 (Rev. 01/14)

- How often records are referenced—daily, weekly, monthly, or annually—and why
- Records media—physical/paper, micrographic, electronic, or optical
- Records size—letter, legal, tab/checks, other
- Records housing—folders, binders, disks, reels, and so on
- Records value—nonessential, important, useful, vital
- Retention requirements

E-mail Records

Electronic messages should accurately reflect the purpose of intended communications, decisions, or completion of actions. Metadata associated with electronic message records are particularly important because they provide information by which those records are located and managed. Metadata for electronic message records fit into three broad categories: content metadata, records management metadata, and records utilization metadata. Metadata are used to ensure the authenticity, reliability, integrity, and usability of an electronic message record.[1]

Is an e-mail message ever an official record?

E-mail messages, instant messages (IMs), or text messages sent and/or received within an organization may be considered records or nonrecords, depending on their content. E-mail is a primary form of business communication that reduces mailing costs. These messages are included on a records retention schedule in appropriate records series. E-mail, text, or instant messages that need to be stored for longer periods should be printed and filed with other physical/paper records. The print copy of the e-mail or text message becomes the official record, and the original message should be deleted from the e-mail system or device. Some e-mail programs will allow users to archive important messages for longer periods.

Records and information managers must work with IT departments to develop official policies regarding e-mail retention. Some organizations routinely purge/delete all e-mail after 30 days. Other organizations allow each user to determine what to retain as long as the user is following the organization's retention policy. E-mail users must be trained to delete unneeded documents.

Records Captured from Computers, Tablets, and Other Devices

Ensuring that documents and information created or submitted on a company's intranet, website, or social media are included in retention policies and schedules is an important concern for many records and information managers. Records and information employees will need to determine whether a record exists only on the website, the company intranet, on a tablet or smartphone, or on social media. If it is determined to be a record, it should be captured and transferred to the RIM system for storage and retrieval. Wikis or blogs maintained within departments or with customers, and clients may contain business-related information that needs to be transferred to the RIM system and included in the records retention schedule. If the same record exists in multiple locations, sometimes referred to as *shadow records*, where is the official copy? The organization needs a policy that addresses these records. Generally, when materials are posted to an organization's website, the materials qualify as records. If the materials have not previously been stored in the RIM system, the organization must establish a link between the website, device, or other media and the RIM system. Web records go through the same life-cycle stages as records in other formats. However, these stages are accelerated because websites may be updated frequently.

Many company websites have some forms-based applications. For example, job applicants may complete applications and submit cover letters through employer websites. The company may change or update these forms frequently. Additionally, employees in many organizations are able to go online to make changes to their 401K plans, view their medical claims,

---

[1] ARMA International, *Best Practices for Managing Electronic Messages* (Overland Park, KS: ARMA International, 2013), pp. 6–8.

Why should records of employee online benefit transactions be on a records retention schedule?

and obtain other information about their company benefits. Documents from these online transactions are included in appropriate records series, and they should be retained for the length of time required by relevant regulations, statutes, and company policies. Other organizations must keep track of sales transactions made on their websites. One important effect of the Sarbanes-Oxley Act on organizations is that they must retain more documents and for longer periods of time than previously. No one retention period can fit all web records, which need to be scheduled according to function or purpose.

What factors influence retention periods?

After the records inventory is completed, the records and information manager must first decide the value of each record and then how long records are to be retained. Appropriate retention periods are determined (based on the applicable regulations, statutes, records values, and company policies) and

RECORDS MANAGEMENT IN ACTION

Power, Pollution, and the Internet

Jeff Rothschild's machines at Facebook, in Santa Clara, California, had a problem he knew he had to solve immediately. They were about to melt.

The company had been packing a 40-by-60-foot rental space here with racks of computer servers (sort of bulked-up desktop computers, minus screens and keyboards, that contain chips to process data) that were needed to store and process information from members' accounts. The electricity pouring into the computers was overheating Ethernet sockets and other crucial components.

Thinking fast, Mr. Rothschild, the company's engineering chief, took some employees on an expedition to buy every fan they could find—"We cleaned out all of the Walgreens in the area," he said—to blast cool air at the equipment and prevent the website from going down.

That was in early 2006, when Facebook had a quaint 10 million or so users and the one main server site. Today, the information generated by nearly 1 billion people requires outsize versions of these facilities, called *data centers*, with rows and rows of servers spread over hundreds of thousands of square feet, and all with industrial cooling systems.

A yearlong examination by *The New York Times* revealed that this foundation of the information industry is sharply at odds with its image of sleek efficiency and environmental friendliness.

The inefficient use of power is largely driven by a symbiotic relationship between users who demand an instantaneous response to the click of a mouse and companies that put their business at risk if they fail to meet that expectation. The complexity of a basic transaction is a mystery to most users: sending a message with photographs to a neighbor could involve a trip through hundreds or thousands of miles of Internet conduits and multiple data centers before the e-mail arrives across the street.

The term *cloud* is often generally used to describe a data center's functions. More specifically, it refers to a service for leasing computing capacity. These facilities are primarily powered from the national grid, but generators and batteries are nearly always present to provide electricity if the grid goes dark. Using the cloud "just changes where the applications are running," said Hank Seader, managing principal for research and education at the Uptime Institute. "It all goes to a data center somewhere."

Source: James Glanz, "Power, Pollution, and the Internet," *The New York Times*, 22 September 2012, retrieved from http://www.nytimes.com/2012/09/23/technology/data-centers-waste-vast-amounts-of-energy-belying-industry-image.html?_r=0.

included in a records retention schedule (RRS) (see Figure 7.6). The schedule may include retention in active office areas and inactive storage areas, as well as when and if such series may be destroyed or formally transferred to another facility such as an archives for historical purposes. Records destruction decisions are based on the records retention schedule. Employees should not

FIGURE 7.6 **Records Retention Schedule**

RECORDS RETENTION SCHEDULE			
RECORDS SERIES	YEARS ACTIVE	YEARS INACTIVE	TOTAL YEARS
Accounting and Fiscal	3	3	6
Accounts payable invoices	3	3	6
Accounts payable ledger	3	3	6
Accounts receivable ledger	3	3	6
Bank deposit records	3	3	6
Bank reconciliation and statements	3	3	6
Annual audit reports	3	P	P
Administration—Executive			
Letters, e-mail messages, executive	1	1	2
Policy statements, directives	3	P	P
Advertising			
Contracts, advertising	1	2	3 years after term
Drawings and artwork	10	P	P
Samples, displays, labels	5	P	P
Human Resources			
Applications, changes, terminations	1	0	1
Attendance/vacation records	3	4	7
Medical folder, employee	While employed	0	30 years after term
Training manuals	3	P	P
Insurance			
Claims, group life/hospital	1	3	4
Claims, workers' compensation	1	9	10
Expired policies: fire, hospital, liability, life, workers' compensation	1	2	3 years after expiration
Operations			
Inventories	1	0	1
Office equipment records	3	3	6
Requisitions for supplies	1	0	1
Records Management			
Records destruction documentation	3	P	P
Records inventory	1	0	1
Records management policies	1	P	P
P = Permanent *Term = Termination*			
Form 220 (Rev. 01/14)			

decide, on their own, to destroy records. RIM best practices include destroying records based on an official and approved records retention schedule and in the normal course of business. Consequently, records are destroyed regularly as certain records reach the end of their usefulness. Chapter 14 contains more information about the role that records retention plays in a comprehensive RIM program.

Creating the records retention schedule is a cooperative effort among several departments in an organization: legal, tax, information management, and records management as well as other departments that own the records. The length of time—the retention period—may be determined by law for statutory, regulatory, or tax purposes. For other records, such as general business documents, the length of time may be limited to the time of use of a record. The estimate of the frequency of use for current and anticipated business is also important. This time period usually determines how long records should be retained in offices or records centers before they are transferred to an archives or otherwise disposed of. A **records center** is a low-cost centralized area for housing and servicing inactive records whose reference rate does not warrant their retention in a prime office area.

records center: a low-cost centralized area for housing and servicing inactive records whose reference rates do not warrant their retention in a prime office space

Each department has unique needs that the retention schedule must meet. Without cooperative input from all departments in an organization, the records retention schedule will not serve its purpose. In addition, the records and information manager must consider each of the following interrelated aspects when developing a records retention schedule:

1. How long will the records be used—be active?
2. In what form should the records be kept? How accessible should the records be?
3. When should the records be determined inactive? Which records should be transferred off-site and when? How will such records be accessed? Will transferred records maintain their integrity and security?
4. What are the applicable federal, state, and local laws?
5. What are the comparative costs for keeping the records or not keeping the records?
6. When and how will the records be disposed of?

Records retention schedules are based on the value of the *information* contained in the records and *not* on the storage media. Records stored on all media are included in a RRS. However, as discussed in Chapter 12, the life span of the media is important for long-term retention. In some organizations, a separate retention schedule is maintained for electronic/digital records. Other organizations, such as a university for example, may have separate retention schedules for each function, each department, or each degree program.

Could an organization have more than one RRS?

All records users need to comply with the records retention schedule adopted by their organization. Many organizations emphasize the importance of records by conducting Records Week activities centered on cleaning out old records, transferring records, and destroying records. By closely following transfer and destruction timetables, an organization can reduce clutter and improve retrieval time because fewer records will be in storage. Additional space will be available for current records needed for day-to-day decision making. The records retrieval process is discussed next.

RECORDS RETRIEVAL

retrieval: the process of locating and removing a record or file from storage or accessing information from stored data on a computer system

Retrieval is the process of locating and removing a record or file from storage. It is also the action of recovering information on a given subject from stored records. In this section, you learn how to retrieve records by following standard procedures and recommended best practices. Although the procedures discussed here are primarily for paper-based systems, the same procedures apply for retrieving and accessing electronic and image records. Steps for retrieving a record are shown in Figure 7.7.

In what three ways may records be retrieved?

A record or information from it may be retrieved in three ways:

1. **Manually.** A person goes to a storage container and removes by hand a record that a user has requested or makes a note of the information someone has requested from it.
2. **Mechanically.** A person uses some mechanical means such as pressing the correct buttons to rotate movable shelves to the correct location of a record, removing the record manually, or recording information requested from the record.
3. **Electronically.** A person uses some means, such as a computer, to locate a record. The requester is shown the requested information or informed on a screen in a database or in an e-mail file as to where it can be found. The physical record may not need to be removed from storage.

How are records requested?

Requests for stored records may be made orally (in person, over the telephone, or by messenger) or in writing (by fax, e-mail, memo, letter, special physical form, or via an online records request form). A typical request, for example, might be, "Please find the most recent letter from ABC Computer Corp. that forecasts the number of silicon chips the company will produce next quarter." Or, "Please pull the DVD of the chairman's 2013 annual report to stockholders." Or perhaps, "Please retrieve the microfiche of the current price list for auto parts." All these records have previously been stored manually according to an established method of storage. The

FIGURE 7.7 **Records Retrieval Procedure**

STEPS FOR RETRIEVING A RECORD
1. Receive request for stored record or records series—requester or records center employee prepares requisition form.
2. Check index for location of stored record(s).
3. Search for record or records series.
4. Retrieve (locate) record or records series.
5. Remove record(s) from storage.
6. Charge out record(s) to requester: Insert OUT indicator in place of record(s) removed from storage; complete the charge-out log.
7. Send record(s) to requester.
8. Follow up borrowed record(s).
9. Receive record(s) for re-storage.
10. Store record(s) again. Remove OUT indicator. Update charge-out log.

letter, DVD, electronic/digital record, or microfiche must be retrieved from storage and given to the requester quickly. Every minute of delay in finding a record is costly—in user or requester waiting time and in filer searching time—and could possibly lead to loss of money for the company because of a lost sale.

Why are cross-references important?

If filers and requesters use the same filing segment for storing and requesting a record, the system works well. If, for instance, records relating to a company named Mansfield Heat & Air were stored alphabetically under *Mansfield* but requested under *Air Conditioner Company*, the filer would find retrieval extremely difficult by searching in the A section instead of the M storage section. Consequently, good cross-referencing is necessary for efficient retrieval.

Retrieval and Re-Storage Cycle

The same steps followed for retrieving are followed for handling all physical records. Only the specific operating procedures differ. The crucial step—the point at which a problem is most likely to arise—is the first step, with the words used to request a record or information. Ideally, the person who stores a record is also the one who searches for and removes it from storage when it is requested. Realistically, however, a record may be stored by one person and retrieved by someone else when that record or information is requested.

Effective records control enables the filer to retrieve requested records on the first try and to answer correctly these questions:

1. Who took the records?
2. What records are out of storage?
3. When were the records taken?
4. Where will the records be re-filed when they are brought back to storage?
5. How long will the records be out of storage?

Requisition, Charge-Out, and Follow-Up Procedures

Effective records control includes following standard procedures for requesting records, charging them out, and ensuring that they are returned. These procedures, referred to as *requisition, charge-out,* and *follow-up,* may be completed manually or by using an automated system. By following standard procedures consistently, the number of lost or misfiled records can be reduced or eliminated.

Requisition Procedures

Preparing a requisition is the first step in the retrieval process. A request is an in-person, mail, telephone, fax, or e-mail inquiry for information about or from records stored in a records center or an archives. A **requisition** is a written request for a record or information from a record.

requisition: a written request for a record or information from a record

Even if the borrower orally requests the information or record, that request is put into writing and referred to as a *requisition*. The form may be prepared by the requester or completed by the filer from information given orally or in writing by the requester. An organization networked through the

Internet or an intranet may post a variety of forms that users may complete and transmit electronically, including records requisition forms. Two types of requisition forms are described next.

Requisition Form

A frequently used requisition form is a 5-inch-by-3-inch or 6-inch-by-4-inch preprinted card or slip of paper with blanks to be filled in. Figure 7.8 shows an example of a requisition form. A requester or filer may complete a similar computer-generated form in an automated system. Some RIM software is capable of generating a pick list for retrieving a number of requested records. A **pick list** is a list containing specific records needed for a given program or project. A filer can use a pick list to retrieve all records on the list. The records are then sent as a group to the requester. The same list can be used to return the records to the proper files/locations.

pick list: a list containing specific records needed for a given program or project

Why is preparing a requisition form necessary?

How does using OUT indicators help filers?

When a requisition form is completed, the filer will have answers to the five records retrieval questions previously discussed—Who? What? When? Where? How long? This form may be prepared in duplicate: The original stays in the folder from which the document was retrieved to serve as an OUT indicator. An OUT indicator is a form or document that describes records removed from the files and helps filers quickly find where records have been removed. The copy (usually placed into a tickler file, as discussed in Chapter 6) serves as a reminder to ensure that the record is returned on time.

A copy of a computer-generated requisition form may be printed to serve as an OUT indicator in a paper file. The filer may also be able to insert an electronic flag into the records database to indicate that a record is out of the records center. The electronic requisition form is then sent to an electronic tickler file.

FIGURE 7.8 **Requisition Form**

RECORDS REQUEST	
Name on Record	**Date on Record**
Date Borrowed	**Date Due (Return by this date.)**
Requester Name	**Extension**
Department	**E-mail**
Place one copy into folder. Place one copy into tickler control file.	
Form 209 (Rev. 01/14)	

Usually prepared in duplicate—original stays in folder; copy serves as a reminder.

On-Call (Wanted) Form

on-call form: a written request for a record that is out of the file

wanted form: a written request for a record that is out of the file

Occasionally, a user will request a record that is charged out to another user. A requisition form replacing the record in the file or in the online database identifies who has the record and when it will be returned. The filer should notify the second requester that the record is on loan and when it is scheduled for return to storage. If the second request is urgent, the filer will notify the original borrower that someone else wants the record and ask that it be returned to storage. Notification may be made orally, in writing on an on-call form or a wanted form, or by fax or e-mail. An **on-call form**, or **wanted form**, is a written request for a record that is out of the file (Figure 7.9). This form is similar to an OUT form. A computer-generated form may also be completed and transmitted by fax or e-mail to the records center.

Two copies of an on-call form are made—one copy goes to the borrower; the other copy is attached to the original OUT indicator in storage. When the borrowed record is returned to storage, it is charged out to the second borrower by the standard method of charge-out or by writing on the on-call form the date on which the record was delivered to the second borrower. (Note the Delivered Date column on the form in Figure 7.9.)

In some optical disk and microfilm storage systems, requested information is retrieved and sent to the requester electronically. An optical disk record is retrieved on a computer terminal and faxed or e-mailed to the requester. Microfilm is scanned into a computer terminal and faxed or e-mailed to the requester. In both cases, the official record is not removed from its file. No follow-up procedures are needed because the official record is still in storage.

FIGURE 7.9 **On-Call/Wanted Form**

ON CALL

WANTED BY (Requester Name)		RECORDS WANTED		DELIVERED
DATE	NAME	DATE	DESCRIPTION	DATE
6/15	James Madison	5/30	Hamilton Construction File	7/31

Form 205 (Rev. 01/14)

Prepared as a duplicate—one copy to borrower; one copy attached to original OUT indicator in storage.

Requesters may be instructed to destroy the borrowed record when they have completed their work with it. Note also that physical records can be scanned and transmitted electronically by e-mail, computer fax, or a conventional fax machine. The official record is returned to the file, and the user may destroy the fax or e-mail copy of the official record after use.

Confidential Records Requests

All stored records are considered valuable, or they would not be stored. Some are so valuable that they are stamped *Confidential, Classified, Secret, Vital*, or *Personal.* Do not release these types of records from storage without proper authorization following established procedures and best practices. In some offices, a written request bearing the signature of a designated officer of the organization is required for release of such records. In an electronic/digital system, access to confidential records is limited to those users who know the password. If a copy of a confidential record is sent electronically, it might be encrypted (the words are scrambled into code using a software program) to prevent unauthorized access. When the requester receives the encrypted file, he or she must unscramble/decrypt the file to read it. Some records may be so valuable or confidential that they are not to be removed from storage under any circumstances. These records must be inspected only at the storage container or in a secure room. The signature of someone in authority is required before the inspection is allowed. A requisition form is usually not needed; however, a record of the persons inspecting the records may be kept.

Manual Charge-Out Procedures

charge-out: a control procedure to establish the current location of a record when it is not in the records center or central file, which can be a manual or automated system

Why is keeping track of who has borrowed records necessary?

Charge-out is a control procedure to establish the current location of a record when it is not in the records center or central file, which can be a manual or automated system. A record is charged out to the borrower who is held responsible for returning it to storage by an agreed-upon date. A standard procedure for charging out and following up records should be observed each time a record is borrowed, regardless of who removes material from storage. Taking less than one minute to note the name of a person borrowing a record will save hours spent searching for a lost or misplaced record. Borrowers seem to be more conscientious about returning records to storage when they know that records have been charged out in their names. Typically, supplies needed to charge-out records consist of the following:

1. OUT indicators to show that records have been removed from storage
2. Carrier folders to transport borrowed records while the original folder remains in the file
3. Charge-out log

OUT Indicators

When a requested record is located, it is removed from storage, and an OUT form is inserted in place of the record. An OUT form shows where to re-file the record when it is returned. OUT indicators are explained in more detail in Chapter 6. If several records are removed from storage, they may be placed into a folder, referred to as a *carrier folder*, to ensure that the records stay together during transport to the user.

OUT Indicator Disposal

When a borrowed record is returned to storage, the OUT form inserted while the record was gone must be removed immediately. Any charge-out information written onto the OUT form is crossed out, and the form is stored for reuse. In some offices, OUT forms are kept for tallying purposes—to see how many records are being requested, to determine the workload of employees, and to see which records are being used frequently and which are not. Totals may be kept daily, weekly, monthly, or yearly as determined by the standard procedure in effect. Requisition forms removed from files may be destroyed. Any forms filed in electronic/digital tickler files may also be deleted.

Automated Charge-Out Procedures

In automated systems, bar codes and RFID tags can be used to charge out records. A bar code printed on a label affixed to a record, folder, or records center storage box is similar to an electronic product code (EPC) printed on a can of food in a supermarket or on a price tag on a pair of jeans in a department store. As discussed briefly in Chapter 6, records may be indexed and bar coded to identify their places in the files and other information about the records. When a requester presents his or her bar code identifier—often printed on an employee name tag—and the requested file is located, the bar code on the record is scanned. An electronic form is created when the bar code on the record is scanned, indicating whether the record is checked out, to whom, and for how long. Copies of the form may be printed or stored electronically. A bar code representing the electronic form may be printed and affixed to an OUT indicator and placed into the file where the requested record should be re-filed. When the record is returned, the bar code is scanned again; the OUT indicator is located; the record is returned to the file; and the requester is "cleared" of any borrowed records.

How do bar codes or RFID tags improve records charge-out?

Folders and records may be rapidly checked out using RFID tags by simply passing them over the top of the reader. Many folders can be read at once, and a list of them displayed on a screen. A similar process can be used to scan folders into a box for archiving.

Follow-Up Procedures

follow-up: a system for ensuring the timely and proper return of materials charged out from a file

What factors affect the length of time that records may be borrowed?

The filer responsible for retrieving and charging out records from storage is also responsible for checking in the records on their return. **Follow-up** is a system for ensuring the timely and proper return of materials charged out from a file. The length of time that records may be borrowed from storage depends on (1) the type of business, (2) the number of requests received for the records, (3) the use of a copying machine, and (4) the value of the records.

Experience shows that the longer records remain out of the files, the more difficult their return becomes. Many organizations stipulate a period of a week to 10 days, with two weeks being the absolute maximum amount of time records may be borrowed. Other organizations allow less time because records can be copied easily and quickly, and the original may be returned to storage within a few hours. Extra copies should be destroyed when they are no longer needed. Following up on a borrowed record may mean calling a borrower, sending an e-mail, or sending a written request as a reminder that borrowed records must be returned to storage. If no other requests for the same records have been received, the date that the records are to be returned may be extended.

Follow-Up for Confidential Records

The rule concerning confidential records is generally that the records (if they may be borrowed) must be returned to storage each night. A special reminder often is used to ensure that these records are returned. This reminder may be a note prominently displayed, a special flag, or some other type of signal. The same charge-out procedures used for other records are also used for confidential records. However, an additional reminder to obtain the record before the end of the day also is used. Because the memory jogger must remind the filer that confidential records are out of storage and must be returned, it must be something unusual.

Charge-Out Log

charge-out log: a written or electronic form filed by dates that records are due back in the inactive records center

Usually, an organization will have a charge-out log on which to record information for all records as they are removed from storage. A **charge-out log** is a written or electronic form used for recording the following information:

1. What record was taken (correspondent name or subject title on the record and date on the record)
2. When the record was taken (date borrowed)
3. Who took the record (name of person, extension number, e-mail address)
4. Date due for returning the record
5. Date returned
6. Date overdue notice was sent
7. Extended date due

The charge-out log should be kept current and used in the follow-up procedure. Refer to Figure 7.10 for an example of a portion of a charge-out log.

RECORDS TRANSFER

records transfer: the act of changing the physical custody of records with or without change of legal title or moving them from one storage area to another

As indicated on the sample records retention schedule shown in Figure 7.6 on page 162, records may be stored in an active records area for a period of time before being moved to another storage area when they are no longer accessed regularly. **Records transfer** is the act of changing the physical custody of records, with or without change of legal title. In other words, records are moved from one storage area to another, but the same company usually still owns them.

Why are records transferred?

Records are transferred when they are no longer used frequently. As records age, they are less frequently accessed and become inactive. Consequently, dates on the records are also considered when deciding to transfer records. In most cases, the active files contain the current year's records plus those of the immediate past year.

records disposition: the final destination of records after they have reached the end of their retention period

The final phase of the records life cycle is disposition. **Records disposition** is the final destination of records after they have reached the end of their retention period in active and/or inactive storage. Records may be transferred to an archives for retention, or they may be destroyed. Inactive storage may be housed on-site or off-site. On-site storage is storage of inactive (usually) records on the premises of an organization. Off-site storage is a potentially secure location, remote from the primary location, at which inactive or vital records are stored.

FIGURE 7.10 **Charge-Out Log**

CHARGE-OUT LOG

Name on Record	Date on Record	Name of Person Borrowing Record	Ext. or E-mail	Date Borrowed	Date Due	Date Returned	Date Overdue Notice Sent	Extended Date Due
Ardmore Car Sales & Service	9/23	J. Wood-Covington	2046	10/01	10/07		10/08	10/14
123 Buckle My Shoe Day Care	2/14	D. Mattingly	dmattingly@xyz.net	10/15	10/22	10/20		
The Flooring Store	4/02	M. Nelson	mnelson@xyz.net	10/16	10/23	10/23		
Greene Café	6/10	K. Bartoli	2058	10/20	10/27		10/28	11/02

Form 211 (Rev. 01/14)

archives: records that are preserved because of their historical or continuing value; also the building or area where archival materials are stored

Archives are the records created or received and accumulated by a person or an organization in the conduct of affairs and preserved because of their historical or continuing value.

Archives also may refer to the building or part of a building where archival materials are located. An archives is used for permanent storage. An archivist is a person professionally educated, trained, experienced, and engaged in the administration of archival materials, including the following activities: appraisal and disposition, acquisition, preservation, arrangement and description, reference service, and outreach to historical societies and individuals or groups interested in preserving documents and other important or historical records.

The US government, most US states, colleges and universities, and corporations store important historical records in an archives. These records may include physical documents, photographs of important events, and other records media. The US National Archives and Records Administration (NARA) maintains public vaults that display hundreds of records—originals or facsimiles of documents, photographs, maps, drawings, and film or audio clips that are important historical records for the nation. Visitors may view documents ranging from important treaties and legislation to letters to and from a former president and citations for military bravery. Universities in which faculty and staff researchers have made important discoveries will have copyright and patent information to protect for long periods of time. These documents and related information are stored in the universities' archives.

In the disposition phase of the records life cycle, decisions are made to (1) destroy a record, (2) retain a record permanently, or (3) transfer a record to inactive storage. Records transfer is made according to an established and approved retention schedule, as described earlier. If records are transferred, the main basis for making that decision is often the active or inactive use of the record.

What is the difference between inactive and archive records?

When should records be transferred?

active records: frequently used records needed to perform current operations

inactive records: records that do not have to be readily available but which must be kept for legal, fiscal, or historical purposes

archive records: records that have continuing or historical value and are preserved permanently by an organization

Records analysts define three groups of records according to the degree of records activity: **active records, inactive records**, and **archive records**. Figure 7.11 describes the three groups.

Sometimes records transfer decisions are made on the basis of dates on the records. The following reasons also greatly influence when and why transfer takes place:

1. No more active records storage space is available.
2. Costs of more storage equipment and extra office space are rising, and less costly areas of nearby storage or off-site storage become attractive alternatives.
3. Stored records are no longer being requested and therefore are ready for transfer.
4. Workloads are lighter, and time is available for records transfer activity.
5. A retention event has occurred. Case or project records have reached a closing or ending time (the contract has expired; the legal case is settled or closed).
6. Established organizational policy requires every department to transfer records at a stated time.

FIGURE 7.11 **Records Activity**

RECORDS ACTIVITY		
ACTIVE RECORDS	**INACTIVE RECORDS**	**ARCHIVE RECORDS**

• Needed to perform current operations
• Used frequently
• Located near user
• Accessed manually or online
• Accessed three or more times a month
• Stored in very accessible equipment in active storage area or online
	• Do not have to be readily available
	• Kept for legal, fiscal, or historical purpose
	• Accessed less than 15 times a year
	• Stored in less expensive storage area
		• Kept for their continuing or historical value
		• Preserved permanently
		• Used to:
		  • Maintain public relations
		  • Prepare commemorative histories
		  • Preserve corporate history
		  • Provide financial, legal, personnel, product, or research information
		  • Provide policy direction
		• Stored in less-expensive storage area, often off-site

Transferring records that are no longer used regularly has three advantages:

1. Records transfer helps to reduce equipment costs because inactive records may be stored in less-expensive cardboard containers.
2. Cabinets or shelves formerly used by the transferred files provide additional space for new active files.
3. The space in drawers, cabinets, shelves, or computer storage is increased because files are no longer crowded, which improves efficiency of storage and retrieval of active files.

Once the decision to transfer is made, the records and information manager must find answers to four important questions:

1. What records are to be moved?
2. How are the records to be prepared for transfer?
3. When are the records to be transferred?
4. Where are the transferred records to be stored?

Answers to the first three questions depend on the transfer method selected and the organization's records retention schedule. The answer to the *where* question depends on the method selected and on the availability of in-house (on-site) or off-site records storage areas. After answering those questions, the records and information manager then follows perpetual or periodic transfer procedures to move the selected records.

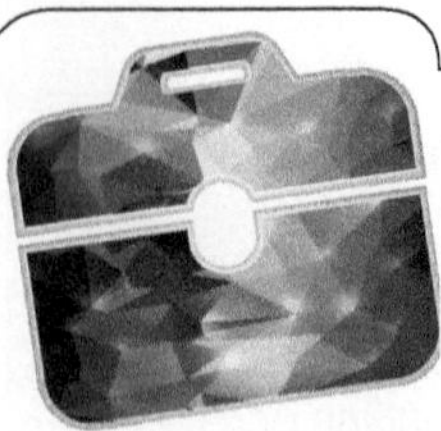

CAREER CORNER

Records Management Specialist

The following job description is an example of a career opportunity in an investment company.

GENERAL INFORMATION

The records management specialist will assist in the continuing development and implementation of a company-wide records management program.

RESPONSIBILITIES

- Perform analytical and interpretive tasks related to records issues.
- Assist in records inventories, evaluate and recommend records management software, write procedures, and train records users.
- Monitor and report departmental compliance to records retention policies.

EXPERIENCE AND EDUCATION

- Bachelor's degree preferred; a minimum of two years' college education
- Strong knowledge of records management systems and records retention
- Experience with records management systems that generate electronic records

Transfer Methods

Two of the most commonly used methods of transferring records are the perpetual transfer method and the periodic transfer method. Each method is discussed in this section, along with the procedure required to ensure efficient records transfer.

Perpetual Transfer Method

perpetual transfer method: a method of transferring records continuously from active to inactive storage areas whenever they are no longer needed for reference

Under the **perpetual transfer method**, records are continually transferred from active to inactive storage areas whenever the records are no longer needed for reference. Examples of records that can be transferred by the perpetual method include student records after graduation; closed legal cases; research projects when results are finalized; medical records of cases no longer needing attention; prison and law-enforcement case records; and completed construction or architectural jobs.

Electronic records and nonrecords should be perpetually transferred from storage on a hard drive to storage on microfilm or optical disks (see Chapter 12 for more on microfilm and optical storage media). E-mail messages should be routinely deleted if they are not official records. The perpetual transfer method is not recommended for business documents or records that are referred to often and must be available quickly.

Periodic Transfer Method

periodic transfer method: a method of transferring active records at the end of a stated period of time—usually 1 year—to inactive storage

The **periodic transfer method** is a method of transferring active records at the end of a stated period of time—usually one year—to inactive storage. Records are moved from current files into inactive storage sites on a scheduled basis. Guides remain in the active storage containers. However, new folders are prepared for records that are then allowed to accumulate in active storage until the next transfer period. All folders in the active records system are transferred to inactive storage at the end of the specified period. No guides are used in the inactive files. Inactive records file drawers or shelves are labeled by year, such as January 1–December 31, 2012, and may include alphabetic ranges. If records are systematically transferred annually, new folders are prepared for the active records system at the beginning of each year. Electronic records dated within the specified time frame are also transferred to inactive storage. (See Chapter 12 for more on electronic storage media.)

one-period transfer method: a method of transferring records from active storage at the end of one period of time, usually once or twice a year, to inactive storage

A commonly used periodic method of transferring records at the end of one period, usually once or twice a year, is called the **one-period transfer method.** Records are transferred at the end of one period (6 months or 1 year). For example, a records manager may decide on October 1 to transfer records dated January 1 through June 30, 2014. Consequently, filers will check all active folders for records dated between January 1 and June 30, 2014, and will transfer only those records to inactive storage. Any records in the active folders or active electronic files dated after June 30, 2014, remain in the active records system, and new records will continue to accumulate in the active records system. New folders will be prepared for inactive storage and will be labeled the same as the active folders or the active electronic files. Because of lowered costs of electronic media, individual electronic records might not be removed from a CD, DVD, or other optical or image media in order to reduce labor costs. New media will be used in the active records system for the next six months or a year. Active records accumulated from July 1 through December 31, 2014, will be transferred to the previously prepared folders in the inactive storage system at a date determined by the records manager. Active electronic records media accumulated during the same time frame will also be transferred to the inactive system at that time.

The main advantage of the one-period transfer method is the ease of operation. The main disadvantage is that some frequently requested records will be in inactive storage, and users must make frequent trips to the inactive storage area. Records for some correspondents will occasionally need to be retrieved from both active and inactive storage if the requested records cover several time periods.

Transfer Procedures

After the transfer method is determined, transfer procedures are communicated to every department. Before the transfer begins, the records and information manager must ensure that adequate storage equipment is available and at the correct location to receive transferred records.

Records are transferred either to inactive or archive (permanent) storage. Inactive storage indicates that the record may be infrequently referenced. At the end of the retention period, inactive records are destroyed. Records stored in an archives must be kept permanently; however, the records may still be referenced. Because some records may have historical value, a special display area may be created for those records. Often, records are transferred to a records center. Transfer procedures for inactive and archival records are the same.

What is the purpose of a transmittal form?

Preparing records for transfer involves completing the necessary transfer forms and boxing the records for inactive or archival storage. Figure 7.12 shows an example records transmittal form. This form also serves as a records center receipt. Note that information on the form should be keyed or clearly handwritten because it will be attached to the outside of a storage box and used to locate inactive records that may be requested at a later date. Also note that information on the form is about the contents of a box, such as a description of the records series, the time span of the records, the department name, and the retention information.

Although some organizations use a multicopy records transfer form at the time that records are transferred, other organizations use a transmittal

FIGURE 7.12 **Records Transmittal and Receipt**

	Records Transmittal and Receipt	Complete and send original and one copy of this form to the records centre with each box of records transferred to the center.					Page 1	of 1 Pages
Transfer Authorization	Transferring Department: Legal	Date of Transfer: 1/20/20__						
Contact	Signature of person releasing records (Name and telephone No.): Karen Garcia Records Manager							
Records Center Receipt	Records Received by (Signature and title): Alfonso Torino	Date Received: 1/20/20__						
Box Number				Shaded Areas for Records Management Use Only				
Sequential No.	Series Description (with inclusive dates of records)	Records Disposal Auth No.	Departmental Retention Schedule Item No.	Location in Records Centre	Retention Period	Disposal Year	Disposal Date	
1265	Closed cases—Fraud-July 01, 2011 thru Dec 31, 2011	25	13					
1266	Closed cases—Criminal-Jan 01, 2012 thru June 30, 2012	26	13					
1267	Closed cases—Copyright-Jan 01, 2013 thru June 30, 2013	27	13					
	Destruction of Records	You will receive one copy of this form when records are ready for destruction. Please sign and return the form to the Records Center. If a change in disposal method or date is necessary, attach a memo that includes the new date and or new method of destruction and reason for the delay.						
		Approval Date	Approval signature for Destruction		Date of Destruction		Destroyed by	

generated by their RIM software. Copies of the records transmittal form, from the multicopy form or additional printed copies of the electronic form, are distributed as follows:

- The transferring department keeps one copy while the box is in transit to storage.
- The original and two copies accompany the box to inactive storage, where the box is logged in, and its location on the storage shelves is noted on all copies of the transmittal form.
- One copy of the form is returned to the sending department for reference when a record from that box is requested. The copy that was first retained in the department is then destroyed because it does not contain the location of the box.

In an automated system, bar codes make the records transfer process much faster. When records are borrowed from an inactive records center or archival storage, the same controls are needed as are used in active storage—requisition, charge-out, and follow-up.

Why is uniform box size needed in a records center?

records center box: a box designed to hold approximately one cubic foot of records, either legal or letter size

If the records center does not provide boxes of uniform size in which to store records to be transferred, the records manager must ensure that all departments use the same size box. Using uniform box sizes facilitates stacking, uses space most economically, and looks neater.

A **records center box** (carton or container) is usually made of corrugated cardboard and is designed to hold approximately one cubic foot (12 inches high by 12 inches wide by 12 inches deep) of records, either legal or letter size. These boxes may have lift-up or lift-off tops or lift-out sides. An example of a records center box is shown in Figure 7.13.

FIGURE 7.13 **Records Center Boxes Hold Approximately One Cubic Foot of Records**

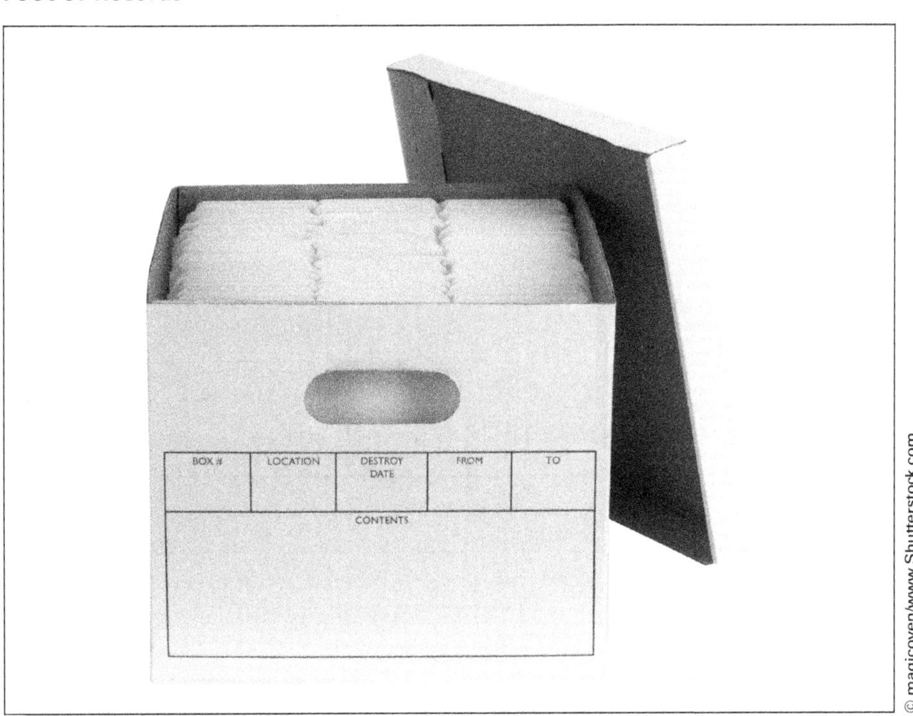

© magicoven/www.Shutterstock.com

RECORDS CENTER CONTROL PROCEDURES

Automation in large records centers is extremely important. It improves productivity, helps center employees provide faster service, and improves system integrity.

How can software improve records center efficiencies?

Records center software combined with bar codes or RFID tags can eliminate many manual tasks. The software should be able to perform the following main functions:

1. Box and/or records inventories
2. Storage management
3. Records and information searches
4. Records retention schedule correlations
5. Destruction methodology correlated with retention schedules
6. Accounting
7. User tracking

Additionally, the software can be programmed to include bar code and RFID tracking, cross-referencing, global searching, off-site storage control, label preparation, document indexing, spell-checking, report generation, audit trails, and more. (Records audits are discussed in Chapter 14.)

By incorporating bar code and RFID technology and having readers connected directly to a computer, records center automation systems can perform these additional functions:

- Locate a box on a shelf.
- Check out/in a box or file.
- Locate a folder in a box.
- Identify a file or box for destruction.
- Charge back faxing, copying, microfilm searches, and other activities to departments that requested such services.[2]

Often, records tracking systems use bar codes or RFID tags to help in retrieval and to eliminate the need for keying input each time a record is requested.

How can records tracking systems improve retrieval accuracy?

Because pertinent information is not keyed each time, input errors are virtually eliminated when bar codes or RFID tags are used. Whether a record is classified as active, inactive, or archival, a tracking system allows instant recall of facts, location, and in some cases, the record itself. Most tracking systems use a database setup to manage records at the document, folder, or box level.

Whether inactive or archival records are stored off-site or within the same building as active records, several control procedures should be in place to ensure appropriate security and accession of the records (Figure 7.14).

Inactive Records Index

Why is an inactive records index considered part of records center control procedures?

First and most important, records must be located. A commercial records center may house records owned by several different organizations; an in-house records center contains records for all departments of one organization. In either case, many different records series are stored on a space-available

[2] ARMA International, Records Center Operations, 3d ed. (Lenexa, KS: ARMA International, 2011), p. 15.

FIGURE 7.14 **Records Center Control Files**

RECORDS CENTER CONTROL FILES	
Inactive Records Index	Contains a complete listing of all stored inactive records
Change-Out and Follow-Up File	Contains requisition forms
Destruction Date File	Contains copies of transmittal forms
Destruction File	Contains copies of transmittal forms after records are destroyed

basis. Consequently, like records series with different dates probably will not be stored near each other. For example, if a request is made for an inactive accounting ledger for July 2012, the filer must locate the box of accounting records for 2012 quickly to find the requested record.

index: a systematic guide that allows access to specific items contained within a larger body of information

inactive records index: an index of all records in the inactive records storage center

Various indexes are useful in locating stored records. An **index** is a systematic guide that allows access to specific items contained within a larger body of information. A records center maintains an index to assist filers in locating inactive records. An **inactive records index** is an index of all records in the inactive records storage center. This index contains details about the inactive records: the dates the records were created, a description of the records series, the department that owns the records, an authorization for transfer to inactive storage, their location in the records storage center, the retention period, and the disposition date.

This information can be manually or electronically maintained and is often a continuation of the records transmittal form (Figure 7.12). The transmittal form contains all information needed for an inactive records index. A records center employee completes the location part of the form by checking the available space in the center and assigning space for the box(es). Records center software can generate the records transmittal form with a bar code or a RFID tag and an adhesive backing to affix to the box containing the records. A copy of the transmittal form is stored in the software's destruction date file (discussed later).

Charge-Out and Follow-Up File

As with active records, charge-out and follow-up procedures must be followed for inactive and archive records. When someone from the Accounting Department, for example, requests accounts payable records for July 1, 2013, through December 31, 2013, a requisition form is completed. The filer scans the inactive records index, noting the location of the requested box of records. Then the filer physically goes to that location in the records center, finds the correct box, and removes the correct record(s). One copy of the requisition form is used as an OUT indicator and is placed inside the box. Last, the requisition information is filed or entered into the charge-out and follow-up file.

charge-out and follow-up file: a tickler file that contains requisition forms filed by dates that records are due back in the inactive records center

A **charge-out and follow-up file** is a tickler file that contains requisition forms filed by dates that records are due back in the inactive records center. If a record is not returned by the date due, written reminders, telephone calls, faxes, or e-mail messages are used to remind the borrower to return the record(s) to the center. Electronic charge-out and follow-up files can be programmed to provide daily reports of records due and send notices to borrowers. Borrowers may return the borrowed record(s) or request an extension via reply e-mail.

Destruction Date File

How are records destroyed?

records destruction: the disposal of records of no further value beyond any possible reconstruction

Records destruction is the disposal of records of no further value by incinerating (burning), macerating (soaking in a chemical solution to soften the paper, then bailing it), pulping (shredding and mixing with water, then bailing), or shredding. Destruction is the definitive obliteration of a record beyond any possible reconstruction—nothing can possibly be recovered from the record. Shredders that can shred records in all media formats, including disks, CDs, and micromedia, are available. Some records that do not contain confidential information may be sold for recycling. Many organizations find that contracting with service providers to destroy their records is more cost-effective than purchasing the supplies and equipment and hiring workers to carry out the destruction.

destruction date file: a tickler file containing copies of forms completed when records are received in a records center

Records center control procedures include maintaining records that document when and how records are destroyed. A **destruction date file** is a tickler file containing copies of forms completed when records are received in a records center. This file may be physical or electronic, and the forms, filed by destruction dates, may be physical or electronic. Destruction dates for each records series are determined when a records retention schedule is created, and these dates are recorded on records transmittal forms. Another copy of the transmittal form can be placed into the destruction date file. Documents in this file are moved into the destruction file after the documents are destroyed.

Before the destruction date arrives, the records center will notify the department that owns the records that the destruction date is approaching.

destruction notice: a notification of the scheduled destruction of records

A **destruction notice** is a notification (memo, listing, form, e-mail message, etc.) of the scheduled destruction of records. This notice reminds departmental employees that some of their records will soon be destroyed, even though the department manager signed a records destruction authorization form when the records were transferred to the records center. That authorization form is kept on file in the records center. Notice that the records transmittal and receipt in Figure 7.12 on page 176 includes a records disposal authorization number. This number is assigned when the records are transferred to the records center. If a written authorization is on file, the number in that column is all that is needed to proceed with the destruction.

Why are some records not destroyed on the scheduled date?

destruction suspension: a hold placed on the scheduled destruction of records

If, after receiving the destruction notice, the department manager determines that the inactive records continue to have value, destruction may be suspended. Records retention policies and best practices should include provisions for suspending records destruction when a lawsuit or other legal actions are pending or are in process. A **destruction suspension** (sometimes referred to as a *records hold or legal hold*) is a hold placed on the scheduled destruction of records that may be relevant to foreseeable or pending litigation, governmental investigation, audit, or special organizational requirements. Records for which destruction has been suspended are often referred to as *frozen records*.

Destruction File

destruction file: a file that contains information on the actual destruction of inactive records

Whether records are destroyed by a service provider or by records center employees, the destruction must be witnessed or proof provided by a certificate of destruction. A **destruction file** contains information on the destruction of inactive records. Usually, the type of destruction is determined at the time the records are transferred to the records center. This information is recorded on the transmittal forms in the destruction date file, which are moved to the

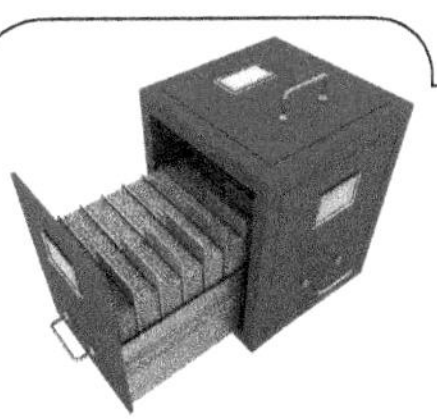

MY RECORDS

Retain and Dispose of Records

Do you have a fear of throwing away documents because you might need them some day? Do you know which records you need to keep and for how long?

To reduce the volume of your paper records, you need to dispose of records you no longer need on a regular schedule. Ask yourself these basic questions to help determine which records to keep and which ones to destroy:

- Is the information important to my life, personal interests, or job?
- Has this information become outdated? Can I find a more current document?
- How easily can I replace this document if I need the information later?

A suggested retention schedule for personal records appears below. If you have specific questions about retaining your records, ask an accountant or attorney.

FILE TYPE	RETENTION	FILE TYPE	RETENTION
Family Records		**Employment Records**	
Birth certificate	Permanent	Contracts	4 years after completion
Diploma	Permanent	Correspondence	4 years after leaving job
Divorce settlement	Permanent	Pay stubs	1 year
Marriage certificate	Permanent		
Military service	Permanent	**Taxes**	
Naturalization papers	Permanent	Federal income tax forms	7 years
Passport	Until receipt of renewed passport	State income tax forms	7 years
Pet papers	For life of pet	**Legal and Financial Records**	
Social security	Permanent	Deeds	Permanent
Will	Permanent	Contracts (mortgage, promissory notes, leases) still in effect	Permanent
Medical Records		Expired contracts	7 years
Details of surgeries, diagnosis, procedures	Permanent	Credit card statements	1 year
Medicines taken	Permanent	Bank statements	1 year
Product Receipts and Warranties			
Currently owned	Permanent		
Sold or recycled	1 year		

destruction file after the records are destroyed. These forms are filed by department names and dates on which destruction was carried out. Records managers maintain and dispose of records as part of the record life cycle. Proper control procedures ensure that the right record is available to the right person at the right time and that records no longer needed are destroyed properly. Electronic destruction files in the RIM software allow for easy entry of essential information regarding the destruction dates, destruction methods used, and department names. Necessary physical forms may be scanned and stored electronically as well.

At least once a year, go through your files and safely dispose of everything that is no longer needed. Cross-cut shredding is a safe way to dispose of any physical records that contain your name, Social Security number, driver's license, account numbers, address, and bank information.

CHAPTER REVIEW AND APPLICATIONS

KEY POINTS

- A records retention program establishes policies and procedures for what documents to keep, where to keep them, and how long to keep them.
- A records inventory is a survey of all records maintained by an organization.
- A retention period is the length of time that records must be retained according to operational, legal, regulatory, and fiscal requirements.
- A records retention schedule (RRS) shows how long to maintain records.
- Retrieval is the process of locating and removing a record, a file, or information from storage.
- Follow-up is a system for ensuring the timely and proper return of materials charged out from a file.
- Records that are no longer used frequently are transferred to a records center or to an archives for permanent storage, or they are destroyed.
- Archives are the records created or received and accumulated by a person or organization and preserved because of their historical or continuing value.
- Records transfer helps reduce equipment costs because inactive records are stored in less-expensive cardboard containers.
- Records center software, along with bar codes and RFID tags, can perform box inventories, charge in/out records and boxes, locate a box on a shelf, locate a record in a box, and perform numerous other important records and information functions.
- Records center control files include an inactive records index, a charge-out and follow-up file, a destruction date file, and a destruction file.

TERMS

active records
archive records
archives
charge-out
charge-out and follow-up file
charge-out log
destruction date file
destruction file
destruction notice
destruction suspension
follow-up
inactive records
inactive records index
index
nonrecord
office of record
official record
on-call/wanted form
one-period transfer method
periodic transfer method
perpetual transfer method
pick list
radio frequency identification (RFID)
record copy
records center
records center box
records destruction
records disposition
records inventory
records retention program
records retention schedule
records series
records transfer
requisition
retention period
retrieval

REVIEW AND DISCUSS

1. Why is a records retention program useful to an organization? (Obj. 1)

2. List and describe each of the four values of records. Provide a record example for each value. (Obj. 2)

3. What is a records inventory? Discuss why an inventory is conducted and what is included in the inventory. (Obj. 3)

4. Describe a records retention schedule, and explain why one is prepared and the purpose it serves. (Obj. 4)

5. What is records retrieval? Name at least three ways that requests for stored records may be made. (Obj. 5)

6. Explain the steps in a manual charge-out procedure. (Obj. 5)

7. Explain how records are charged out in an automated records center. (Obj. 5)

8. What is the purpose of using follow-up procedures for borrowed records? (Obj. 5)

9. List six reasons for transferring records. (Obj. 6)

10. Describe two methods of records transfer. (Obj. 6)

11. List five capabilities of typical records center software. (Obj. 7)

12. An inactive records center usually maintains four control files. Discuss these files. (Obj. 8)

APPLICATIONS

7-1 Determine Retention Periods (Objs. 1, 4)

Data File

1. Open the Microsoft® Access data file *7-1 Retention Schedule*. Open the Records Retention Schedule table.

2. Refer to the records retention schedule in Figure 7.6, page 162, to find retention periods for the records listed below. Enter the retention data in the Years Active, Years Inactive, and Total Years database fields.

   Records
   Expired liability policy
   Records inventory
   Bank deposits
   Advertising contracts
   Annual audit reports
   Policy statements
   Records management policies
   Requisitions for supplies
   Training manuals
   Executive correspondence
3. Sort the table by the Records Series field and then by the Records field.

4. Create and print a report to show the records retention schedule.
   - Include all fields in the Records Retention Schedule table.
   - Group records by the Records Series field. Sort by the Record field in ascending order.
   - Choose Stepped layout and Landscape orientation.
   - Name the report "Records Retention Schedule Report."
   - Print the report.

5. Create a query to show all records with "P" in the Total Years field. Display the Records Series, Record, and Total Years fields in the query results. Save the query as "Total Years Query." Print the query results table.

7-2 Solve Retrieval Problems (Objs. 1, 4, 5)

You and two other students have been invited to assist the owners of a small clothing company to gain better control of their records. The two owners of Creative Designs design, create, and sell silk ties for men. A variety of designs are used, including various holiday and sports themes in addition to their own creative, whimsical designs. Currently, the company consists of the two co-owners, one sales representative, and one administrative assistant. Temporary workers are often called in to help prepare a large order for shipping. The administrative assistant is responsible for preparing files for storage, filing all records, and retrieving records as needed. However, everyone in the company has access to the files, and they often remove records if the administrative assistant is helping prepare a shipment to a major retailer.

Because the company is small, few records controls are being used. Sometimes an owner is unable to locate the sales records for a specific buyer, and no one knows who has a custom-design client's records. Misfiling occurs frequently because someone is in a hurry when records are refiled, and file users often stack records to be refiled wherever space is available. The administrative assistant spends unproductive time searching for misfiled records and records that should be in storage but are not.

The owners plan to expand the product line to include matching dress shirts, which will mean more employees and more records.

1. Work with your team members to prepare a list of recommendations to help Creative Designs improve its records management. Include the kind of records procedures you would recommend for this growing company and additional supplies or equipment needed to provide adequate control of records.
2. Key the list and submit it to your instructor.

7-3 Recommend Records Transfer Methods (Obj. 6)

Which transfer method—perpetual, periodic, or one-period—would you recommend for each of the following records situations? Explain your decision.

1. Home improvement store: employment applications, general correspondence, property mortgage.

2. Medical clinic office: medical case files of deceased patients.

3. Law office: client folders from the past 10 years.

4. Exercise gym and spa: all folders relating to advertising activity—news releases, publicity photographs, and advertising activity reports. All records were created in the current year.

5. Condominium builder: all folders related to a high-rise condominium that has recently been completed. All units are sold, and the grand opening was held the last Saturday of last month. The folders contain records of subcontractors, new owners, insurance carriers, and governmental agencies that issued required permits.

7-4 Learn about Web Resources for Managing E-mail Records (Objs. 1, 4)

The National Archives in the United States provide guidance for a variety of records management topics. Go to the US National Archives & Records Administration website: www.archives.gov. Click **A–Z Index** under **Resources**. Click **R**. Click **Records Management**. Click **Email Management**. Click **Bulletin 2013-02: Guidance on a New Approach to Managing Email Records (Capstone)**. List the advantages of using the Capstone Approach.

SIMULATION

Job 8 Requisition and Charge-Out Procedures

Job 9 Transfer Procedures

Continue working with Auric Systems, Inc. Complete Jobs 8 and 9.

ADDITIONAL RESOURCES

For data files, Microsoft® Access tutorials and more, go to www.cengagebrain.com.

CHAPTER 8

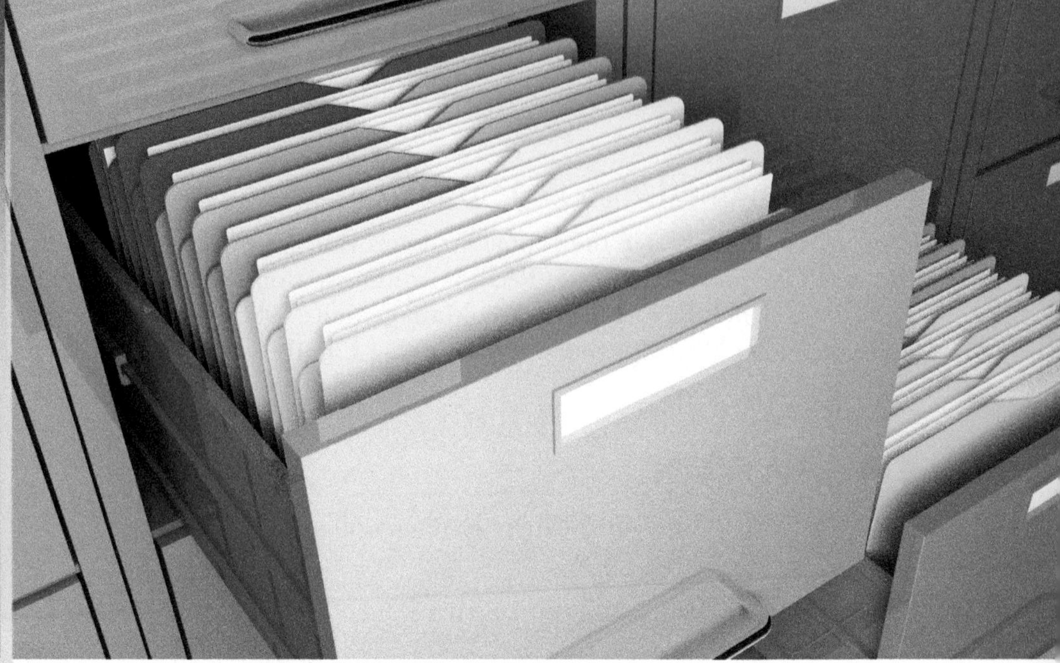

Subject Records Management

LEARNING OBJECTIVES

1. Define *subject records management.*
2. List advantages and disadvantages of storing and retrieving records by subject.
3. Compare the dictionary and encyclopedic subject file arrangements.
4. Describe the guides, folders, and labels used for subject records storage.
5. Describe four indexes and their use for subject records management.
6. List the steps used when storing and retrieving records stored by their subjects.
7. Use computer software to prepare an index for subject records.
8. Store and retrieve records following subject records procedures.

Courtesy of Dr. Bruce Dearstyne

ON THE JOB

Dr. Bruce Dearstyne, an Adjunct Professor at the College of Information Studies, University of Maryland, teaches courses in program management, project management, and information management. Prior positions include professor at the College of Information Studies and program director at the New York State Archives and Records Administration. He has written articles for ARMA's journal, *Information Management, and, in 2009,* ARMA published his book, *Managing Records and Information Programs: Principles, Techniques, and Tools.*

Dr. Dearstyne predicts the following changes in records and information within the next two to three years:

- Continuing shift from tangible (paper) records to electronic formats as the most common/default records format;
- Continued increase in the volume and variety of digital information created and delivered through a variety of channels and devices, particularly mobile devices, complicating the challenge of distinguishing records from nonrecords information;
- Further growth of "big data" and the use of "analytics" for extracting and distilling meaningful, useful information from it; and
- Continued increase in legal concerns and considerations, particularly surrounding the role of records in e-discovery and other legal proceedings.

Dr. Dearstyne also advises beginning students studying for a career in records management that they will need to develop two sets of skills: leadership and communication. They will need the ability to redefine program mission, redesign programs and set new directions, and the ability to explain and interpret what records management is, why it is important, and how it should be applied.

SUBJECT RECORDS STORAGE AND RETRIEVAL

You have already studied the alphabetic method of storing and retrieving records by name—names of individuals, businesses, and organizations. Two other alphabetic storage methods—subject and geographic—are also widely used. In this chapter, you learn how and when to arrange records by their subjects. Geographic records management, a filing method in which records are arranged by geographic location, is presented in Chapter 10.

Why store records by subject?

subject records management: an alphabetic system of storing and retrieving records by their subject or topic

Subject records management is an alphabetic system of storing and retrieving records by their subject or topic. Subject filing is recommended when the range of topics used within an organization is broad and may include letters, e-mail messages, reports, clippings, catalogs, research data, product development plans, and inventory lists. In such a case, a topical arrangement becomes the logical way in which to arrange information.[1] Sometimes, documents cannot be filed by any other filing characteristic.

File users expect records that pertain to the same subject or topic to be stored together. Consequently, subject storage is the preferred storage method in many organizations. Subject records storage is used in any type of business or organization that has a large volume of stored records. A small organization may use a limited list of subject titles (also referred to as *headings*) for coding, storing, and retrieving records. However, a large organization may have an extensive list of main subject titles as well as numerous subdivisions of those titles. Filing by subject has advantages and disadvantages, as shown in Figure 8.1.

FIGURE 8.1 **Advantages and Disadvantages of Filing by Subject**

SUBJECT FILING	
ADVANTAGES	DISADVANTAGES
• Subjects are easier to remember than names. • Related records are easier to find. • Related records are not scattered throughout the files. • Files can easily be expanded by adding subdivisions to main subject titles. • Subject filing is appropriate for storing large volumes of records. • Security is provided because business and individual names are not visible to unauthorized persons who may not know the subject under which a record is filed.	• Main subject titles and subdivisions may overlap as the list of subject titles grows. • Concise, clearly defined, and uniformly stated subject titles may be difficult to select. • Inconsistent subject title coding on records can make storage and retrieval difficult. • Users may not remember the exact titles or be unfamiliar with the subject titles and may have more difficulty finding records. • Planning and maintenance are required to ensure that approved subject titles are used consistently. • Subject filing is the most expensive storage method because experienced filers are required. • An experienced records analyst may be required to create the subject titles to ensure that the most logical subjects are selected. • Indexing, coding, and cross-referencing take more time because each record must be read carefully and thoroughly.

[1]ARMA International, *Establishing Alphabetic, Numeric and Subject Filing Systems* (Lenexa, KS: ARMA International, 2005), p. 4.

Arranging records by subject categories, such as topic, organizational function, department, service, product, or project, is logical and improves retrieval for certain records. As you study a variety of filing methods, you will learn how components of one or more filing methods can be combined for efficient records storage and retrieval. The alphabetic method is often combined with other methods. Although an organization's records may be filed alphabetically by name, some records are kept together under subject headings, such as APPLICATIONS, PURCHASE ORDERS, and RENTAL CAR CONTRACTS, because use of these records would require such groupings. Arranging records according to organizational functions, such as ACCOUNTING, HUMAN RESOURCES, MARKETING, and SALES, is often used in large organizations.

What filing method is often combined with other methods?

Subjects are easy to recall, and subject records storage is the only logical, efficient method of storing and retrieving certain records. Many people think records are best remembered and retrieved by subject. As a result, many types of businesses and industries file their records using the subject method. A rule of thumb for choosing an appropriate filing method is to match the method to the most logical way for file users to request records. Office workers sometimes use alternate, synonymous terms for a single topic when filing by subject. Therefore, cross-references and indexes are necessary when using subject filing. Subject indexes and cross-referencing are explained later in the chapter.

The selection of a word or phrase to use as a subject title (the filing segment) is of prime importance when using the subject storage method. One person should be responsible for selecting subject titles. That person must be thoroughly familiar with the material to be stored and have considerable knowledge of every phase of the operations and activities of the business. If all file users have authority to add subject titles to a subject filing system, the same type of records content soon becomes stored under two or more synonymous terms. Such storage of related records in two or more places separates records that should be stored together and makes retrieval of all related records difficult.

Why should only one person be responsible for adding or changing subject titles?

The subject title must be short and clearly descriptive of the material it represents. Once a subject title has been chosen, everyone in the organization must use it. Additional subject titles must be chosen so that they do not duplicate or overlap any subject previously used. Good subject selection requires file users to agree on the subjects to be used; flexibility to allow for growth within the selected subjects and for expansion to add new material; and simplicity so that users can understand the system. Once subject titles have been selected, all file users must employ them consistently. Preparation and use of necessary indexes or taxonomies ensure consistent use of selected subject titles.

Why is choosing subject titles so important?

Remember the following important subject filing guidelines:

1. Select subject titles that best reflect stored records, are meaningful to file users, and are easy to remember.
2. Select subject titles that have only one interpretation.
3. Use one-word subject titles whenever possible.
4. Use plural titles whenever possible.

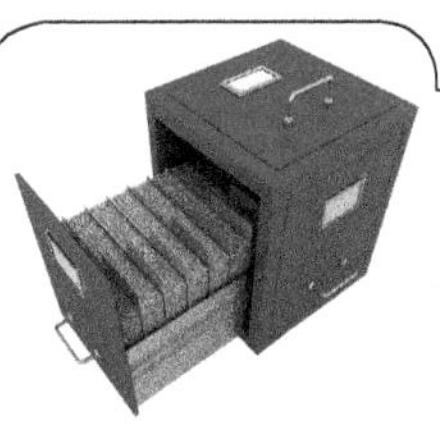

MY RECORDS

Subject Filing

Would the subject method be a good way to file your personal records? How can you set up your records for filing by subject?

You can use a bellows folder with subject categories to file your financial records. These folders are useful for many storage purposes. Labels include alphabetic subdivisions, subjects, and a place to write your own labels. Subject categories vary with the manufacturer of the folders and may include the following:

Automobile	Bank Records	Income Taxes	Insurance Records
Medical and Dental	Unpaid Bills and Receipts	Utilities	Miscellaneous

If you have a filing cabinet, you can also create your own folders. The following categories may serve as a guide for you:

Bank Records	Car	Charity	Education
Investments	Medical and Dental	Miscellaneous	Mortgage/Rent
Payroll	Income Taxes	Utilities	Pet Records

To help all members of your family understand your subject filing, create and print a master index of your subjects. You and your family can brainstorm all the subjects that are likely for your family's needs. Here are some sample categories:

Family and Friends
- Family information
- Pet information
- Important phone numbers
- Frequently called numbers
- Address/phone directory

Home and Automobile
- Home maintenance
- Home repairs
- Household appliances
- Vehicle maintenance
- Mileage record

Inventory
- Home inventory
- Book inventory
- Video/DVD inventory
- Audio inventory
- Photograph documentation

Food and Shopping
- Groceries needed
- Meal planner
- Recipe instructions
- Mail/Internet order record
- Monthly spending record

Cleaning and Chores
- Family chore chart
- Kids' schedule
- Cleaning checklist
- Cleaning schedule

Health, Exercise, and Medical
- Balanced diet log
- Nutrition worksheet
- Exercise log
- Walking log
- Quick health info
- Doctor visits
- Medication schedule

Things to Do
- People to visit or contact
- Places to go
- Movies to see or rent
- Books to read

Special Occasions
- Birthdays
- Gift ideas
- Holiday card record

5. Provide for the occasional use of alternate, synonymous, or related subject titles.
6. Consider combining filing methods when subdividing and sub-sorting records in large subject filing systems. For example, subdivide records first by subject and then alphabetically by location or name, numerically by record or document number, or chronologically by date.
7. Designate one person to manage the subject titles—to select the titles and to add new titles as needed.

SUBJECT RECORDS ARRANGEMENTS

Physical and electronic records may be stored in two alphabetic subject arrangements: (1) dictionary and (2) encyclopedic. The definitions of these two terms are easy to remember when you relate them to the arrangement of words in a dictionary versus the arrangement of information in an encyclopedia. A dictionary contains a list of words in alphabetic order. An encyclopedia contains a list of words and related topics in alphabetic order. Both subject arrangements are explained and illustrated in the following paragraphs.

Dictionary Arrangement

dictionary arrangement: a single alphabetic filing arrangement in which all types of entries (names, subjects, titles, etc.) are interfiled in alphabetic order

A **dictionary arrangement** is a single alphabetic filing arrangement in which all types of entries (names, subjects, titles, etc.) are interfiled. Characteristics of the dictionary arrangement are listed in Figure 8.2. In the subject dictionary arrangement, subject folders are arranged behind A-to-Z guides in correct alphabetic order by subject title. Generally, the dictionary subject arrangement is not recommended if the volume of records is greater than could be stored in two file drawers. However, the dictionary arrangement is used regardless of the number of records if the subject topics are easily identified without the necessity of using subdivisions.

Figure 8.3 shows a small office file arranged in straight dictionary order. A-to-Z guides are one-fifth cut and occupy first position in the file. Special guides are one-fifth cut and are in second position. Two special guides in Figure 8.3 are CUSTOMER SERVICES and SALES. These special subject guides mark exceptionally active subjects, making them conspicuous and easier to find.

FIGURE 8.2 **Characteristics of the Dictionary File Arrangement**

DICTIONARY FILE ARRANGEMENT
Labels on primary guides are the letters A to Z in alphabetic order.
Special guides are used to identify subject folders that are referenced often.
General subject folders are used to store all records relating to the subject title.
Captions on general subject folders include the letter of the alphabet as well as the subject title.
Subject titles are not subdivided.

FIGURE 8.3 **Dictionary Arrangement of Subjects**

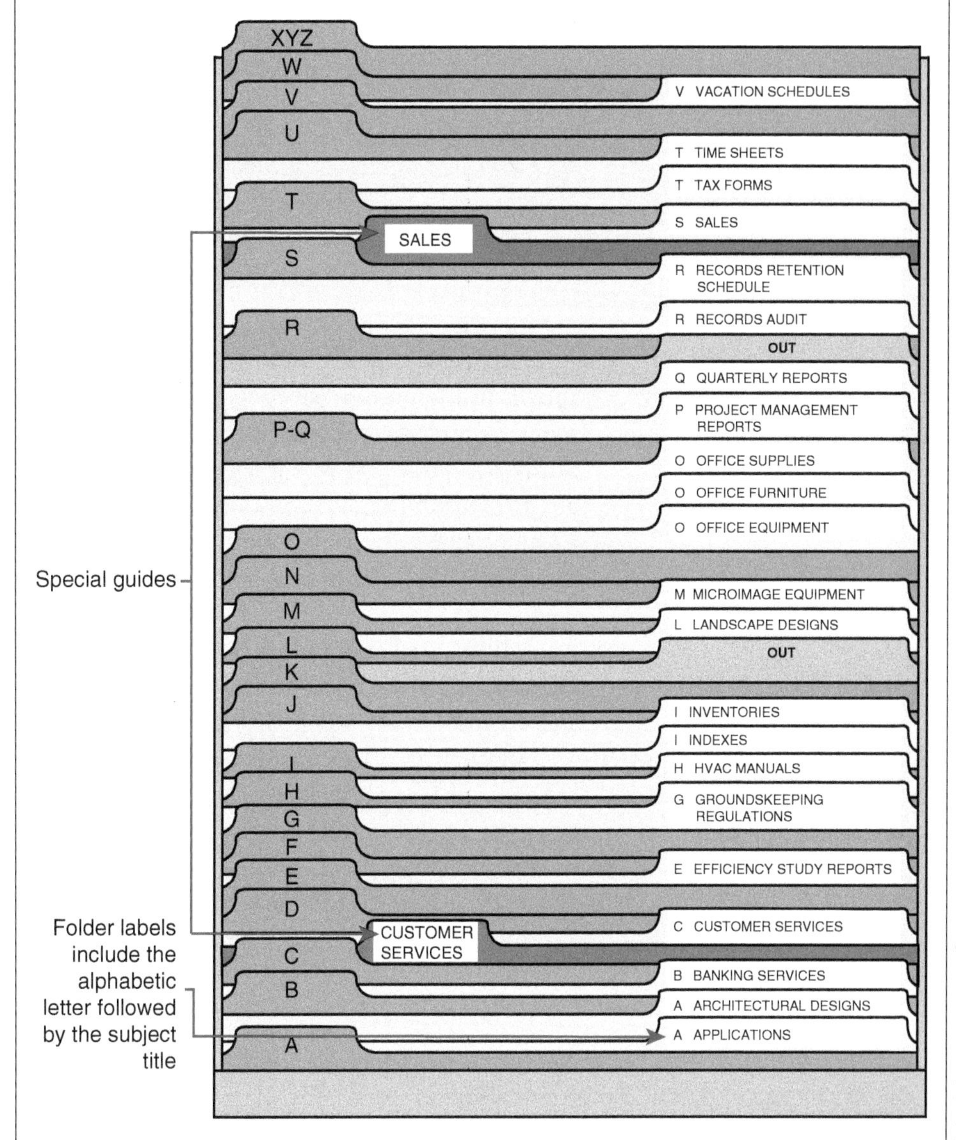

When is a subject dictionary arrangement no longer considered as a dictionary arrangement?

All general folders labeled with subject topics and OUT guides are one-third cut. They occupy the third position in the file.

So far, subdividing general subjects into more specific subdivisions has not been necessary. If records accumulate and make dividing the general subjects into more specific subdivisions necessary, the arrangement would no longer be considered a dictionary arrangement.

Encyclopedic Arrangement

encyclopedic arrangement: a subject filing arrangement in which records are filed under the specific subtitle to which they relate

The **encyclopedic arrangement** is a subject filing arrangement in which records are filed under broad, major subject titles and then under the specific subtitle to which they relate. Titles and subtitles in physical and electronic subject RIM systems are arranged alphabetically. Characteristics of the encyclopedic arrangement are listed in Figure 8.4.

FIGURE 8.4 **Characteristics of the Encyclopedic File Arrangement**

ENCYCLOPEDIC FILE ARRANGEMENT
Primary guide captions are general subject titles.
Secondary guide captions are subdivisions of the general subject titles.
Folder captions include the main subject titles and the subdivisions.
A general subject folder with the same label caption as the primary guide is inserted behind the last subdivision folder for all subjects.

Why subdivide main subject titles?

Figures 8.5 through 8.8 show encyclopedic arrangements of the subject file shown in Figure 8.3. As the number of records increases, the file arrangement requires specific subject subdivisions for quicker access to filed records. Study the guide and folder captions in Figures 8.5 through 8.8. *Main subjects* are printed on the label captions of the primary guides. These guides are one-fifth cut and in first position. Secondary guides in second position also have one-fifth-cut tabs. These guide labels bear the *subdivision* of the main subjects. The secondary guides may also include the primary guide captions such as those illustrated in Figure 8.9 on page 198. However, because guides are not removed from the file when storing and retrieving records, repeating the main subject title on the secondary guide is not necessary.

Why do subject folder captions include both main titles and subdivisions?

On the other hand, because they are removed from the file when storing and retrieving records, *folder* label captions include the main subjects and the secondary guide captions. If necessary, additional subdivisions of the first subdivision may be made for the specific subject titles. If necessary, the correspondent name may be included on the label. A comprehensive folder label helps ensure that a borrowed folder will be returned to its correct file location. One-third-cut folders are recommended.

FIGURE 8.5 **Encyclopedic Arrangement of Subjects A–E**

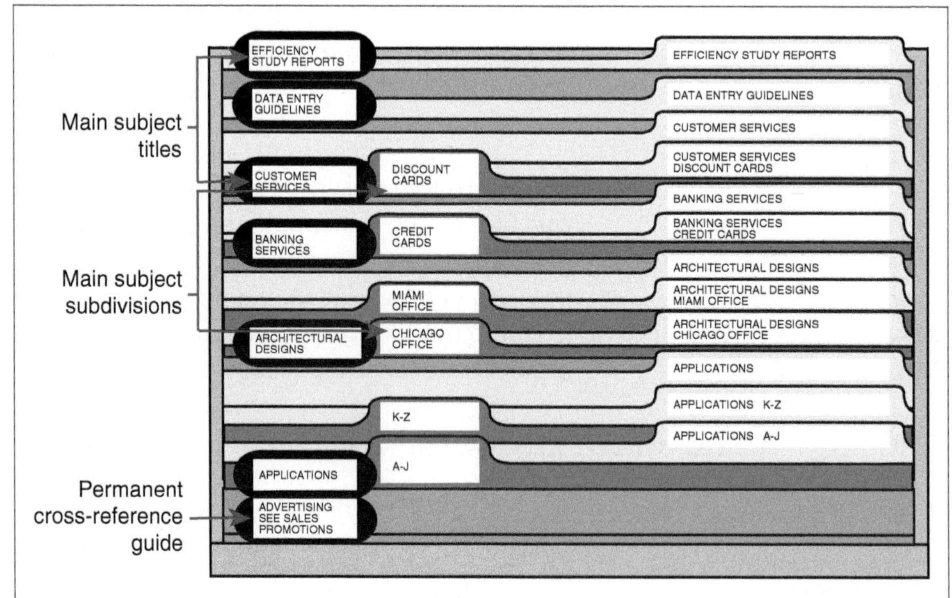

FIGURE 8.6 **Encyclopedic Arrangement of Subjects F–N**

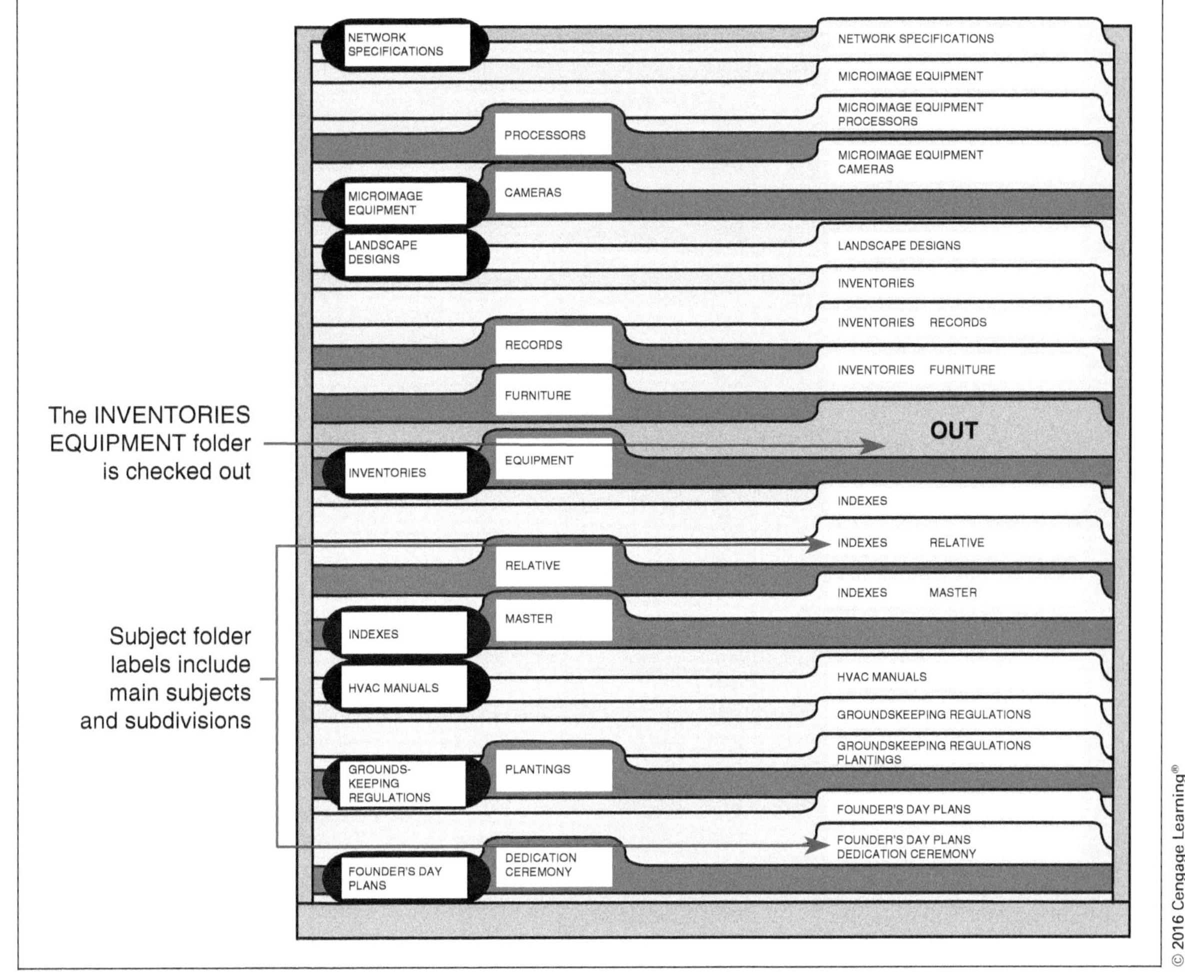

Once again, OUT indicators are in third position with all general folders. OUT guides are usually of a distinctive color that is easily visible to show the location of a removed folder.

Most of the same general subject folders in Figure 8.3 have been maintained in the encyclopedic file arrangement shown in Figures 8.5 through 8.8. Specific subject folders have been added where subjects are subdivided by the secondary subject guides. Note the general subject folder for BANKING SERVICES in Figure 8.5. Although a subdivision folder for CREDIT CARDS has been added, the general BANKING SERVICES subject folder remains. The general folder holds records pertaining to other banking services information that does not fit into the credit card category.

How should general folders be managed?

When is a new subdivision added?

General folders need to be checked regularly to determine whether some records could be moved into a new specific folder. When the number of records for other related subject topics has accumulated to the predetermined number that warrants a specific folder, a new subdivision should be added, the index updated immediately, a new secondary guide prepared, and a new subdivision folder prepared. General subject folders are placed after subdivision or specific subject folders so that filers will first look for a subdivision to avoid filing all records in the general folder.

FIGURE 8.7 **Encyclopedic Arrangement of Subjects O–S**

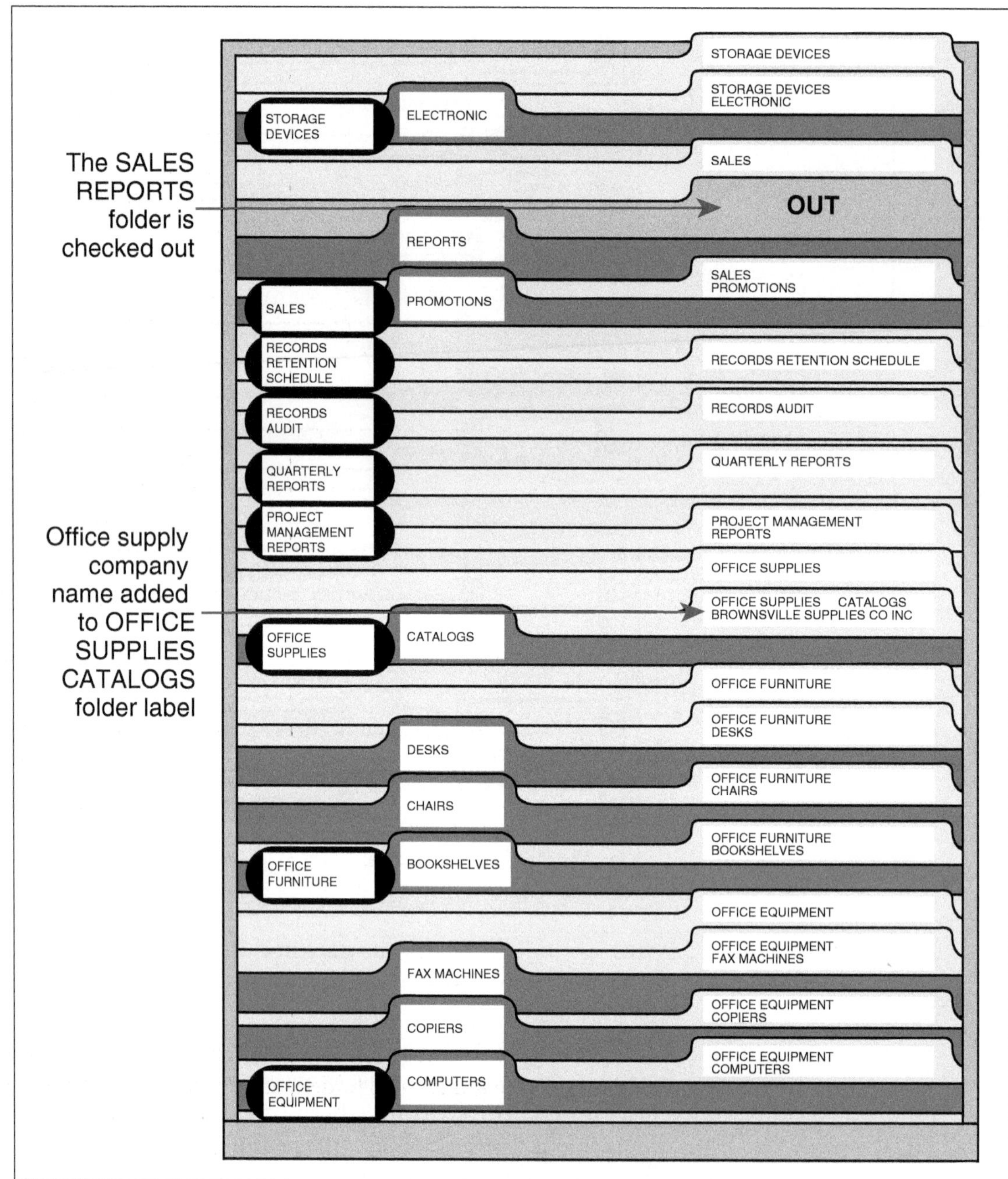

When general folders become crowded and no specific subject subdivisions are possible, other means of subdividing records may be used. Notice that the APPLICATIONS general folders are subdivided by sections of the alphabet—A–J and K–Z in Figure 8.5.

In Figure 8.6, the INVENTORIES general subject is subdivided by types of inventories—equipment, furniture, and records. The name of an office supply company catalog—Brownsville Supplies Co., Inc.—has been added to the folder label for OFFICE SUPPLIES CATALOGS in Figure 8.7.

How is color used in subject filing?

Color can be used effectively with subject filing. Very often, each subject label will have a color band that is repeated on all guides and folders for that subject. Sometimes, all captions of one subject will be one color, and the

FIGURE 8.8 **Encyclopedic Arrangement of Subjects T–V**

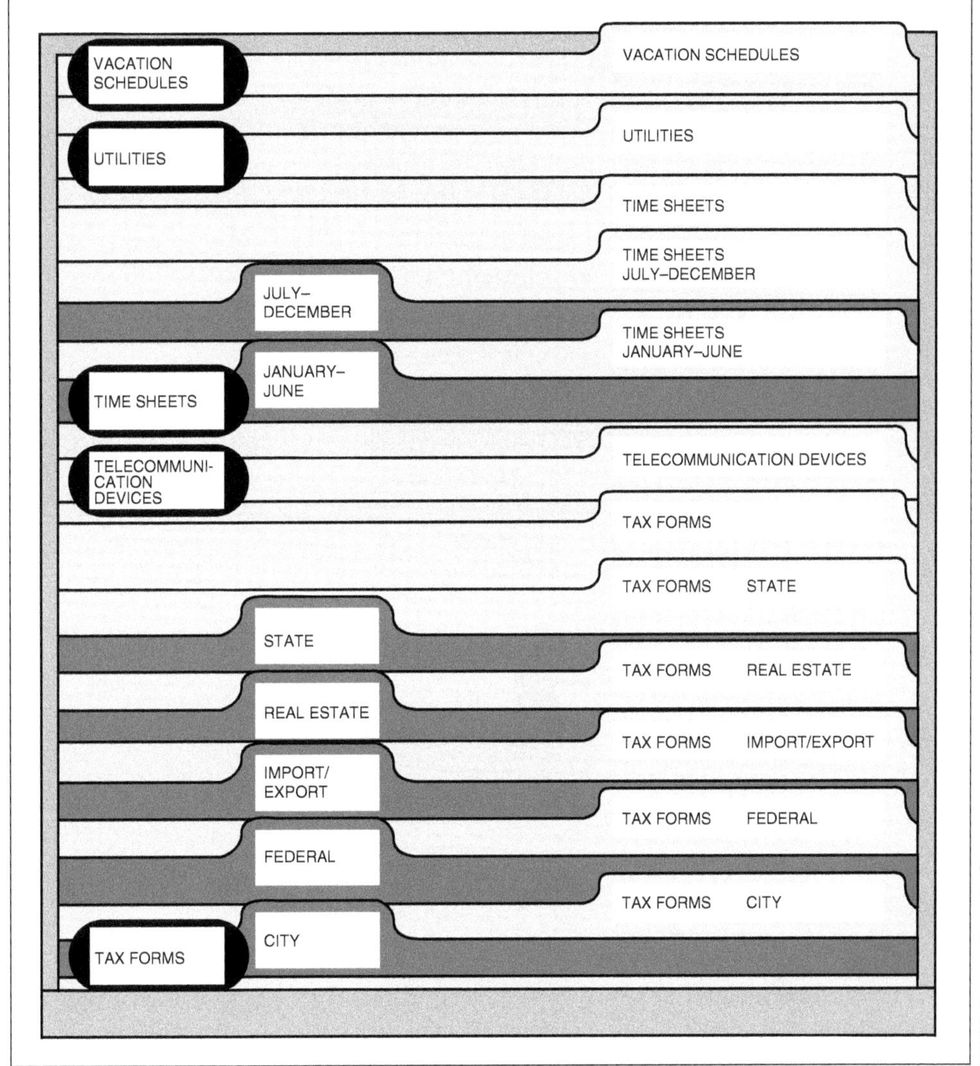

color changes when the subject title changes. A third possibility is for each subject to have guides and folders of only one color, with a change of color used for guides and folders of the next subject. Using a colored folder for all general subject folders can also be effective. Although the use of color can speed the filing process and reduce misfiles in any filing system, using color does not take the place of careful selection of meaningful subject titles in a subject filing system.

SUBJECT FILING SUPPLIES

Supplies used for the subject arrangement of physical files include guides, folders, labels, and OUT indicators, all of which were explained in Chapter 6. The use of OUT indicators when charging in and charging out records was discussed in Chapter 7. Because more information is keyed on guide and folder label captions for subject filing than for alphabetic name files, preparing records for subject storage is slightly more challenging than for alphabetic records.

Guides and Labels

Guide labels used in subject records storage are determined by the subject titles used. If subject titles are long, subject codes or abbreviations may be used. Subject coding is explained in more detail on pages 205–207. Figure 8.9 shows an example of primary and secondary guides. The primary guide caption contains the main subject title; the secondary guide caption contains the main subject and its subdivision. Because guides are not removed from a storage container during storage and retrieval, a primary guide caption can be omitted on a secondary guide, as shown in Figures 8.5 through 8.8 on pages 194–197.

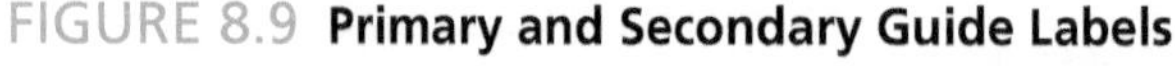

FIGURE 8.9 **Primary and Secondary Guide Labels**

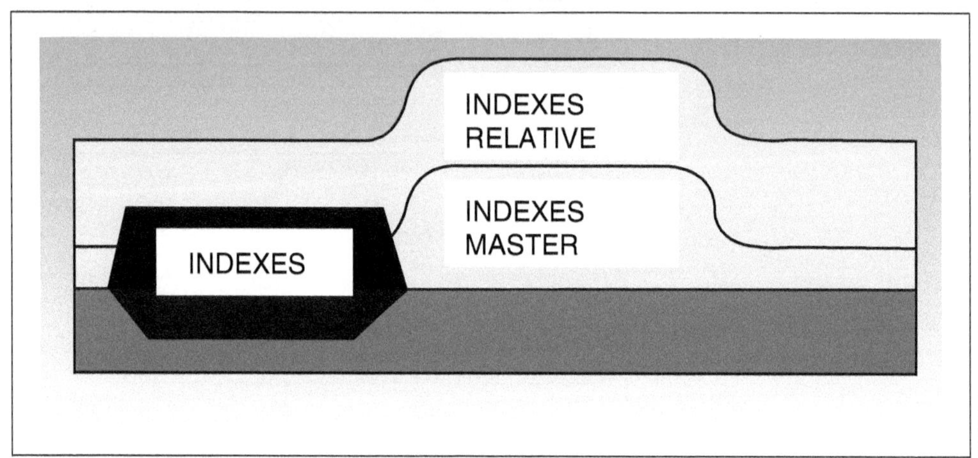

Why does subject filing require customized guide and folder labels?

Subject filing requires customized labeling of guides and folders that matches subjects and subdivisions. Adhesive labels are available from a variety of suppliers and in a variety of sizes and colors. Packages of labels include directions for using the label function in word processing software programs. The software program label function enables preparation of many different label sizes and styles, as shown in Figure 8.10. Label templates may be downloaded from label suppliers' websites. A template allows a user to key several captions on a template and print the entire sheet of labels or only a portion of the sheet Blank tab inserts for one-third-cut or one-fifth-cut metal or plastic tab sizes can be purchased in strips for attaching computer-generated adhesive labels.

Where are captions printed on primary guide labels or inserts?

Captions on all guides in the records system should have consistent spacing and style. All primary guide label captions should begin near the left edge and near the top of the label. The label function of software (word processing or database) uses preset margins for each label selection. When using these settings, be sure the label captions begin at the same point on all labels.

Labels are easier to read with information in a straight line rather than staggered. Key the information in all capitals with no punctuation. Decide whether to use complete subject titles, abbreviated titles, or subject codes, and follow this format consistently. Mixing styles of captions complicates filing and retrieval.

FIGURE 8.10 **Consistent Labels Can Be Prepared Using the Label Feature of Software Programs, or by Downloading Label Templates from Label Suppliers' Websites**

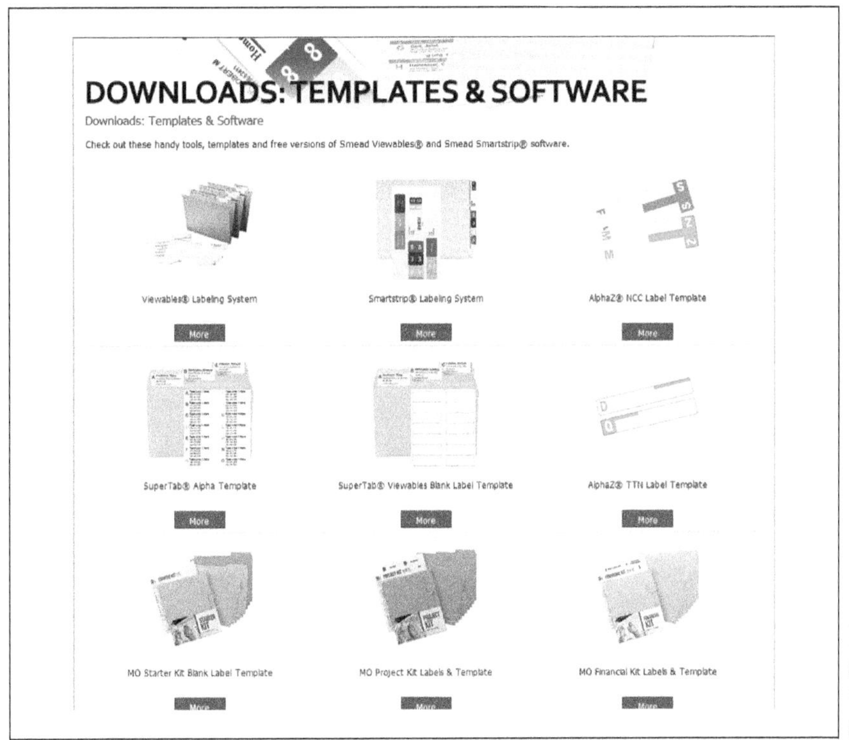

Folders and Labels

Where are captions printed on folder labels?

Folder label captions include the primary or main subject title and all necessary subdivisions. As discussed previously, comprehensive label captions help ensure that borrowed folders are returned to the correct file locations. One-third-cut folders are preferred. Adhesive folder labels are available in a variety of sizes and may be printed using a laser or an inkjet printer. The label size should match the tab cut of the folder. Use the label function of word processing software for preparing labels, or follow the directions for label formatting that is packaged with the labels. The main subject title should begin near the left margin and as near as possible to the top of the label or the bottom of a color bar on the label. Key the *subdivision* 0.5 inch to the right of the main subject title or under the first letter of the first line. Key the label in all capitals with no punctuation, as shown in Figure 8.11. Be precise and consistent with folder label preparation. Attention to this detail creates a neat, readable, straight-line filing system.

FIGURE 8.11 **Subject Folder Labels**

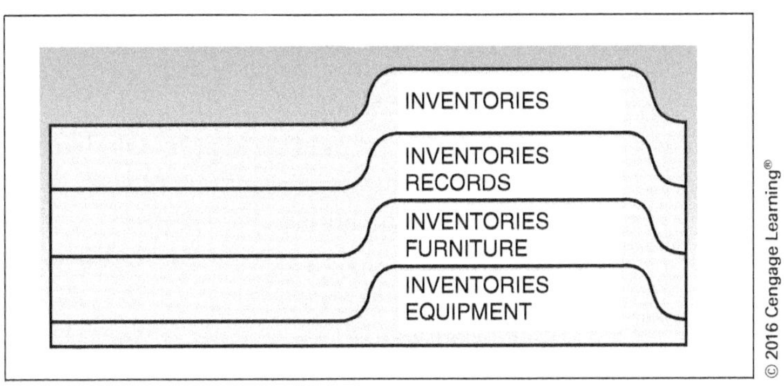

Color-code folder labels for each subject guide to reduce misfiles. Bar codes can be added for electronically tracking records. Bar codes and color codes for folders and labels in subject records storage relate to the first, second, and sometimes third letters in subject titles. Supplies and services for color coding and bar coding are available through companies offering records and information management products. These companies can be located through the *Yellow Pages* or on the Internet. The ARMA International website has a buyer's guide listing vendors of filing supplies and records management products. Some of these companies offer records and information management products and services applicable to subject records systems, as well as other records systems. Their websites not only provide information about their companies but also give helpful hints for setting up and maintaining records management systems.

OUT Indicators

What information should be written on an OUT guide when a subject record is borrowed?

An OUT guide appears in the file samples in Figures 8.3 through 8.7 on pages 193–196. You may want to review OUT indicators and the charge-out and follow-up procedures discussed in Chapters 6 and 7. Follow the same procedures for subject filing that you applied in alphabetic name filing. The only difference is that you will use subject titles, rather than individual or organization names, to identify records.

SUBJECT INDEXES

Why does a subject file require an index?

You learned about the importance of using an index when storing and receiving records in Chapter 7. Because filers may not know all subjects used in a subject file, they cannot go directly to a file to locate a record. A subject file requires an index and therefore is considered an indirect access filing method.

Indirect access: a method of access to records that requires prior use of an external index

Indirect access is a method of access to records that requires prior use of an external index. Users must refer to an index to determine whether a subject has been established in the system and, if it has, the location of a record before they can store or retrieve the record from the main file. Alphabetic filing is considered a direct access filing method because a specific record or name in a file can be found without first referring to an index to find its location. **Direct access** is a method of access to records without reference to an index or other filing aid. The filer goes directly to the file without first referring to a list of names for the location of the record in the files, as you learned in Chapter 6.

Preparation of Indexes

Indexes are electronic/digital or printed lists. Although most indexes are created in text files or databases, a print copy of the index should be available in the files storage area. It should be kept in a designated location, and users should always return it to the same location. Indexes are usually included in RIM software as well. Making additions, deletions, and corrections to an index can be done quickly and easily on a computer, using either word processing or database software. Because the computer can be used to search and sort the index, finding specific subject titles and keeping an electronic index up-to-date are easy.

What four types of indexes are used in the subject records storage method?"

The following four types of indexes are valuable, and often necessary, when using the subject records storage method:

- Master index
- Relative index
- Numeric index
- Name index

Master Index

master index: a printed alphabetic listing in file order of all subjects used as subject titles in the filing system

A **master index** is a printed alphabetic listing in file order of all subjects used as subject titles in the filing system. The master index is also referred to as the *master list, subject index*, or *subject list.* Even if computer access to the master index and relative index is available, keep an updated printed copy in the front of the file drawer with the physical files. This practice is important to maintain consistent coding and filing of records by subject. Without frequent referrals to these indexes, misfiles and duplicate subject titles are likely to occur. For a large volume of records in a complex filing system, use of electronic indexes saves time in locating specific records. The index should be updated as new subjects are added and old ones are eliminated or modified. When new subjects are added, refer to the index to avoid assigning a subject title that is already in the system. Figure 8.12 is a master index of the portion of the file illustrated in Figure 8.3 on page 193.

FIGURE 8.12 **Master Index for a Subject File**

MASTER INDEX-SUBJECT FILE

Applications*
Architectural Designs
  Chicago Office
  Miami Office
Banking Services
  Credit Cards
Charitable Donations
Customer Services
  Discount Cards
Data Entry Guidelines
  Formatting
  Keystrokes
Efficiency Study Reports
Founder's Day Plans
  Dedication Ceremony
Groundskeeping
  Regulations
  Plantings
HVAC Manuals
Indexes
  Master
  Relative
Inventories
  Equipment
  Furniture
  Records
Landscape Designs
Microimage Equipment
  Cameras
  Processors
New York Branch Office
Office Equipment
  Computers
  Copiers
  Fax Machines
Office Furniture
  Bookshelves
  Chairs
  Credenzas
  Desks
Office Supplies
  Catalogs
  Invoices
Project Management
  Reports
Quarterly Reports
Records Audit
Records Retention
  Schedule
Sales
  Projections
  Promotions
  Reports
Storage Devices
  Electronic
Tax Forms
  City
  Federal
  Import/Export
  Real Estate
  State
Telecommunication
  Devices
Time Sheets*
Utilities
Vacation Schedules

*Divided folders do not need to be listed in the master index.

For physical filing systems, store a hard copy of the index, as an outline of the file contents, at the front of the file for ready access to all users. Without a master index, file users must scan all drawers or shelves of records to locate subject titles. New file users can familiarize themselves with the subject storage system quickly by referring to a master index. In addition, reference to the master index ensures that only preselected subject titles are used for filing and retrieving records.

Relative Index

relative index: a dictionary-type listing of all possible words and combinations of words by which records may be requested

A more complex subject file may require a relative index. A **relative index** is a dictionary-type listing of *all* possible words and combinations of words by which records may be requested. The word *relative* is used because the index includes not only all subject titles used in the system but also synonyms for subjects or any *related* subject titles that filers might consider logical topics for storing and retrieving records.

Study the relative index in Figure 8.13. Notice the entry for Advertising, which is not used as a subject title in the system. The relative index refers the filer to Sales Promotions—the subject title selected for storing and retrieving advertising materials. This type of index serves as a vast cross-reference device because it contains all subjects by which a record might be requested. When someone requests a record by a subject that is not the one selected for use in the system, check the relative index to see whether that subject title has been included. If not, add the requested subject to the index listing with the correct subject title beside it.

Referencing the relative index helps filers avoid duplication of subject titles and locate subjects when records are requested by unfamiliar terms. The relative index often contains both SEE and SEE ALSO cross-references. These notations help to suggest related materials and alternative file locations.

Numeric Index

numeric index: a current list of all files by the file numbers

The numeric index will become more meaningful after you study Chapter 9 and learn to assign numbers to subject file headings. Filers can file and retrieve numbers faster than words or letters because they can read numbers more quickly. When numbers are used to identify specific subjects, a numeric index is needed. A **numeric index** is a current list of all files by the file numbers. Such an index shows numbers assigned to subject titles and helps filers avoid reusing the same numbers when new subjects are added to the storage system.

Name Index

name index: a listing of correspondents' names stored in a subject file

Customarily, subject records storage does not require an alphabetic index of names of individuals or companies. However, documents filed in a subject arrangement *do* require a name index. A **name index** is a listing of correspondents' names stored in a subject file. The name and address of each correspondent are included in the index, as well as the subject under which each name is stored. Names are arranged alphabetically in text or database files and may be printed. Because records are sometimes requested by the name of an individual or a company, a name index containing this information can save time that would otherwise be spent searching for a record by subject.

FIGURE 8.13 **Relative Index for a Subject File**

RELATIVE INDEX-SUBJECT FILE			
SUBJECT TITLE	**FILED UNDER**	**SUBJECT TITLE**	**FILED UNDER**
Advertising	Sales Promotions	Import/Export Tax Forms	Tax Forms
Applications	Applications	Indexes	Indexes
Architectural Designs	Architectural Designs	Inventories	Inventories
Banking Services	Banking Services	Landscape Designs	Landscape Designs
Bookshelves	Office Equipment	Master Index	Indexes
Cameras	Microimage Equipment	Miami Office	Architectural Designs
Catalogs	SEE Office Supplies	Microimage Equipment	Microimage Equipment
Charitable Donations	Charitable Donations	Network Specifications	Network Specifications
Chairs	Office Furniture	Office Equipment	Office Equipment
Chicago Office	Architectural Designs	Office Furniture	Office Furniture
City Tax Forms	Tax Forms	Office Supplies	Office Supplies
Computers	Office Equipment	Plantings	Groundskeeping Regulations
Copiers	Office Equipment	Processors	Microimage Equipment
Credenzas	Office Equipment	Project Management Reports	Project Management Reports
Credit Cards	Banking Services	Quarterly Reports	Quarterly Reports
Customer Services	Customer Services	Real Estate Tax Forms	Tax Forms
Data Entry Guidelines	Data Entry Guidelines	Records Inventory	Records Inventories
Dedication Ceremony	Founder's Day Plans	Records Audit	Records Audit
Desks	Office Equipment	Records Retention Schedule	Records Retention Schedule
Discount Cards	Customer Services	Relative Index	Indexes
Efficiency Study Reports	Efficiency Study Reports	Sales	Sales
Electronic Storage Devices	Storage Devices	Sales Projections	Sales Projections
Equipment Inventory	Inventories	Sales Promotions	Sales Promotions
Fax Machines	Office Equipment	Sales Reports	Sales Reports
Federal Tax Forms	Tax Forms	State Tax Forms	Tax Forms
Formatting	Data Entry Guidelines	Storage Devices	Storage Devices
Founder's Day Plans	Founder's Day Plans	Tax Forms	Tax Forms
Furniture Inventory	Inventories	Time Sheets	Time Sheets
Groundskeeping Regulations	Groundskeeping Regulations	Utilities	Utilities
HVAC Manuals	HVAC Manuals	Vacation Schedules	Vacation Schedules

STORAGE AND RETRIEVAL PROCEDURES

All the steps for storing and retrieving physical correspondence records studied in Chapters 6 and 7 are as important in the subject filing method as they are in any other storage method. A brief description of each step, together with an explanation of its application to the subject method, follows. The steps are summarized in Figure 8.14.

FIGURE 8.14 **Subject Filing Storage and Retrieval Procedures**

STEPS FOR STORING AND RETRIEVING SUBJECT RECORDS

Step 1: Inspecting

- Check for release mark.

Step 2: Indexing

- Read entire record carefully.
- Select filing segment from text.
- Verify that subject is in master index.
- Select filing segment from the master index if not in the text.

Step 3: Coding

- Code the main subject and any subdivisions where they appear in the text.
- Insert diagonals between the units, underline the key unit, and number remaining units of the filing segment.
- Write the subject at the top right of the record if it is not in the text.
- Underline cross-reference subjects with a wavy line, insert diagonals between the units, and number all units, starting with 1.
- Write the correct cross-reference subject title in the margin if it is not exactly right in the text. Underline it with a wavy line and number all units.
- Place an X in the margin beside the cross-reference subject.

Step 4: Cross-Referencing

- Prepare a cross-reference sheet for all alternative subjects, or photocopy the record.
- File the cross-reference sheets, or copies, under the alternative subject title(s).

Step 5: Sorting

- Sort by main subject titles, then by subdivisions.

Step 6: Storing

- File records coded for subject subdivisions in appropriate subdivision folders.
- File records coded for the main subject only into the general subject folder.
- File records in the appropriate folders in alphabetic order by correspondent names; the latest date is in the front of the folder.

Step 7: Retrieving

- Use the master or relative index to locate records.

Inspecting

Checking a record to determine whether it is ready to be filed is known as inspecting. Every record in any records and information management system should be inspected to verify that it has been released for filing. Whatever action the record requires should be taken or noted for later action prior to storing the record. Do not store a record until a written notation (called a *release mark*) by someone with authority indicates that it is ready for storage. A release mark might be a code or check mark, a punched symbol, a person's initials, a stamped notation, or some other agreed-upon mark. In Figure 8.16, *JJ* is the release mark used to indicate that the letter is ready for storage.

Indexing

Indexing, or classifying, is the mental process of determining the subject filing segment to be used in storing a record. Because each record must be read carefully (as shown in Figure 8.15), this step takes more time with the subject method than with other storage methods. If a record relates to only one subject, indexing is simple. The filer simply selects the correct subject from the master index. If someone else has previously indicated the subject under which a record is to be stored, recheck the accuracy of the subject selection. If a record contains information about more than one subject, you must determine the most important subject by which to store the record. Then cross-reference the other subject(s).

FIGURE 8.15 **Indexing for Subject Records Storage Requires Reading the Document to Determine the Subject**

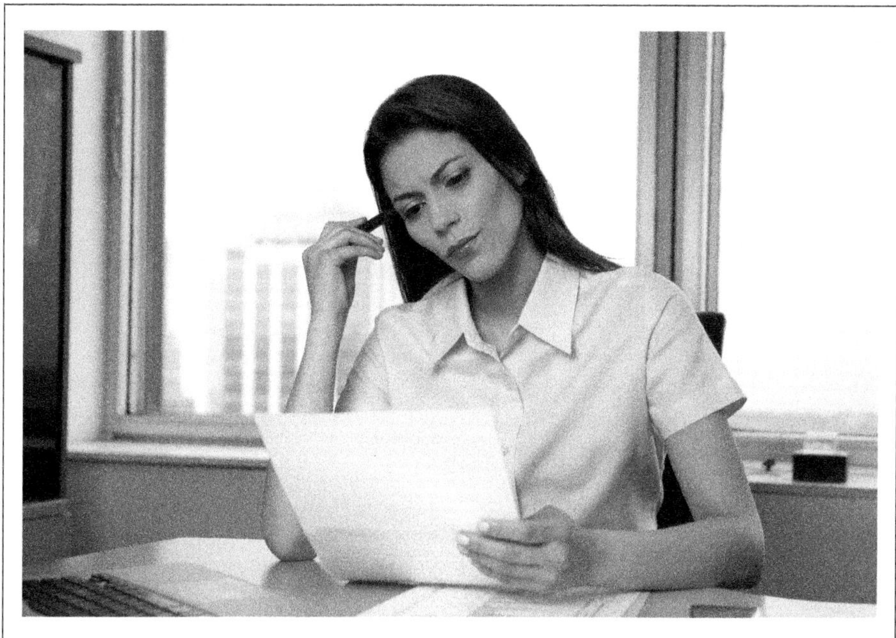

Coding

In Chapter 3, you learned that coding means marking the filing segment on the record. Code the main subject title and any subdivisions by placing diagonals between the units, underlining the key unit, and numbering the remaining units in the filing segment where they appear on the record. Code the correspondent's name by placing diagonals between the units and continuing the numbering of the units (Figure 8.16). If the subject is not mentioned in the record, write it clearly at the top of the record. Some filers prefer to write the filing segment in color in the upper right margin of the record. The subject title is therefore more visible in the file. When more than one subject is indicated, code only the most important one; cross-reference all other subjects in some distinctive manner. For example, the subject to cross-reference in Figure 8.16 is underlined, and an X is placed in the margin opposite the subject. The correct cross-reference subject title and subtitle SALES PROMOTIONS/ TELEVISION are written and coded in the margin. Diagonals are placed between the units, and all filing units are numbered.

FIGURE 8.16 **Record Coded for Subject Record Storage**

2 3
Sales / Promotions / Magazine

4 5 6
Demirchyan /Advertising /Agency

1530 Park Avenue, New York, NY 10126-5701
Tele: 212.555-0177 Fax: 212.555.0136

May 16, 20-- 11:00 A.M.

May 15, 20--

Ms. Angie Brown-Duran
Duran Designs, Inc.
600 E 52 Street
New York, NY 10022-2844

Dear Angie

The magazine advertising media kit you requested for *Design Creator's* magazine is on its way. Note that the new full-color page rate is $15,650; the black/white page, $10,275. A copy of your ad is enclosed and ready for your approval. We should meet the publication deadline for the September issue with no problem.

If you are still considering television, you might be interested in XYC-TV's monthly advertising schedule for June. *HGTV* and *The Garden Show* rates are easily within your budget. We will be happy to show you some ideas for 30-second commercials if you want to pursue TV advertising. X Sales / 2 Promotions / 3 Television

Design Creators is offering an incentive to first-time advertisers. It is offering an 8 percent discount to all advertisers booking space in the next two issues. An 18 percent discount is offered to advertisers contracting space in the next four issues. We can discuss these issues at our meeting on Tuesday.

Sincerely JJ

Ani McCord

Ani McCord
Advertising Director

psm

Enclosure

Do not rely on memory to determine the subject under which a record should be stored. Consult the master or relative index to be sure that you have selected and coded the filing segment correctly.

Why would using subject codes save coding time?

Coding in an alphabetic subject filing system may include an entire subject title such as PURCHASING. However, abbreviations can simplify coding in a large, complex subject filing system because writing subjects on records, especially subjects of more than one word, can be done much quicker with abbreviated subject codes. Create an abbreviation with the first alphabetic character of the subject title followed by the next one or two consonants such as PRC for PURCHASING, or use the first character of each word in a multiple-word subject heading such as RRS for RECORDS RETENTION SCHEDULE. Because the codes may consist of as many as six characters, PRCH may be more easily remembered for PURCHASING than PRC. Consistency is essential when developing a subject code system in which two- to six-character abbreviations are used. Everyone using the system must understand the codes and how to develop new ones when necessary. If abbreviations are used, the master index should show codes as well as complete subject titles. Be sure to write subject letter codes on each record, and include them on individual folder label captions, along with the subject title.

CAREER CORNER

Human Resources Records Administrator

The following job description is an example of a career opportunity in a manufacturing company.

GENERAL INFORMATION

The records administrator manages employee-related files such as medical, vacation, discipline, and performance review records.

RESPONSIBILITIES

- Ensure that employee file requests have proper authorization.
- Implement and maintain standard employee folder organization.
- File and retrieve all employee-related records.
- Comply with the company's records retention schedule for human resources records.
- Produce periodic statistical reports of employee demographic information.

EXPERIENCE AND EDUCATION

- High school diploma or equivalent
- Two to three years' administrative experience
- Excellent verbal and written communication skills
- Ability to properly handle confidential and sensitive information
- Strong attention to detail and organization
- Strong database software and report writing experience

Cross-Referencing

Cross-references help filers locate stored records. When file users request a record under a topic other than its subject title, add a cross-reference under that topic. Code the document as suggested previously, and prepare a cross-reference sheet such as the one shown in Figure 8.17. File users looking for the document under its alternative subject title SALES PROMOTIONS/TELEVISION are sent to the original record's file location, SALES PROMOTIONS/MAGAZINE. If a record refers to several important subjects, consider

FIGURE 8.17 **Cross-Reference Sheet for Subject Records Storage**

CROSS-REFERENCE SHEET

Name or Subject

Sales / Promotions [2] / Television [3] / Demirchyan [4] / Advertising [5] / Agency [6]

Date of Record

May 15, 20--

Regarding

Magazine and television advertising

SEE

Name or Subject

Sales Promotions Magazine Demirchyan Advertising Agency

Date Filed 5/15/20-- By JJ

filing photocopies of the record under the different subject titles involved. This procedure eliminates the need for preparing several cross-reference sheets for that record. Sometimes a permanent cross-reference guide is placed in the storage container.

In Figure 8.5 on page 194, for example, a permanent guide labeled ADVERTISING, SEE SALES PROMOTIONS has been placed into the file in the primary guide position. Do not file records behind the permanent SEE guide. The SEE guide is there only to direct filers to the correct storage location.

Sorting

Sorting arranges records in filing order according to the records and information management system used. Use some kind of A-to-Z sorter to sort physical records to be stored alphabetically by subject. Sort records by main subject titles; then sort records by subdivisions. Time spent sorting records before filing saves filing time. Filers will be able to file and move in one direction through a filing system rather than moving backward and forward through drawers or shelves of stored records.

RECORDS MANAGEMENT IN ACTION

Technology "Brings Lawyer and Client Closer"

Rob Sanders and his assistant Commonwealth attorneys in Covington (Kentucky) now use their iPads more than their legal pads.

"It keeps prosecutors connected to the office 24/7," Sanders said. "It makes the office more efficient and more responsive. They go everywhere."

Spouses Christine and Chad Cooper used to go every day to the downtown office of the large law firm where they worked. Now, they do most of their work in cyberspace from their St. Bernard home or just about anywhere else they choose. "Our clients don't have to pay for Italian marble in our lobby," Chad Cooper said.

They and many other lawyers are taking advantage of technology in the courtroom and in private practices to advance the digital evolution of their profession.

Those changes are mirrored by, and perhaps a product of, the expectation of information easily accessed at any time by both lawyer and client.

The one-pound iPad can store hundreds of pictures, court documents, and videos that can be played to juries during trial. It replaces boxes of paper files, giving prosecutors anytime access, via cyberspace, to digital documents.

Source: Kimball Perry, Cincinnati.com, 2 June 2013, retrieved June 3, 2013 from http://news.cincinnati.com/apps/pbcs.dll/article?AID=/201306030522.aspx.

Storing

Storing (also called *filing*) places the hard copy into an appropriate location or saves the electronic record. For manual filing, careful placement of records into folders is always important. Be sure that the subject folder label caption agrees with the filing segment coded on the record. Raise the folder slightly before inserting the record to be sure the record enters the folder completely. Remove records that are in disarray, jog them, and return them neatly to the folder. Records sticking out of folders can obscure guide and folder label captions.

When filing documents into subject folders, file records in alphabetic order according to the names of the correspondents. Then for each correspondent, arrange the records by the date of the document with the *most recent date in front.*Place each record in its folder with its top to the left so that the record will be in correct reading position when the folder is opened.

Retrieving

Understanding the subject records system is critical to finding and removing (retrieving) records from storage. Use indexes to help locate records. In addition, follow the retrieval procedures described in Chapter 7. As with other methods of records storage, retrieval procedures for subject records management make use of OUT indicators to show information about records that have been removed from storage. Knowing who has taken the records, the contents of those records, when the records were borrowed, and when the records will be returned is the only way to maintain control over a records retrieval system. Follow-up also is necessary to ensure that records are returned, extend the charge-out time, or direct attention to any matters needing future action or consideration.

CHAPTER REVIEW AND APPLICATIONS

KEY POINTS

- Subject records management is an alphabetic system of storing and retrieving records by their subject or topic.
- Subject records may be filed in a dictionary or an encyclopedic arrangement.
- Supplies used for the subject arrangement of files include guides, folders, labels, and OUT indicators.
- The subject records storage method requires the use of indexes and is therefore considered an indirect access filing method.
- The master index is an outline of the file and lists all subject titles and subdivisions in alphabetic order as they appear in the file.
- The relative index lists all subject titles and subdivisions in a straight alphabetic, dictionary order.
- When numbers are used to identify specific subjects, a numeric index—a current list of files by the file numbers—is maintained.

- Letters filed in a subject arrangement require a name index.
- Maintain control over the records storage system by carefully inspecting, indexing, coding, cross-referencing, sorting, and storing records.
- Keep a charge-out record of all borrowed records and a follow-up system that ensures their safe return to storage.

TERMS

dictionary arrangement
encyclopedic arrangement
indirect access
master index
name index
numeric index
relative index
subject records management

REVIEW AND DISCUSS

1. Define *subject records management*, and explain why this system is the best choice for filing certain records. (Obj. 1)

2. Give two reasons that an organization might have a subject filing arrangement for records rather than arranging their records alphabetically by individual or company names. (Obj. 1)

3. List three advantages and three disadvantages of using the subject records storage method. (Obj. 2)

4. What do you consider the most important advantage and the greatest disadvantage to arranging records by subject? (Obj. 2)

5. Name two alphabetic arrangements of subject records storage, and explain how the two arrangements are alike and how they differ. (Obj. 3)

6. What two criteria determine which alphabetic arrangement to use for a subject records system? (Obj. 3)

7. What supplies are needed when using the subject storage method? Describe the placement of subject titles on guide and folder label captions. (Obj. 4)

8. Explain how color can be used with subject labels or folders to help locate records and reduce misfiles. (Obj. 4)

9. Name and describe four indexes used with subject records storage. (Obj. 5)

10. Which two indexes are essential for all subject files? Name two types of computer software that can be used to prepare subject file indexes. (Objs. 5 and 7)

11. Explain the procedure for storing and retrieving records in a subject records storage system. (Obj. 6)

12. When filing letters into subject folders, how are records arranged in the folder? (Obj. 8)

APPLICATIONS

8-1 Prepare a Master Index for a Subject File (Objs. 5 and 7)

Use database software to complete a master index for subject records files for a small business. Some records have already been entered into the database. You will add records and sort the database, query the database to show only a portion of the master index, and create a report showing the complete index.

Data File

1. Download the data file *8-1 Master Index* to a computer or a removable storage device, and then open it with Microsoft® Access.

2. Enter records into the Master Index table for the remaining files listed below. For records with only main subject titles, enter only the main subject title in the Main field. For records with main titles and subdivisions of main titles, enter the main title in the Main field and the subdivision title in the Sub field. (You will add subdivisions for some main titles already in the index.) Save the table.

Main Title	Subdivision
Utilities	
Utilities	Natural Gas
Utilities	Electric
Utilities	Water
Accounting	Credit Cards
Reports	
Reports	Annual Reports
Reports	Quarterly Reports
Reports	Monthly Reports
Accounting	Loans

3. Use the Advanced Filter/Sort feature to sort the Master Index table by the Main field, then by the Sub field to place the index into alphabetic order.

4. Create a query based on the Master Index table. The query results should display the Main field in the first column and the Sub field in the second column. The query results should show all records that have Office Equipment in the Main field. Sort the Main field in ascending order and the Sub field in ascending order. Save the query as "Office Equipment Query." Run the query and print the query results.

5. Create and save a report to show all the data in the Master Index table. The data should be sorted in ascending order by the Main field and then by the Sub field. Choose Tabular layout. Name the report "Master Index Report," and print it.

8-2 Create a Relative Index (Objs. 5 and 7)

Data File

1. Download the data file *8-2 Relative Index* to a computer or a removable storage device, and then open it with Microsoft® Access.

2. Enter records into the Relative Index table for the remaining files listed below. Enter the data into the Subject Title and the Filed Under fields. Sort the table by the Subject Title field. Save the table.

Subject Title	Filed Under
Resumes	Applications
Cars	Vehicles
Trucks	Vehicles
Charities	Contributions
Banking	Accounting

3. Create a report to show all data in the Relative Index table. Show the Subject Title data in the first column of the report and Filed Under data in the second column of the report. Sort the Subject Title field in ascending order. Choose Tabular layout. Save the report as "Relative Index Report," and print it.

8-3 File or Retrieve Records by the Subject Method (Obj. 8)

Refer to Figure 8.3, "Dictionary Arrangement of Subjects," on page 193 to file/retrieve the following records. Indicate where each record would be located by writing the complete folder label caption for each. If more than one subject location is possible, list other subjects that should be used for cross-referencing.

1. A new manual for the air-conditioning system

2. A report from a recent workflow efficiency study

3. A job application from Anthony Timmons

4. A letter from an office products vendor about filing supplies

5. A notice of price change on an order you have placed for filing cabinets

6. Last month's sales report

7. A memo about the date that the records audit will begin

8. Weekly time sheets for Records and Information Department employees

9. Vacation schedules for the Accounting Department

10. A price quote from a lawn and garden center to landscape a recreational area

8-4 Use the Internet to Locate Supply Vendors (Obj. 4)

Office supplies needed for preparing guides and folders for a subject records management system are available from local office products stores, various discount stores, and from online vendors. Use the Internet search engine of your choice to locate office supplies vendor websites. Search for filing supplies for a subject filing system.

1. Locate two vendors of guides and folders and two vendors of label software.
2. Go to these vendor websites and review their products.
3. Key a summary paragraph of what you learned by reviewing these sites. Describe how the guides, folders, and label software that you found would be suitable for a subject filing system. Send the summary to your instructor by e-mail.

SIMULATION

Job 10 Subject Business Document Filing

Continue working with Auric Systems, Inc. Complete Job 10.

ADDITIONAL RESOURCES

For data files, Microsoft® Access tutorials and more, go to www.cengagebrain.com.

CHAPTER 9

Numeric Records Management

LEARNING OBJECTIVES

1. Define numeric records management, and list three reasons for its use.
2. Describe the components of a consecutive numbering storage method and procedures for this method.
3. Describe how to convert an alphabetic records arrangement to a consecutive numeric records arrangement.
4. List advantages and disadvantages of consecutive numeric records storage.
5. Compare and contrast consecutive, terminal-digit, and middle-digit numeric records storage.
6. Define *chronologic records storage*, and explain its use.
7. Compare and contrast block-numeric, duplex-numeric, decimal-numeric, and alphanumeric coding.
8. Explain how computer indexes and database software can be used with numeric records management.

Courtesy of Lisa Thompson

ON THE JOB

When Purchase Cancer Group in Paducah, Kentucky, began to run out of storage space in the office and the cost of storing older records in a warehouse was increasing each month, physicians and staff began looking for ways to cut expenses. A large number of patient charts had accumulated in the 20 years since the practice was established; so, they decided that the monthly storage bill was a place to start.

Lisa Thompson, office manager, said, "We began by looking at the amount of time spent looking for patient charts." When a patient or healthcare professional called, the patient's chart would be given to the person handling the call. However, because physicians and staff would often lay charts onto their desks or in different areas of the office, the chart could not be located in a timely manner. Everyone in the practice understood that, in a few years, an electronic medical records (EMR) system would be required. The staff had always been proactive in handling issues; so they chose to convert to an EMR system that could be implemented as soon as possible.

All patient records, insurance bills, explanations of benefits (EOBs), and other insurance correspondence are scanned into the electronic system, and inactive records are no longer sent to an off-site storage company. Patient records may be accessed by name, date of birth, or social security number.

Reprinted with permission of Lisa Thompson.

NUMERIC RECORDS STORAGE AND RETRIEVAL

numeric records management: any classification system for arranging records that is based on numbers

Why use numeric records storage?

The records and information management (RIM) storage methods you studied in previous chapters were alphabetic—records were arranged in alphabetic order by name or subject. In this chapter, you learn how to store records in numeric order. As its name suggests, **numeric records management** is any classification system for arranging records that is based on numbers.

Numeric records management is often used in organizations that store and retrieve very large numbers of records and that have a need to preserve confidentiality of their records and information. Numbers used in storing records are assigned to records to identify their locations in a file. The number can be preprinted on the record (such as a purchase order or invoice number), or it may be assigned to the record based on the type of numeric filing arrangement. Records are filed by number in ascending order—from the lowest to the highest number.

Numbers are impersonal; the information they represent is dependent on the numbering system and is not immediately accessible to persons other than users of the system. Anyone who happens to see an open file drawer, file shelf, or file folder cannot readily identify the contents.

The use of numbers for identification and classification of data is part of everyday work routines. Most people appreciate the speed and accuracy of using numbers. Today, the list of numbers that each individual uses, and must therefore remember, is long. For example, almost every US citizen has a Social Security number, and all US citizens have ZIP Codes. Citizens of other countries also have postal codes to remember. Thousands of people in the United States and other countries have a home telephone number, a work telephone number, at least one cellular telephone number, and maybe a pager number to remember as well. Many people also have auto license plate numbers, code numbers for entering their places of work or their condominium buildings, passwords for accessing their computers at work, and personal identification numbers (PINs) for using their debit cards. Those individuals who establish online accounts or register with various websites have user IDs and passwords to remember. Medical office personnel ask patients for their dates of birth because patient records are stored in numeric order by date of birth. Patient names may also be on the folder labels, but the folders are stored in numeric order. When you order a pizza, the order clerk at the local pizza shop may ask for your telephone number. Your name, address, and the kind of pizza you last ordered shows on the computer screen when your telephone number is entered.

In this chapter, numbering methods for numeric filing are categorized as follows:

- Consecutive numbering
- Nonconsecutive numbering
- Numeric coding used in combination with geographic or subject filing

The components and procedures for filing physical records numerically are similar for all numeric records management systems. Expanding files is easy with a numeric filing system. An unlimited set of available numbers (compared with the limitation of 26 alphabetic characters) allows the addition of numbers, folders, and storage units without transferring current files. In an alphabetic file, adding files in one section of the alphabet requires moving folders in all drawers or on all shelves that follow the expanded section.

CONSECUTIVE NUMBERING

consecutive numbering method: a method in which consecutively numbered records are arranged in *ascending* number order—from the lowest number to the highest number

What does *consecutive* mean?

Filers using the most frequently used method of numbering records for storage assign numbers to records in sequence. Also called *serial, sequential,* and *straight numeric,* the **consecutive numbering method** is a method in which consecutively numbered records are arranged in *ascending* number order—from the lowest number to the highest number. Consecutive numbers follow one after another without interruption. Numbers begin with 1, 100, 1000, or any other number, and progress upward. Office forms, such as invoices, sales tickets, and purchase orders, are numbered consecutively. Although these forms may be filled out at various locations within a business, they come together in the file in consecutive numeric sequence.

Consecutive numbers are often assigned to customers and clients, and their letters are stored by consecutive numbers. Because a record may be requested by a name or topic rather than by a number, an index must be referenced to locate a numbered record. A numeric RIM system is considered an indirect access system because an index is used to locate a record in the file. As an indirect access system, numeric filing is ideal for storing electronic records where label space for record identification is often limited. An index is prepared to show the contents of the records and their assigned file code numbers. The index lists records by name, subject, creator, date, department, location, function, or a combination of these elements. Indexes required for numeric RIM storage are discussed in detail later in the chapter.

Consecutive Numbering Components

What are the components of the consecutive numbering method?

Components of the consecutive numbering method consist of (1) a numeric file, (2) an alphabetic file, (3) an accession log, and (4) an alphabetic index. Physical files use the following supplies for this storage method:

1. Numbered guides and folders for the numeric file
2. Alphabetic guides and folders for the general alphabetic file
3. Database software (or a lined book) for an accession log
4. Database or word processing software for an alphabetic index

Numbered Guides and Folders

Figure 9.1 shows a file drawer of consecutively numbered individual file folders in a straight-line arrangement. Primary guides, numbered 250 and 260, divide the drawer into easy-to-find numeric segments. Consecutively numbered individual folders 250 through 259 are placed behind a corresponding guide number for Section 250.

How many folders should be between guides?

Usually, one guide is provided for every 10 folders. Folders can show the names of the businesses, organizations, or individuals to the right of the number on the label, if secrecy is not a factor. However, when office policy requires names in addition to assigned code numbers, the names are not in alphabetic order. Folders are arranged in consecutive numbered order; therefore, someone with unauthorized access to files would have difficulty locating a particular person's file.

Guide captions are available in a variety of formats: (1) Guides may have numbers already printed on their tabs; (2) numbered labels may be inserted into slots on the tabs; (3) self-adhesive numbers may be attached to tabs; or (4) numbers may be keyed onto guide labels.

As discussed in Chapter 8, software and label templates are available for printing guide and folder label captions. RIM supply companies can also

FIGURE 9.1 **Consecutive Numbering Arrangement**

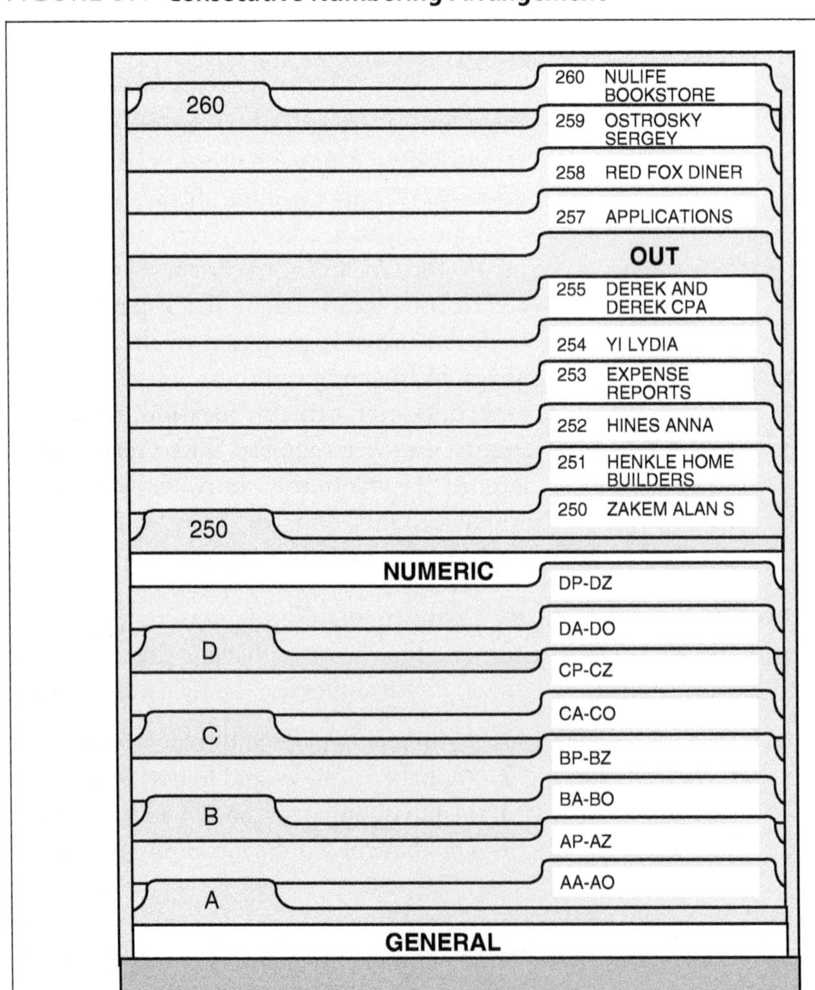

FIGURE 9.2 **Labels with Color-Coded Numbers Call Attention to Misfiles**

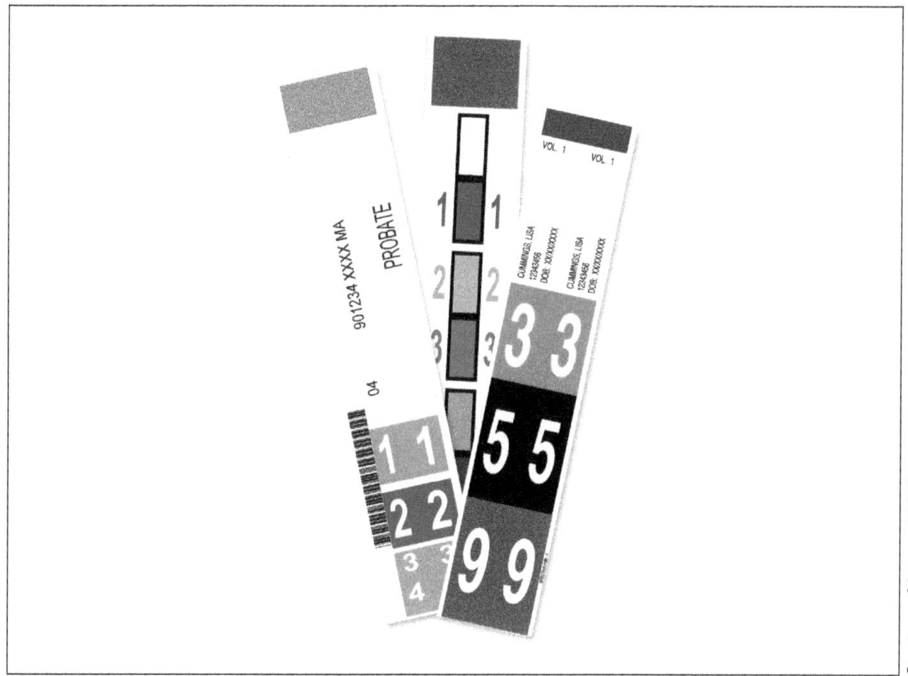

Courtesy of Ames, a TAB Company

produce customized labels from an organization's database information saved to a disk or CD. Figure 9.2 illustrates computer-generated labels with color-coded numbers. The numbers and colors call attention to misfiles, and bar codes provide electronic tracking of records. Avoid handwriting or hand printing on guide labels. Handwriting lacks uniformity of placement and style, making numbers difficult to read and unattractive.

Alphabetic Guides and Folders

What is the purpose of the general alphabetic file in a numeric system?

Perhaps you wonder what a general alphabetic file is doing in numeric records storage. A general alphabetic file, found in many numeric arrangements, holds records of correspondents whose volume of communications is small. Some offices prepare individually numbered folders for correspondents as they enter the file. With this procedure, a general alphabetic file is not needed. In most offices, individually numbered folders are not prepared until a predetermined number of documents (usually five or more) have accumulated for one correspondent or when a correspondent's file is expected to be active. Until an individual numbered folder is prepared, documents are stored in general alphabetic folders in a general alphabetic file in the same manner as names are stored using the alphabetic method.

The general alphabetic file should be placed at the beginning of the numeric file because expansion occurs at the end of a consecutively numbered arrangement. In Figure 9.1, only a portion of the alphabetic file is shown. The general alphabetic file contains a centered primary guide labeled GENERAL followed by lettered guides. In large records systems, alphabetic-lettered guides follow the primary guide to show the alphabetic divisions. In small systems, alphabetic-lettered guides may not be needed; instead, folders with alphabetic captions are arranged in alphabetic order behind the GENERAL guide. The general alphabetic folders hold records of correspondents who have not yet been assigned numbers.

Accession Log

accession log: a serial list of numbers assigned to records in a numeric storage system; also called an *accession book* or *numeric file list*

Why is the accession log referenced before records are coded for numeric storage?

The **accession log**, also called an *accession book* or *numeric file list,* is a serial list of numbers assigned to records in a numeric storage system. This log provides the numeric codes assigned to correspondents, subjects, or documents, as well as the date of the assignment. The next number available for assignment is obtained from this log. An accession log prevents a filer from assigning the same number twice. Correspondent names and subjects are entered into the accession log in indexed order. Figure 9.3 shows an accession log created in a computer database.

Although a lined book is often used for the accession log, a computer-generated log is simpler to prepare, use, and update. Database software is used in large records systems that have more than 1000 records or several people accessing the files on a daily basis. Number code assignment can be made automatically with appropriate computer programming.[1] You can store numerous items of information about each record in one or more tables and use the Query or Report function to generate lists or reports that show all or any part of this information. In smaller records systems, an accession log can easily be produced using a word processing program. The accession log information includes the file number, the correspondent name or subject in indexed order, and the date on which the record was added to the file.

FIGURE 9.3 **Accession Log**

FILE NO	NAME OR SUBJECT	DATE
525	Norwood Christian Church	5/18/20--
526	Astroturf Applications	5/10/20--
527	Liang Yang	7/12/20--
528	EZ Service Center	11/22/20--
529	A1 Moving & Storage	4/21/20--
530	Unique Web Designs	2/2/20--
531	Colyer James	10/15/20--
532	Happy Time Florist	9/18/20--
533	Borrowed Time Antiques	12/2/20--
534	SmithHarrison Makita	9/1/20--
535	BT Heating & Cooling	8/17/20--

[1]ARMA International, *Establishing Alphabetic, Numeric and Subject Filing Systems* (Lenexa, KS: ARMA International, 2005), p. 1.

Alphabetic Index

alphabetic index: a reference to a numeric file, organized alphabetically, that is used when the name or subject is known, but not the assigned number

A numeric records storage system cannot function without an alphabetic index. An **alphabetic index** is a reference to a numeric file, organized alphabetically, that is used when the name or subject is known, but not the assigned number. For a numeric-subject system, it may be called a *relative index*.[2] The index is typically a list of correspondent names or subjects for a numeric file. The assigned file codes are listed for records stored in the numbered file, or a G is entered as the code for records stored in the general alphabetic file. Filers reference the alphabetic index to determine where records for correspondents are located in the filing system.

How does using a database help filers in numeric storage and retrieval?

A computer file is recommended for the alphabetic index because of its speed and efficiency in locating records. The same database table can be used to store information for an accession log and an alphabetic index. Figure 9.4 shows a partial alphabetic index generated from a database. Cross-references are in bold print.

FIGURE 9.4 **Alphabetic Index**

NAMES AND SUBJECTS	FILE NO.	SEE
A1 Moving & Storage	529	
Astroturf Applications	526	
Borrowed Time Antiques	533	
BT Heating & Cooling	535	
Colyer James	531	
Easy Service Center	**528X**	**EZ Service Center**
EZ Service Center	528	
Happy Time Florist	532	
Harrison Makita Smith	**534X**	**SmithHarrison Makita**
Harrison Tom Mrs	**534X**	**SmithHarrison Makita**
Liang Yang	527	
Norwood Christian Church	525	
Smith Makita	**534X**	**SmithHarrison Makita**
SmithHarrison Makita	534	
Unique Web Designs	530	
Yang Liang	**527X**	**Liang Yang**

To retrieve a record, the first source of location information is the alphabetic index, to see whether a code for the subject or correspondent's name has been assigned. If a code is not found, the filer then checks the general alphabetic file to locate the record. Because rapid retrieval of a record can be important, keeping all names and subjects in one index is more efficient than looking in multiple locations. With all names and subjects in the index, a filer

[2]Ibid., p. 9.

follows the same pattern for retrieving all records. Each correspondent and subject in the index has a different file code number or the letter G. Because the alphabetic index serves as the records location source for all file users, the index should be accurate and up-to-date.

When information about each correspondent and subject is stored in a database, locating information about that correspondent or subject is quick and easy, using the database Find or Query function. Because of the ease of obtaining information from a database, you may want to add addresses or other information. This information in a database is also useful for printing mailing labels.

When creating a database, you can use the AutoNumber feature to assign file number codes automatically. If you want to use another numbering system, simply include a File Code Number field and enter the number. The data can be sorted on the File Code Number field in descending order so that the highest number shows on the first line of the list, allowing you to determine quickly the next number for assignment. The data can also be sorted by name to create an alphabetic name index. The database can be used for an onscreen check of the assigned file code number for a correspondent or subject. Using the Find feature, you can go directly to a record to obtain information, as shown in Figure 9.5.

FIGURE 9.5 **"Find" Dialog Box in Access**

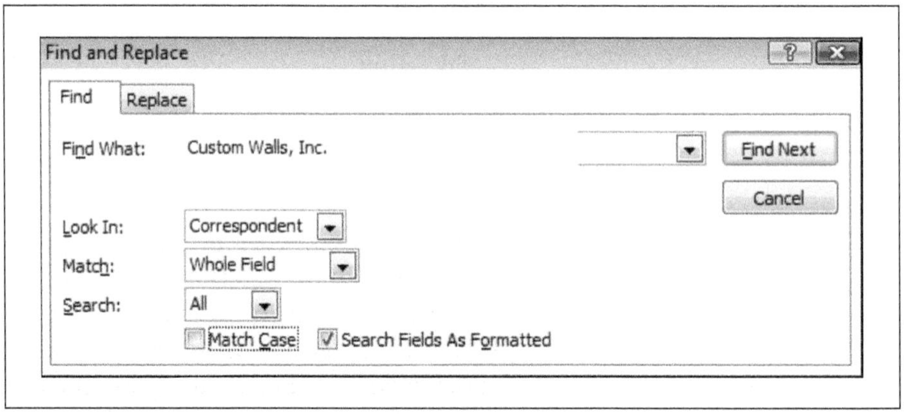

Source: Microsoft

Storage and Retrieval Procedures

What step in the storage procedures for numeric storage is not needed in other storage methods?

The steps for storage (inspecting, indexing, coding, number coding, cross-referencing, sorting, and storing) and retrieval (requisitioning, charging out, and following up) are as important in the numeric method as they are in all other RIM storage methods. In addition, the step of number coding is required in the procedure for numeric storage. All records are inspected, indexed, and the filing segment coded before a number or a G is assigned. The procedures to follow in storing and retrieving records in numeric systems are discussed next. Steps for coding numeric records are listed in Figure 9.6.

FIGURE 9.6 **Coding Procedures for Numeric Storage**

STEPS FOR CODING RECORDS FOR NUMERIC STORAGE
Coding
• Code the filing segment.
• Write an X in the margin beside cross-reference names or subjects.
• Underline the cross-reference name or subject with a wavy line.
Sorting
• Sort records that do not have preprinted numbers alphabetically before referencing the alphabetic index.
Number Coding
• Consult the alphabetic index for each record.
• Write the assigned file code number or a G in the upper right corner of the record.
• Assign the next available number—if a number has not been assigned—or a G.
• Enter the new file code number into the accession log.
• Write the code number or a G in the upper right corner of the record.

Inspecting and Indexing

Inspect records for release marks. Then index to determine the filing segment by which to store each record.

Coding

Code the filing segment and identify any needed cross-references by marking an X in the margin and underlining the cross-reference name or subject with a wavy line. Sort alphabetically any records that do not have preprinted numbers before consulting the alphabetic index to see whether a file code number or a G (GENERAL) has been assigned. For correspondents' names or subjects with numbers already assigned or preprinted on the record, code the record with the file code number by writing the assigned number in the top right corner of the record. The letter in Figure 9.7 shows the coded correspondent name and the code number already assigned to the name. Number 122 is written in the upper right corner of the letter. For correspondents or subjects with the letter G already assigned, the record will be stored in the general alphabetic file. Code the record with a G in the upper right corner.

For new correspondents or subjects with no assigned code number, write the letter G in the upper right corner of the documents. Make a database entry for the new correspondent or subject and indicate the file location to be G. Place the record into an alphabetic sorter for later storage in the general alphabetic file. The letter in Figure 9.8 on page 227 shows a document coded for the general alphabetic file.

FIGURE 9.7 **Coded Letter for Number File**

2 3 4 5 122

L/&/M/Advertising/Agency

80 Second Avenue
New York, NY 10022-1421
Telephone: 212-555-0146 Fax: 212-555-0187
www.l&mads.com

September 24, 20--

SEP 25, 20-- 11:03 A.M.

Ms. Graciella Melena
Melena & Daughters, Inc.
600 E. 52 Street
New York, NY 10022-2844

Dear Ms. Melena

1 2 3

Your ad with Kirkman/Products,/Inc. is well under way. Executives at Kirkman are more than a little excited about the advertising tie-in with your company. We have a two-page ad for spring distribution we would like to share with you and Juan Ramos, Advertising Director at Kirkman. X

Juan is eager to complete the work on this campaign. By the way, Kirkman is also willing to supply a personal appearance of one of its product designers for your spring exhibition. Kirkman has agreed to pay $47,000 for the first spring as if you will handle all productions costs. We can work out these arrangements in more detail at our joint meeting.

Melena & Daughters and Kirkman Products are uniquely compatible, Graciella. This cooperative effort crates a far more dynamic campaign for today's market than we could have developed from an independent effort. We are eager to show you what we have done.

I will call you next week to arrange a convenient time for a joint ad presentation.

Sincerely

L & M ADVERTISING AGENCY

J. R. McGuire RLG

J. R. McGuire, Advertising Coordinator

kac

FIGURE 9.8 **Coded Letter for Alphabetic File—Numeric Method**

2 G

4325 21 St., New York, NY 10022-1345
Telephone: 212-555-0197 Fax: 212-555-0198

June 5, 20--

JUN 7, 20-- 12:30 P.M.

Ms. Graciella Melena
Melena & Daughters, Inc.
600 E. 52 Street
New York, NY 10022-2844

Dear Ms. Melena

Last week I met with your friend Diane Pruiksma regarding the renovation of our office complex at 4325 21 St. here in the city. She suggested that I look at your work on the Theater Arts Building because she thought it was close to the type of makeover we are considering for our corporate offices.

Several employees from our company toured the building last week and agreed that it is an impressive piece of work. We are interested in knowing what you and your staff would propose for us. We have very specific needs in mind, but some creative projects we would leave to you.

Let me know how you would like to proceed. We prefer a meeting at our locations so that we can show you the changes in layout, communications services, and office equipment we have in mind. We are also eager to hear your suggestions and hope that you can prepare a proposal by the end of August.

Now that we have agreed to renovate, we are eager to get started. We are looking forward to an early meeting time that will be convenient for everyone.

Sincerely

Sumiyo Maekawae RLG

Sumiyo Maekawa

dsr

Number Coding

To assign file code numbers to a correspondent or subject, follow these steps:

1. When using a database accession log, create a new record. Key the correspondent's name or subject and current date (and other information) into the appropriate fields, and assign the next file code number. If a database is not used, make entries into the physical accession log to record the assigned number or the letter G for the name or subject.
2. Write the assigned number code on the record in the upper right corner.
3. If any cross-references are needed, enter the cross-reference name or subject into the database alphabetic index with the assigned file code number followed by an X at the end of the number (e.g., 122X). Key the name into the SEE field for the location of the record in the file.
4. Prepare a new folder with the file code number on its tab. Add the correspondent's name or the subject to the tab label if office policy requires this information.
5. Place the record into the folder with the top to the left, and place the folder into a number sorter for later storage in the numbered file.

Cross-Referencing

Where are cross-reference sheets filed in the numeric method?

Code all units in the cross-reference name or subject that has an X beside it in the margin. If the cross-reference name or subject does not exactly match the name or subject in the alphabetic index, write the correct cross-reference name or subject on the document, underline it with a wavy line, and number all units. *Do not store cross-references in numbered file folders.* File all cross-references in the general alphabetic file. Enter all cross-references into the database, as described previously in step 3. To call attention to cross-references in a database name file, consider using all capitals or bold type.

Sorting

Why are records sorted more than once for numeric storage?

Perform an initial alphabetic sorting before assigning file code numbers or the letter G to the records. After consulting the alphabetic index, write assigned codes in the upper right corners of the records, and assign all other necessary codes before placing the records into numeric or alphabetic sorters. If rough sorting was done as you prepared the records, move the sorter and its contents to the storage area. However, if you prefer to perform like tasks together, sort all records after you have indexed, coded, and prepared cross-reference entries. A quick sort before storage saves time. Stacking the numbered records in random groups by hundreds, for example, eliminates moving back and forth from drawer to drawer or shelf to shelf while storing records.

Storing

Store all records coded with numbers in correspondingly numbered folders with the most recent date on top. Store records coded G in the general alphabetic folders. Store them first alphabetically, according to the units in the filing segments, and then by dates within each name group, with the most recent date on top. File all cross-references into the alphabetic file.

Office policy determines the point at which accumulated records in the general alphabetic file require the assignment of a permanent code number. When that accumulation has occurred, remove the records from the general file, and take the following steps:

Why is the accession log referenced before records are coded for numeric storage?

1. Consult the accession log to determine the next available number. Enter the name of the correspondent or the subject and the file code number into the database file or the physical accession log. Record the current date.
2. Locate the correspondent's name in the alphabetic index. Replace the G with the file code number.
3. Locate all cross-references for the subject or correspondent's name. In the alphabetic index database, change the G on all cross-reference entries to the file code number followed by an X.
4. Re-code all records removed from the general file by crossing out the G and writing the assigned file code number above or beside it.
5. Prepare a new folder with the assigned file code on its tab (and possibly the correspondent's name or the subject).
6. Place all records into the new folder. Place the record with the most recent date on top.
7. Place the numbered folder in its correct numeric sequence into the number file.

CAREER CORNER

Job Description for Records Administrator

The following job description is an example of a career opportunity in records and information management in a law firm.

GENERAL INFORMATION

The records administrator is responsible for firm-wide records and information management, including off-site records centers. The records administrator reports to the managing partner.

RESPONSIBILITIES

- Supervise daily operations of all records centers.
- Manage records management software.
- Implement a records retention and destruction program, and ensure compliance in all records centers.

EXPERIENCE AND EDUCATION

- Bachelor's degree; CRM preferred
- Five years' experience in legal records management
- Demonstrated supervisory skills and experience
- Excellent oral and written communication skills
- Proficiency in office suite software and RIM software

Retrieving

When you remove records from numeric storage, use requisitions, OUT indicators, and a charge-out log in the same way you used them for alphabetic and subject records storage. With a database table, you can include an OUT Date field, Borrower's Name field, and Date Borrowed field to record charge-out information. When a record is removed from the file, an entry is made into the database table. To ensure the safe return of borrowed records, follow the same procedures described in Chapter 7. If OUT information is kept in the database, a filter or query could be used to show all borrowed OUT files, sorted by date.

Converting to Numeric Storage

Why would an organization change its storage system from alphabetic to numeric?

An organization may decide that a numeric arrangement would provide quicker RIM storage and retrieval than an existing alphabetic arrangement. Security may be another consideration for changing from alphabetic storage to consecutively numbered storage. A number on a storage container or file folder does not convey information to inquisitive persons. However, a name on a folder is instantly recognizable to anyone who sees it. File users may prefer an indirect access storage method that allows for a variety of useful indexes to locate stored records such as a database master index. Whatever the reason for a conversion, the procedure is time-consuming but not difficult.

The following steps convert an alphabetic file arrangement to a consecutively numbered arrangement:

1. Prepare numbered guides for every 10 folders in storage according to the sequence of numbers decided upon, such as 1–10–20, 100–110–120, 1000–1010–1020, and so on.
2. Remove each individual folder from storage, and assign a file code number from the accession log. Enter the filing segment for each correspondent name or subject into the database or accession log beside the assigned number. Enter the date.
3. Prepare a numbered label and affix it to the folder, or add the newly assigned number to the older label. Caution: Do not remove general folders from alphabetic storage; the reason is explained later in the chapter.
4. Key each filing segment for cross-references into an alphabetic index database. Key the assigned file code number and an X into the database.
5. Remove and destroy all cross-reference sheets and SEE ALSO cross-references from individual folders because the database now replaces those sheets. Database records can be sorted as needed or located without sorting by using the Find function.
6. Remove any permanent cross-reference guides within the group of folders being converted to the numeric method, and make database entries for the information on the guides.
7. Code each record in every folder with its newly assigned file code number in the upper right corner of the record.
8. Return the numbered folders to storage in correct numeric sequence.

How does using a database help filers in numeric storage and retrieval?

9. Create the general alphabetic file by coding all remaining records with the letter G. (All individual folders from alphabetic storage were converted to numbered folders and filed numerically.)
10. Key the name of each correspondent or subject in every general folder into the database. Database records can be sorted as needed or located with the Find function without sorting.

Advantages and Disadvantages

Every storage method has advantages and disadvantages. Consecutive numbering is no exception, as shown in Figure 9.9. This indirect access method has advantages for storing electronic records, such as CDs and DVDs, where labeling space is often limited. A numeric code identifies the records.

FIGURE 9.9 **Advantages and Disadvantages of Consecutive Numeric Storage**

CONSECUTIVE NUMERIC RECORDS STORAGE	
ADVANTAGES	**DISADVANTAGES**
1. Re-filing of numerically coded records is rapid because people recognize number sequences better and faster than alphabetic sequences. **2.** Expansion is easy and unlimited. New numbers can be assigned without disturbing the arrangement of existing folders or other stored records media. **3.** Transfer of inactive records is easy because the lowest numbers are the oldest records and are stored together. **4.** All cross-references are in the general alphabetic name database and do not congest the drawers or shelves where numbered records are filed. **5.** Security is provided because names do not appear on numeric captions on guides, folders, electronic records, and other records media. **6.** All records for one customer bear the same numeric code, keeping related records together. **7.** Time and effort in labeling is minimized because numbers can be affixed much more quickly than names, subjects, or project titles. **8.** Misfiled records are detected easily—numbers out of sequence are easier to detect than misfiled records arranged alphabetically.	**1.** Consecutive numeric is an indirect access method that requires reference to an alphabetic index. **2.** More guides are necessary for the numeric method; therefore, the cost of supplies can be higher. **3.** Consecutive numeric storage is more time-consuming than other methods. Records must first be sorted alphabetically and then resorted numerically prior to storage. Resorting is eliminated with a database and use of the Find function to locate specific names or numbers in the records file. **4.** Congestion occurs around the end of the file where new records are added. Records with the highest numbers are typically the most current and most active records. **5.** Numbers can be easily transposed, which causes misfiles.

A database record for each item shows this number, along with the originator's name, department, subject, special project, or any other meaningful category. The database record can be as comprehensive as necessary to identify and locate records. Even when CDs and DVDs are reused, the file code number remains the same; only the information in the record fields is updated. A complete list of correspondents' names, addresses, and other information is available from the alphabetic index or a correspondent database. These database files could be searched by any of the fields of information to find a particular record. Numeric database files are used frequently for inventories of equipment and supplies. Each item is assigned an identifying number, and pertinent fields of information are added to the database for data entry and retrieval.

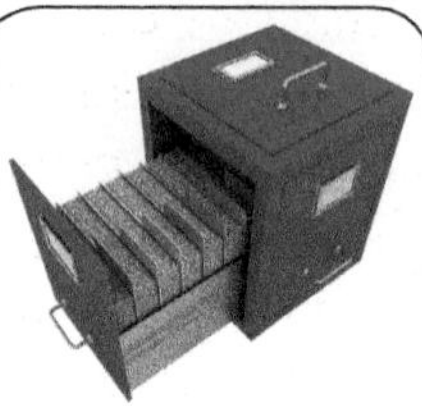

MY RECORDS

Home Inventory

What is a home inventory? Should you create a home inventory?

Creating a home inventory is a good idea. An inventory lists the value of your possessions and helps you keep track of warranties, receipts, and other information about the items in your home. Use the inventory to determine your homeowner's or renter's insurance needs as well as to provide details about your possessions in case of loss.

CREATE AN INVENTORY

To create an inventory, start by listing the rooms in your home. Next list the items in each room. You can find sample home inventory sheets on the Internet by using the search term *homeowner's inventory*. Here are sample inventory headings: Item, Model, Serial Number, Year Purchased, Cost, and Present Value.

MAINTAIN YOUR INVENTORY

Follow these suggestions for maintaining a home inventory:

- Keep receipts of major purchases to prove the value of an item in case of loss.
- Store warranties and/or user manuals with the receipt of the item.
- Photograph the contents of each room. Show cabinets and closets with open doors. If a closet is a walk-in, photograph inside the closet.
- Set a specific date to update the inventory annually, such as the beginning or end of Daylight Savings Time or the anniversary of an important family event.
- Store the photos and a copy of your inventory sheet in a safe place such as a safe deposit box or a fire-resistant box.
- When you replace possessions, update the inventory and remove all records about the old item. Make sure the records for the new item are stored.

Don't wait for a disaster to strike before you complete a home inventory!

NONCONSECUTIVE NUMBERING

nonconsecutive numbering: a system of numbers that has blocks of numbers omitted

Nonconsecutive numbering is a system of numbers that has blocks of numbers omitted. Records arrangements based on these nonconsecutive numbers use a sequential order that differs from a consecutive order of numbers normally read from left to right. This section explains the use of three of these methods: terminal-digit, middle-digit, and chronologic storage.

Terminal-Digit Storage

terminal-digit storage: a numeric storage method in which the last two or three digits of each number are used as the primary division under which a record is filed, and groups of numbers are read from right to left

Terminal-digit storage is a numeric storage method in which the last two or three digits of each number are used as the primary division under which a record is filed. Groups of numbers are read from right to left. The digits in the number are usually separated into groups by a space or hyphen.

The disadvantage of congestion that can occur at the end of a consecutive numeric storage area is eliminated with terminal-digit storage. This records storage method separates large numbers into groups of digits, which are easier to read. The terminal-digit storage method is used most effectively with thousands of folders whose numbers have reached at least five digits (10,000 or more). The words *terminal digit* refer to the end digits of a number (091 38 0297). Numbers may be assigned sequentially, or the digit groups may mean something specific. For example, the first group of numbers may be a customer identification number; the second group may indicate a sales district, salesperson, or department; the third group may indicate a date, branch office, or department.

Which set of digits in a terminal-digit number are the terminal digits?

The number may be a product number in which various groups of numbers refer to a sales department and/or a particular manufacturer or wholesaler. The numbers can have a variety of meanings, or they can simply be a sequentially assigned numeric code number.

The groups of numbers are identified as primary, secondary, and tertiary numbers reading from right to left.

TERTIARY (FOLDER NUMBER)	SECONDARY (GUIDE NUMBER)	PRIMARY (OR TERMINAL) FILE SECTION, DRAWER, OR SHELF NUMBER
35	14	65

An arrangement of numbers in terminal-digit sequence would look like the following illustration. The numbers in bold determine the correct numeric order in the file. The front of the file is at the top of the illustration.

786	67	**1258** (Front of File)
231	55	**2187**
189	40	**2891**
303	**99**	2891
947	28	**6314**
287	**29**	6314
502	64	**9284**
498	64	**9485**
502	64	9485 (End of File)

FIGURE 9.10 **Terminal-Digit Arrangement**

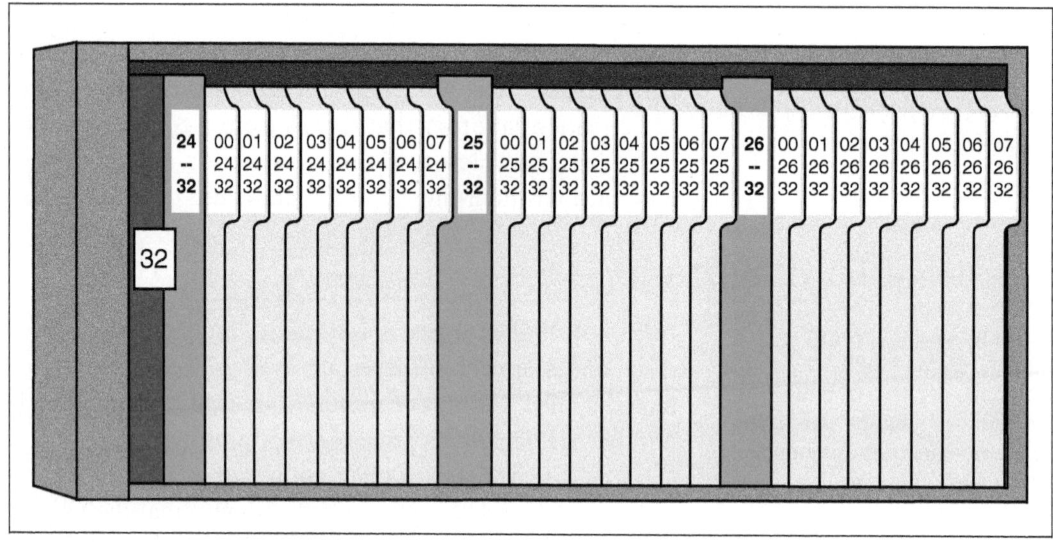

Primary numbers usually indicate a drawer or shelf number. If the volume of records stored is great, more than one drawer or shelf may be needed to hold all records with numbers ending in the same terminal (or primary) digits. Figure 9.10 shows the arrangement of folders in a portion of shelf 32.

The secondary numbers determine the primary guide captions. The section of the shelf shown begins with guide 24–32. If space had permitted, the entire 32 section would show guide 00–32 at the front of the drawer. Records are arranged behind each guide by the tertiary numbers—the digits at the extreme left of the number.

As new folders are stored, new guides are added to separate each group of 10 folders. The first section of the file shown in Figure 9.10 (the 24–32 section) has been expanded in Figure 9.11 by the addition of folders numbered

FIGURE 9.11 **Expansion of Terminal-Digit Arrangement**

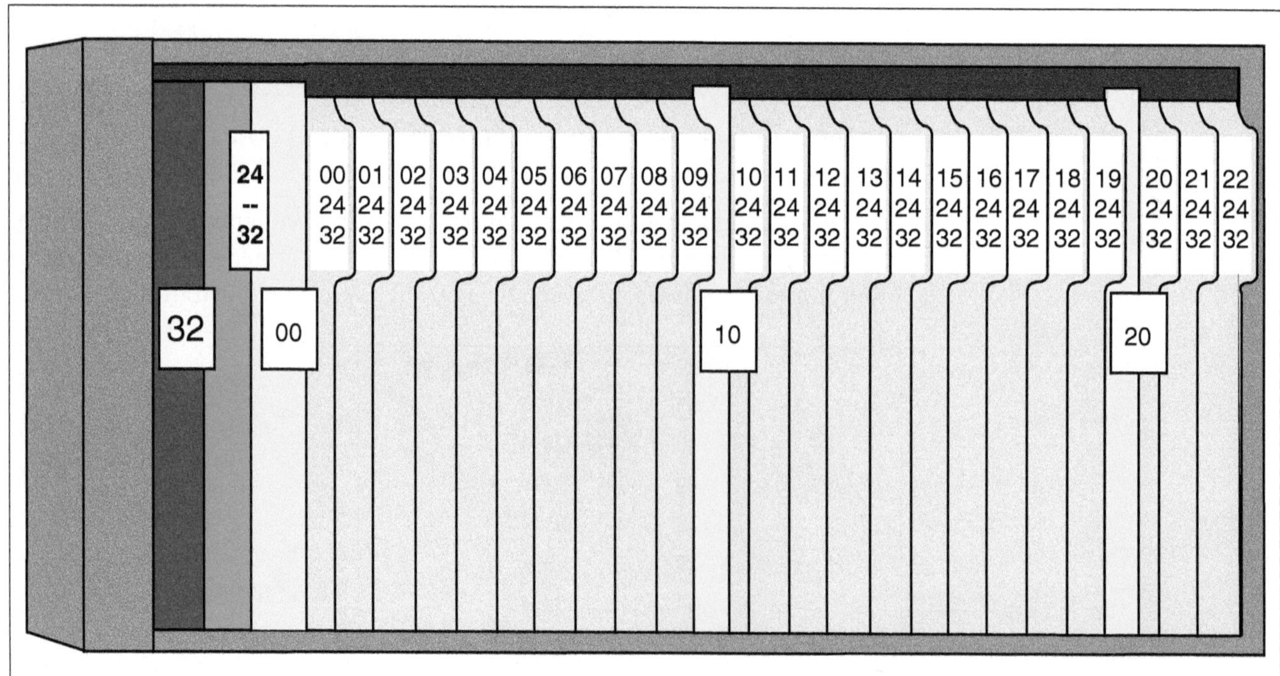

08–24–32 through 22–24–32. The tertiary numbers have increased from 00 through 07 to 00 through 22. Therefore, secondary guides 00, 10, and 20 were added in first position, and the primary guide for 24–32 was moved to the second position of the file shelf.

Why are records numbered 05 25 32 and 05 25 33 stored in different locations?

When sequentially numbered records, such as 05 25 32 and 05 25 33, are added to terminal-digit storage, these new and typically more active records are filed in different file locations. Distributing current records throughout a storage area avoids congestion in one particular storage area. Remember that in consecutive numeric storage these records would be stored next to each other at the end of the storage area.

Middle-Digit Storage

middle-digit storage: a numeric storage method in which the middle digits are used as the primary division for organizing the filing system

Middle-digit storage is another method of nonconsecutive numbering. Similar to terminal-digit storage, using this method avoids working with large numbers and overcomes the disadvantage of congestion at the end of the storage area. Middle-digit refers to the middle group of digits in a large number. **Middle-digit storage** is a numeric storage method in which the middle digits are used as the finding aid to organize the filing system. This method uses the middle two or three digits of each number as the primary division under which a record is filed. Groups of numbers are read from the middle to left, to right. Primary numbers are in the middle; numbers to the left are secondary; and numbers to the right are tertiary, or last.

SECONDARY (GUIDE NUMBER)	PRIMARY (FILE SECTION, DRAWER, OR SHELF NUMBER)	TERTIARY (FOLDER NUMBER)
35	14	65

An arrangement of numbers in middle-digit sequence would look like the following: the numbers in bold determine the correct numeric order:

947	**28**	6314 (Front of File)
287	**29**	6314
189	**40**	2891
231	**52**	2187
498	**64**	9485
502	64	9284
502	64	**9485**
786	**67**	1258
303	**99**	2891 (End of File)

FIGURE 9.12 **Middle-Digit Arrangement**

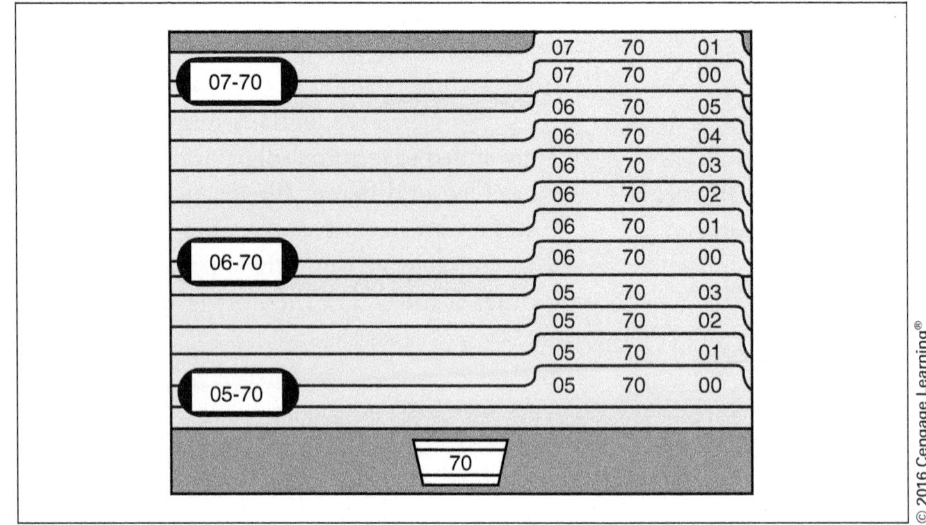

In Figure 9.12, all records with middle digits 70 are stored in one section. The digits on the left determine record sequence within the 70 drawer, followed by the digits on the right. The left digits determine the primary guide captions **05**–70, **06**–70, and **07**–70.

In the middle-digit method, blocks of sequentially numbered records are kept together. However, records are distributed through the files in blocks of 100. Records numbered 10 **70** 00 to 10 **70** 99 are filed together in one section; 10 **71** 00 to 10 **71** 99, in the next file section. The middle-digit method has additional value when the middle digits identify someone or something specific, and related records need to be kept together. If the middle digits represent a sales representative or a sales district, for example, all records for that individual or location are kept together in one block.

Chronologic Storage

chronologic storage: a method by which records are filed in date sequence, either in reverse sequence (with the most recent date on top) or forward sequence (with the oldest record first)

Chronologic storage is a method by which records are filed in date sequence, either in reverse sequence (with the most recent date on top) or forward sequence (with the earliest or oldest date on top). Users often refer to a chronologic file as a *chron file.* Exact chronologic storage is not well suited to letters or e-mail messages because of the need to keep together all records from, to, and about one individual or organization. Chronologic storage is often used for daily reports, deposit slips, freight bills, statements, and order sheets that may be best stored by date.

The chronologic principle is followed in all methods of storage as records are placed into folders. The most current records are at the front or back of the folder, thereby keeping the most recent records easily accessible. Tickler files are one form of chronologic storage. A tickler file may be kept electronically in a program such as Microsoft Outlook, as shown in Figure 9.13. You may want to refer to the discussion of tickler files in Chapter 6.

FIGURE 9.13 **Tickler File in Microsoft Outlook**

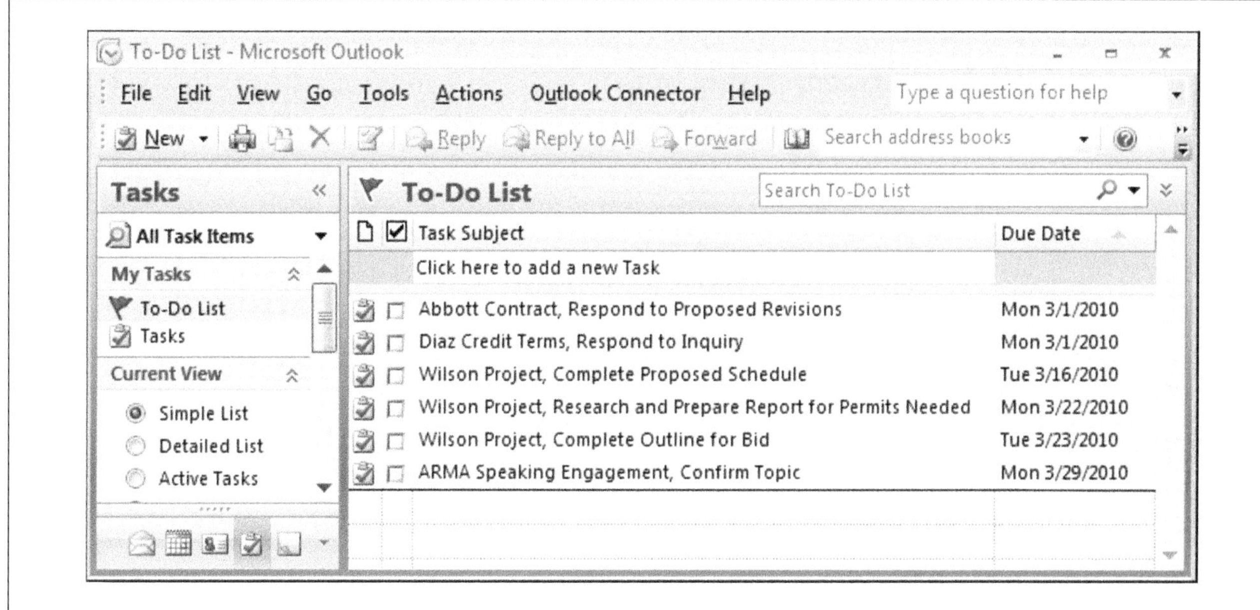

Source: Microsoft

OTHER NUMERIC CODING SYSTEMS

Numbers are sometimes added to encyclopedic arrangements of subject and geographic filing methods. Numbers help to eliminate misfiles in subject and geographic files that contain main subject divisions and numerous subdivisions. Numeric coding methods described in this section allow for coding necessary subdivisions.

Block-Numeric Coding

block-numeric coding: a coding system based on the assignment of number ranges to subjects

Block-numeric coding is a coding system based on the assignment of number ranges to subjects. Groups of numbers represent primary and secondary subjects such as the encyclopedic arrangement of a subject file discussed in Chapter 8.

Major subject divisions are assigned a block of round numbers, such as 100, 200, 300. Then, each subdivision is assigned a block of numbers within the major block of round numbers, such as 110, 120, 130. The more file expansion expected, the larger the blocks of numbers. The subdivision 110, for example, allows for additional subject subdivisions of subjects (111 to 119).

Duplex-Numeric Coding

duplex-numeric coding: a coding system using numbers (or sometimes letters) with two or more parts separated by a dash, space, or comma

Like block-numeric coding, duplex-numeric coding is also used in subject or geographic filing systems that contain major categories and subdivisions. **Duplex-numeric coding** is a coding system using numbers (or sometimes letters) with two or more parts separated by a dash, space, or comma.

How many subdivisions are possible with duplex-numeric coding?

An unlimited number of subdivisions is possible with this coding system. Subject subdivisions are added sequentially, however, and may not follow a strict alphabetic order. Notice that PAST BUDGETS comes before FUTURE NEEDS in the following example because FUTURE NEEDS was added to the file *after* PAST BUDGETS.

```
10  BUDGETS
    10-1        ACCOUNTING DEPARTMENT
                10-1-1  PAST BUDGETS
                10-1-2  FUTURE NEEDS
                10-1-3  RECEIPTS
    10-2        ENGINEERING DEPARTMENT
                10-2-1  PAST BUDGETS
                10-2-2  FUTURE NEEDS
    10-3        INFORMATION SYSTEMS DEPARTMENT
                10-3-1  PAST BUDGETS
```


Decimal-Numeric Coding

decimal-numeric coding: a numeric method of classifying records by subject, in units of 10 and coded for arrangement in numeric order

Decimal-numeric coding is a numeric method of classifying records by subject in units of 10 and coded for arrangement in numeric order. An unlimited number of subdivisions is permitted through the use of digits to the right of the decimal point.

Where is decimal-numeric coding most often used?

This method is used for classifying library materials and where large numbers of records arranged by subject or geographic location must be permanently grouped and when these records are subdivided into smaller groups.[3] It is called the *Dewey Decimal Classification (DDC) system.*

The system has nine general classes or main divisions (100–900). A tenth division (000) is used for records too general to be placed in any of the nine main divisions. Each main division can be divided into nine or fewer parts (110, 120, to 190). These nine parts can be divided further into nine additional groups (111, 112, to 119). Decimals are added for further divisions (111.1, 111.1.1). The DDC is not commonly used in an office. However, the use of decimals to subdivide records is a practical alternative to the dashes, spaces, and commas used in duplex-numeric coding to subdivide records.

Alphanumeric Coding

alphanumeric coding: a coding system that combines letters and numbers, in combination with punctuation marks, to develop codes for classifying and retrieving information

Alphanumeric coding is a coding system that combines letters and numbers, in combination with punctuation marks, to develop codes for classifying and retrieving information. Main subjects are arranged alphabetically, and their subdivisions are assigned a number. After all main subjects are determined, they are given a number (usually in groups of 10 or 100 to provide for expansion). More elaborate variations of this system may use

[3] ARMA International, *Establishing Alphabetic, Numeric and Subject Filing Systems* (Lenexa, KS: ARMA International, 2005), p. 15.

both letters and numbers and have numerous subdivisions as shown in the following example.

MGT-MANAGEMENT
    MGT-01 RECORDS MANAGEMENT
        MGT-01-01 STORAGE EQUIPMENT
        MGT-01-02 FILING SYSTEMS
            MGT-01-02-01 PHYSICAL
            MGT-01-02-02 ELECTRONIC
            MGT-01-02-03 PROCEDURES MANUAL
        MGT-01-03 ELECTRONIC RECORDS RETENTION SCHEDULE
        MGT-01-04 VITAL RECORDS RETENTION SCHEDULE
    MGT-02 SALES MANAGEMENT
        MGT-02-01 ADVERTISING

RECORDS MANAGEMENT IN ACTION

Preserving the World's Heritage

CyArk is a 501(c)(3) nonprofit organization dedicated to protecting the history of cultural heritage sites through advanced digital scanning, modeling, and photography techniques. Since 2003, the organization has modeled a number of locations, including Mt. Rushmore, Pompeii, and the ancient Mayan city of Tikal. In order to ensure that the world's cultural heritage is preserved for generations to come, CyArk worked with Iron Mountain, Crossroads Systems, and Spectra Logic to implement a comprehensive data protection, management, and archiving solution.

Far more detailed than even the best photograph, these models provide incredibly accurate, realistic views of every aspect of a particular site, giving them numerous applications for educational and cultural tourism settings. CyArk's model of Mt. Rushmore, for example, allows viewers to see the individual chisel marks on Teddy Roosevelt's mustache.

Newer, advanced technologies have helped CyArk capture more facets of each site it surveys. They are also requiring the organization to manage a greater volume of data than it did in the past. With fewer than 15 employees and a nonprofit designation to uphold, handling such a significant—and growing—amount of data put an incredible strain on CyArk's staff. It also raised concerns that the organization's existing storage and archiving process, which used expensive disk drives and stored backup data inside a local bank vault, would not provide the economies or security CyArk needed to safeguard data in perpetuity and further its mission goals.

Iron Mountain saw these challenges as an opportunity to deploy a cutting-edge solution that combines the cost efficiency and longevity of tape with the Linear Tape File System (LTFS) open standard. The company enlisted the assistance of Crossroads Systems and Spectra Logic.

As the first enterprise-level archive product to deploy LTFS, Crosswords Systems StrongBox® solution is a file-based, intelligent caching appliance that enables an entire tape library to appear like a standard disk on Network Attached Storage (NAS). CyArk can take the raw data from the field, enter it onto a server, and automatically transfer it into the LTFS library.

Any data that CyArk selects using the StrongBox interface is written to two high-capacity LTO-5 tapes—the first of which is stored locally in a Spectra Logic T950 library. The library also continuously monitors the health of the tape and the data residing on it.

Source: Iron Mountain Knowledge Center, retrieved from http://ironmountain.com/Knowledge-Center/Reference-Library/View-by-Document-Type/Case-Studies/C/CyArk.aspx

DATABASES FOR NUMERIC STORAGE

Earlier in this chapter, you read how database software can simplify creating the accession log and the alphabetic index required for a numeric file. All necessary information can be kept in one table for ready access and updating. When you design database queries to sort file code numbers for the accession log, remember that the computer sorts within a database field from left to right. With terminal-digit or middle-digit numeric storage, use a separate field for each part of the number to aid in sorting and preparing the accession log and alphabetic index. For example, with terminal-digit numbering, set up three fields in the database table for the numeric code: Tertiary, Secondary, and Primary. Enter the numeric code for each group of numbers in its correct field. Data entry is simplified and less prone to error if the order of the numeric codes in the table matches the normal left-to-right reading sequence.

To sort these numbers as an accession log and determine the next number to be assigned, create a query to display fields in this order: Primary, Secondary, and Tertiary. Then sort each of these three columns in descending order. The query results would be displayed as shown in Figure 9.14.

FIGURE 9.14 **Terminal-Digit Accession Log Query Results**

Primary	Secondary	Tertiary	Name or Subject	Date
9485	64	502	WXTV	9/30/20--
9485	64	498	Cleaning Supplies	9/14/20--
9284	64	502	Chou Meiling	10/02/20--
6314	29	287	Balawi Vincent	10/03/20--
6314	28	947	GlorePost Dorothy CPA	9/24/20--
2891	99	303	LaPlata Motor Sports	9/04/20--
2891	40	189	McCutchen Alex Jr	9/17/20--
2187	55	231	Brentwood Apartments	9/18/20--
1258	67	786	Applications	9/04/20--

Note that the numbers in the query results are in reverse order to the numeric file code to allow the last four digits (Primary field) to be sorted first, the middle digits (Secondary field), second, and the first three digits (Tertiary field), last. The last number assigned—502 64 9485—is shown at the top of the list. The next number available for assignment is 503 64 9485.

A list similar to that used for terminal-digit numbering can be generated to produce a sorted list of numeric codes for middle-digit numbering. Numeric codes for middle-digit numbering would be entered on the query design with the middle set of numbers (Primary field) first; the left-most set of numbers (Secondary field), second; and the last group of numbers (Tertiary field), third. Sorting for these three fields would follow the same order. The middle-digit numbers could be sorted from only two fields (by combining the Primary and Secondary numbers into one field because they read from left to right and would be sorted in that order). However, using the same practice for either method of numbering reduces confusion and also increases the flexibility to change later to terminal-digit or consecutive numbering without changing the table.

When using the accession log for a nonconsecutive numbering system, the number on the top line of the query results table may not show the next number to be assigned. Remember that in a particular office, the Primary number may indicate a drawer or shelf; the Secondary number, the section of the shelf or drawer; and the tertiary number, the order of the file in that section.

Another office may have different categories assigned for the number groupings. For example, the first group of numbers could indicate a customer identification number; the second, a branch office; and the third, a department. The appropriate grouping for a specific record would determine where to look on the database-generated accession log to locate the next number to be assigned. For a large volume of records, however, you may need to use the database Filter function to show only the categories that pertain to the group of records that you are coding.

A convenient feature for database records is the ability to sort and print mailing labels. Mailing labels must be pre-sorted to take advantage of bulk mailing rates. Computer-generated mailing labels can be sorted by ZIP Code without entering parts of the ZIP Code into separate fields because these numbers are sorted in sequential order as read from left to right.

CHAPTER REVIEW AND APPLICATIONS

KEY POINTS

- Records can be numbered consecutively, numbered in combination with geographic locations or subjects, or stored in nonconsecutive filing arrangements.
- Components of the consecutive numbering method include (1) a numbered file, (2) an alphabetic file, (3) an accession log, and (4) an alphabetic index.
- The accession log is a serial list of numbers assigned to records in a numeric storage system. It also provides the next number available for assignment.
- The alphabetic index is a reference to a numeric file, arranged alphabetically. It is used when the number code for a name or subject is not known. Because the index must be referenced before storing or retrieving a record, numeric records storage is an indirect access method.
- Steps for storing records in a numeric system include inspecting, indexing, coding, number coding, cross-referencing, sorting, and storing.
- Terminal-digit storage creates an even distribution of consecutively numbered records throughout a numeric system, and middle-digit storage allows blocks of related records to be stored together sequentially.
- Chronologic storage is used in some aspect of almost every filing method. Records from the same correspondent are arranged in folders by date, and tickler files are arranged by date to serve as reminders of due dates.
- Block-numeric coding and duplex-numeric coding combine numeric codes with subject or geographic categories, and alphanumeric coding uses alphabetic subject abbreviations with a numbering system.
- Computer databases are important for efficient numeric records storage. Improved efficiency of records management derives from the computer's ability to select particular records quickly, to identify their numeric code, to sort records so that a specific record or numeric code is located quickly, and to prepare lists and reports from stored information in a variety of formats.

TERMS

accession log
alphabetic index
alphanumeric coding
block-numeric coding
chronologic storage
consecutive numbering method
decimal-numeric coding
duplex-numeric coding
middle-digit storage
nonconsecutive numbering
numeric records management
terminal-digit storage

REVIEW AND DISCUSS

1. Define *numeric records management*, and list three reasons for storing records by the numeric method. (Obj. 1)

2. Why is expansion easier with numeric than with subject filing? (Obj. 1)

3. List and describe the components of consecutive numeric storage. (Obj. 2)

4. What steps are used when preparing records for numeric storage? (Obj. 2)

5. Explain why records in numeric storage may be coded with either the letter G or a number. (Obj. 2)

6. When are records transferred from the general alphabetic file to the numbered file? (Obj. 2)

7. Why should a general alphabetic file be placed at the beginning, rather than at the end, of a consecutively numbered storage arrangement? (Obj. 2)

8. How are cross-references prepared in the consecutive numbering method? How are they numbered? (Obj. 2)

9. When an alphabetic arrangement is converted to a consecutively numbered arrangement, where will the general folders in the alphabetic file be located in the numeric storage arrangement? Will records in these folders be coded with a number? Why or why not? (Obj. 3)

10. List at least three advantages and three disadvantages of consecutive numeric records storage. (Obj. 4)

11. Explain how numbers are sorted in consecutive numbering, terminal-digit numbering, and middle-digit numbering. (Obj. 5)

12. Give at least one way that terminal-digit and middle-digit numbering are alike and one way that they are different. (Obj. 5)

13. Define chronologic storage and explain how it is used. (Obj. 6)

14. Give at least one way that block-numeric, duplex-numeric, decimal-numeric, and alphanumeric coding are alike and one way they are different. (Obj. 7)

15. What are two ways that database software makes numeric data storage and use easy and fast? (Obj. 8)

APPLICATIONS

9-1 Arrange Physical Files (Obj. 5)

1. Manually arrange the numbers below in terminal-digit order.
2. Manually arrange the numbers below in middle-digit order.
3. Manually arrange the numbers below in consecutive order.

24 15 38	18 03 01	16 74 34	17 34 60	27 11 82	21 32 71
21 33 71	26 00 02	17 33 60	19 31 01	27 10 82	20 33 70
29 17 50	16 74 32	29 17 51	18 31 02	17 31 01	27 11 42

9-2 Sort Database Records (Obj. 5)

The numbers in Application 9-1 have been entered into a database table so that they can be sorted for terminal-digit, middle-digit, and consecutive numbering. The first group of two digits is in the Group 1 field; the second group of two digits is in the Group 2 field; and the third group of two digits is in the Group 3 field.

Data File

1. Download the data file *9-2 Number Arrangements* to a computer or a removable storage device, and then open it with Microsoft® Access.

2. Create a query based on the Number Arrangements table to sort the numbers in terminal-digit filing order. Sort in descending order. Save the query as "Terminal-Digit Order," and print the query results.
3. Create a query based on the Number Arrangements table to sort the numbers in middle-digit filing order. Sort in descending order. Save the query as "Middle-Digit Order," and print the query results.
4. Create a query based on the Number Arrangements table to sort the numbers in consecutive filing order. Sort in descending order. Save the query as "Consecutive Order," and print the query results.
5. Use the query results to check your answers for steps 1–3 in Application 9-1.

9-3 Learn More About Decimal-Numeric Coding (Obj. 7)

Decimal-numeric coding, or the Dewey Decimal Classification (DDC) system, as stated earlier, is used in libraries and other organizations. The Online Computer Library Center (OCLC®), Inc., is a nonprofit, membership, computer library service and research organization dedicated to the public services of furthering access to the world's information and reducing library costs. Answer the following questions based on information found on the OCLC website.

1. Go to www.oclc.org.

2. Where is the world headquarters of the Online Computer Library Center (OCLC) organization located?

3. Search the site, using the search term *DDC*. Click the link to the Dewey Decimal Classification (DDC) system. What is the current print edition of the DDC?

4. Return to the OCLC homepage. Click About. Click Careers at OCLC (at the bottom of the page). Click Our locations. Click the map stickpins to locate another location in the United States and two locations outside the United States.

SIMULATION

Job 11 Consecutive Number Document Filing

Job 12 Terminal-Digit Numeric Document Filing

Continue working with Auric Systems, Inc.

Complete Jobs 11 and 12.

ADDITIONAL RESOURCES

For data files, Microsoft® Access tutorials and more, go to www.cengagebrain.com.

CHAPTER 10

Geographic Records Management

LEARNING OBJECTIVES

1. Explain the need for geographic records management and the kinds of organizations that might use this method.
2. Describe the geographic records storage method and procedures for this method.
3. Explain the use of an alphabetic index in the geographic storage method.
4. Describe the types of cross-references used in the geographic storage method and how they are stored.
5. Describe how files are arranged using compass terms and how this method differs from general alphabetic filing.

© GrabMaps/www.Shutterstock.com.

ON THE JOB

Dr. Eugenia K. Brumm, CRM, FAI, a director in the Records and Information Management Practice in the Legal Operations Consulting area at Huron Consulting Group, has been in the records management field for 20 years as a practitioner, consultant, and academic. Dr. Brumm observed, "Over the past several years, my consulting projects have brought me into a variety of very large, global organizations. Only a handful of these organizations have stored a significant amount of physical records in centralized locations. In some instances, the centralized locations—off limits to unauthorized personnel—are staffed by personnel who control access to the records and handle records requests and checkout. Such situations often are found in highly regulated industries, such as pharmaceutical, and in confidential information departments such as Human Resources. Staff members in the centralized locations follow basic storage and retrieval procedures for hard-copy records.

In other instances, according to Dr. Brumm, small department-specific, physical records repositories are set up on the honor code. Users can retrieve hard-copy files and, according to procedure, are required to complete an OUT card. File users often do not follow proper procedures. As a result, the missing files and records, as well as the disturbance of the file plan within these file rooms, make retrieval difficult for all users.

GEOGRAPHIC RECORDS STORAGE

What are some specialized fields that use storage methods based on location?

geographic records management: a method of storing and retrieving records by location using a geographic filing system

geographic filing system: the classification of records by geographic location usually arranged by numeric code or in alphabetic order

You have already studied numeric storage and alphabetic storage by name and by subject. In this chapter, you learn a third storage method closely related to subject records management that uses alphabetic and numeric filing and indexing rules. Some types of information, especially in specialized activities, are more easily accessed based on location within a facility, a locality, a state or province, a country, or a continent. Business activities spanning wide geographic areas demand intelligent business decisions based on location. Specialized fields, such as natural sciences, the oil and gas industry, property records in city/county/state or federal governments, and the facility management profession, use storage methods based on location.

Geographic records management is a method of storing and retrieving records by location using a geographic filing system. A **geographic filing system** is the classification of records by geographic location usually arranged by numeric code or in alphabetic order.[1]

In this age of e-commerce and dot.com companies, communication and commerce, even for small businesses, can involve a worldwide audience. The automobile industry is an example of a widespread international business operation. American automobile manufacturers, such as General Motors and Ford, do not limit their markets or component purchases to this country, and companies from countries such as Japan produce and sell a variety of cars in the United States. Even state and local governments establish branch offices in other countries to promote foreign trade. Clearly, the global economy creates business opportunities that extend to locations all around the world. High-tech communications and satellite networks facilitate interactions for multiple locations worldwide.

Scientific institutions that conduct research and house the results of the research may use geographic storage for documentation as well as specimens collected in the field. For example, a large natural sciences academy includes a herbarium that houses plant collections. It is the primary repository and source of information for many well-known botanists. The herbarium uses a regional geographic filing system for storing materials about specimens collected from around the world and housed at the herbarium. The file plan includes local (nearby states alphabetic by name), other parts of North America north of Mexico (with states, and then provinces, in alphabetic order), Latin America (all of western hemisphere from Mexico south), Europe, the Middle East, Africa, Asia, and the Pacific Islands (including Australia and New Zealand). Figure 10.1 shows the arrangement of records by region for the specimen files. The materials are also used to generate color-coded maps of the geographic system.

In another example, a major oceanography library has an outstanding collection of expedition reports and over 78,000 maps. The map collection includes a large collection of hydrographic/bathymetric charts. The map collection is arranged alphabetically by national hydrographic agency and then in a geographic filing arrangement within each agency.

[1]ARMA International, *Glossary of Records and Information Management Terms*, 4th ed. (Lenexa, KS: ARMA International, 2012), p. 13.

FIGURE 10.1 **Herbarium Files**

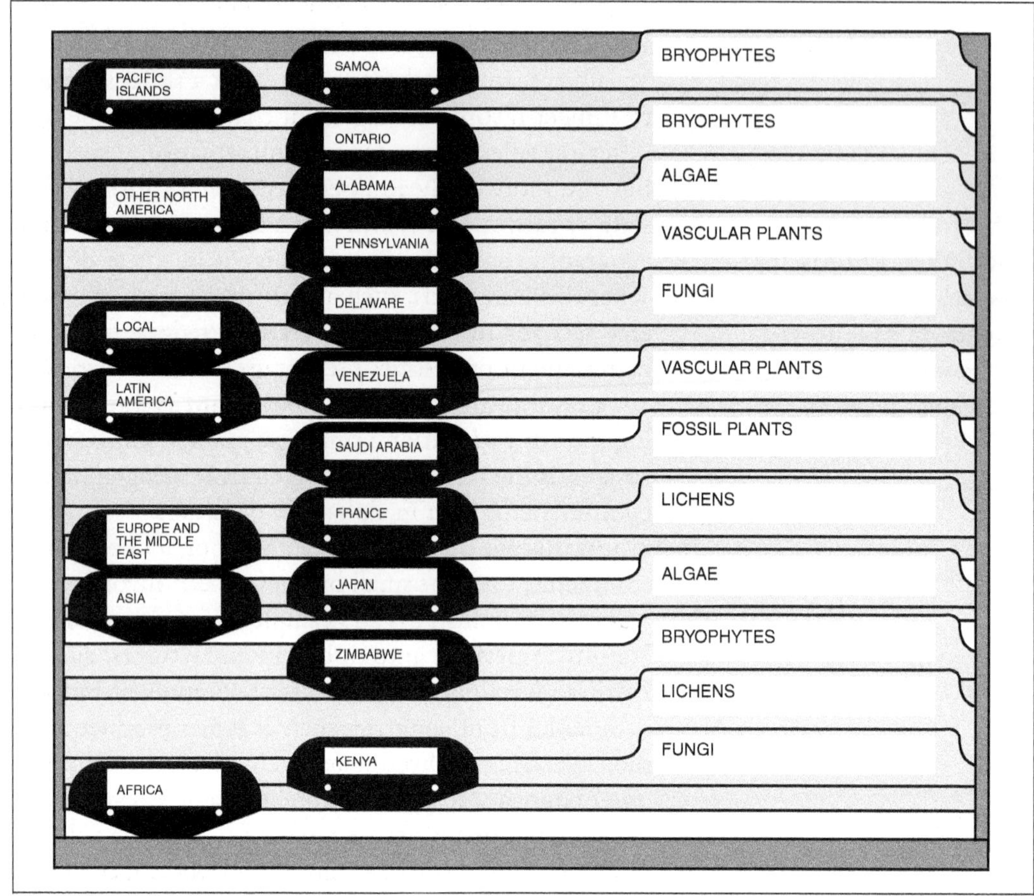

The oil and gas industry needs to track oil and gas resources by location worldwide. A major oil company files its information related to specific oil wells (as shown in Figure 10.2) by a standard numbering system established by the American Petroleum Institute that is used to code the material by location.

FIGURE 10.2 **Petroleum Companies May Use Geographic Records Equipment**

The ID number includes codes for state, county, and oil well number. For example, ID#42-501-12345 would be state #42 (Texas), county #501 (Harris County), and Oil Well #12345.

Records of property such as homes, businesses, new developments, parks, and government offices are important for proving ownership, for obtaining necessary permits, and for responding to 911 calls or other emergencies. Finding ownership, responding to emergencies, or issuing permits is faster and more efficient when the records are arranged by location.

What types of organizations might use geographic records management for facilities management?

Some large corporations, government agencies, and universities monitor and track the maintenance of a great number of buildings, grounds, and equipment through facility management. In addition, new construction or reconstruction must also be monitored and related to existing records. For example, a large university tracks construction projects on campus. The campus map is divided into 26 alphabetic sectors, starting in the east with A and ending in the west with Z. Each time a building was added in a sector, a new code was created, A01, A02, A03 through Z07, and so on. The building codes translated into coordinates such as A1 or B52 and so on.

To track projects, a number is added to the end of the building code. For example, A01-04 is the fourth renovation on building A01 (Science Center). The codes include the type of construction. For example, 1 is off campus, 2 is renovation, 3 is original construction, and 4 is infrastructure (across sectors/ buildings). A project code that reads 3-Z01 is the original construction of the first building in sector Z, which coordinates with a particular building such as the Medical Center.

A similar example is a large gas and electric utility that uses coordinates internal to the plant to identify the location of equipment (fittings, valves, subsystems, pipe runs, compressors, etc.), and each piece of equipment or pipe run has a tag number associated with it. The tag number is entered into a database to access the specification sheet, drawing, bill of materials, and operations and maintenance manual for the item. The tag number is comprised of several components. It includes the area number of the gas plant (170), then the system type (s5steam, o5oil, g5gas), then the line number or system number it was located on (221), and finally a size and item number (8-1234). So tag #170-G-221-8-1234 is

- in gas plant area 170,
- a gas system (G),
- gas line number 221,
- 8 inch, and
- item #1234.

What other types of businesses might use geographic records storage?

Other examples of businesses that may store records by the geographic method include:

- Multinational companies with plants, divisions, and customers outside the boundaries of the United States
- E-commerce businesses that need information about customer locations and target sales areas

- Insurance companies, franchised operations, banks, and investment firms that have many branches (possibly sales offices) at different geographic locations within the United States and have a high volume of intracompany physical communications
- Businesses that are licensed to operate in specific states and whose records are kept according to those states
- Utility companies (electricity, gas, telephone, water) whose utility facilities and services and customers are listed by location within their service area
- Real estate agencies that list their properties by areas such as foreign countries, divisions of countries or cities, groupings of subdivision names, or streets within a metropolitan area
- Scientific and other publications that file photographs and slides by location

CAREER CORNER

Job Description for Medical Records Technician

The following job description is an example of a position with the Department of Veteran Affairs, Veteran Affairs, Veterans Health Administration

GENERAL INFORMATION

The individual in this position reviews patients' medical records to extract medical, laboratory, pharmaceutical, demographic, social, and administrative data.

RESPONSIBILITIES

- Ensure maintenance and accuracy of diagnostic and procedural statistics for facility.
- Select and assign codes from the current version of one or more coding systems, depending on regular/recurring duties.
- Identify the principal diagnosis and procedure for inpatient discharges.
- Codes diagnoses for VA registries such as Agent Orange, Ionizing Radiation, Persian Gulf, Prisoner of War, and so on.

EXPERIENCE AND EDUCATION

- Knowledge of medical terminology, anatomy, disease process, treatments, diagnostic tests, and medications to ensure proper code selection
- At least 2 years' experience that demonstrates ability to perform the duties, OR
- Associate's degree with a major field of study in medical records technology/health information technology that was accredited by the American Health Information Management Association (AHIMA) at the time that the program was completed, OR
- Experience/education combinations such as an associate's degree in a field other than medical records/health information will substitute for 18 months of required experience, OR
- Completion of a course for medical technicians, hospital corpsmen, medical service specialist, or hospital training obtained in a training course given by the US Armed Forces or the US Maritime Service may be substituted on a month-for-month basis for up to one year of experience
- English language proficiency

Source: Adapted from www.usajobs.gov/GetJob/ViewDetails/360788300, accessed February 22, 2014.

geographic information system (GIS): a computer system designed to allow users to collect, manage, and analyze large volumes of data referenced to a geographic location by some type of geographic coordinates such as longitude and latitude

Many geographic filing systems are used to support an internal geographic information system. A **geographic information system (GIS)** is a computer system designed to allow users to collect, manage, and analyze large volumes of data referenced to a geographic location by some type of geographic coordinates such as longitude and latitude. It lets the user query or analyze a database and receive the results in the form of a map. Geographic information systems are increasingly considered essential components of effective engineering, planning, and emergency management operations.

ADVANTAGES AND DISADVANTAGES OF GEOGRAPHIC RECORDS STORAGE

Like any records system, geographic records management has advantages and disadvantages; however, when information is requested and referenced by location, records need to be stored by location. In these situations, the advantages outweigh the disadvantages. This section describes advantages and disadvantages of geographic records management.

Advantages

Why use geographic records storage?

The principal advantage of geographic storage is that operations relating to a specific location are filed together. It provides reference to information specific to certain geographic areas for making decisions about those locations or for compiling statistics relative to the locations. For example, storing records by building name and location is a means of monitoring all maintenance activity for that building. An analysis of records can be used constructively to note (1) the types of equipment that must be maintained and how often maintenance is done; (2) the kinds of maintenance or operational problems that have occurred most often and how soon equipment must be replaced; (3) the buildings that require the most maintenance and resources to do that maintenance; or (4) the buildings that must be updated to meet new codes. If equipment is moved from one building to another, geographic file guides and folders are easily rearranged. Each geographic area in storage is a unit or a group, and the shift of groups of records is easily accomplished by moving an entire group from one file location to another.

Disadvantages

What makes using geographic records storage time consuming?

The principal disadvantage of geographic storage is that the user must know the geographic location, or an index must be created and maintained. For instance, customer records filed by location require an alphabetic index of all their names and addresses. If the location of a customer is not known, an alphabetic index must be referenced to learn the location before a record can be filed or retrieved from the geographic file. Like the subject and numeric storage methods, geographic storage may require two operations to store and retrieve a record—a check of the index for the correct file location and then the physical search of the file. Another disadvantage of the geographic method is the complexity of the guide and folder arrangements that may be required in some large systems. For example, a geographic arrangement takes more time to establish than an alphabetic name or subject file when the nature of the organization requires many subdivisions. Storing and retrieving records can be more time consuming, too, because reference must be made first to an area (such as a state), then to a location within that area (such as a city), and finally to a name and address.

Why are cross-references needed in a geographic storage system?

Cross-references are necessary in the geographic storage system for both alphabetic filing methods and numeric filing methods. Alphabetic cross-references may include, for example, names of organizations having more than one address or organizations located at one address and doing business under other names at other locations. Although place names are typically sequenced alphabetically, geographic arrangements sometimes combine alphabetic and numeric arrangements. Records from global locations are sometimes written in the native language of the country producing the record. At the very least, city and country names are written in the native language. In some instances, the English language equivalent of the city/country name may be different.

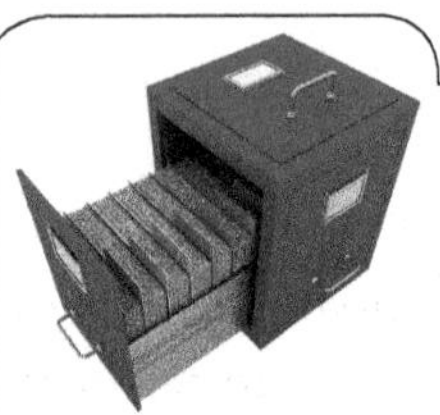

MY RECORDS

Sharing Your Information on Social Media Sites

Using social media sites, such as Facebook, can be an enjoyable way to share personal information and express your opinions with family and friends. It is also a way to keep updated on activities and events happening in each other's lives and to share photos and videos. Through Twitter, you can share your opinion with celebrities as well as the media. You can also synch your accounts so that whatever you tweet or post on another social media site will automatically appear on your Facebook page.

Once you share information through a social media site, it cannot be retrieved, and you are responsible for the content of that information. Anything shared with friends or others becomes information that resides in their social media accounts. That information could again be shared with other friends who could share it still again.

One way of keeping your information within a circle of friends and family is to create a group and invite only select members. By adjusting the privacy settings, outside access to information posted by members, to the group, can be restricted.

However, even deactivating your Facebook account will not immediately remove your own data, and some information may be retained for legal purposes or at Facebook managers' discretion to improve their services.

Twitter cautions users with this statement posted in their terms of service: "What you say on Twitter may be viewed all around the world instantly." Twitter also states that their "Services are primarily designed to help you share information with the world."

In summary, any personal information that you share through a social media site can become public knowledge and shared with individuals for whom it was not intended. The best policy is not to post onto social media sites any information that you want to keep private.

Source: Facebook Data Use Policy, https://www.facebook.com/about/privacy/your-info, accessed January 17, 2014.

Source: Twitter Privacy Policy, https://twitter.com/privacy, accessed January 20, 2014.

For instance, Mumbai, India, is known in many US organizations as Bombay, India, and Firenze, Italia, is known as Florence, Italy. The records are usually filed in the order of the US known name, so a cross-reference to other languages is required.

The advantages of using geographic records management outweigh these disadvantages for business operations requiring information accessed by geographic location.

GEOGRAPHIC RECORDS STORAGE ARRANGEMENTS

The geographic arrangement of records in an office depends upon the following:

- The type of business
- The way reference is made to records (i.e., by building, by state, by ZIP Code, by geographic region, by country)
- The geographic areas related to records

The geographic arrangement can be as simple as a file of city streets or countries of the world. More complex systems include subdivisions and are arranged in order from major to minor geographic units; for example, (1) country name, (2) state name or state equivalent (provinces, for example), (3) city name, and (4) correspondent's name. In general, the filing segment in geographic records storage includes geographic filing units first, followed by the correspondent's name. If geographic areas are subdivided by subject, such as Accounts Receivable, Sales, or Purchasing, the subject area would be considered second and then the correspondent's name. Subdivisions by subject may be appropriate for centralized records in a company that maintains extensive business operations through branch offices in different locations. The location of the branch office could be subdivided by operational functions and then by correspondent names. Most likely, such centralization of records would be through centralized electronic records accessed in various company sites through an intranet.

Compass Terms

compass point: any of 32 horizontal directions indicated on the card of a compass

compass term: a compass point used as part of a company name or subject

How are filing segments containing compass terms coded?

Some records and file guides in geographic filing use compass point terms. A **compass point** is any of 32 horizontal directions indicated on the card of a compass.[2] A **compass term** is a compass point used as part of a company name or subject. For example, Southern Mutual Life Insurance Corporation contains a compass term (Southern). When filing records with compass terms, each word or unit in a filing segment containing compass terms is considered a separate filing unit. If the term includes more than one compass

[2] Dictionary.com, http://dictionary.reference.com/browse/compass+point?s=t, accessed February 18, 2014.

point, the term should be treated as it is written.[3] This procedure is the same procedure that you learned earlier for alphabetic filing of company or organization names. The following table shows examples of indexed names that contain compass terms.

Examples of Names with Compass Terms

	FILING SEGMENT	INDEXING ORDER OF UNITS			
	Name	**Key Unit**	**Unit 2**	**Unit 3**	**Unit 4**
1.	North West Plumbing Inc.	North	West	Plumbing	Inc
2.	North Western Imaging	North	Western	Imaging	
3.	North-West Computer Co.	Northwest	Computer	Co	
4.	Northwest Kitchens	Northwest	Kitchens		
5.	Northwestern Refrigeration Co.	Northwestern	Refrigeration	Co	

How can geographers and other scientists use compass terms in scientific document filing?

Compass terms are frequently applied to technical studies conducted by geographers, geologists, geophysicists, and other scientists studying the earth's surface. To maintain a geographically organized file in these circumstances, the compass term is treated as an adjective and is placed after the name. Again, this procedure is used only in scientific document filing. The table below shows examples of names that contain compass terms indexed for scientific document filing.

Examples of Names with Compass Terms (Scientific Document Filing)

	FILING SEGMENT	INDEXING ORDER OF UNITS FOR SCIENTIFIC DOCUMENT FILING		
	Name	**Key Unit**	**Unit 2**	**Unit 3**
1.	North Andreas Fault	Andreas	Fault	North
2.	Northwest Mackinaw Island	Mackinaw	Island	Northwest
3.	Ohio	Ohio		
4.	Eastern Pacific Rim	Pacific	Rim	Eastern
5.	Southern Point Island	Point	Island	Southern
6.	Tennessee	Tennessee		

Dictionary Storage Arrangement

dictionary arrangement: an arrangement of records in alphabetic order (A–Z).

A **dictionary arrangement** for geographic records is an arrangement of records in alphabetic order (A–Z). All types of entries in the system (names, subjects, titles, etc.) are interfiled. Use the dictionary arrangement when filing

[3] ARMA International, *Establishing Alphabetic, Numeric and Subject Filing Systems* (Lenexa, KS: ARMA International, 2005), p. 21.

single geographic units such as all streets, all cities, all states, or all countries. Two guide plans may be used: the lettered guide plan or the location name guide plan.

What are two commonly used guide plans?

Lettered Guide Plan

lettered guide plan: an arrangement of geographic records with primary guides labeled with alphabetic letters

A **lettered guide plan** is an arrangement of geographic records with primary guides labeled with alphabetic letters. The lettered guide plan can be used in any geographic arrangement. For a large volume of records stored geographically, alphabetic guides cut storage and retrieval time by guiding the eye quickly to the correct alphabetic section of storage.

Figure 10.3 shows a dictionary arrangement of records by country in a lettered guide plan. Primary guides are one-fifth-cut lettered guides arranged in a straight line in the first position (from left to right). General country folders are third-cut folders arranged in a straight line in the third position (far right) in the file drawer. As you can see, a lettered guide plan may be excessive in a file consisting of only a few diverse names.

Location Name Guide Plan

location name guide plan: an arrangement of geographic records with primary guides labeled with location names

A **location name guide plan** is an arrangement of geographic records with primary guides labeled with location names. Use the location name guide plan when location names are few but diverse.

FIGURE 10.3 **Dictionary Arrangement of Records, Lettered Guide Plan**

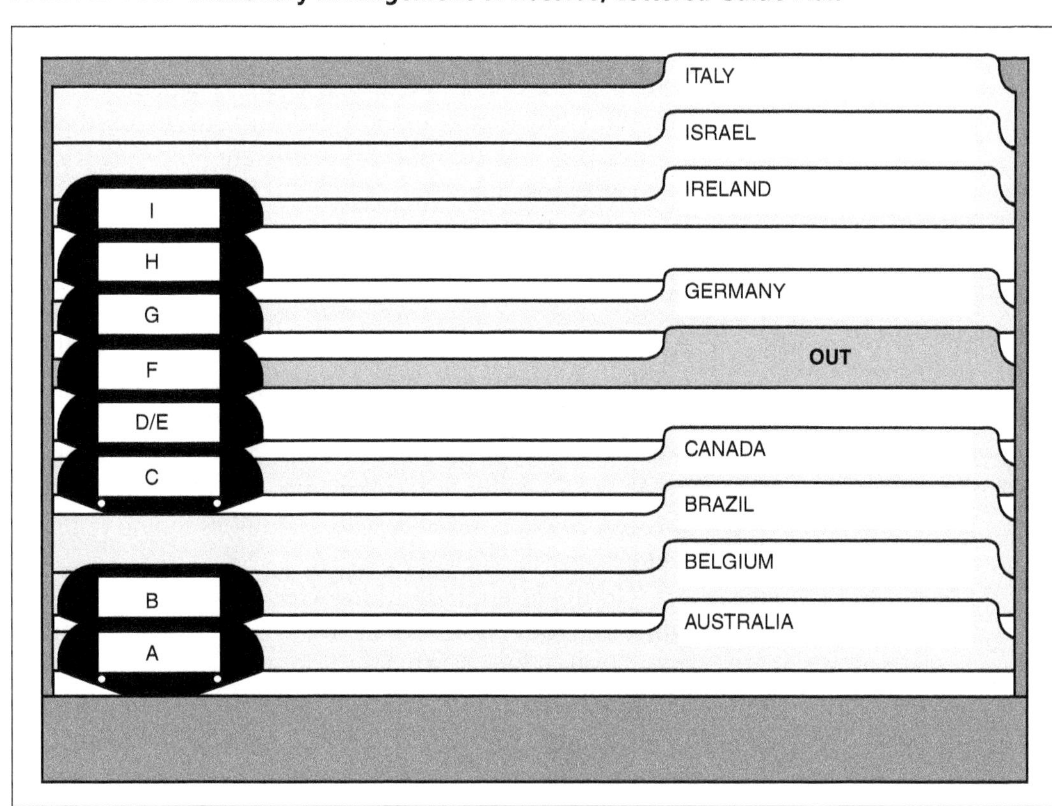

FIGURE 10.4 **Dictionary Arrangement of Records, Location Name Guide Plan**

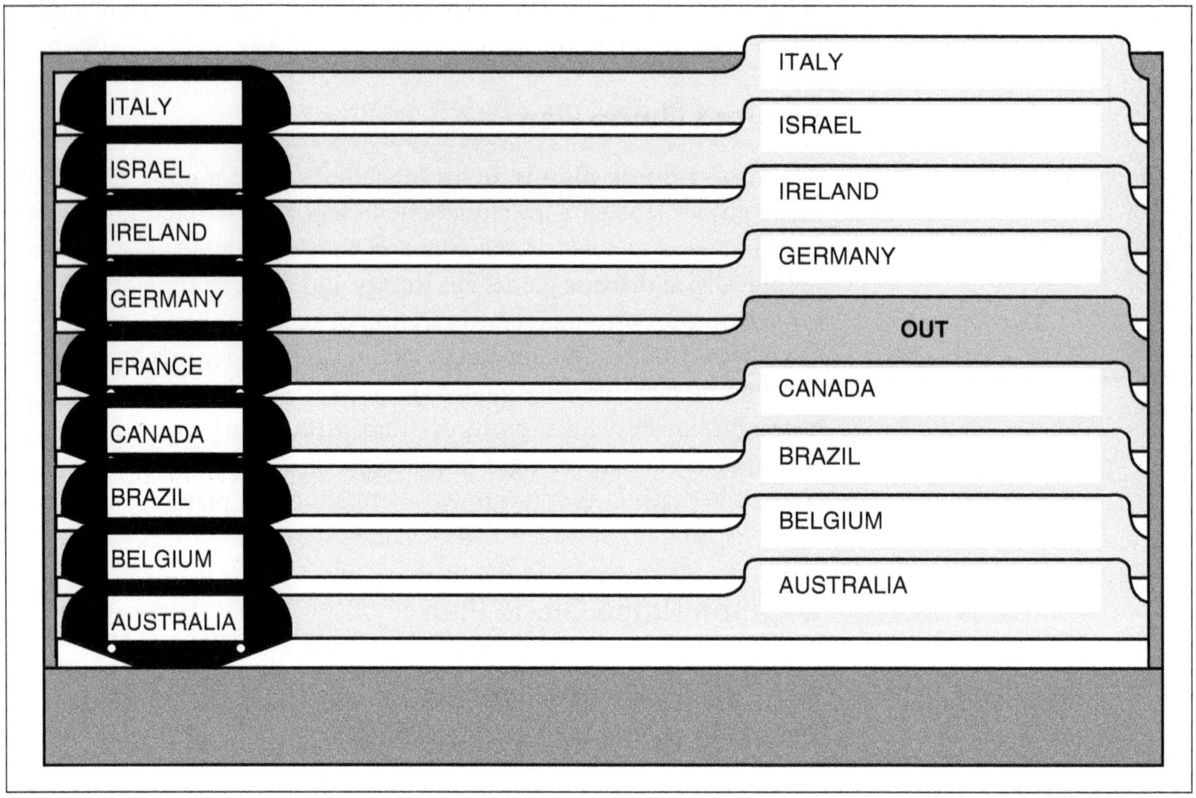

Figure 10.4 shows a location name guide plan in a dictionary arrangement of foreign country names. Primary guides are one-fifth-cut country name guides arranged in a straight line in first position. General country folders are one-third cut, arranged in a straight line in the third position (far right side). Figures 10.3 and 10.4 show the different guide plans in a dictionary arrangement of identical records.

Encyclopedic Storage Arrangement

encyclopedic arrangement: The alphabetic arrangement of major geographic divisions plus one or more geographic subdivisions also arranged in alphabetic order

An **encyclopedic arrangement** is the alphabetic arrangement of major geographic divisions plus one or more geographic subdivisions also arranged in alphabetic order. Similar to the dictionary storage arrangement, the encyclopedic arrangement makes use of either a lettered guide plan or a location name guide plan. Guides in a storage system provide sufficient guidance to speed the storage and retrieval of records. Guides should not dominate a storage area and become an efficiency barrier.

Although lettered guides with closed captions require more thought when filing (i.e., A–D, E–H, I–P), they provide a means of using fewer lettered guides. Figures 10.5 and 10.6 illustrate geographic records storage in an encyclopedic arrangement. Compare the guide plans used for these identical records: Figure 10.5 uses a lettered guide plan, and Figure 10.6 uses a location name guide plan. The major geographic units in the illustrations are state names; the subdivisions are city names. Refer to the illustrations as you study the following detailed explanations of the file arrangements, the guide plans, and the folder contents.

Lettered Guide Plan

What kinds of guides and folders are needed in the lettered guide plan?

Figure 10.5 shows part of a drawer of New York and North Carolina records stored by the lettered guide plan. Refer to Figure10.4 as you study the following arrangement description.

1. First position: fifth-cut primary guides for the state names NEW YORK and NORTH CAROLINA, the largest geographic division in this storage plan.
2. Second position: fifth-cut secondary guides. These alphabetic guides divide the states into alphabetic sections. Each guide indicates the alphabetic section within which records with city names beginning with that letter are stored. Secondary guide tabs are numbered consecutively so that they will be kept in correct order.

FIGURE 10.5 **Encyclopedic Arrangement of Records, Lettered Guide Plan**

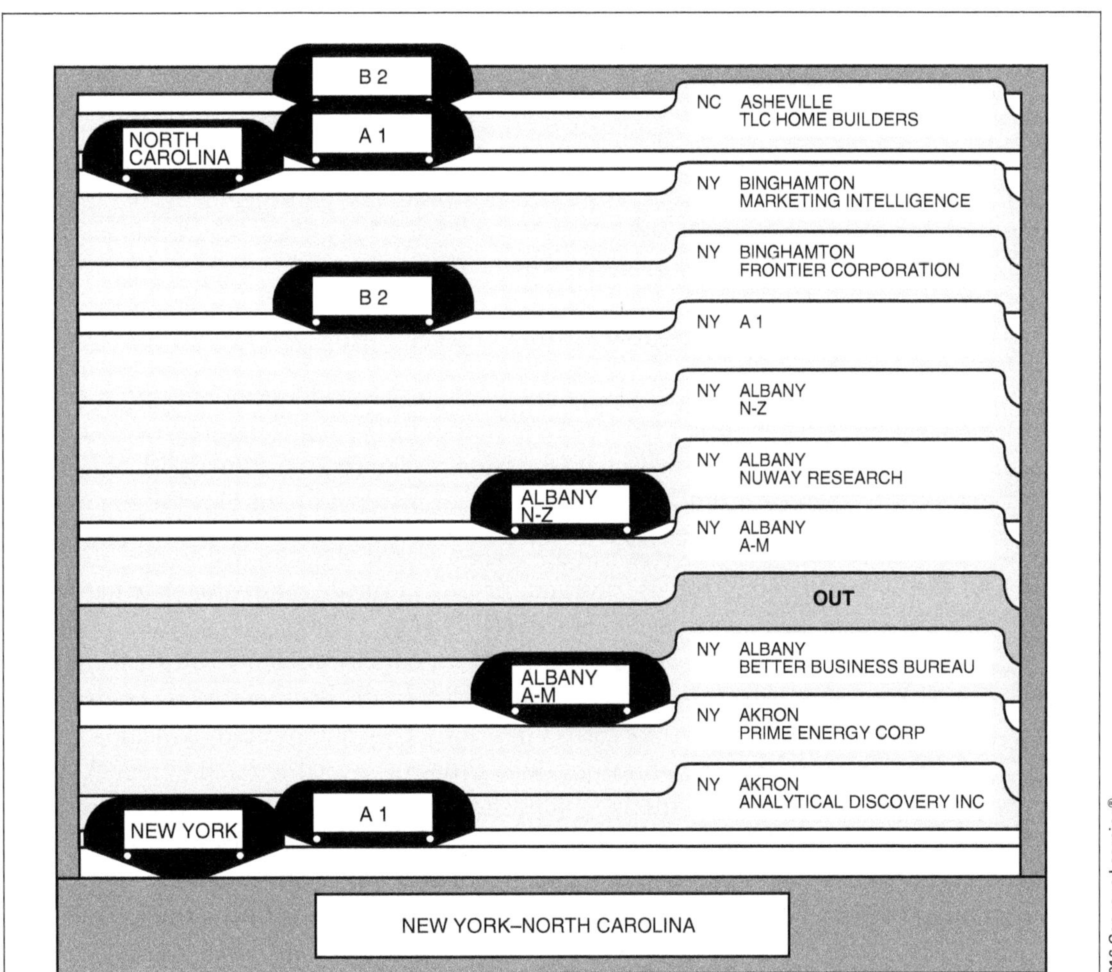

3. Third position: fifth-cut special guides. Special city guides indicate cities that have a high volume of records. The guides ALBANY A–M and ALBANY N–Z provide a separation of correspondents' names in the city section.
4. Fourth Position: one-third-cut folders, third-position tabs, arranged in a straight line at the right of the file drawer. (Your eye moves left to right across the contents of the file.) Notice the three kinds of folders used in this file arrangement: general alphabetic state folders, special city folders, and individual folders.
5. Each secondary guide is accompanied by a corresponding general alphabetic city folder, which is placed at the end of that alphabetic section. The folder has the same caption as that of the secondary guide. Each general alphabetic folder contains records from correspondents located in cities with names beginning with the letter of the alphabet on the folder. For instance, the general A 1 folder might contain correspondence from organizations and individuals in New York cities such as Adams, Akron, Alabama, and Amsterdam, but not from Albany because that city has its own special city folders.
6. Special city folders accompany the special city guides (NY ALBANY A–M and NY ALBANY N–Z).
7. Individual folders are arranged alphabetically by city and then by correspondents' names. Label captions for individual folders include names of the correspondents' states and cities on the first line. The correspondents' names are on the second line.
8. OUT guides are also in fourth position. OUT guides are one-third cut with third-position tabs, and they mark the location of a borrowed folder.

What type of folder is placed at the end of an alphabetic section in the lettered guide plan?

Location Name Guide Plan

Probably the most frequently used location name guide plan arrangement is one that uses state names as the first filing segment (or country names for international operations). Figure 10.6 shows part of a drawer of New York and North Carolina records stored by the location name guide plan. Refer to Figure 10.6 as you study the following arrangement description:

1. First position: fifth-cut primary guides for state names NEW YORK and NORTH CAROLINA.
2. Second position: fifth-cut city guides. AKRON is the first city guide after the NEW YORK state guide. Because the city guides stay in the drawer in their correct positions, they do not need to include the state name.
3. Third position: fifth-cut special lettered guides A–M and N–Z. These special guides show an alphabetic division of correspondents' names in the city of ALBANY section. Special guides speed the location of active or high-volume records.
4. Fourth position: all folders, one-third-cut, third-position tabs. Notice that a general city folder bearing the same caption as the city guide comes at the end of the folders behind each guide.

How are special guides used in the location name guide plan?

FIGURE 10.6 **Encyclopedic Arrangement of Records, Location Name Guide Plan**

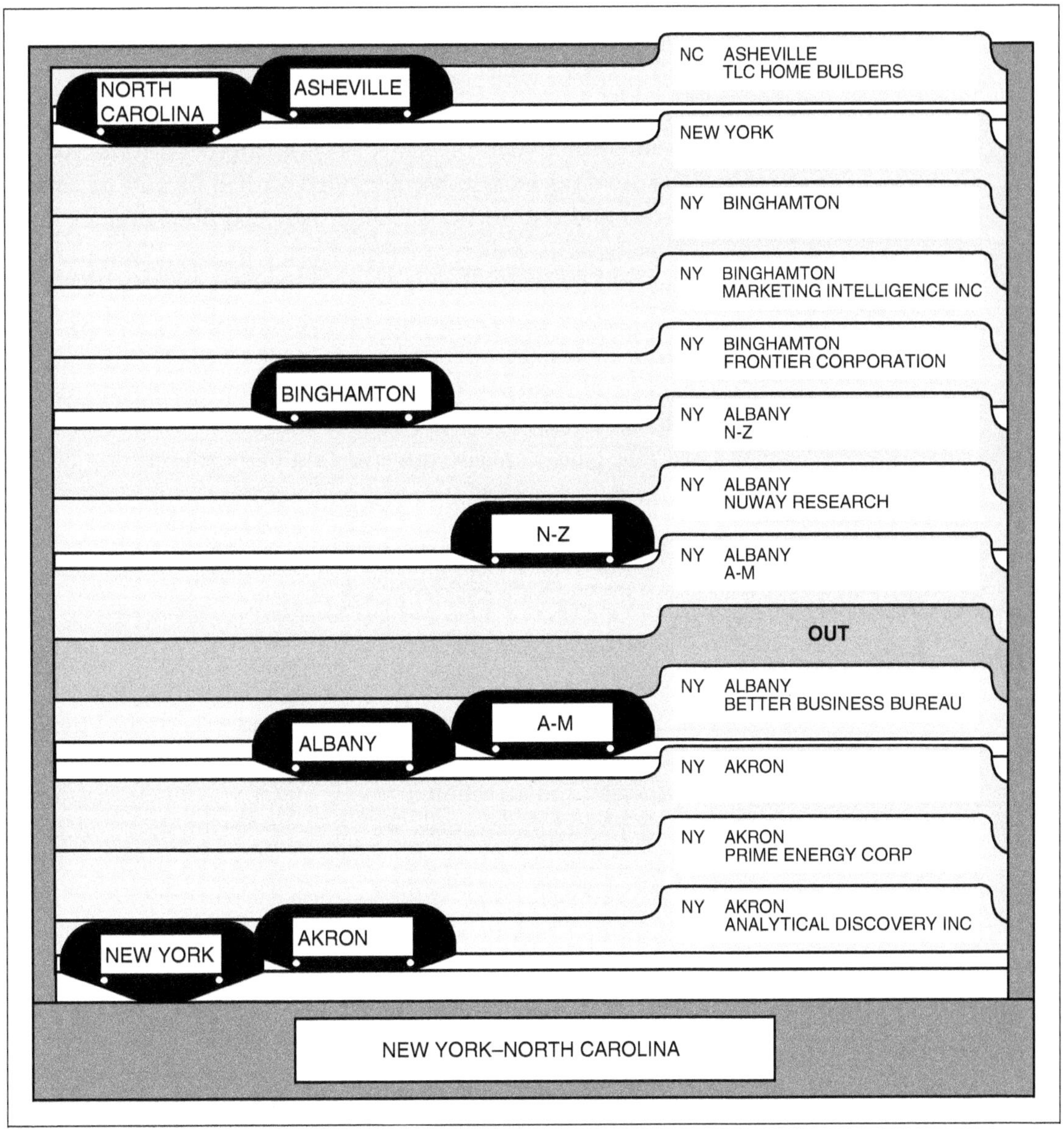

5. The general state folder for NEW YORK is at the end of the NEW YORK section. File documents from other cities in New York in this general state folder when no general folder for those cities is in the file. Arrange records alphabetically in the general state folder by city name first, followed by the correspondent's name. If correspondents' names are identical, use the street name and house number to determine correct order. Store all records from the same correspondent in chronologic order with the most recent record in front.
6. A general city folder is used for every city guide used in the file drawer. Place the general city folder at the end of the city subdivision. ALBANY has two general city folders, one for correspondents' names beginning

with A to M and a second general city folder for correspondents' names beginning with N to Z. Store all records in general city folders alphabetically by correspondents' names. Arrange records from the same correspondent with the most recent record in front. When records begin to accumulate for one correspondent, say five or more, consider opening an individual folder for that correspondent.

7. Individual folders are arranged alphabetically by name within their state and city sections. Folder label captions include the state and city locations as well as correspondents' names. Because folders will be removed from the file, the comprehensive caption helps to prevent misfiles when borrowed records are returned to storage. Arrange records in individual folders with the most recent record in front. Be sure to store all records in folders with the top of the document at the left of the folder.
8. OUT guides are also one-third cut in fourth position in the file drawer.

GEOGRAPHIC RECORDS STORAGE INDEXES

You are already familiar with indexes because you studied the use of alphabetic and master indexes in Chapter 8, Subject Records Management, and alphabetic indexes and accession logs in Chapter 9, Numeric Records Management. Because geographic records are arranged first by location and then by company or individual names, the correspondent's location must be known before a record can be located. If the location of a correspondent is not known, the filer must use an alphabetic index.

Numeric File List

As you learned in Chapter 9, a numeric file list, also called an *accession log*, is a serial list of the numbers assigned to records in a numeric storage system. The list is used to determine the next number available for assignment. In the examples described on pages 248 and 249 of this chapter, a numeric list would be used to determine the next oil well number, the next building number, the next project number, or the next equipment item number.

Alphabetic Index

Why would an alphabetic index be needed in a geographic storage arrangement?

The alphabetic index lists all correspondents or subjects in geographic storage. This index can be a database index or a printed list. For numeric files, the alphabetic index includes the assigned file codes for records stored in a numbered file. The index would include an entry for each identification number assigned to each file (i.e., account number, oil well number, customer number). Figure 10.7 shows an example of the alphabetic index for numeric geographic files.

FIGURE 10.7 **Alphabetic Index for Numeric Geographic Files**

ALPHABETIC INDEX FOR OIL WELLS	
OIL WELL	NUMBER
Harris County, Texas, Oil Well #12345	42-501-12345
Harris County, Texas, Oil Well #13567	42-501-13567
Jones County, Oklahoma, Oil Well #6789	40-403-6789
Rainer Parish, Louisiana, Oil Well #2468	45-203-2468

However the index is maintained, it must be easy to update and keep current. Names or subjects will be added, deleted, or changed. The index should include appropriate information. For example, in an alphabetic index, the correspondent's name and full address or the full subject name should be used. Figure 10.8 is a database alphabetic index for geographic records storage. Correspondents' names are in alphabetic order in column one. The state, city, and street locations are shown in the remaining columns. All correspondents are listed in the index, including correspondents whose records are stored in general city and state folders.

When information for an index is stored in a database, filers can access an individual name on the screen without looking for the name on a printed list. Even with the capability to check electronic indexes, a printed copy of the index should be available.

FIGURE 10.8 **Alphabetic Index for Geographic Files**

ALPHABETIC INDEX					
INDEXED NAME	STATE	CITY	BLDG	STREET	SEE ALSO
Analytical Discovery Inc	NY	Akron	4873	Center St.	
Armor Supply Center	NY	Cortland	1601	Fourth St.	
Better Business Bureau	NC	Asheville	389	Main St.	NY Albany
Better Business Bureau	NY	Albany	150	Rowan St.	NC Asheville
Computer Magic	NY	Geneseo	38	Main St.	
Echo Power Equipment	NY	Cherokee	174	Military Rd.	
Frontier Corporation	NY	Binghamton	20	Shuman Blvd.	
Kerry Company The	NY	Albany	204	Delaware Ave.	
Marketing Intelligence Inc	NY	Binghampton	451	Dunbar Rd.	
Nuway Research	NY	Albany	44	Broadway	
Prime Energy Corp	NY	Akron	2470	Miles Rd.	
TLC Home Builders	NC	Asheville	20	River Dr.	

Master Index

What is a master index?

A master index, as noted in Chapter 8, is a complete listing of all filing segments in the filing system. Figure 10.9 is a database master index for correspondents. States were sorted first, then the city names, and finally the correspondents' names.

FIGURE 10.9 **Master Index for Correspondents**

MASTER INDEX				
STATE	CITY	INDEXED NAME	BLDG	STREET
NC	Asheville	Better Business	389	Main St.
NC	Asheville	TLC Home Builders	20	River Dr.
NY	Akron	Analytical Discovery Inc	4873	Center St.
NY	Akron	Prime Energy Crop	2470	Miles Rd.
NY	Albany	Better Business Bureau	150	Rowan St.
NY	Albany	Kerry Company The	204	Delaware Ave.
NY	Albany	Nuway Research	44	Broadway
NY	Bath	Marketing Intelligence Inc	451	Dunbar Rd.
NY	Binghamton	Frontier Corporation	20	Shuman Blvd.
NY	Cherokee	Echo Power Equipment	174	Military Rd.
NY	Cortland	Armor Supply Center	1601	Fourth St.
NY	Geneseo	Computer Magic	38	Main St.

The master index shows at a glance the geographic units covered in the filing system and is especially useful to new filers. A printed copy of the index is kept in the front of the file drawer or another readily accessible location. If the alphabetic index is prepared with database software and names are kept updated, queries can be created for viewing or printing an updated alphabetic or master index at any time; or an individual record can be viewed or printed. Other software packages that allow resorting and moving of columns can also produce a master index.

GEOGRAPHIC RECORDS STORAGE AND RETRIEVAL PROCEDURES

Supplies used in the geographic method are similar to those used in other storage methods—guides, folders, and OUT indicators. You may want to review the section on filing supplies in Chapter 6 before continuing with the discussion of storage and retrieval procedures.

What steps are used when storing geographic records?

The same basic steps for storing records in alphabetic, subject, and numeric methods (inspecting, indexing, coding, cross-referencing, sorting, and storing) are also followed in the geographic method. Minor differences are explained in the following paragraphs. Retrieval procedures (requisitioning, charging out, and following up) are also basically the same.

Inspecting and Indexing

Check to see that the record has been released for storage (inspect) and scan the letter for content to determine its proper place in storage (index). In Figure 10.10, the handwritten letters JK indicate that the letter is released for storage.

FIGURE 10.10 **Letter Coded for Geographic Filing**

3 4 5
Stratford /Group /Inc.
Educational Consultants
2 1
49 Kimberly Lane, Raleigh,/ NC 76000-4127
Phone: (919) 555-0143 Fax: (919) 555-0123

May 4, 20--

May 07, 20-- 11:05 A.M.

Dr. Michael L. Kelley
Alfred State College
10 Upper College Drive
Alfred, NY 14802-3643

Dear Dr. Kelley

Your request for 50 brochures explaining in detail the programmed learning materials we have available for use in summer workshop programs has been referred to our Burbank, California, office.

Interest in this exciting and novel material has been extremely high, and we are pleased that professors are finding it so worthwhile. Because of the extraordinary number of requests for this brochure, it is temporarily out of stock. We expect a new supply within the next two weeks, however, and will send you 50 copies as soon as we receive them.

Thanks for letting us provide you with helpful materials for your workshop.

Sincerely

Johandra Linfoot

Johandra Linfoot
Educational Consultant

JK

dw

2 1
Branch Office: 2964 Broadway, Burbank,/CA 91500-1217 X

Coding

Code the document for geographic storage by marking the correspondent's *location* (address) first. Code by underlining the filing segment—Raleigh, NC, in Figure 10.10. Write numbers above or below the filing segment to show the order of indexing and alphabetizing units. Then code the correspondent's name—Stratford Group, Inc., in Figure 10.10—by placing diagonals between the units and numbering the succeeding units. Figure 10.10 shows a letter coded for the geographic storage method, including a cross-reference as described in the "Cross-Referencing" section below.

After coding documents, consult the alphabetic index to see whether the correspondent is currently in the system. If not, add the new correspondent's name and address to the index.

Cross-Referencing

What names require cross-referencing?

Cross-referencing is as necessary in the geographic storage method as it is in the alphabetic or numeric storage methods. In Chapters 3, 4, and 5, personal and business names are listed that may require cross-references. Additional cross-references may be needed for (1) names of organizations having more than one address and (2) organizations located at one address and doing business under other names at other locations. When a foreign country name is translated into its English equivalent, a cross-reference to the other language is also required.

Filers coding a letter or other form of physical document will first code the geographic location by underlining the filing segment, inserting diagonals between filing units, and numbering the units to show their rank in indexing order. The correspondent's name is indexed last. When an alternative location is mentioned in the letter, it is underlined with a wavy line, diagonals are inserted between units, and units are numbered. An X is placed beside the cross-reference location. (See Figure 10.10.)

In the geographic storage method, insert cross-references in both the alphabetic or numeric index and the storage file. In the numeric index, prepare an entry for each identification number assigned to each file (i.e., account number, oil well number, customer number). In the alphabetic index, prepare an entry for every name by which a correspondent may be known or by which records may be requested. For the letter shown in Figure 10.10, a cross-reference shows a branch office located in another city. A filer might look for a record from the Stratford Group, Inc., in either of these two locations.

Four types of cross-references can be used: (1) cross-reference sheets that are stored in folders to refer filers to specific records, (2) photocopies of coded records that are placed in the alternative locations to serve as substitutes for cross-reference sheets, (3) cross-reference guides that are placed into storage as permanent cross-references, and (4) SEE ALSO cross-reference notations on sheets or on folder tabs. Each of these cross-references is explained in the following paragraphs.

cross-reference sheet: a sheet placed in an alternative location in the file that directs the filer to a specific record stored in a different location other than where the filer is searching

A **cross-reference sheet** is a sheet placed in an alternative location in the file that directs the filer to a specific record stored in a different location other than where the filer is searching. The cross-reference sheet in Figure 10.11 is made for the branch office indicated on the letter shown in Figure 10.10. The original letter is stored in the N section of geographic storage (NORTH CAROLINA), but the cross-reference sheet is stored in the C section (CALIFORNIA).

FIGURE 10.11 **Cross-Reference Sheet for Geographic Method**

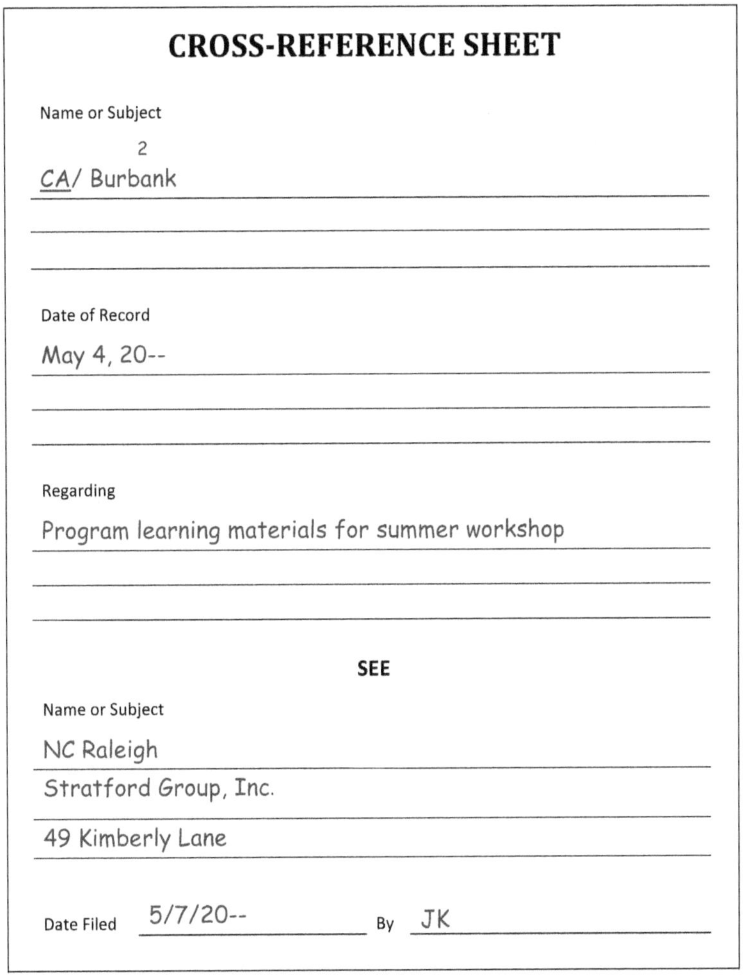

CROSS-REFERENCE SHEET

Name or Subject

2
CA/ Burbank

Date of Record

May 4, 20--

Regarding

Program learning materials for summer workshop

SEE

Name or Subject

NC Raleigh
Stratford Group, Inc.
49 Kimberly Lane

Date Filed 5/7/20-- By JK

Making photocopies of records after coding them for geographic storage saves time by eliminating the tasks of writing the filing segments onto cross-reference sheets and then coding them. The photocopy serves as the cross-reference sheet.

cross-reference guide: a special guide that serves as a permanent marker in storage indicating that all records pertaining to a correspondent are stored elsewhere

A **cross-reference guide** is a special guide that serves as a permanent marker in storage indicating that all records pertaining to a correspondent are stored elsewhere. For example, the cross-reference guide in Figure 10.12

FIGURE 10.12 **Cross-Reference Guide for Geographic Method**

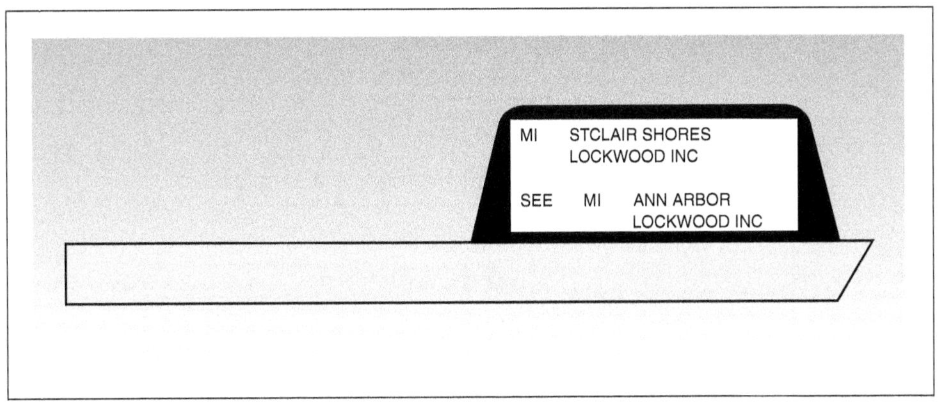

shows that all records for Lockwood, Inc., are stored under the home office location in Ann Arbor, MI, not the branch office location in St. Clair Shores, MI. The words ***Ann Arbor*** must be written onto each record when it is coded. The cross-reference guide is stored according to the location on the top line of its caption in alphabetic order with other geographically labeled guides and folders.

SEE ALSO cross-reference: a notation on a folder tab or cross-reference sheet that directs the filer to multiple locations for related information

How do the cross-references in Figures 10.13 and 10.14 differ from each other?

A **SEE ALSO cross-reference** is a notation on a folder tab or cross-reference sheet that directs filers to multiple locations for related information. If a company has two addresses and records are stored under both addresses, two SEE ALSO cross-references would be used. For example, if Windsor Publishing Co., Inc., conducts business in Houston, TX, and also in Wichita Falls, TX, the references would indicate that information for this company can be found in two storage locations.If these SEE ALSO cross-references are sheets of paper, they are kept as the first items in their respective folders so that they will not be overlooked (see Figures 10.13 and 10.14). Instead of being

FIGURE 10.13 **Cross-Reference Sheet for SEE ALSO Cross-References**

CROSS-REFERENCE SHEET

Name or Subject

2
TX / Houston

3 4 5 6
Windsor / Publishing / Co. / Inc.

1313 North Sixth Street

Date of Record

Regarding

SEE ALSO

Name or Subject

TX Wichita Falls

Windsor Publishing Co., Inc.

2264 Evanston Avenue

Date Filed 11/4/20-- By JK

FIGURE 10.14 **Cross-Reference Sheet for SEE ALSO Cross-References**

CROSS-REFERENCE SHEET

Name or Subject

2 3

TX / Wichita / Falls

3 4 5 6

Windsor / Publishing / Co. / Inc.

2264 Evanston Avenue

Date of Record

Regarding

SEE ALSO

Name or Subject

TX Houston

Windsor Publishing Co., Inc.

1313 North Sixth Street

Date Filed 11/4/20-- By JK

written onto separate cross-reference sheets, this SEE ALSO information may be keyed onto the tabs of the two folders for the Windsor Publishing Co., Inc. (See Figure 10.15.) Figure 10.16 on page 268 shows a cross-reference entry in a database record.

FIGURE 10.15 **SEE ALSO Cross-References on Folder Tabs**

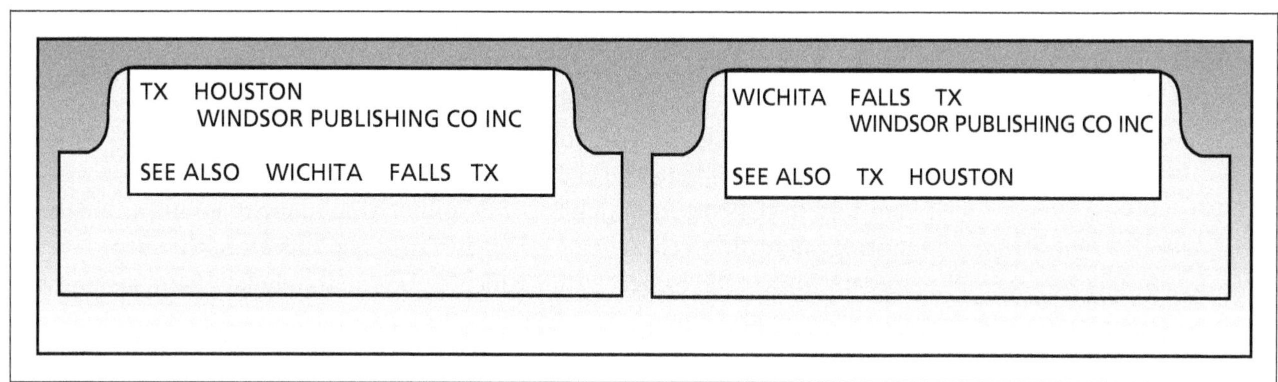

FIGURE 10.16 **Cross-Reference in a Geographic Database**

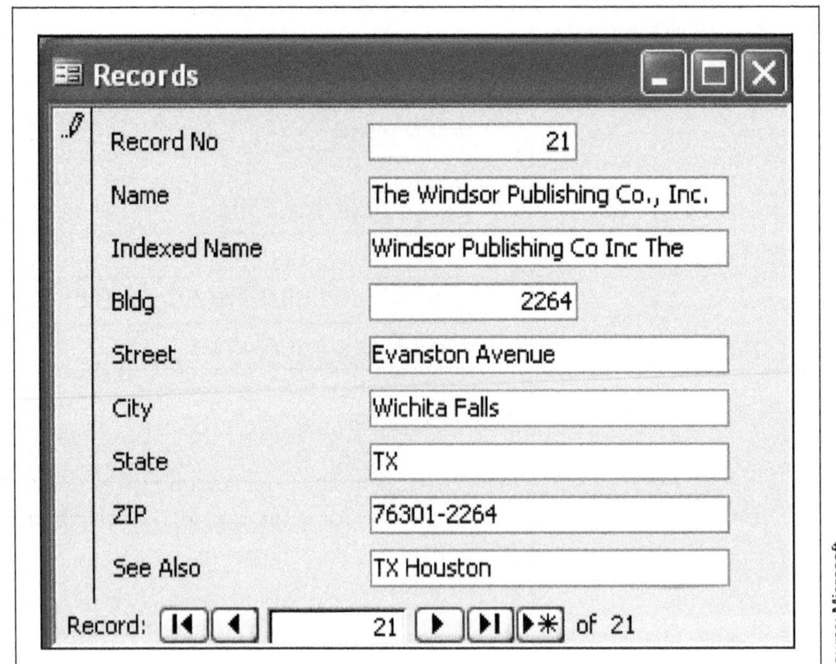

Sorting

What two ways of sorting may be used in the geographic storage method?

Sort records numerically by file code or alphabetically by location. If alphabetic, sort first by the largest geographic unit such as country or state name; then sort by the first subdivision such as state equivalent or city; finally sort by correspondents' names in alphabetic order.

Storing

Individual correspondents' folders, special city folders, alphabetic subdivisions of cities with their corresponding general folders, general folders for alphabetic grouping of cities, and general state or regional folders may be part of a geographic records storage arrangement. Therefore, placing a record into the wrong folder is easy to do. Because of the complexity of a geographic arrangement, be extremely careful when storing.

Lettered Guide Plan

Assuming that the alphabetic arrangement is by state and city, look for the primary state guide. Then use the lettered guides to locate the alphabetic state section within which the city name falls. After finding that section, look for an individual correspondent's folder. If you find one, store the record in that folder in chronologic order with the most recent record on top.

If an individual folder for the correspondent is not in the file, look for a general city folder. If a general city folder is in the file, store the record according to the correspondent's name in the same manner as in an alphabetic arrangement. If a general city folder is not in the file, store the record in the general alphabetic folder within which the city name falls. Again, arrange the city names according to the rules for alphabetic indexing.

Within a city, arrange the names of correspondents alphabetically; group the records of one correspondent with the most recent date on top.

If identically named correspondents reside in one city, follow the rules for filing identical names. (See Chapter 5 for review.)

When enough correspondence has accumulated to warrant making a separate folder for a specific city, a specific geographic section, or an individual correspondent, remove the records from the general folder, and prepare a new folder with the geographic location on its tab as the first item of information. Then prepare a similarly labeled guide, if one is needed, for the folder. Finally, place the folder and guide in their alphabetic positions in storage.

Although requirements for preparing a separate folder for a specific geographic location vary, a good rule of thumb is this: When five or more records pertaining to one specific geographic location (such as a state, city, or region) accumulate, prepare a separate folder for that location.

Location Name Guide Plan

Again, assuming that the arrangement is by state and city, find the primary state guide, and look for the correct city name on a secondary guide. If a city guide is present, search for an individual correspondent's folder. If one exists, store the record in the folder according to date.

If an individual folder is not in the file, store the record in the correct general city folder according to the geographic location of the correspondent

RECORDS MANAGEMENT IN ACTION

Sears Replaces Retail Stores with Data Centers

Recognizing that the world needs less space for retail and more space to store data, Sears plans to turn some Sears and Kmart locations into data centers and disaster recovery spaces. A new Sears subsidiary will be tasked with converting some of the more than 2,500 Sears and Kmart properties to data storage facilities equipped with servers, chillers, and backup generators. It also plans to top many of its buildings with telecommunication towers.

Sean Farney, who built and managed Microsoft's 700,000-square-foot Chicago data center is leading the subsidiary, Ubiquity Critical Environments. Seventy-one percent of the US population lives within 10 miles of a Sears store.

A 127,000-square-foot Sears location on the south side of Chicago will serve as the first data center. Although many businesses have stacks of servers jammed into back offices to store data, as well as stand-alone facilities, the "growing sophistication, cost and power needs of these systems are driving companies into leased spaces at a breakneck pace," according to a recent report exploring "cloud factories," from *The New York Times*.

Sears' mall-based retail locations as well as those that have been downsized to smaller retail footprints are seen as better options for disaster recovery facilities. Traditionally located in industrial areas, businesses are said to be looking for other locations for business continuity centers, such as one with a nearby Starbucks or other retail, according to Mr. Farney.

Sears' management believes that as wireless users grow, holes in coverage are being created that Sears' rooftops could fill. "When malls were being built, they gravitated to the intersection of freeways and highways, and Sears got entry to all of them," according to Mr. Farney.

Source: Tom Ryan, Contributor, Forbes.com, *Retail Wire: Plugged In*, May 31, 2013, retrieved 1/17/14 from http://www.forbes.com/sites/retailwire/2013/05/31/sears-replaces-retail-stores-with-data-centers/.

Source: Twitter Privacy Policy https://twitter.com/privacy (Accessed January 20, 2014).

and then by name, in alphabetic order with other records within the folder. If more than one record is stored for a correspondent, arrange the records chronologically with the most recent date on top.

If a general city folder is not in the file, place the record in the general state folder, first according to the alphabetic order of the city name and then by the correspondent's name and street address (if necessary), according to the rules for alphabetic indexing.

Retrieving

What are the retrieval procedures?

Retrieving a record from a geographic file involves these five steps:

1. Asking for the record (requisition)
2. Checking the alphabetic or numeric index to determine the location of the record
3. Removing the record from the files
4. Completing charge-out documentation for the record
5. Following up to see that the record is returned to storage within a specified time

Requisition

Requests for a record stored by geographic arrangement may identify it by location, by numeric file code, or by correspondent's name. If the request is made by location, finding the record should be simple. If the request is made by name or number, however, refer to the alphabetic index or a computer database to locate the file containing the record.

Charge-Out

After you have located and retrieved the record, charge it out in the same manner that you charge out records in any other storage method. Be sure to insert an OUT indicator at the storage position of the record. A Charge-Out field can be added in a records database and shown in the alphabetic index.

Follow-Up

Follow-up procedures used to secure the return of borrowed records are the same for the geographic method as those used with any other storage method. Use a tickler file or another reminder system to be sure that records are returned to storage at designated times and to remind yourself of records that need to be brought to someone's attention in the future. If OUT information is recorded in a database table, this information can be sorted by date and used as a tickler file.

CHAPTER REVIEW AND APPLICATIONS

KEY POINTS

- Geographic records management is grouping and storing records by location.
- Companies that need information by location to make good business decisions are likely to choose geographic records management.
- Many geographic filing systems are used to support an internal geographic information system.
- Geographic records storage requires a more complex system of guides and folders than other types of records storage, and storing and retrieving records can be more time consuming.
- Some records and files in geographic filing use compass point terms that require the use of unique filing rules.
- Two basic arrangements are commonly used in geographic storage: the dictionary arrangement and the encyclopedic arrangement. The arrangement used depends upon whether subdivisions of the geographic units are necessary.
- Either the lettered guide plan or the location name guide plan can be used. Whether the files contain a small number of diverse names or a large number of similar names will likely determine the guide plan.
- Because geographic records are arranged first by location, then by company or subject, and then by individual names, the correspondent's location must be known before a record can be located.
- An alphabetic index lists all correspondents or subjects in geographic storage. For numeric files, the alphabetic index includes the assigned file codes for records stored in a numbered file.
- A master index, which shows at a glance the geographic units covered in the filing system, is also helpful and is especially useful to new file users.
- Except for indexing and coding, the storage and retrieval procedures for geographic storage are similar to those used for other storage methods.
- Indexing and coding require looking first at the location of the document and then at the name, the document subject, or project title being stored.
- Cross-references should be placed in both the alphabetic index or numeric index and the storage file.

TERMS

compass point
compass terms
cross-reference guide
cross-reference sheet
dictionary arrangement
encyclopedic arrangement
geographic filing system
geographic information system
geographic records management
lettered guide plan
location name guide plan
SEE ALSO cross-reference

REVIEW AND DISCUSS

1. Why is arranging records by location important? (Obj. 1)

2. Name three kinds of businesses that are likely to use the geographic method of storage. (Obj.1)

3. What are the advantages and disadvantages of the geographic storage method? (Obj. 2)

4. Explain how the dictionary and encyclopedic arrangements of geographic records differ. (Obj. 2)

5. Explain the difference between the lettered guide plan and the location name guide plan. (Obj. 2)

6. Describe the arrangement of guides and folders in an encyclopedic arrangement of a geographic file using the lettered guide plan. The geographic units covered in the arrangement are state names and city names. (Obj. 2)

7. Explain how an alphabetic index is used in geographic records storage. (Obj. 3)

8. Explain how indexing and coding for the geographic method are different from indexing and coding for the alphabetic method of records storage. (Obj. 2)

9. List three types of cross-references used in the geographic method and state where they are placed or stored in the filing system. (Obj. 4)

10. When may files be arranged using compass terms? How does using compass terms to arrange files differ from general alphabetic filing methods? (Obj. 5)

APPLICATIONS

10-1 Selecting a Geographic Arrangement (Obj. 2)

For each of the following scenarios, identify the most efficient geographic arrangement, and explain the reasons for your choices. Identification of this arrangement should include as many of the following elements as appropriate: major and minor geographic units, encyclopedic or dictionary arrangement, lettered guide plan or location name guide plan. Key and print your answers.

1. A large aerospace company keeps its facility and equipment maintenance records by building code. The buildings and equipment include:
   - Assembly Plant: Belt 1, Belt 2, Motor 456, Motor 123, Lathe 3
   - Research Center: Computer 72, Mega Server 6, Small printer, Large printer
   - Fire Station: Hose 3, Hose 5, Extinguisher 23, Ladder 9
   - North Testing Laboratory: Oven 17, Microscope 43, Centrifuge 12
   - South Testing Laboratory: Oven 18, Microscope 21, Centrifuge 5
2. The home office of a large food processing/packing plant is located in Iowa. The company maintains records to and from branch offices in three regions of the United States—Western, Northeast, and South Central—as well as in Japan, Canada, and England.
3. A newspaper publisher in Scranton, PA, maintains a file of all streets in the city. The street name file identifies paper carriers who distribute home delivery to those locations. The newspaper also has mail subscribers in the states of Pennsylvania, New York, Ohio, and West Virginia.
4. A garment manufacturer maintains records by its operations in 10 cities. City locations include the following:

United States
Los Angeles, CA
Philadelphia, PA
Detroit, MI

Central America
Managua, Nicaragua
León, Nicaragua

Canada
Calgary, Alberta
Montréal, Quebec
London, Ontario

South America
Cuernavaca, Morelos, Mexico
Zamora, Michoacán, Mexico

10-2 Compass Terms (Obj. 5)

1. Assume that the names listed in the table below are to be filed in a scientific document file that uses compass terms. Code the names by writing the units in the appropriate columns. The indexing order of the first name is shown below as an example. In the Order column, number the names to show the order in which they would be placed into the files.

Order	Name	Key Unit	Unit 2	Unit 3
a.	East Cumberland Lake	Cumberland	Lake	East
b.	Eastern Shore Park			
c.	East Avon Park			
d.	North River Preserve			
e.	Northern Plateau			
f.	Southwest Mackinaw Island			
g.	Northern Ohio Fault			
h.	East Ridder Fault			
i.	Western Pacific Rim			

2. Assume that the names listed in the table below are to be filed in an alphabetic subject file (not a scientific document file). Code the names by writing the units in the appropriate columns. In the Order column, number the names to show the order in which they would be placed into the files.

Order	Name	Key Unit	Unit 2	Unit 3
a.	East Cumberland Lake	East	Cumberland	Lake
b.	Eastern Shore Park			
c.	East Avon Park			
d.	North River Preserve			
e.	Northern Plateau			
f.	Southwest Mackinaw Island			
g.	Northern Ohio Fault			
h.	East Ridder Fault			
i.	Western Pacific Rim			

10-3 Geographic Indexes (Objs. 2 and 4)

1. Create a new *Microsoft® Access* database file named *CH10 Indexes*. Create a table named Records. Create the following fields in the table and set the primary key.

Field Name	Field Type
Record No	Number (primary key)
Name	Text or Short Text
Indexed Name	Text or Short Text
Bldg	Number
Street	Text or Short Text
City	Text or Short Text
State	Text or Short Text
ZIP	Text or Short Text
See Also	Text or Short Text

2. Enter records for names shown below in the Records table. For names with more than one address, enter each record separately, and enter cross-reference information in the See Also field. (This information may seem unnecessary when all records are viewed. When an individual record or a subset of the records is viewed, however, this data alerts users that the same name is filed in another location.)

Record No	Name and Address	Record No	Name and Address
1	John Powers Electronics 24 Delaware Ave. Rochester, NY 14623-2944	11	Wilkes Tree Farm 400 Stanton Christiana Rd. Newark, DE 19713-0401
2	Indian River Community College 3209 Virginia Ave. Fort Pierce, FL 34982-3209	12	Beverly Plumbing 1000 Gordon Rd. Rochester, NY 14623-1089
3	Computer Land, Inc. 30 Shepherd Rd. Springfield, IL 62708-0101	13	Electric City, Inc. 3201Southwest Traffic Way Kansas City, MO 64111-3201
4	Portland Cement Co. 12000 Lakeville Rd. Portland, OR 97219-4233	14	Abba D Plumbing 901 S. National Ave. Springfield, MO 65804-0910
5	Penn Valley Community College 3300 Southwest Traffic Way Kansas City, MO 64111-3300	15	Pioneer Center Furniture 560 Westport Rd. Kansas City, MO 64111-0568
6	Cerre Ceramic Studios 7250 State Ave. Kansas City, KS 66112-7255	16	Amy's Sports Center 874 Dillingham Blvd. Honolulu, HI 96817-8743
7	Toby Leese Tack Shop 175 University Ave. Newark, NJ 07102-1175	17	Genesis Cinema 1325 Lynch St. Jackson, MS 39203-1325
8	John Powers Electronics 10 State St. Rochester, NY 14623-2944	18	Computer Magic 84 Center St. Springfield, MA 01101-2028
9	City Office Supplies 4281 Drake St. Rochester, MI 48306-0698	19	Computer Magic 24 Fourth Ave. New York, NY 10018-4826
10	Armstrong State College 11935 Abercorn St. Savannah, GA 31419-1092	20	The Computer Store 2847 14th St. New York, NY 10018-2032

3. Create a query named "Alphabetic Index" based on the Records table. Include the Indexed Name, State, City, Bldg, Street, and See Also fields in the query results. Design the query to sort by Indexed Name, then by State, then by City, and then by Street fields. Print the query results table.

4. Create a query named Master Index based on the Records table. Include the State, City, Indexed Name, Bldg, Street, and See Also fields. Design the query to sort by State, then by City, then by Indexed Name, and then by Street fields. Print the query results table.

10-4 Research Geographic Filing Uses (Obj. 1)

1. Using an Internet search engine of your choice, conduct a search using the exact phrase *geographic filing system.*

2. From the results list, find sites for at least two businesses or institutions that describe their use of a geographic filing system. Do not include course outlines or course descriptions at colleges or universities.

3. Follow the links to the business or institution website. Read and summarize the use of a geographic filing system for the business or institution. Send an e-mail to your instructor with a summary of your findings.

SIMULATION

Job 13 Geographic Filing

Continue working with Auric Systems, Inc. Complete Job 13.

ADDITIONAL RESOURCES

For data files, Microsoft® Access tutorials and more, go to www.cengagebrain.com.

PART 2 Electronic Records Management

CHAPTER 11

Electronic Records File Management

LEARNING OBJECTIVES

1. Describe each stage of the electronic records life cycle.
2. Describe classifying electronic records using metadata, taxonomies, and file plans.
3. Discuss retention and disposition of active and inactive electronic records.
4. Describe electronic database elements and how to locate information in a database.
5. Describe how databases can be used in records management and e-commerce.

Photo ©Beth Artis

ON THE JOB

Brock Miller is currently the president of the Oregon Chapter of ARMA and the executive director for Accu NW, a records management company that began in 2008 as an entrepreneurial startup of the larger family business GSS Inc., which was incorporated in 1948. As a small business, Accu NW provides records scanning, storage, and shredding services in Oregon and Washington. Brock has an MBA from the Huntsman School of Business at Utah State University, and prior to leading Accu NW, he worked in operational excellence, marketing, and project management, which is a great background for building and operating a records management services company. In addition to his busy work schedule, Brock writes a monthly column for the Oregon ARMA Chapter newsletter, highlighting the practical applications of the Principles.

When establishing services with a customer for his company, Brock and the Accu NW team work intensely to identify metadata, file plans, and/or indexing requirements for records to be scanned and stored either electronically or physically. Scanning services can be provided at Accu NW or at the customer site.

Accu NW is determined to deliver the information they manage for their customers in a straightforward, effective, and prompt way. Customers can call or e-mail and request specific documents and should expect real-time response from this organization. Records can be delivered electronically or by Accu NW personnel. Physical records are destroyed at the end of their retention period only with explicit permission from the customer.

Brock demonstrates that opportunity exists for the entrepreneur in the records management field who is prepared to innovate and work very hard. Brock's advice for individuals interested in a records management career include getting a minor in Information Technology and understanding the Principles as taught by ARMA in a comprehensive way. Additionally, they should also define themselves as records managers who think and behave as leaders.

You have worked with the alphabetic filing rules in Chapters 3, 4, and 5. You learned how to index and code personal and business names following the 10 rules. This chapter addresses electronic files management during all stages of the electronic records life cycle as well as metadata, taxonomies, file plans, and how databases work.

ELECTRONIC RECORDS LIFE CYCLE

electronic records life cycle: consists of five phases: creation, classification, use and distribution, retention and maintenance, and disposition

As the number of computer files increases, the need to organize electronic files is more important than ever. In this section, you learn how the records life cycle is applied to electronic file management. The **electronic records life cycle** consists of five phases: creation, classification, use and distribution, retention and maintenance, and disposition. Figure 11.1 shows the records life cycle for electronic files. Each phase of the electronic records life cycle is described in this chapter.

The major difference between the electronic and physical records life cycle is that when an electronic record is created and saved, it is also classified. When you choose the electronic file name, file folder, or subfolder where the document will reside, you are classifying the record. Later in the chapter you learn about classifying documents using metadata, taxonomies, and file plans.

FIGURE 11.1 **Electronic Records Life Cycle**

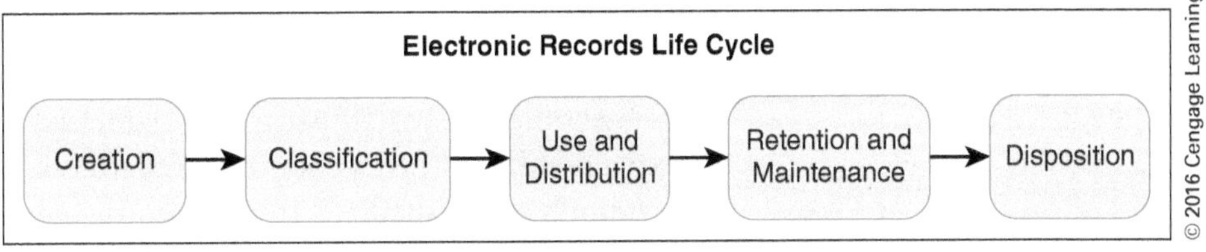

Creation of Electronic Records

How are electronic files created?

Electronic files are created in specific software applications such as Microsoft® Word, Excel, Access, e-mail applications, and many others. When the application is opened, the user starts keying the needed information in a new document. Creating and storing (saving) the document is the first step in the records life cycle. One way to save a document the first time is to choose Save or Save As from the File menu. When the Save As dialog box opens, navigate to the proper drive and folder. Then, key a file name that is meaningful to the task that you are performing. A **file name** is a unique name given to a file stored for computer use that must follow the computer's operating system rules. If the user does not change the drive or folder, Windows will automatically save a new document to the Documents folder in one of the libraries on the hard drive or in the cloud (OneDrive®).

file name: a unique name given to a file stored for computer use that must follow the computer's operating system rules

Specific software applications create specific file formats. For example, Microsoft® Word 2007, 2010 and 2013 create a Microsoft® Word document (.docx). If you are using an older version of Microsoft® Word, such as 97 or 2003, the document type is .doc. In current Windows operating systems, the file format is not readily listed. In older versions of Windows and DOS, file names were limited to eight characters for the file name and three characters for extensions: "12345678.123" was the number of characters you could use to name a document. Apple computers use long file names, thereby making it possible for more descriptive names. Windows currently allows long file names and inserts the automatic document type. Microsoft® Excel 2007, 2010 and 2013 create spreadsheets (.xlsx); Excel 97 or 2003 creates spreadsheets (.xls). Microsoft® Access 2007, 2010 and 2013 create a database (.accdb): Access 97 or 2003 creates a database (.mdb).

Because these applications are editable, they are not good candidates for long-term storage unless the organization has a good RIM software program. Another document format that can be set is **portable document format (pdf)**, which is the Adobe Acrobat standard. Users can easily save a file as a pdf and set the properties so that the document cannot be altered. Another document format, tagged image format (tif or tiff), can also be set so it cannot be edited or changed.

portable document format (pdf): Users can easily save a file as a pdf and set the properties so that the document cannot be altered

Compressed file format is another document format that saves a file that uses less storage space. A number of compressed file formats exist, zip being the most common. Windows Explorer has a built-in file compressor that uses the zip extension.

Electronic documents are stored as bytes on computer storage devices. In many offices, electronic files are stored on a computer's hard drive, on shared drives, on a local area network (LAN), or in the cloud. Some workers might use external storage devices. Removable external storage devices include devices such as CDs, DVDs, external hard drives, and USB flash drives. These devices are removable; thus, the user can take a device from one computer and use it on another. Whatever type of storage device is used, the data should be stored using metadata, taxonomies, and/or file plans (all are explained later in this chapter). Regardless, workers need to follow the organization's established electronic records management policies and procedures when storing records.

Folder Structure

Dividing storage space into folders is an important part of managing electronic information. A **folder** (or directory) is a subdivision of storage space created by the operating system of a computer. An **operating system** is an organized collection of software that controls the overall operations of a computer. A folder can contain many files. For example, you might have a folder for this class named "Records Management." You might save a file in the folder named "Chapter 11 Review Questions." For documents created using the Windows operating system, you are directed to a Library where you can create folders.

folder: (or directory): a subdivision of storage space created by the operating system of a computer

operating system: an organized collection of software that controls the overall operations of a computer

Creating folders on any storage device is easy. As with many operations on a computer, different procedures can be used to achieve the same result. Figure 11.2 shows the Windows Explorer application that comes with the Microsoft Windows operating system. To create a new folder using this program, the user can choose Organize from the menu bar and select New folder or right-click in the list of folders, choose New, and then Folder. The new folder appears with the name "New folder." The user then changes the name of the folder to a meaningful name.

FIGURE 11.2 **Windows Explorer New Folder**

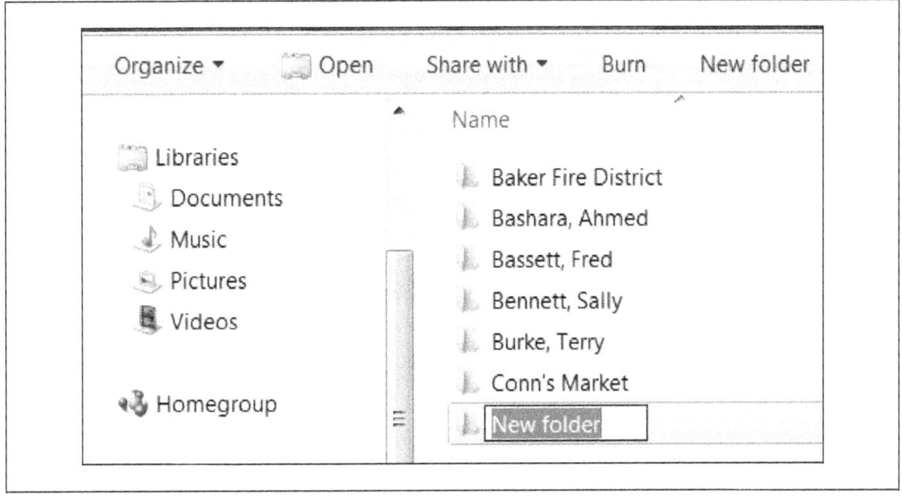

Source: Microsoft

Folders (sometimes called *subfolders*) can be created within other folders, which allows the user to create a folder structure. For example, suppose that you work for Safety First, a company that sells smoke alarms, fire extinguishers, and other fire prevention products. You handle routine correspondence to customers who regularly buy Safety First products. Safety First has a LAN where shared folders are available for any of the office workers. Figure 11.3 shows a partial listing of customer folders.

Your task is to look up some information in an e-mail that you sent to Fred Bassett. You would open the Customers folder, the Bassett, Fred subfolder, and then the appropriate file. Documents from or to a new customer would mean creating a folder for the customer name. Documents (such as e-mails or draft versions of contracts) for the new customer would be stored in the customer's folder. When many files are stored in one customer's folder, creating subfolders to organize the files by year may be helpful. These subfolders are shown in Figure 11.3 in the Burke, Terry folder.

FIGURE 11.3 **Customer Folders on a Drive**

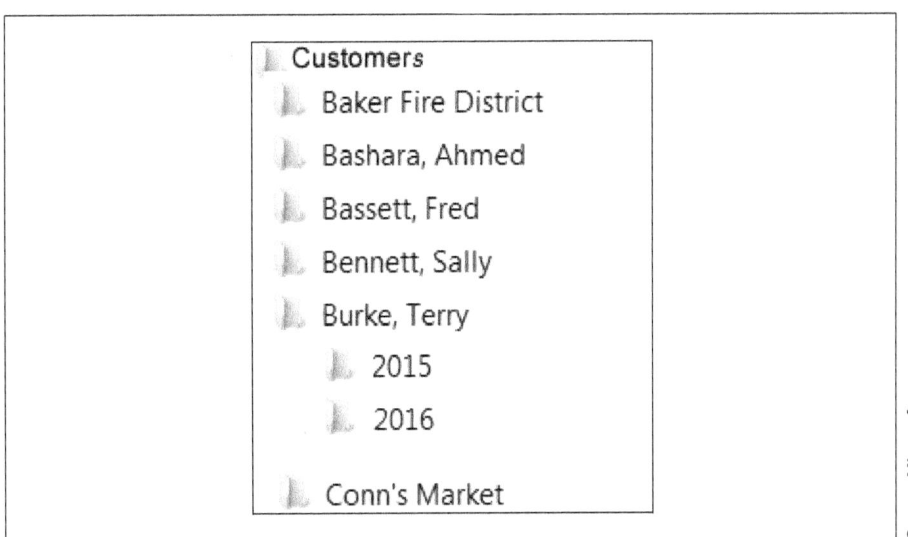

Source: Microsoft

MY RECORDS

Reduce the Flow of Unsolicited Information

Is your e-mail inbox overflowing with unwanted offers?
Are telemarketers calling at all hours?

Although you may not be able to stop completely the ever-increasing flood of information, taking the following steps will help to reduce the volume of unwanted junk mail, spam, and telemarketing calls that you receive:

DECREASE JUNK MAIL

- Access the Direct Marketing Association's DMAchoice website to add your name and address to the residential file of customers who do not wish to receive promotional mail at home.
- When you enter a sweepstakes, fill out product warranty cards, or provide personal information on a form for any reason, write on the form: "Please do not sell my name or address."

DECREASE SPAM

- Do not fill out an online registration form (newsletters and mailing lists usually require them) unless the site's privacy policy clearly states that the data will not be shared with other people without your approval.
- Read any online form carefully before you transmit personal information through a website. Some sites require you to deselect a check box to opt out of future communications with that particular company or related companies.
- Don't display your e-mail address in public forums such as newsgroup postings, chat rooms, or websites.
- Use two e-mail addresses—one for personal messages and one for newsgroups and chat rooms.
- Report unwanted spam e-mail to the Federal Trade Commission (FTC), and send a copy of the offending e-mail to your ISP (Internet service provider).
- Disconnect from the Internet when you're away from your computer. This prevents hackers from accessing your computer.
- Be cautious about opening any attachments or downloading files from e-mails you receive. Don't open an e-mail attachment—even if it looks like it's from a friend or coworker—unless you are expecting it or you know what it is. If you send an e-mail with an attached file, include a message explaining what the attachment is.
- Download free software only from sites you know and trust. It can be appealing to download free software—like games, file-sharing programs, and customized toolbars. But remember that free software programs may contain malware.

STOP UNWANTED TELEMARKETING CALLS

- Register your telephone number(s) on the National Do-Not-Call Registry to block calls permanently. Remember to include your cell phone number. A link to this site is provided on the website for this textbook.
- If you receive an unwanted telemarketer call, interrupt the caller and say, "Please permanently remove my number from your calling list." If the same company calls again, they are violating the law.

Source: Federal Trade Commission, Consumer Information, SPAM, http://www.consumer.ftc.gov/articles/0038-spam, accessed January 15, 2014.

Folder structure should be designed to facilitate finding files quickly. A shallow folder structure has many folders at the same level. Consequently, the user has to look through a long list of folders to find the one needed. A deep folder structure has folders within folders within folders. Seeing the logic of the folder structure can be difficult when too many levels of folders are used.

Which is the most effective type of folder structure?

A folder structure that is neither too shallow nor too deep is ideal, as you will learn in the taxonomy and file plan section of this chapter. The structure should have enough levels of folders to organize files in a meaningful way, but not so many levels that the structure is hard to understand. Choose meaningful names for folders and files for quick retrieval of files. Most operating systems allow the use of long file names.

File Names

Using meaningful file names is an important part of managing electronic files. An organization may have procedures in place for naming files and folders explained later in this chapter. If no procedures or guidelines exist, think about how the data might be requested when you need to retrieve it. In the earlier Safety First example, you write to Conn's Market to answer a question about changing the company's credit terms. You might name the document "Conn's Market credit terms 5-6-16." The document would be stored in the customer's folder. The complete list of folders and file name would be Customer Correspondence (first folder), Conn's Market (second folder), and Conn's Market credit terms 5-6-16 (file name). Using a date in the file name helps to distinguish different files about the same topic within the customer's folder.

In Chapters 8, 9, and 10 you learned about subject, numeric, and geographic filing methods. Any of these methods are appropriate for organizing your electronic files and folders.

CLASSIFICATION OF ELECTRONIC RECORDS

Why is classifying electronic records important?

The value of records increases when users know that they can retrieve the needed electronic documents. Classifying records provides the means to locate, group, retrieve, and manage documents. Having well-indexed records reduces financial and legal risks, improves standards compliance, and enhances productivity. Unless a good quality classification system is built into a document or RIM computing application, the system will fail to perform one of its primary purposes—locating and retrieving the document-based information. Chapter 13 gives examples of RIM software programs such as SharePoint®.

Classification of records should not be taken lightly. Classification involves planning and making decisions such as what to classify and which classification terms to use. In physical storage systems, indexing involves units and sometimes subjects. Classifying electronic records is similar in that *units* become *fields* and *subjects* become *keywords*. Classification fields can be used to categorize documents, to track creation or retention dates, or to enter subject matter. Classifying a computer record is the process of deciding the name or code by which it will be stored and retrieved, following the policies and procedures of the RIM software management programs or another system. If the organization has a file plan and metadata, employees are more likely to file electronic documents properly. Electronic files are often carelessly identified with abbreviations as file names that only the record creator could interpret. The file name "brdmtgmins" illustrates a file name that means nothing to anyone other than the person creating it. "Board Meeting Minutes 9-15-14" is a much clearer file name and would aid retrieval.

Full-text indexing provided by software capable of optical character recognition (OCR) eliminates the need for someone to read and manually index documents using keywords. OCR software "reads" a scanned document or page and indexes every word to track its location. Consequently, you can find documents by using any word or phrase in them.

Physical records are located by looking into a particular file cabinet, into a certain drawer, and into a specific file folder. Electronic records are located using metadata, taxonomies, and file plans. A well-designed and organized electronic records system is needed to make electronic records retrieval easier.

Metadata

metadata: structured information that describes, explains, locates, or otherwise makes it easier to retrieve, use, or manage an information resource

The simplest definition of metadata is data about data. **Metadata** is structured information that describes, explains, locates, or otherwise makes it easier to retrieve, use, or manage an information resource.[1] Another definition is "Data describing context, content, and structure of records and their management through time."[2]

Did you know that search engines, such as Google, Yahoo, or Bing, use <meta name = "description" . . . > on the html source pages to find matching terms for a search? The principle of metadata is at work on web pages too.

For records and information management, metadata is descriptive data with specific properties about a particular record. An example of metadata is a description of the American Gothic painting. The painting itself is the work of art; the metadata are the facts about the painting, which are shown in Figure 11.4.

FIGURE 11.4 **Metadata for the American Gothic Art**

Title: English: American Gothic
Artist: Grant Wood
Year: 1930
Type: Oil on beaverwood
Dimensions: 29¼ × 24 5/8 in (74.3 cm × 62.4 cm)
Location: The Art Institute of Chicago, Chicago, Illinois

[1]ARMA International Glossary for Records and Information Management Terms, 4th ed.
[2]ISO 15489—Records Management.

Metadata by itself is not a record and is essential for the management of information. Some records may contain metadata about other records. An example is a database that lists the metadata for a records series such as payroll records.

RIM-related metadata contained with the electronic records aids with capturing, registration, classification of records type or series, storage, and maintenance of records.

When you create a document in Microsoft® Word, the program automatically adds basic metadata to it. Find the properties on the File menu on the left side of the screen. Figure 11.5 shows a screen capture of what that metadata looks like for the Microsoft® Word document that was used as a manuscript for the "Classification of Electronic Records" section of this chapter.

FIGURE 11.5 **Basic Metadata in Word**

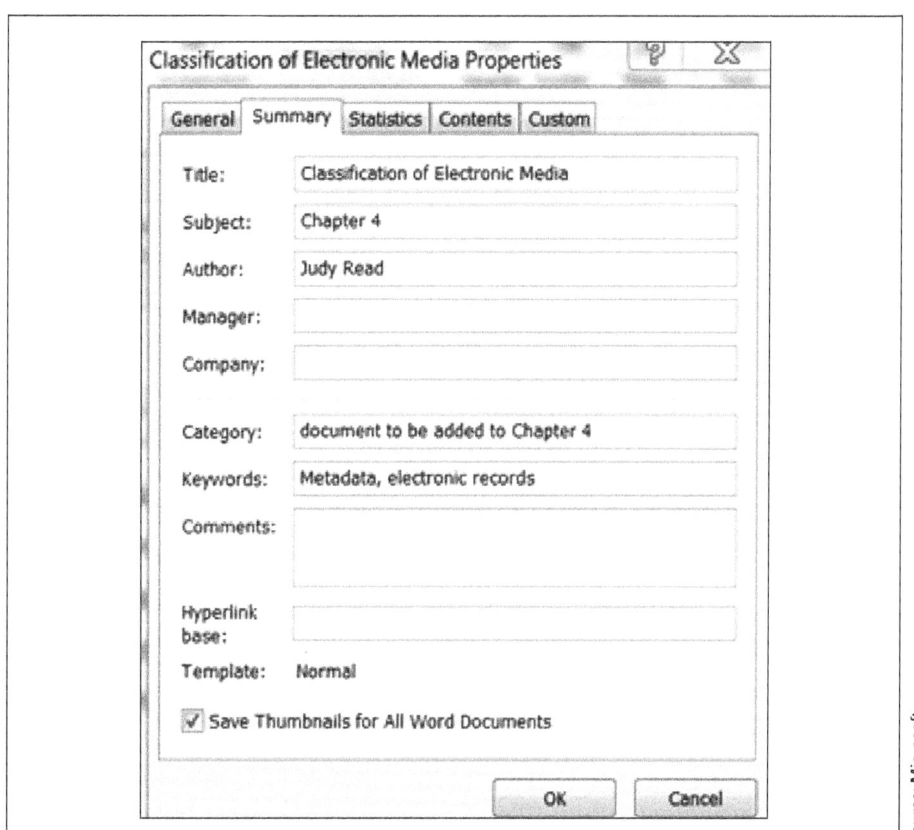

Source: Microsoft

Common Metadata Elements

The basic metadata descriptors identify the title, subject, author, manager, company, category of the record, keywords, and any comments. A hyperlink base is provided as a default in Microsoft® Word 2010 and 2013. (If SharePoint is used to maintain a company intranet or Internet presence, the address of the hyperlink is listed. Example: https://mycompany.com/). Each of these "fields" describes the document, which is why they are called *metadata.* Figure 11.6 shows 13 metadata elements that are most often used in RIM software programs.

The automatic classification of the unique identification, author, department, and so on are what make metadata work in a RIM system. Records

FIGURE 11.6 **Most Common Elements (or Fields) for Metadata**

ELEMENTS (OR FIELDS)	DESCRIPTION OF WHAT THE ELEMENT DOES
Unique Document ID	A numeric or alphanumeric value from the organization's file plan that is assigned to the document
Creation Date	The date that the document was created or received and could be different from the date that the document was declared a record
Creator/Author ID	The individual (or system such as payroll) who created the document
Business Unit	The department associated with the creator/author
Format	The file format used to create and store the document such as docx, pdf, xlsx, and so on
Subject/Title of Document	A brief, high-level description of the document or a set of keywords
Declaration Date	The date when the "draft" version became the final version or a record is declared
Record Owner	The department that is responsible for the management of the record
Record Custodian	The records management department most likely to assume responsibility for maintaining the record and/or has joint interest in the access to and preservation of the record
Qualified for Disposition	A standardized category associated with the length of time that a record must be kept to meet legal, regulatory and/or business requirements
Security Level	Identifies the sensitivity and criticality of information based on the need for information confidentiality, integrity, and availability
Vital Records Indicator	Indicator notating that the record is essential to resume and/or continue operations in the event of a disruption
Status	An indication of whether the document is a record, work in progress, or for reference.

Source: Adapted from "Metadata for Records Management 101: A Standards Based Approach," by Jennifer Best and Jason Sterns of New York Life Insurance Company at the 2012 ARMA International Conference, Chicago, IL, September 23–25.

managers can assist end users in understanding metadata when working with RIM software programs such as SharePoint.

The next section shows how metadata works with Excel invoices. For our example, we will use a hypothetical company named Electronic Slates, Inc. Electronic Slates assembles, sells, and distributes computer tablets.

The invoice business process uses Excel and accounting software to create the invoices and adapts the metadata that Excel provides. Find the properties from the File menu on the left side of the metadata panel screen capture. Here are two views of the metadata for an invoice using

FIGURE 11.7 **Metadata Panel in Excel**

Document Properties ▾ Location: C:\kg40-10\Chapter 4\Electronic Slates Invoices\Invoice 1112.x * Required field ×

Author:	Title:	Subject:	Keywords:
Rod Simmons	1112	Invoice	Blue, Black, Silver, Optional Keyb
Category:	Status:		
06-10-102	Record		

Comments:

Excel. Figure 11.7 shows the metadata panel at the top of the spreadsheet, and Figure 11.8 shows a screen capture of the custom metadata.

The Category box shows the file plan described later in this chapter. The Title box shows the invoice number. The author is Rod Simmons. Each of these "fields" is a clue to how to find the document. The Location box is the best field in which to find the record.

The Custom items show that this record, Invoice 1112, was checked by the records coordinator, the record is scheduled for disposition on 02/28/16, and the finance department "owns" the record.

The metadata from any of the Office programs can be used in an XML database using the SharePoint interface. From there, users can search on any of the fields to find out more about the record, including its file location.

FIGURE 11.8 **Custom Metadata in Excel**

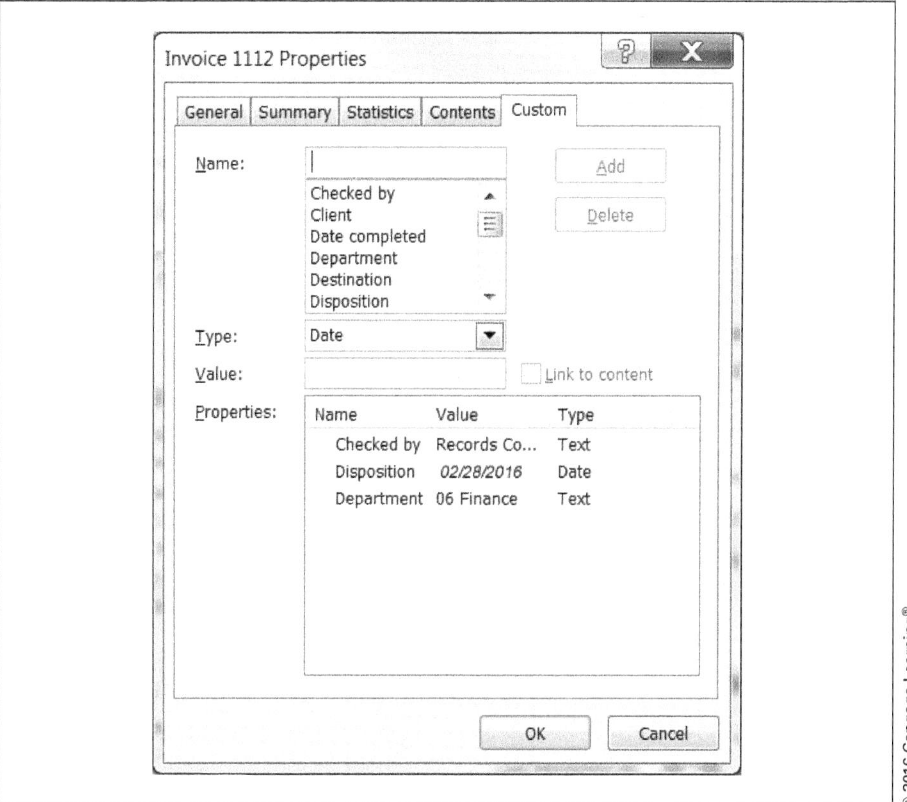

Taxonomies

Both taxonomies and file plans can be similar in terms of how they are designed. This chapter introduces you to taxonomies and file plans that are currently used in our example company Electronic Slates, Inc.

taxonomy: a high-level, hierarchical classification system for documents and records that facilitates the management of recorded information throughout its life cycle

A **taxonomy** is a high-level, hierarchical classification system for documents and records that facilitates the management of recorded information throughout its life cycle. A common taxonomy that many people are aware of is the classification of the animal kingdom using phylums, classes, order, family, genus, and species as shown in Figure 11.9. The entire order is a hierarchy: the number of choices in each level gets smaller. Another example is the Dewey Decimal Classification used in libraries to classify subject areas, shown in Figure 11.10.

FIGURE 11.9 **Animal Kingdom Classification**

CLASSIFICATION	EXAMPLE
Kingdom	Animalia (includes all animals)
Phylum	Chordata (includes all vertebrate animals)
Class	Mammalia (includes all mammals)
Order	Carnivora (includes carnivorous mammals)
Family	Felidae (includes all cats)
Genus	Panthera (includes the great cats)
Species	Panther (includes all types of panthers)

FIGURE 11.10 **Dewey Decimal System Example**

CLASSIFICATION	EXAMPLE
300	Social Science
340	Law
345	Criminal Law
345.06	Evidence

Many taxonomies are based upon the subjects pertinent to the organization. Creating a taxonomy for an organization is a project involving members of the information technology, records and information management, legal, and business function departments.

An enterprise-wide taxonomy usually contains three levels. An area is the highest level, usually corresponding to a key business area (Sales and Marketing is the example in Figure 11.11). The second level is a specific business function within the business area (Sales and Marketing). The third level is specialization that is a process within a function. In Figure 11.11, the Sales function includes Training, Contacts, and International Sales. The Marketing function includes Market Research and Customer Development.[3]

---

[3]http://www.doculabs.com/wp-content/uploads/downloads/2011/12/Doculabs-Answers-Ten-Questions-on-Taxonomy-v1.01.pdf, 2007, accessed December 10, 2013.

FIGURE 11.11 **Business Taxonomy for Sales and Marketing Functions**

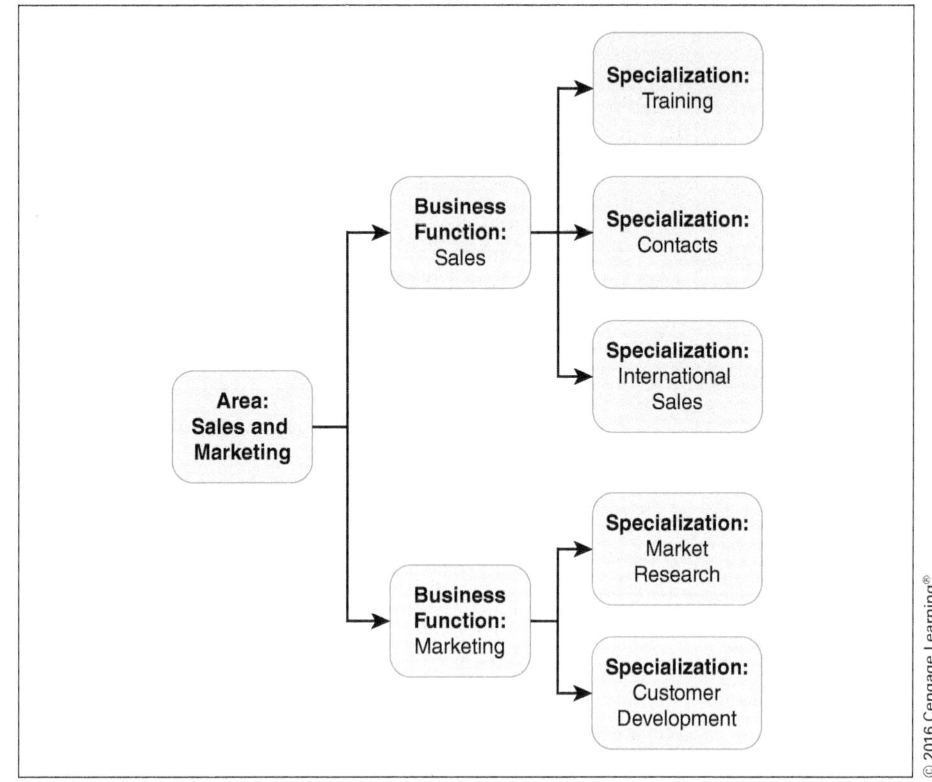

What aids are available to help classify documents?

Supplemental information is often required to improve knowledge workers' ability to classify particular documents. Data maps, thesauri, and indexes are developed. Procedures are implemented, and the users can then decide where to store the records.

File Plans

file plan: a classification scheme that defines and identifies all files, including indexing and storage of the files, and referencing the disposition schedule of each file

A **file plan** is a classification scheme that defines and identifies all files, including indexing and storage of the files, and referencing the disposition schedule of each file. This broad definition goes hand in hand with a comprehensive retention schedule. The file plan is a collaborative effort among records management, information technology, legal, and business functions departments. Chapter 7 presents information about using retention schedules.

Figure 11.12 shows the taxonomy and file plan for Electronic Slates, Inc., based on the main business functions of the company. As a builder, seller, and distributor of computer tablets, the main business functions are **Administration, Assembly, Distribution, Human Resources**, and **Finance**. Each function is assigned a two-digit number. The secondary folder shows a specialization within the business functions. Each specialization is assigned a two-digit number. The tertiary folders are for individuals or companies, and each is assigned a three-digit number, which creates a file plan number and a unique identifier for that individual or organization.

FIGURE 11.12 **Taxonomy and File Plan for Electronic Slates, Inc.**

TITLE				
PRIMARY	SECONDARY	TERTIARY	DESCRIPTION	FILE NO.
02 Administration	10 Travel		Travel applications forms, approvals, policies	02-10
	20 Insurance		Insurance coverage, policies, renewals	02-20
	30 Records Management	101 Information Governance	Policies for creation to disposition of records	02-30-101
		201 Records Inventory	Current and historical records inventory	02-30-201
		301 Archives	Archive policies, current and historical inventory	02-30-301
		401 Disposition	Disposition policies current inventory	02-30-401
		501 File Plan	Current file plan documents and agreements	02-30-501
03 Assembly	10 Components	250 IM Chips	Drafts and master contracts, negotiations, cancellations, and terminations to all contracts	03-10-250
		175 Byte, Inc.		03-10-175
	20 Process	370 Chip Control, Inc.	Engineering reports and contracts	03-20-370
04 Sales and Distribution	10 Contracts		Draft and master contracts for distributors of the tablets	04-10
	20 Reporting		Reports to regulating government entities	04-20
	30 Sales	100 Gene Vershum	Sales receipts, contracts	04-30-100
		150 Tyler Young		04-30-150
		300 Jill Napen		04-30-300
05 Human Resources	10 Employees	307 Able, Albert	Employee files including offer letters, contracts, disciplinary records, promotions	05-10-307
		601 Flint, Errol		05-10-601
		310 Tudor, Henry		05-10-310
	20 Policies	100 Workplace Safety	General policies on employment and workplace safety, business, conduct, etc. Drafts and approved copies	05-20-100

continues on next page

FIGURE 11.12 *(continued)*

TITLE				
PRIMARY	SECONDARY	TERTIARY	DESCRIPTION	FILE NO.
06 Finance	10 Accounts Receivable	102 Albany Baptist Seminary	Accounts Receivable: Invoices	06-10-102
		175 Big Box Store		06-10-175
		225 Explorer Energy		06-10-225
		280 Georgia Labor Dept.		06-10-280
		420 Meridian Hospital		06-10-420
		720 Simmons Insurance		06-10-720
		840 Tualatin School District		06-10-840
		324 Health Care HMO		06-10-324
		375 East Coast Electric & Gas Co.		06-10-375
		462 Mississippi Wholesalers		06-10-462
		512 Buyers Warehouse		06-10-512
		583 Technical & Career College		06-10-583
		636 Salem Brooms Base-ball Club		06-10-636
		691 Finest Office Products		06-10-691
		704 Allen Gates Foundation		06-10-702
	20 Accounts Payable		Accounts Payable	06-20
	60 Tax	Return 2010	Tax Return including challenges, supporting documents, notices of assessments, etc.	06-60-2010
		Return 2011		06-60-2011
		Return 2012		06-50-2012
		Return 2013		06-50-2013
		Return 2014		06-50-2014

Source: Miller, Bruce. Managing Records in Microsoft SharePoint 2010, published by ARMA International, Overland Park, KS, 2012.

Using the preceding table, here are two examples of how taxonomies and file plans work together to generate unique file plan numbers. The file numbers show the location of the records pertaining to the number.

1. An e-mail is distributed announcing that A. Able has been promoted to CFO of the company. A Human Resources staff person would classify this document as a record and store it in the employee's file. The taxonomy includes Human Resources 04, Employees 10, and Albert Able 307. Therefore the file number for the document announcing Albert Able's promotion is the unique identifier 04-10-307.
2. An e-mail is sent from IM Chips that advises a temporary shortage of the system boards for the tablets. A tropical storm has damaged the factory, and production will be halted for at least a week. The component manager notifies the records specialist that several documents

will be created. The documents so far will be put into a folder for the IM Chips, file number 03-10-250. The e-mail addresses assembly (03), components (10), IM Chips (250). As you can see from the description, it deals with their contract.

How are file plan numbers used?

In summary, file numbers or unique identifiers help with classification. These examples show how taxonomies and file plans work together to help records management flow efficiently through the phases of the records life cycle.

Use and Distribution

The next phase of the records cycle is distributing and using the information contained in the electronic folders and files. Distribution can be through electronic channels described as follows; or files can be printed and sent by regular mail, by facsimile, or by courier.

E-Mail

Documents can be created in Word, Excel, Access, and other programs and then attached to an e-mail message for distribution. The user can also key the information in a program such as Word and copy and paste the information into an e-mail. Electronic mail is the most common type of internal communication for organizations.

What is the most common type of written internal communication for businesses?

What chapter provides procedures for setting up files to hold correspondence?

Depending on the e-mail software used, folders can be created to help organize messages. Using the example of the Safety First business, you could send documents within the company via e-mail to communicate with people in other departments such as the shipping or accounting department. If you receive an inquiry from a customer, you could access the order number from the company database and know which stage of processing has been completed. You could then send an e-mail to the department that is currently working on the order. When your inquiry is answered, you could forward the information to the customer.

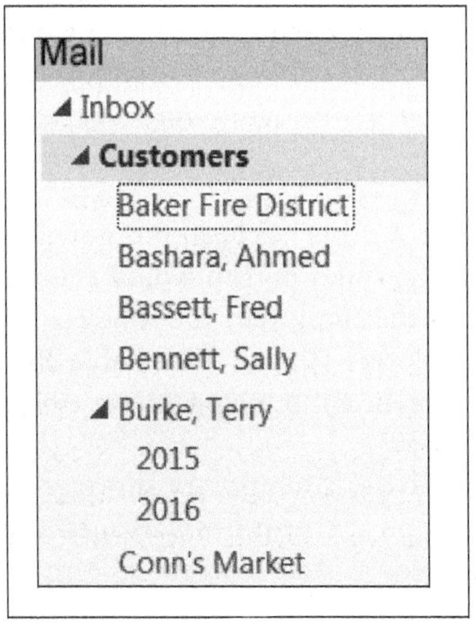

FIGURE 11.13 **Customer Folders in Microsoft Outlook**

For customers who order many products from the company, create a customer name folder into which you store all e-mails to and from the customer. If you have a few customers who only order once or twice a year, you can create a folder named "A" for all customers whose names begin with an A. The procedures for setting up files to hold physical correspondence are given in Chapter 6. With a little adaptation, the same procedures can be followed for e-mail folders.

All phases of the records life cycle can be completed using e-mail software in conjunction with SharePoint software. SharePoint is discussed further in Chapter 13. Figure 11.13 shows a folder structure in Microsoft Outlook organized by customer names. In this program, you can create folders by right-clicking on the Inbox icon and then keying the name of the folder.

E-mails that are records must be transferred to a proper recordkeeping system for long-term storage. When e-mail messages are part of an organization's records system—physical or electronic—users may transfer e-mail to a subdirectory (folder) on a local hard drive, network drive, or other electronic storage medium. If RIM software is used to manage and identify information, appropriate metadata must be entered into the records management system when an e-mail message is placed into it.

E-mail messages, including text and instant messages, transmitted through an organization's e-mail system are usually considered the organization's property and therefore are subject to management under an organization's RIM program. Tweets may also be considered organization property when sent and received at an organization's offices and containing work-related information. E-mail and Internet use is monitored in many organizations. E-mail messages containing information about programs, policies, decisions, or important transactions, may have ongoing value. Consequently, records retention policies may apply. Users decide whether the e-mail is a record, a nonrecord, or work in progress, based on the information in the message. If it is a record, the e-mail is filed under the appropriate file number based on the taxonomies and file plan of the organization.

Other Digital Communications

Text messages, tweets, and instant messages are similar to telephone messages because they are useful for only a short period of time. However, these media types can become records and be subject to e-discovery proceedings. If these communications do become records, they must be transferred and stored in the proper recordkeeping system.

Blogs, wikis, Internet forums, webinars, and podcasts are used for evaluation, review, and discussion in business and social settings. All five of these media can be archived and referenced for additional review or research.

Intranets

HTML (HyperText Markup Language): the language the Internet browsers such as Internet Explorer, Google Chrome, or Mozilla Firefox interpret and display

Many organizations post internal documents such as procedure manuals, reference documents, a personnel directory, and correspondence on a secure intranet site where employees see and use distributed information. **HTML (Hyper Text Markup Language)** is the language the Internet browsers, such as Internet Explorer, Google Chrome, or Mozilla Firefox, interpret and display. Users may also be allowed to download documents to their computers. The information technology (IT) Department works with RIM professionals to update and manage the intranet site. An intranet site allows employees access through password-protected user names.

What is the main advantage of using an intranet site?

Some companies do not allow access to the intranet site unless employees are using a company computer. Many companies do not print and distribute manuals to everyone in the organization; instead, the information is posted on an intranet site. Because the information is available on the intranet and updated regularly, the documents are not made available in printed form, and the company saves the cost of printing.

RECORDS MANAGEMENT IN ACTION

Metadata and Your Privacy

Metadata are essential for electronic records classification, storage, and retrieval. With the vast increase in the number of mobile devices and individuals accessing the Internet, metadata can provide a detailed account of daily communication and online activities. Privacy becomes a concern if such information is misused.

So what metadata are generated when you use your smartphone or access the Internet? Here are some examples of metadata that are being generated.

- ***Phone calls:*** phone number of the caller, unique serial numbers of phones involved, time of call, duration of call, location of each participant, telephone calling card numbers.
- ***E-mail:*** sender's name, e-mail and IP address; recipient's name and e-mail address; date, time, and time zone; unique identifier of e-mail and related e-mails; and subject and status of the e-mail.
- ***Facebook:*** your name and profile bio information that you have provided, including, birthday, hometown, work history and interests, your username and unique identifier, your subscriptions, your location, your device, activity date, time and time zone, your activities, likes, check-ins, and events.
- ***Twitter:*** your name, location, language, profile bio information and URL; when you created your account; your username and unique identifier; tweet's location, date, time, and time zone; tweet's unique ID and ID of tweet replied to contributor IDs; your follower, following, and favorite count; and your verification status.
- ***Google search:*** your search queries, results that appeared in searches, and pages that you visit from search.
- ***Web browser:*** your activity, including pages you visit and when; your IP address; Internet service provider; device hardware details; operating system and browser version; and cookies and cached data from websites.

As you can see, metadata can be used to identify your communication patterns as well as physical activities.

Source: Oliver Laughland, Metadata: is it simply "billing data," or something more personal? theguardian.com, December 2, 2013, http://www.theguardian.com/world/2013/dec/02/metadata-should-it-be-dismissed-as-billing-data-or-is-it-personal-material, accessed December 4, 2013.

Source: Guardian US interactive team, A Guardian guide to your metadata, theguardian.com, June 12, 2013, http://www.theguardian.com/technology/interactive/2013/jun/12/what-is-metadata-nsa-surveillance#meta=1111111, accessed December 4, 2013.

An intranet site is usually organized by a hybrid method of storage, which you learned about in Chapters 8, 9, and 10. Search engines are available on most large company intranets so that the user can find the appropriate information. An IT Department is usually in charge of a company intranet site. However, IT works with a team of workers from all departments of the company to help test the site and help guide its evolution.

Shared Folders

Another place for distribution and use of electronic documents is on shared drives or folders on the company's local area network (LAN). An organization may have access to the cloud as a shared resource. The LAN may be set up so that certain departments have the use of a particular shared drive. For example, department workers have the right to create, save, edit, modify, and delete files and folders on the shared drive. Some shared drives are available to everyone in the company. Other shared drives are limited to specific staff or departments. Confidential information is usually on a restricted drive available only to employees who are cleared to access confidential information.

Search Features

Which Windows function can help you find a file?

Programs or features that allow users to search for files on a computer drive, LAN drives, or intranet are important tools for electronic records management. On a computer that uses **Microsoft® Windows**, for example, users can search by file name, date, or text on any drive on the computer and/or any drives to which the computer connects. The word "sharepoint" is in the Windows Explorer search shown in Figure 11.14. The search is set for the hard drive of the computer.

What are working and storage copies?

Data is a valuable organizational resource, and users want and need to have access to that data from many locations, sometimes in different time zones. For effective storage management of electronic media, storage copies must be differentiated from working copies. *Working copies* are intended for ongoing information processing and reference requirements. *Storage copies* are created to satisfy retention requirements. The most active or working copies of electronic records are usually stored where they can be quickly accessed. That location may be inside a computer on a hard drive, on shared drives, on the organization's intranet, or in the cloud.

FIGURE 11.14 **Search Using Windows Explorer**

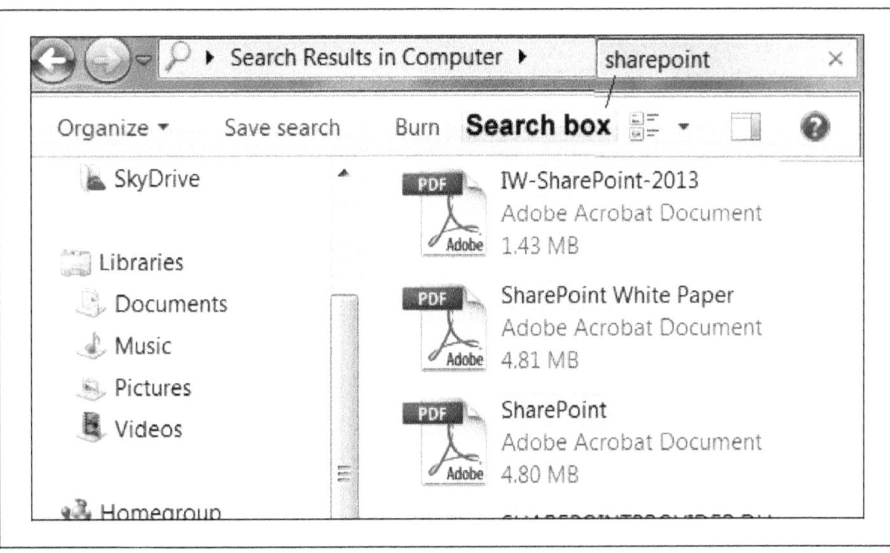

Source: Microsoft

RETENTION AND MAINTENANCE

The next phase of the records life cycle is retaining the files. In Chapters 2 and 7, you learned that a records retention schedule is used to specify how long to keep the records in an organization. Based on retention schedules, maintenance of electronic files follows regularly scheduled times to keep or dispose of the files.

E-Mail Retention Policies

Why do e-mail users need to be cautious about what they write in e-mail on their employer's computers?

As mentioned previously, e-mail, text messages, and tweets may be obtained as evidence during e-discovery procedures. Damaging evidence can often be found in messages that senders or receivers thought were deleted. Because the e-mail server makes daily backups of all files, including e-mail messages of any type, copies of messages sent and deleted may still be in the backup file. In addition, software programs often make several copies of files and place them in different addresses. Computer forensic experts may be able to recover these files.

Security issues stemming from unsuspected file copies call for the following measures:

- Implement an organization-wide e-mail policy that requires regular purging of files that are no longer active or needed for future operations or historical records.
- Follow the established e-mail policy and do not put anything into an e-mail message that you would not want repeated or used in court.
- Protect your password.
- Always log off the system properly so that no one else can create, change, or damage records on your computer.

Moving and Copying Files and Folders

Files and folders can be moved from one folder to another as part of managing electronic records. Moving electronic files that are over a year old, for example, to a different folder leaves fewer files in the original folder, and the more active files are easier to find. At the Safety First business, customer files older than a year are moved to removable storage devices. On the removable drive, the same alphabetic system with a folder labeled with the customer name is used. The dates are noted in the folder name also.

The Copy command in programs such as Windows Explorer is used to create a duplicate of a file or a folder. The copy may have a different name than the original file or folder, or it may have the same name if it is stored in a different drive or device. Copying allows files to be available in two or more locations. For example, with the employer's permission, an employee can copy a file to a removable storage device and then edit the file on his or her home computer. When the employee returns to work, the updated file is copied to the work computer. Having files readily available can be a convenience to the employee. However, keeping unnecessary copies of files should be avoided, to make the best use of storage capacity on hard drives or other devices. In addition, having copies on multiple devices can cause problems and confusion when changes are made to one copy on one device and not to the others.

Data Migration

Data migration is used to copy electronic folders and files onto new media as it becomes available and as older media reach their life expectancy. Implementing a data migration procedure ensures that today's electronic storage can be read with devices used in the future.

Backing Up and Restoring Data

backup: a copy of electronic files and/or folders as a precaution against the loss or damage of the original data

A **backup** is a copy of electronic files and/or folders as a precaution against the loss or damage of the original data. Users should follow a regular schedule to back up vital and important electronic records. Many LANs use software that automatically makes copies of some or all data on the network on a regular schedule.

If data is lost or damaged, it can be restored using backup copies. The process of restoring backup copies ensures that the electronic files can be used again without interruption to the flow of business.

DISPOSITION

Inactive Records Storage and Archives

When records are transferred to inactive files or archives, systematic storage according to standard filing procedures apply. Storage copies, sometimes called *master copies*, of electronic records are usually recorded onto removable magnetic, optical, or solid state media. These copies often contain inactive records that were transferred from hard drives, and they are seldom referenced. Storage copies may be used only for making additional working copies in the event that existing working copies are damaged. Storage copies also are used to recover and restore information if a system failure or other disaster occurs. The long-term quality of magnetic storage media has not been determined. Because magnetic records can be damaged by extreme temperature or proximity to magnetic charges, vital records should be stored on a more permanent medium for archival storage.

Why are storage copies (master copies) not used in daily operations?

Optical discs have a predicted life expectancy of approximately 10–20 years.[4] However, retrieving records from optical disc storage requires computer equipment and software, which can become obsolete and impact retrieval of records created on that hardware and software. Newer versions of some software and hardware accept earlier versions and save the records in the new version. However, media format or size may change, which will make locating the specific type of disk drive difficult. As a result, microfilm remains a popular medium for long-term storage of vital records with a life expectancy of 100 years.[5] Although many media formats and equipment have been replaced or become obsolete, older media will often be located when a records inventory is conducted. Maintaining a current inventory of electronic records helps RIM managers develop effective retention schedules for those records. RIM managers are also better able to make data migration decisions—determining which records need to be migrated and to what media.

---

[4]Source: ARMA online Essentials in RIM Micrographics Course, http://www.arma.org/r1/professional-development/certificate-programs/essentials-of-rim-certificate, accessed November 2011.

[5]Ibid.

Inactive Records Retention

What are total retention periods?

Records and information managers need to develop total life cycle retention periods. Retention periods should be assigned according to records series. A *total retention* period, required for most records retention schedules, reflects the length of time that the data should remain in computer accessible form. After that time has expired, all data should be purged from all storage devices supporting the system.

Although some businesses maintain and manage their inactive and archival records in house, others have found that outsourcing these records to commercial vendors is more cost effective. Some issues to consider when deciding to outsource include the cost of onsite storage space, storage equipment and containers needed to meet the continuing increase in the number of inactive records as the business grows, personnel costs in managing the inventory, and destruction of the records when retention periods end.

Disposition of Records

The final step in a records life cycle is disposition. The inactive record can either be destroyed or preserved indefinitely. If a record is to be destroyed, it must be done correctly and completely. If electronic information is in directories and subdirectories, a software file manager can sort the files by date and identify records due for disposition (retain or destroy). Ways to dispose of electronic records are presented in Figure 11.15.

How is information erased from magnetic disks?

To dispose of information on a magnetic disk, the file(s) must be deleted, and the space the files occupied on the disk must be overwritten to make recovering the information almost impossible. When users delete files, the space is marked for reuse, but the information is not physically removed or erased from a disk. With the help of commonly used utility programs, a user may restore deleted files that have not been overwritten. If the electronic storage space is erased but is still available for reuse, the record can be

FIGURE 11.15 **Disposition Procedures for Electronic Records**

Magnetic disks	Delete file(s) from the disk, and overwrite the space with new information. Defragmentation and disk scanning software can overwrite areas of a hard disk or diskette that are no longer being used
Magnetic tapes	Mark files for deletion and overwrite the space. Usually, all files must be restored to a hard disk, the marked files deleted, and the remaining files written to the tape. Delete the files restored from the hard disk after they are written to the tape. Use defragmentation and disk scanning software to overwrite the disk.
CD-ROM	Restore all files to a hard drive, delete selected files, and write or burn remaining files onto a new CD-ROM. Destroy original CD-ROM by shredding.
CD-R, CD-RW	Restore all files to a hard drive, delete selected files, rewrite remaining files to the same disc.

recovered. The record's information could still be subject to e-discovery proceedings. The fact that the record was simply deleted could give the appearance of covering up information and make matters worse for the organization during e-discovery.

Three primary methods are used for destroying electronic records:

- Software Erasure Programs
- Degaussing—a procedure that involves applying a strong magnetic field to tapes and hard drives to remove the magnetically recorded data
- Shredding the electronic records[6]

CDs, DVDs, or USB flash drives used to store confidential data should be shredded to completely destroy the records.

Businesses and organizations may use a combination of these methods in destroying electronic records. Some businesses and organizations will destroy the records in house, whereas others will outsource some or all records destruction.

In summary, the electronic records life cycle is a way to organize records from creation through disposition. The classification phase is an important part of electronic records management. Metadata, taxonomies, and file plans help in identifying records, where they are stored, and how long to keep them.

ELECTRONIC DATABASES

If you completed the applications for Chapters 3, 4, and 5, you have created or edited electronic files using a database program, Microsoft® Access. As with physical records, electronic files should be managed so that you can retrieve the data quickly when needed.

database: a collection of related data stored on a computer system

An electronic **database** is a collection of related data stored on a computer system. The data can be used with various applications but managed independently of them. For example, records in a database that contain names and addresses can be used to create personalized e-mails with a word processing program. Databases are organized especially for rapid search and retrieval of specific data. People have been using databases on large mainframe computers for over 50 years. A variety of database programs are available for personal computers as well. Microsoft® Access is a popular database program.

Database Elements

tables: a set of data organized into fields and records (columns and rows)

field: a set of one or more characters treated as a unit of information

A database contains **tables** that hold the data. Data in a table are organized in fields and records. A **field** is a set of one or more characters treated as a unit of information. The combination of characters forms words, numbers, or a meaningful code. For example, your first name, middle name, and last name could each be entered into a separate field. Your date of birth, Social Security number, telephone number, and the month and year that you finished high school are all examples of facts about you. Each fact could be entered into a separate field.

---

[6]Source: Adapted from ARMA Online Course Essentials of RIM Electronic Record Management, accessed November 2011.

record: all the fields related to one person or organization

All the fields related to one person or organization make up a **record.** Records related to one subject or topic (customers, students, orders) are usually stored in one or more related tables. A database can also contain several other objects such as forms and reports. Figure 11.16 shows a database created with Microsoft® Access.

FIGURE 11.16 **Database from Microsoft® Access**

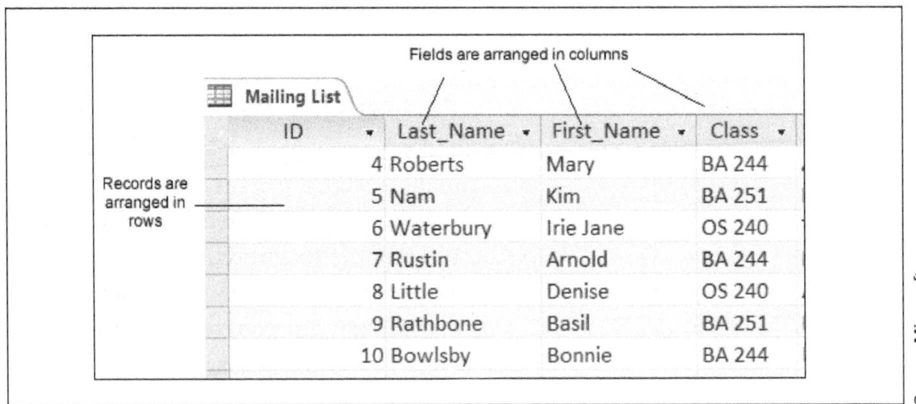

ID	Last_Name	First_Name	Class
4	Roberts	Mary	BA 244
5	Nam	Kim	BA 251
6	Waterbury	Irie Jane	OS 240
7	Rustin	Arnold	BA 244
8	Little	Denise	OS 240
9	Rathbone	Basil	BA 251
10	Bowlsby	Bonnie	BA 244

A field has a unique name and a specified number of characters, and it contains a defined type of information. Commonly used field types are text fields (sometimes called *alphanumeric fields* for letters, numbers, symbols, and punctuation) and number fields. Other typical field types are date fields, logical fields, and memo fields.

Why is a primary key assigned?

When using database software, the user must assign a field as a primary or unique key. The database will not allow the same data to be entered into the primary key field for more than one record. The primary key creates a unique identifier for each record. For example, when you change a service to your cell phone, the person making the change asks for your phone number (which is unique to you). Your phone number is entered as the search criteria in the database. The database then finds and displays your personal information.

Can you use a word processing program to create a database?

On which field can you sort data?

Word processing and spreadsheet software can contain simple databases. A relational database program such as Microsoft® Access, MySQL, or Oracle allows more flexibility in working with the information in the database. When a document is set up in database format with fields (whether the document is in a word processing, spreadsheet, or database program) sorting on any field is possible. The procedures vary depending on the software. Usually a field or column is selected. The type of sort is defined: ascending (A–Z, 1–10) or descending (Z–A, 10–1). The sort command is carried out, and the list is placed into alphabetic or numeric order by the chosen field. Several words can be entered into the same field and the correct alphabetic order is maintained.

Finding Information in a Database

Finding a specific piece of information in a database is easy. Use the Find feature to enter the data that you want to find such as a name, address, or phone number. Tell the database to search all fields or selected fields; give the command to start the search; and the information will display on the screen within seconds. What if you don't know the exact name you wish to find? In this case, you can enter the first few letters of the last name. When that information displays on the screen, scroll through the records until you find the correct one. You may need other information (such as a birth date) to validate that the name is the correct one.

A database is useful for sorting various fields alphabetically. As you learned in Chapters 3, 4, and 5, an alphabetic listing of customer names makes looking up a particular customer much easier. Database software can sort records using fields in a database. If you want to sort the database by the city in which customers live, simply sort on the City field. If you want to sort the database by the Postal code for a large customer mailings, sort on the Postal Code field. If you want to sort the database by the city and then alphabetically by customer, the database will return this information with the proper query. Remember that the purpose of sorting data is for retrieval—finding and using information again. A **query** is a database object used to instruct the program to find specific information. For example, Figure 11.17 shows the design view of a query in Microsoft® Access and the resulting query table.

query: a database object used to instruct the program to find specific information

Figure 11.18 on page 302 shows a portion of a report based on the query shown in Figure 11.17. Customers are grouped alphabetically by city, and then sorted by name. Queries also help a user summarize information. For example, a jewelry store has a database of customer names, addresses, phone numbers, warranty information, and lists of merchandise purchased organized by the dates of purchase. The store manager is having a sale on rings. The manager wants to know which customers had purchased rings in the last two years. The query would ask the database to sort the Purchase field and then identify the beginning and ending years. The database would return a list of customers in sorted order by the Purchase field for the last two years. The manager could then target advertising to those customers.

FIGURE 11.17 **Query Design and Results**

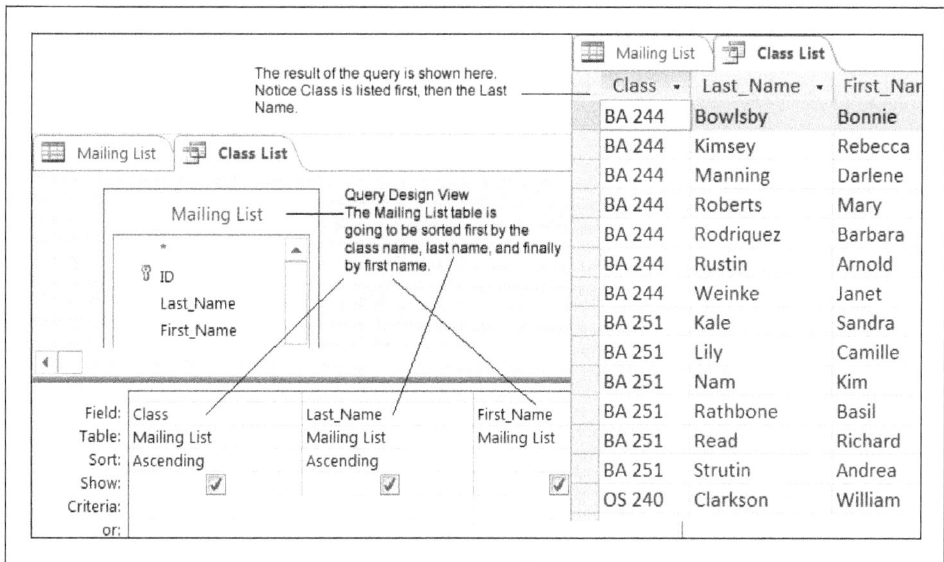

Source: Microsoft

FIGURE 11.18 **Microsoft® Access Report Based on Query Results**

City Sort

City	Last Name	First Name	Class
Aloha			
	Little	Denise	OS 240
	Nelson	Rick	OS 240
	Roberts	Mary	BA 244
Beaverton			
	Bowlsby	Bonnie	BA 244
	Clarkson	William	OS 240
	Manning	Darlene	BA 244
	Miller	Todd	OS 240
	Nam	Kim	BA 251
	Rathbone	Basil	BA 251
Portland			
	Deetz	Evelyn	OS 240
	Kale	Sandra	BA 251
	Kimsey	Rebecca	BA 244
	Lily	Camille	BA 251
	Rustin	Arnold	BA 244
	Strutin	Andrea	BA 251
	Weinke	Janet	BA 244
Tigard			
	Read	Richard	BA 251
	Rodriquez	Barbara	BA 244
	Thomas	Roberto	OS 240
	Waterbury	Irie Jane	OS 240

Source: Microsoft

USING DATABASES IN RECORDS MANAGEMENT AND E-COMMERCE

Many records departments create a database index of their physical and/or nonpaper records. For example, a database is created that contains the names, addresses, and telephone numbers of subscribers of the symphony. An electronic database allows rapid creation of mailing labels to notify customers of special concerts or other events to help generate more sales.

In Chapter 2 you learned about e-commerce and how RIM professionals work with IT professionals to manage electronic records created via the Internet. E-commerce is another way of doing business using electronic resources. Most organizations have a web presence, and many allow some type of dynamic interaction with visitors to their websites. The dynamic interaction usually involves filling out a form, clicking Send or Submit, and receiving some type of response on the web page.

CAREER CORNER

Job Description for Records Specialist I, II, or III

The following job description is an example of a career opportunity with a wholesale electric power supplier.

The Records Specialist position is responsible for maintaining the corporate records center functions that include classification and coding of material for integration into the corporate Enterprise Content and Records Management (ECRM) system. Duties include search and retrieval of records from various physical and electronic locations, providing imaging support services, and providing instruction and records expertise to other functional areas regarding records retention and storage processes in accordance with policy, program, and procedures. The Records Specialist will manage records using various data repositories

The position level will be based on the qualifications and experience of the selected candidate.

QUALIFICATIONS

- A Experience requirements for Records Specialist III: Minimum six (6) years of general office/file center environment experience, including three (3) years of working in a records center/corporate repository environment.
- B. Experience requirements for Records Specialist II: Minimum four (4) years of general office/file center environment experience, including two (2) years of working in a records center/corporate repository environment
- C. Experience requirements for Records Specialist I: Minimum two (2) years of general office/file center environment experience, including one (1) year of working in a Records Center/corporate repository environment
- AA/BA/BS preferred
- Combination of education and work experience providing competencies to perform the required responsibilities specific to position
- Experience with records inventory projects, including analysis and interpretation of records content for data capture within ECRM systems
- Working knowledge of library and records management techniques, procedures, and methodologies
- Must be proficient in multiple software applications and records specific hardware/software

What is the relationship between a form on a web page and an organization's database?

The server computer that houses the web pages sends instructions from the HTML document to the web server application software, which in turn queries or displays the database.

The application server software acts as a translator between the form on the web page and the data in the database. Filling out a form and clicking Submit causes the server application software to create a new record in the database. If you signed up for an electronic newsletter, for example, a record is created indicating your e-mail address. When the newsletter is sent the next time, you will receive a copy in your e-mail inbox. If you change your e-mail address, you fill out another form on the web page. Clicking Submit updates your record in the database.

If you were to contact the organization in person or over the phone, the customer service representative would access the same database. Your record would be found by searching using a unique field. In the case of the newsletter example, the unique field would be your e-mail address. A bigger role for databases in e-commerce is played when the transaction for services or merchandise is completed. The dynamic form on the web page not only accesses the database but also starts the procedure for products to be "picked" off the warehouse floor, sent to shipping, and then sent to the customer. The payment part of the transaction is completed via electronic fund transfer (EFT) or other automated process. The customer receives the product, and a credit card is charged for the amount of the product. The customer receives a credit card statement showing the bill for this product.

What are examples of push technology and pull technology?

push technology: allows a central server to notify a computer or cell phone when an event occurs

pull technology: occurs when the user initiates the request for the data each time

With **push technology**, e-mail, texts, calendar updates, and other data are automatically delivered to a smartphone or other mobile device based on the user's profile. Push technology also allows a central server to notify a computer or cell phone when an event occurs. The event is usually a new piece of content such as a tweet or a new e-mail.

Pull technology occurs when the user initiates the request for the data each time. A computer or cell phone asks the server if any new content is available, then the server provides the computer or cell phone with the new information. Shopping on the Internet is an example of pull technology.[7]

Databases on personal computers, LANs, intranet, or the Internet are useful tools to help manage records and information. Chapter 13 simulates an electronic content management system using databases in conjunction with metadata, taxonomies, or file plans.

[7]Source: PCMag.Com Encyclopedia "definition of push technology," http://www.pcmag.com/encyclopedia/term/49977/push-technology, accessed January 2014.

CHAPTER REVIEW AND APPLICATIONS

KEY POINTS

- Electronic records have a life cycle, as do physical records. The stages of the electronic records cycle include creation, classification, use and distribution, retention and maintenance, and disposition.
- Tools (such as Windows Explorer) are available on computers to manage all phases of the records life cycle.
- Using meaningful file names is an important part of managing electronic files.
- Using metadata (data about data) helps in retrieving electronic records.
- Organizations create taxonomies and file plans to make classifying electronic records easier by following a hierarchical structure.
- An electronic database is a collection of related data stored on a computer system. In a database, data is stored in tables containing fields and records.
- The Find or Query feature of database software can be used to find information. Reports can be made from the data in a table or query results.
- Databases are an integral part of e-commerce. Web server and web application software use a form on a web page to create or append records.
- In an e-commerce transaction for services or merchandise, the dynamic form on a web page not only accesses the database but also starts the procedure for products to be sent to the customer. The payment part of the transaction is completed via electronic fund transfer (EFT).

TERMS

backup
database
electronic records life cycle
field
file name
file plan
folder (or directory)
HTML (HyperText Markup Language)
metadata
operating system
portable document format (PDF)
pull technology
push technology
record (computer record)
table
taxonomy
query

REVIEW AND DISCUSS

1. Name and briefly describe the five stages of the electronic records life cycle. (Obj.1)

2. You are taking the following classes: WR 121 English Composition, SOC 104 Introduction to Sociology, HST 201 History of Western Civilization, and BA 244 Records Management. List the folder names that you will create to store electronic files for each of your classes. (Obj. 2)

3. In what ways does metadata aid in managing records? (Obj.2)

4. Name at least three common metadata elements used in RIM software programs. (Obj.2)

5. Explain how taxonomies and file plans work together to create a file classification system. (Obj. 2)

6. What does "Total Retention Period" mean for electronic records? (Obj.3)

7. Why should employees be careful about what they write in e-mails on their employers' computers? (Obj.3)

8. Name the three primary methods for destroying electronic records. (Obj. 3)

9. Describe the relationships among tables, fields, and records in a database. (Obj. 4)

10. What is the purpose of a database query? (Obj. 4)

11. Describe how a database is used during an e-commerce transaction. (Obj. 5)

12. Describe the difference between push and pull technology as related to e-commerce. (Obj. 5)

APPLICATIONS

11-1 Create a Logical Folder Structure (Obj. 6)

Data File

1. Copy the folder named "Sheraden Investment Services" found in the data files to your hard drive or other storage device.

2. Study the list of files contained in the folder. The files are also listed below. Open some of the files to see the type of data they contain. Determine how to organize the files into a meaningful folder structure.
3. Create a logical folder structure with appropriate folders and subfolders. Move appropriate files to their folders. Submit your work as your instructor directs.

File Names	
Abbott Kenneth 2015	McAllister Vicky Annual
Abbott Kenneth 2016	Reston Brenda 2015
Abbott Kenneth Annual	Reston Brenda 2016
Abbott Paul 2015	Reston Brenda Annual
Abbott Paul 2016	St Amand Dennis 2015
Abbott Paul Annual	St Amand Dennis 2016
Annual Appointment Letter	St Amand Dennis Annual
Demarco David 2015	TenPass Margaret 2015
Demarco David 2016	TenPass Margaret 2016
Demarco David Annual	TenPass Margaret Annual
Investment Summary	Thatcher Linda 2015
McAllister Vicky 2015	Thatcher Linda 2016
McAllister Vicky 2016	Thatcher Linda Annual

11-2 Classify E-Mail Messages (Obj. 3)

E-mail messages may be considered records or nonrecords, depending on their content and continuing value to an organization. Work with a classmate to complete the following:

1. Read the description of each of the following e-mail messages, and decide whether the message should be considered a record and stored in the records and information system.
2. Create a directory system for storing the e-mail files that you decide are records. For all these messages, create a meaningful file name for the record and a meaningful name for the directory where the record will be stored on a hard drive. Assume that your operating system allows the use of long file names.

	Message Date	Message Contents
a.	11/04/20--	A coworker indicates that a meeting at 9:00 a.m. next Friday is convenient for her.
b.	11/04/20--	Your supervisor describes new procedures for handling purchase orders.
c.	11/04/20--	The vice president of Human Resources explains the new medical savings plans available to all employees.
d.	11/05/20--	A coworker wishes you happy birthday.
e.	11/05/20--	A coworker provides routing instructions for a report that you are preparing.
f.	11/05/20--	A vendor, Broadway Computer Services, Inc., lists details of a new contract being negotiated.
g.	11/06/20--	An outside contractor, Kingsmill Roofing, gives an estimate for completing a roofing project.
h.	11/06/20--	A coworker who is having trouble accessing online files and wonders whether you are having the same problem.
i.	11/07/20--	Questions are sent to Broadway Computer Services, Inc., regarding the contract being negotiated.
j.	11/07/20--	The Finance Department's administrative assistant summarizes decisions made at a department meeting and listing action items.
k.	11/07/20--	Request to Monica Ortega, CPA, for a bid for the annual tax audit.
l.	11/07/20--	Your supervisor informs all employees that she will be out of the office next Wednesday.

11-3 Classify Documents for Electronic Slates, Inc.

Refer to Figure 11.12, Taxonomy and File Plan for Electronic Slates, Inc., on pages 290–291. You have received the following documents listed and described in the following table. In the column marked File No., add the appropriate number. Some documents may not "fit" with the file plan: The documents may not be records.

Document Format	Description	FILE NO.		
		Primary	Secondary	Tertiary
Word	Official Transcript for Henry Tudor			
E-mail	Agenda for Records Department meeting next week			
PDF	Report from Chip Control, Inc., on the Assembly process			
E-mail notice of invoice payment	Tualatin School District for $18,370.00			
Word	Final version of the current compliance report from the Occupational Safety and Health Administration (OSHA)			
E-mail	Invitation to the retirement party for your supervisor			
E-mail notice of invoice payment	Meridian Hospital for $16,130.00			
Billing Statement	From Byte, Inc., for $3647.00 for system boards			
E-mail notice of invoice payment	Big Box Store for $22,025.00			
E-mail	Performance Review for E. Flint			

ADDITIONAL RESOURCES

For data files, Microsoft® Access tutorials and more, go to www.cengagebrain.com.

CHAPTER 12

Electronic Media and Image Records

Photo by Judith M. Read-Simmons

ON THE JOB

Geri McCrae is a Systems Administrator with the Oregon Employment Department. Geri finds her job enjoyable because each day can provide unique problems and challenges to be resolved. Her duties include modifying, scanning, and imaging software programs to capture new and modified unemployment insurance (UI) information. This information is then integrated into the department mainframe computer. As part of her duties, she tests the changed programming for accuracy and completeness and repairs any problems that might occur.

Although the Employment Department has encouraged employers and UI claimants to use electronic processes, a multitude of various paper documents still must be manually scanned. Geri is responsible for ensuring that the correct metadata are captured and the documents are classified correctly for retrieval.

In addition, Geri monitors logs and transactions that occur between the image system and the mainframe; maintains user logon and access permissions for several hundred department employees; and continually troubleshoots for document, workflow, and hardware/software issues.

Geri advises students interested in records and information management careers to gain a basic knowledge of computers, software, and database management.

LEARNING OBJECTIVES

1. Define *electronic records* and *image records*.
2. Define *magnetic, optical,* and *solid state media* and list two types of each media.
3. Discuss records safety and security.
4. Explain managing information on mobile devices.
5. Explain the advantages and disadvantages of a Bring Your Own Device (BYOD) policy for organizations.
6. List and describe four factors related to microfilm quality.
7. Discuss microfilming processes.
8. Discuss image records retention.

ELECTRONIC AND IMAGE RECORDS

electronic record: a record that can be readily accessed or changed and is stored on electronic storage media

image record: a digital or photographic representation of a record on any medium such as microfilm, optical disk, or solid state devices

An **electronic record** is a record that can be readily accessed or changed and is stored on electronic storage media. An electronic record is often referred to as a *machine-readable record*—digitized and coded information that must be translated by a computer or other type of equipment before it can be understood. An **image record** is a digital or photographic representation of a record on any medium such as microfilm, optical disc, or solid state devices.

Electronic records may contain quantitative data, text, images, or sounds that originate as an electronic signal. A document created with word processing software and stored as a computer file is an electronic record. A printed physical copy of that document is not an electronic record; it is a physical record. A database index of a subject filing system is an electronic record. A computer-generated, printed physical copy of the subject index or a copy on microfiche is a physical record.

Electronic Media

Electronic media include magnetic, optical, and solid state media. Electronic media can store and retrieve a document faster than other storage media. Each of these media has advantages and disadvantages for their usage. Electronic document formats include digitized images generated by document scanners and character-coded data or text produced by word processing software, e-mail systems, or other computer programs. Each format (physical, photographic, and electronic) has distinct attributes that can satisfy specific life cycle and records retention requirements. However, no format is superior in every circumstance. Each medium is discussed next.

Magnetic Media

magnetic media: a variety of magnetically coated materials used by computers for data storage

Magnetic media are a variety of magnetically coated materials used by computers for data storage. The first *hard disk drive (HDD)* was introduced by IBM in 1956. The technology has evolved since then; however, the basic principle on how they work has not changed. HDDs are basically metal platters with a magnetic coating that allows data storage. A read/write head on a movable arm accesses the data on the spinning platter.

The first hard disk drives for personal computers were only 20 KBs (kilobytes) in the 1980s. Storage capacity of up to 4 TBs (terabytes) is now available for desktop and laptop computers. Cloud software as a service (SaaS) includes server farms with the largest hard drive capacities.

Two types of widely used magnetic media are listed in Figure 12.1.

FIGURE 12.1 **Magnetic Media**

Hard disk	A thin, rigid metal platter covered with a substance that holds data in the form of magnetized spots
Redundant array of independent disks (RAID)	A computer storage system consisting of over 100 hard disk drives, contained in a single cabinet, that simultaneously send data to a computer over parallel paths

Because the moving parts of magnetic media are subject to failure, backups are scheduled regularly. When erased or damaged, data on magnetic media can be restored from backups.

Magnetic tape on reels or in cartridges can be used for storing backups of data, especially for large mainframe computers. RAID configurations provide mass storage with the advantage of spreading data across an array of hard drives, which increases the chance that if one drive fails, data will not be lost. RAID drives are used on server computers for local area networks, intranets, and the Internet. Desktop units are also available.

When HDD magnetic disks become full, they must be replaced with higher capacity drives, or additional hard drives must be purchased. Using hard drives with removable media or using external hard drives has several advantages:

- Removable media can be stored in locked cabinets, vaults, or other secure locations to prevent unauthorized access.
- Removable disks can be used in other computer systems with compatible drives.
- Removable disks can be used to back up conventional hard drives and to restore electronic records if a hard drive fails.
- Removable hard disks can be used with an identical device if a removable hard drive fails.

Optical Media

optical media: a high-density information storage medium where digitally encoded information is both written and read by means of a laser

Optical media is a high-density information storage medium where digitally encoded information is both written and read by means of a laser. Optical media include optical discs, compact discs (CDs), computer output to laser disc (COLD), digital videodiscs (DVDs), and optical cards. An optical disc is a platter-shaped disc coated with optical recording material. Optical media is read by optical disc drives, which can be CD, DVD, or BD (Blu-ray). The newest laptops do not always come with an optical drive.

Optical discs are electronic image media. The storage capacity and durability of optical discs allow the capture of text as well as graphic, photographic, and animation images for viewing on a computer screen. Some types of optical media are listed in Figure 12.2.

What is the difference between a CD-R and CD-RW?

CD-ROMs (Compact Discs - Read Only Memory) were developed first for audio storage, and they gradually evolved to data storage. Additional CD formats—CD-R (recordable), CD-RW (rewritable), and BD-R (recordable Blu-ray disc)—have contributed more options for records and information management storage applications. CDs provide safe and reliable media that can store images for long periods of time. CDs store databases, documents, directories, publications, and archival records that do not need alteration. CDs do not require special hardware or software to retrieve information; however, the storage capacity is limited. A standard CD can hold from 12,000 to 15,000 documents.

COLD (Computer Output to Laser Disc) technology combines the capabilities of scanning documents created on another system and linking them to COLD documents (computer-created records saved by laser to optical discs). This combination of digital image scanning of physical documents, optical disk storage, and search capabilities of database software

FIGURE 12.2 **Optical Media**

CD-ROM Compact disk-read-only memory	A high-density digital disk storage medium that can be read only. It cannot be written on
CD-R Compact disk-recordable	A write-once optical disk
CD-RW Compact disk-rewritable	An erasable optical disk
COLD Computer output to laser disk	A technique for the transfer of computer-generated output to optical disk so that it can be viewed or printed without using the original program
DVD Digital videodisk or versatile disk	A read-only optical storage medium that stores approximately 130 minutes of full-motion video
DVD-R Digital videodisk-recordable	A recordable DVD
DVD-RW Digital videodisk-rewritable	A rewritable DVD
BD-R	A recordable Blu-ray disk
Optical Card	A small electronic device about the size of a credit card that contains electronic memory and possibly an imbedded integrated circuit

facilitates development of a computerized records storage and retrieval system for both active and long-term records. Many organizations still use COLD technology.

What is one solution to the high-storage capacity needed for multimedia files?

Full-motion video requires huge amounts of storage space. Some solutions to the high-storage capacity needed for multimedia are the digital videodiscs (DVDs), external hard drives, and/or solid state devices. DVDs are also used in long-term data storage applications. DVD-R and DVD-RW media have extended their use to include data storage.

Solid State Media

solid state drives (SSDs): provide data storage on interconnected flash memory chips where the data are retained even when the device is not plugged into a power source

Solid state drives (SSDs) provide data storage on interconnected flash memory chips. The data are retained even when the device is not plugged into a power source. SSDs are high-performance plug-and-play storage devices that have no moving parts. SSDs represent advancement in storage technology, random access speeds, multitasking ability, and outstanding durability and reliability. Ultra-thin laptops and tablet computers often contain 2.5 inch SSD rather than a hard disk drive (HDD).[1]

flash drive: a read/write device that attaches to a computer and is usable as a standard hard drive

The most common type of SSD is the flash drive, as shown in Figure 12.3. Small portable drives, such as flash drives or scan cards or disks, are solid state devices. These storage devices are true digital media. A **flash drive** is a read/write device that attaches to a computer and is usable as a standard hard drive. Flash drives may also be called *USB drives, jump drives, thumb drives, and memory sticks.*

[1]http://www.storagereview.com/ssd_vs_hdd, accessed May 3, 2014.

FIGURE 12.3 **Example of a Flash Drive**

© Ingvar Bjork/www.Shutterstock.com

A flash drive, as shown in Figure 12.3, consists of a small printed circuit board encased in a hard plastic covering. These devices are provided by a variety of vendors and have various names. Storage capacities range from 4 GB to 512 GB. They may be carried in pockets, attached to key rings, or worn around the neck on a lanyard (cord). A flash drive can be plugged into a USB port directly, or it can be plugged into to a hub that is plugged into a USB port. A USB hub allows two or more USB devices to be plugged in via one USB computer port. Fingerprint recognition for security is available on some flash drive models as well. Flash drives may be used to carry files to another computer for working in another location or to back up computer data. With sufficient memory, a flash drive can be used to back up an entire personal computer hard drive. In many cases flash drives are replacing CDs and DVDs as "media of choice."

How does a flash drive plug into a computer?

A *secure digital (SD) card* is another type of SSD. These tiny memory cards are used in various devices: smartphones, car navigation systems, e-books, digital cameras, personal computers (as shown in Figure 12.4), and tablets. SD cards may also be called *smart cards* and are available with storage capacities as high as 4 GBs. For example, an SD card from your camera can be inserted into an SD slot on your printer. You can then print your photos. Wireless flash drives are now available in 16 to 32 GB sizes, because the memory is actually an SD card that is used to transfer photos, music, videos, and contact information from your smartphone.[2] The advantages of using an SD card include high data transfer rates and low battery consumption. SD cards also use flash memory, which means that a power source is not required to retain stored data.

FIGURE 12.4 **Example of a Secure Digital (SD) Card**

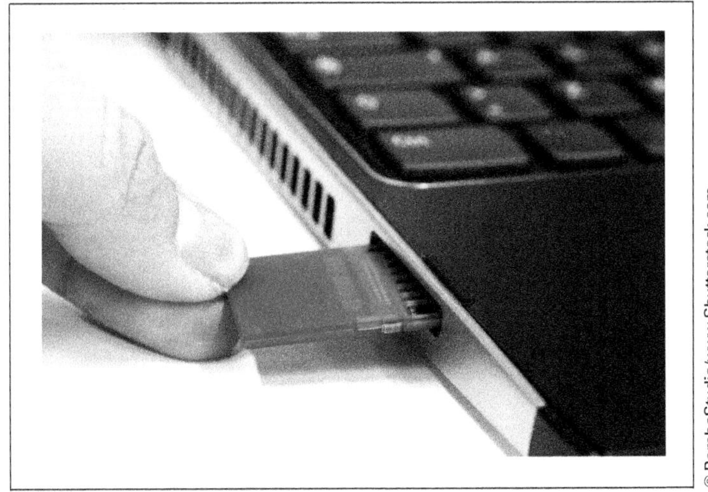

© RomboStudio/www.Shutterstock.com

Smart cards may be used for secure access to buildings, for student IDs, for medical devices, and to store automobile service histories. They may be preloaded with specific currency amounts for use in ATMs and debit card purchases. When that amount is depleted, the card may be reloaded with the same or a larger amount. Optical memory cards may be used to store medical images and personal medical records, for access/entry cards, and for immigrant ID cards.

[2]https://www.sdcard.org/consumers/cards, accessed January 2, 2014.

What are the advantages and main disadvantage of using SSDs?

Solid state devices are capable of holding larger capacities. The advantages of using SSDs are no moving parts, no heat, no vibration, less power draw on computers, and faster access times. Cost is the biggest disadvantage. HDDs generally cost \$0.15 per gigabyte, whereas SSDs are roughly \$0.50 per gigabyte.

Data Input

Computer data entry most often is done through a computer keyboard. However, other input devices, such as scanners, bar codes, optical character recognition (OCR), fax machines, and various handheld devices are also used. Remember that hard disks and other removable media are also input devices. With voice-recognition software and a microphone, users may enter data by dictating letters, e-mails, messages, or other documents into a computer or by speaking commands to a computer. This technology is especially helpful to individuals who do not have full use of their hands.

scanner: a device that converts an image (text, graphic, or photograph) of a document into electronic form for processing and storage

How does a scanner enter data?

A **scanner** is a device that converts an image (text, graphic, or photograph) of a document into electronic format for processing and storage. A scanner passes light over a document or object and converts it to dark and light dots that become digital code. Scanners may be handheld devices that are passed over an item to be entered or desktop models that scan a document from a flat surface. A desktop document scanner used in RIM applications has an automatic document feeder, which allows a stack of paper to be placed into a tray and automatically brought into the scanner one page at a time. Scanners that do not have an automatic document feeder are designed for graphics and require each page to be manually placed onto the scanner. However, many offices now have hub copiers/printers/scanners, which can make scanning physical documents more convenient for staff.

Do you have an ID card that has a bar code?

Bar code and radio frequency identification (RFID) technology, discussed in Chapters 6 and 7, are also types of scanned data entry. *Bar code* is a coding system consisting of vertical lines or bars set in a predetermined pattern that, when read by an optical reader, can be converted into machine-readable language. In records and information management, bar codes and RFID tags are used for tracking locations of documents, files, or boxes of records. With bar code software, users can print labels from a computer or from a dedicated bar code printer. Bar code labels are placed onto each document or onto the first page of a multipage document that is scanned into a computer. With appropriate software, scanned documents can be separated and assigned to folders much faster than can be done manually. Information assigned to the bar codes can be used for indexing, tracking, and retrieval.

Bar codes and RFID tags are also used to check out items in libraries, to record items shipped and received, and to record items stocked on shelves in supermarkets. This technology is also used to track shoppers' buying habits and for direct advertising to individual customers. A bar code reader is a photoelectric scanner that translates bar code symbols into digital formats so that they can be read by a computer.

optical character recognition (OCR): machine reading of printed or written characters through the use of light-sensitive materials or devices

Optical character recognition (OCR) is machine reading of printed or written characters through the use of light-sensitive materials or devices. A device such as a wand or scanner is used to read special preprinted characters and to convert them into digital format for computer data entry. For example, a department store associate uses OCR scanning to enter prices from a product.

A desktop fax machine scans an image and converts it into digital code enabling transmission to another fax machine or to a computer with an internal fax modem and fax software. A fax modem and software may be installed as part of a computer system to simulate a desktop fax machine's input and output. Fax machines are still used to capture "wet" signatures. Some companies need actual signed documents to meet legal requirements. After a document is retrieved from the fax machine, the document is signed; it can be faxed back to the sender, thus meeting legal requirements.

OCR applications are also used in scanning documents that become images. Better OCR software has made scanning documents more viable. The images are saved as TIFF (tagged image file format). Once in TIF format, the documents cannot be altered. Many companies use this process to scan and digitize physical records. Metadata can be added easily to these records. The OCR software can be set to scan all or only a portion of a document. This information can be input into the enterprise database for records management.

Retrieval Procedures

As the use of electronic records has made electronic media a primary records storage media, storage and retrieval of these records has presented new concerns. Classification (Chapter 11) of electronic records is just as important as indexing physical records, and for the same reason—to locate and retrieve records or information. Information redundancy, media compatibility, and media stability can result in electronic records retention issues.

data warehouse: a collection of data designed to support management decision making

When information is needed that presents a clear picture of business conditions at a single point in time, data may be retrieved from a data warehouse. A **data warehouse** is a collection of data designed to support management decision making. A data warehouse includes systems to extract data from operating systems and a warehouse database system that provides flexible access to the data. *Data warehousing* or *data mining*, as it is sometimes called, generally refers to combining many different databases across an entire organization. Records can be assembled from various applications, platforms (operating systems), and storage devices into formats for presentations to management for decision making or other business purposes. For example, executives may retrieve and assemble electronic records from several departments that will help them assess the profitability of their organization. The concept of data warehousing has been expanded to include enterprise content management, which is addressed in Chapter 13.

Electronic information is stored on a network hard disk, a user's local hard disk, an optical disk, a removable drive, or in the cloud. These files must be identified so that they can be easily retrieved, used, and dispositioned (retained or destroyed).

FIGURE 12.5 **Removable Storage Devices Represented by Icons**

Source: Microsoft

Operating system software, such as Microsoft® Windows, automatically maintains a directory and filename index of files. Computer storage peripherals, such as removable hard drives and CD, DVD, flash drives, or optical disc drives, are often represented by labeled icons shown in Figure 12.5. Storage peripherals and their fixed or removable media are computer-based equivalents of file cabinets. When a storage device is selected, a directory of the device's recording medium is displayed. The root directory is displayed first and provides an overview of the contents. The root directory typically contains subdirectories that are identified by folder icons.

Why is clear and comprehensive labeling of media important?

Magnetic tape cartridges, CDs, DVDs, or other removable data storage devices must be clearly labeled for accurate storage and retrieval. In centralized data processing facilities, much more information may be required on media labels. Information that should be included on these media labels is listed in Figure 12.6. All this information will not fit onto small labels. Consequently, label contents may be limited to brief identifiers, with more complete information recorded into a logbook or database.

FIGURE 12.6 **Label Information—Electronic Records**

LABEL INFORMATION FOR ELECTRONIC RECORDS	
REMOVABLE DATA STORAGE DEVICES	**CENTRALIZED DATA PROCESSING FACILITIES**
1. Department, unit, or organization that created the records	1. Complete listing of files contained on the medium
2. Name of records series	2. Manufacture date for the medium
3. Inclusive dates, numeric series, or other identifying information	3. Security precautions and access restrictions
4. Type of computer on which records were created	4. Type of copy—working or storage
5. Software name and version used to create the records, such as Word	5. Any special attributes of the medium

RETENTION AND MAINTENANCE

As discussed in Chapter 7, electronic records must be included on an organization's records retention schedule and destroyed according to the schedule. Records and information managers have long recognized the importance of records retention for visible records media such as physical and microfilm. The same controls need to be applied to electronic records as well.

Duplicate Records

What is information redundancy?

In many organizations, users may be able to access the same information in machine-readable and human-readable formats. Storing duplicate copies of the same information is called *information redundancy*. Word processing documents may be created, revised, and edited through several versions before a final document is produced. Each version may be printed or kept electronically, with any editing changes marked for review and corrections, and retained to provide a history of development of the document versions.

The computer files may also be backed up for protection and retention. Consequently, one document may be available in several versions and formats, which means redundant information and redundant recordkeeping. RIM is affected by space needs—file cabinet, floor space, and media space for electronic records. During the discovery phase of a lawsuit, electronic records, physical records, and microfilm records may be subject to review by opposing parties. Physical records may be routinely purged and destroyed, but electronic records may not be subject to the same controls. Records retention schedules and policies must apply to electronic records as well as to records in other formats. As you learned from Chapter 11, metadata, taxonomies, and file plans have built-in retention dates.

MY RECORDS

Organizing Photographs

How do you organize your photos? Can you find a particular photo quickly? Are your photos stored safely?

If you are like many people, you have photos both in printed and digital format. Are your printed photos in a shoebox, a drawer, or stacks on a shelf? How about your digital photos—are they scattered on your hard drive or several removable storage devices? Are you able to find and view the photos within a few minutes when you want to see particular photos?

ORGANIZE PRINTED PHOTOS

Follow these guidelines to organize your printed photos:

- Organize your printed photos by location, subject, date, or event.
- Organize and store negatives, using the same system as for the printed photos.
- Store photos in plastic enclosures made of uncoated polyester, polypropylene, or polyethylene.
- Create albums of your photos, using the plastic enclosures stored in a three-ring binder.
- If you place photos in a scrapbook, avoid using adhesives that may cause chemical damage to the photo. Rubber cement and self-stick "magnetic" pages are particularly damaging to photos.*

ORGANIZE DIGITAL PHOTOS

Follow these guidelines to organize your digital photos:

- Centralize your photos for a particular location, subject, date, or event. Windows creates a My Pictures folder inside the My Documents folder. Create appropriate folders inside the My Pictures folder or on your hard drive or removable storage device.
- Make a backup copy of your picture folders to a CD, DVD, or a large flash drive.
- Use photo software that comes with your digital camera or smartphone to help you organize pictures into albums.
- Internet companies have photo websites where you can upload, edit, tag, and back up your photos from your Android and iOS mobile devices. Some of these services are free if you limit the amount of storage space that you use. Other sites allow you to back up your photos for a cost. Still other sites are popular for individuals who wish to have their photos in printed format. These companies will also customize photo products into albums, calendars, coffee mugs, and so forth.

*Source: Geoff Williams, "Tips For Organizing Your Most Priceless Possessions: Your Photos," September 24, 2013, US News and World Report.com, http://money.usnews.com/money/personal-finance/articles/2013/09/24/the-best-ways-to-organize-your-photos, accessed January 15, 2014.

Media Compatibility and Stability

If you have worked with computers for a number of years, you have probably witnessed changes in electronic storage media. For example, new personal computers no longer have floppy drives. They have CD or DVD drives and USB ports for removable storage devices. Records stored on 3.5-inch disks that are in long-term storage may not be recoverable

media compatibility: how well the media and the equipment needed to access information stored on the media work together

Why is media compatibility important?

unless an organization has also stored an older working computer that has a compatible drive and software. Some new laptops do not have CD/DVD drives.

Software also can become obsolete or be discontinued, or a decision can be made to change the software throughout the entire organization. **Media compatibility** refers to how well the media and the equipment needed to access information stored on the media work together. Records created in an obsolete or discontinued software program may no longer be accessible. New software programs that provide backward compatibility with older versions help overcome some software upgrade problems.

Current media may not be compatible with future equipment or software. Operating systems may also change, which will prevent access and retrieval. A Microsoft® Windows operating system may be replaced by a Linux operating system or a newer operating system. RIM managers must look toward the future when selecting storage media and equipment. They need to consider whether what they purchase in 2016 will be compatible with records stored in 2020.

media stability: the length of time the media will maintain its original quality so that it can continue to be used

Why is media stability important?

Media stability refers to the length of time the media will maintain its original quality so that it can continue to be used. The useful life of physical and photographic media is longer than the retention periods for the information stored in these formats. The useful life of hard disk drives depends on the number of times that the media is accessed. The stable life expectancy of electronic records is often shorter than the required retention period for the information stored on the media. The following practices help to preserve electronic records for longer periods.

- Magnetic and optical media should be inspected regularly. Samples may be inspected in large storage collections. Inspection should include a visual inspection as well as retrieval and playback of the information.
- Disks in inactive storage may be refreshed by using defragmentation or disk scanning software, providing that compatible computers are available.
- Other electronic records can be recopied onto new media at predetermined intervals to extend their lives for the required retention period. Periodic recopying is known as *renewing* the media.
- Copying can also be used to transfer information from deteriorating or obsolete media. Digitally coded information can be copied an indefinite number of times without degrading the quality. However, video and audio recordings based on analog signals lose image and/or sound quality with copying. Recopying makes managing electronic records difficult and requires a future commitment of labor and resources, with no certainty that the technology needed to recopy records onto new media will be available (i.e., media compatibility).
- **Data migration** is the process of moving data from one electronic system to another, usually in upgrading hardware or software, without having to undergo a major conversion or re-inputting of data. Electronic records should be inspected and migrated regularly.

data migration: the process of moving data from one electronic system to another, usually in upgrading hardware or software, without having to undergo a major conversion or re-inputting of data

RECORDS MANAGEMENT IN ACTION

Oregon Passes Legislation Protecting Individual Social Media Accounts

Oregon, along with several other states, has passed legislation making it an unlawful employment practice for an employer to require an employee or job applicant to provide his or her username and/or password to their social media accounts. This legislation is an attempt to ensure that information posted on an individual's social websites, such as Facebook or Twitter, is not revealed as a condition of employment and is protected.

Other provisions of the law include prohibiting the employer from

1. compelling an employee or job applicant to add the employer as a contact associated with the individual's social media site;
2. forcing an employee or applicant to access his or her personal social media account in the presence of the employer and in a manner that enables the employer to view the contents; and
3. taking, or threatening to take, any action to discharge, discipline, or otherwise penalize an employee for refusing to provide access to his or her social media account.

However, if the employer is conducting an investigation into employee misconduct or possible illegal activities, the employer can inquire about information that might exist on the individual's social media accounts.

Accessing Electronic Records

Users can access physical records by going to storage areas and retrieving them. These records can be removed from cabinets and other storage containers for reference, or taken to another work area for use (charged out). Electronic records, however, may be stored in remote locations where users cannot see the records or know what type of medium is used.

Workstations connected by a network, intranet, or the cloud allow many users to access data at the same time. Organizations connected to the Internet may allow customers and employees to access forms and other information. Customers may complete forms online and submit them to the organization much faster than by conventional means.

Internet or intranet access also provides the opportunity for creating new records such as online forms. These new records must be incorporated into the records and information management system and retention periods assigned. Freedom of access also raises safety and security concerns.

RECORDS SAFETY AND SECURITY

Safeguarding records against intentional or unintentional destruction or damage and protecting records confidentiality is known as *records protection*. Protecting records, regardless of their media, and ensuring their proper use and control are essential. The cloud or networked computer records systems are vulnerable to outside intruders through Internet access. Safety and security of electronic records are discussed in this section.

Records Safety

What is records safety?

Records safety refers to protecting records from physical hazards existing in an office environment, such as electrical surges, physical damage to CDs and DVDs, high humidity, extreme heat or cold, and natural disasters. The procedures discussed in the following sections apply to controlling and protecting records from physical hazards.

Protective Measures

Users should adopt protective measures for hardware, software, and media. These measures include using surge protectors to protect computer equipment from changes (surges) in electrical voltage and installing locks to areas containing computer files and equipment to protect against misuse or theft.

Why are the right storage environmental conditions important for magnetic, optical, and solid state media?

Optical and magnetic media should not be stored in direct sunlight, placed near radiators, or exposed to heat sources. CD-R media that are not housed in cartridges may be damaged by exposure to light. They should be stored in containers that are stored in closed cabinets. High humidity, extreme heat or cold, exposure to light, electromagnetic sources, dust, smoke, and various storage conditions can damage electronic records; therefore, controlling temperature and humidity and other storage conditions helps protect these records. Dust and other contaminants can infiltrate high-density media housings and render portions of recorded information unreadable. Air conditioning is usually required to control temperature and humidity and to remove pollutants. Media storage areas should be cleaned regularly.

Adequate preparation for and protection from natural disasters, such as floods, fires, and earthquakes, should be provided for all records. Protection from natural disasters involves advance planning to select a second equipment site for emergency operation and for making duplicate copies of vital records for the alternate location. See Chapter 14 for more on disaster preparation and recovery.

Records Conversion and Backup

Records stored on magnetic media should be converted to hard copy, optical disks, flash drives, or microforms for long-term storage. The life expectancy of magnetic records may be limited because of storage conditions. Controlling environmental conditions for long-term storage of magnetic tapes is very important. Vital records should not be on magnetic media for long-term storage.

Why is backing up computer files important?

Backing up computer files and storing the copies in fireproof cabinets or in an off-site location help to protect against the loss of files. Duplicate electronic records made from backup copies can be created quickly and inexpensively.

Protection against Computer Viruses

virus: a computer program that replicates itself into other programs that are shared among systems with the intention of causing damage

Taking measures to prevent computer viruses from destroying data is an essential part of records security. A **virus** is a computer program that replicates itself into other programs that are shared among systems with the intention of causing damage. The opportunity for the introduction of viruses increases when computer users access electronic records from remote locations. Viruses transmitted over the Internet and through e-mail can be particularly destructive.

What can computer users do to prevent viruses from entering their computers via e-mail?

Safety measures involve (a) using virus detection software programs regularly, (b) making backup copies of new software programs onto the cloud or other storage media before installing them onto a computer, and (c) making daily backup copies of data entered. Some removable hard drives can automatically make daily backups. Using virus software that scans for viruses in e-mail and on storage devices from outside sources helps eliminate data damage from viruses. Keeping the virus software updated is essential.

Records Security

Records security refers to protecting records from unauthorized access. Electronic transmission and distribution of records require special security precautions. With wide use of the Internet to conduct business, organizations take careful measures to provide records security and protection from unauthorized access to the information stored on electronic media. Generally accepted security measures are discussed in the following sections.

Security Policies and Checks

Implementing a security policy helps to ensure safe, reliable operation of the records system. Such a policy is based on a detailed study of equipment used, records functions performed, information contained in the principal records, employees having access to the records, and current security devices.

What security solutions do organizations use to limit access to employees?

In many organizations, employees have access only to selected computer drives. These drives may be their shared department drive and their own working drive. Employees must have usernames and passwords to access their computers before they can access files on their personal drive, their department's shared drive, intranet, or the cloud.

Conducting security checks and, when necessary, bonding personnel who use hardware and software in the system are practices that help ensure the safety of records. The company's electronic records security policy should include close supervision of records work as well as holding employees personally accountable for the proper maintenance of company equipment and information.

Security Measures

As a deterrent to crime, some firms program a security warning into their computers for display onto terminal screens. An effective method of controlling access to a computer room is a card reader/combination lock system into which employees must insert their access cards and keys in a personal code before the door will open. Other security systems scan and save the scan of each person's eyes, which is matched each time the same person tries to enter a secure area. Voiceprints are also used in a similar manner. Or individuals may pass their hands under scanners or place their thumbs on a thumb pad to gain approval for access to secure areas.

firewall: a combination hardware and software buffer that many organizations place between their internal networks and the Internet

A **firewall** is a combination hardware and software buffer that many organizations place between their internal networks and the Internet. A firewall allows only specific kinds of messages from the Internet to flow in and out of the internal network. This limitation protects the internal network from intruders or hackers who might try to use the Internet to break into these systems. To prevent spyware from being secretly installed onto computers, many companies incorporate spy detection software as part of their system security measures.

Data Protection

To protect electronic data against unauthorized use, safeguards, such as passwords, digital signatures, or encryption, may be used.

password: a string of characters known to the computer system and a user, who must specify it to gain access to the system

- A **password** is a string of characters known to the computer system and a user, who must specify it to gain access to the system. Passwords alone are not sufficient protection because they can be stolen or guessed. You should not use a real word or variation of your name, your pets' or children's names, your date of birth, a word that can be found in a dictionary, or a word that might logically be guessed. The best password is a mix of letters, numbers, and punctuation marks in a random sequence of at least eight characters. Some security experts recommend developing a meaningful sentence and selecting a combination of letters, numbers, and symbols to represent that sentence in one word—your password.

digital signature: electronic signature, or *e-signature*, consists of a string of characters and numbers added as a code on electronic documents being transmitted by computer

Is a contract signed electronically less legally valid than a written contract or document?

- A **digital signature**, electronic signature, or *e-signature*, consists of a string of characters and numbers added as a code on electronic documents being transmitted by computer. The special software of the receiving computer performs a mathematical operation on the character string to verify its validity. The Electronics Signature in Global and National Commerce Act, passed in 2000, sets national standards for electronic signatures and records and gives them the same legal validity as written contracts and documents. The law provides that no contract, signature, or record shall be denied legally binding status just because it is in electronic form. A contract must still be in a format capable of being retained and accurately reproduced. Credit card companies accept e-signatures at checkout counters in supermarkets, department stores, and other point-of-sale locations.

encryption: the process of converting meaningful information into a numeric code that is only understood by the intended recipient of the information

What types of data are usually encrypted before being sent over the Internet?

- **Encryption** is a method of scrambling data in a predetermined manner at the sending point to protect confidential records. The destination computer decodes the data. Encryption is the process of converting meaningful information into a numeric code that is only understood by the intended recipient of the information. The receiving computer and Internet browser understand the mathematical formulas that turn the information into numeric code and back again into meaningful information. The Internet is a major tool for commercial, proprietary, or sensitive information transmission, and data encryption is a vital security measure. With encryption, organizations can use EDI to transmit highly sensitive information. The most identity-sensitive data are encrypted first. Encrypting data backups that will be shipped off-site is also a priority.

Security for Faxed Documents

Transmitting documents by fax is a communication method used between companies, medical offices, hospitals, and other types of organizations. Unfortunately, many workers in offices where medical documents and other confidential information are received fail to take necessary precautions to prevent unauthorized individuals from access to the fax machine. A fax machine dedicated for confidential material only and located in a less open area provides some security, as does calling ahead to alert the message receiver to watch for a fax.

CAREER CORNER

Records Manager (Archivist)

The following job description is an example of a career opportunity with a public school district.

DUTIES AND RESPONSIBILITIES

- Manage, plan, organize, and implement the operations and staff involved in records management activities; provide leadership and internal consulting services in support of records programs; ensure compliance with local, state, and federal records maintenance and retention laws.
- The Records Manager Archivist provides technical expertise, leadership, and guidance to district and department staff regarding records management, review, and retention activities. Employees in this position must possess extensive knowledge of and ensure compliance with laws governing the collection, destruction, access, review, and archiving of student, business, and public records and documents.
- Manage professional and support staff; direct identification, development, and implementation in the full scope of records management and retention policies and procedures.
- Distribute and interpret state-approved records retention schedules; organize, inventory, and archive district records; provide complete notification, documentation, and physical preparation for destruction of records.
- Supervise the performance of assigned personnel; interview, select, evaluate, and train employees, and recommend transfers, reassignment, termination, and disciplinary actions.

QUALIFICATIONS

- A Bachelor's degree in Information Management, Library Science, or related field, which includes archival training and ARMA Records Management Certification is required. Current membership in the Society of American Archivists is preferred.
- Three (3) years of professional records and archiving management in a large public organization working with digital records systems, indexes, and catalog files. Experience in a lead, supervisory, or management role is preferred.
- Any other combination of training and experience that demonstrates the applicant is likely to possess the required skills, knowledge, and abilities may be considered.

MANAGING INFORMATION ON MOBILE DEVICES

Do you have a smartphone or tablet computer?

Electronic information management is necessary for mobile digital devices, such as smartphones, tablet PCs, computer laptops, and personal digital assistants, whether for business or personal use. Figure 12.7 shows the three most common types of mobile devices.

Tools

Many types of software, such as word processing, spreadsheets, games, and graphics, are available for smartphones, tablets, or personal digital assistants (PDAs). They may come with the device or purchased separately and downloaded onto the device. Many applications or "apps" are free to download.

smartphone: a cell phone with software applications and access to the Internet

tablet computer: a mobile computer that has a touchscreen on which you can directly input data and navigate using your fingers or a stylus

personal digital assistant (PDA): a handheld computer that is portable, easy to use, and capable of sharing information with a desktop or notebook computer

FIGURE 12.7 **Three Mobile Devices**

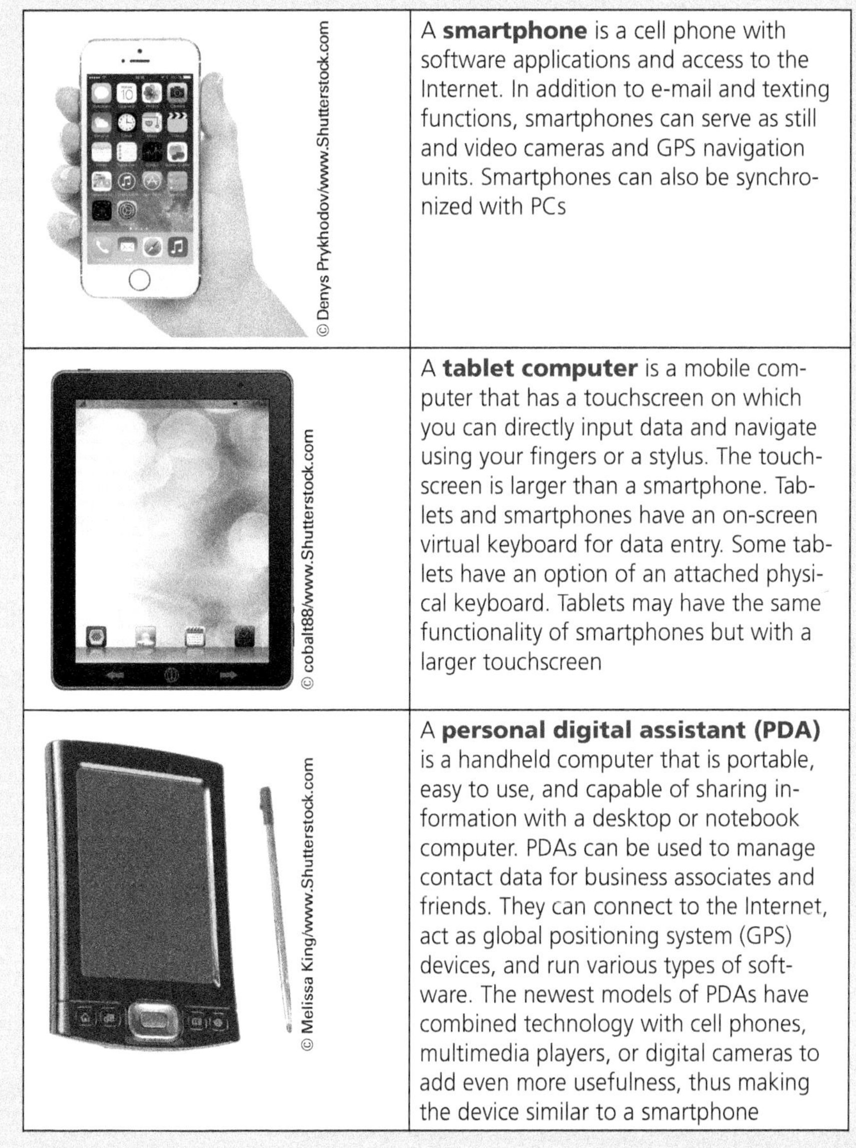

© Denys Prykhodov/www.Shutterstock.com
A **smartphone** is a cell phone with software applications and access to the Internet. In addition to e-mail and texting functions, smartphones can serve as still and video cameras and GPS navigation units. Smartphones can also be synchronized with PCs
© cobalt88/www.Shutterstock.com
A **tablet computer** is a mobile computer that has a touchscreen on which you can directly input data and navigate using your fingers or a stylus. The touchscreen is larger than a smartphone. Tablets and smartphones have an on-screen virtual keyboard for data entry. Some tablets have an option of an attached physical keyboard. Tablets may have the same functionality of smartphones but with a larger touchscreen
© Melissa King/www.Shutterstock.com
A **personal digital assistant (PDA)** is a handheld computer that is portable, easy to use, and capable of sharing information with a desktop or notebook computer. PDAs can be used to manage contact data for business associates and friends. They can connect to the Internet, act as global positioning system (GPS) devices, and run various types of software. The newest models of PDAs have combined technology with cell phones, multimedia players, or digital cameras to add even more usefulness, thus making the device similar to a smartphone
© 2016 Cengage Learning®

Smartphones, tablets, and PDAs come with personal information management (PIM) software already loaded. The programs or features allow users to do tasks such as those listed below. Some tasks may require downloading additional applications (apps) from the Internet.

- Send and receive e-mails.
- Take meeting notes and make to do lists.
- Locate business names, addresses, phone numbers, e-mail addresses.
- Obtain directions to businesses and other organizations.
- Post appointments, using a calendar feature.
- Set reminders and alerts for appointments.
- Post reviews of businesses.
- Utilize online banking, including bill payments and check deposits.
- Post photos and comments to social media sites.
- Perform calculations.

The functionality of each device depends on the number of applications that have been downloaded and the knowledge of the user in managing the information.

Bring Your Own Device (BYOD)

Bring Your Own Device (BYOD): the policy to allow employees to use their own smartphones, tablets, and laptops to access corporate information

With the popularity of mobile devices, many businesses allow employees to use their own smartphones, tablets, and laptops to access corporate information: this policy is called **Bring Your Own Device (BYOD)**. Under BYOD, employees can use devices that they have grown comfortable with for work. On the other hand, businesses can realize cost savings by not having to purchase and provide company-owned devices. Many companies require employees to cover the costs of their device(s), including purchase, maintenance, repair, and data plan expenditures.

Device Information Security

What steps can organizations take to make their information on employees' devices more secure?

Organizations must establish security policies and procedures when BYOD is granted. Because the device and the corporate information that resides upon it belong to the employee, sensitive information can be lost. For instance, what happens to the information if the device is lost or stolen or when the employee leaves the company? Data and information can be lost even when the device is upgraded to the latest version.

Possible security measures that businesses could take include limiting access to corporate information, that is, e-mail only, password, and timeout protection; and limiting the types of apps that can be downloaded onto the device. These apps may contain viruses that could upload the information without detection.

Other measures that businesses and other organizations can take in protecting confidential information include the following:

- Encryption on employer-owned laptops and other mobile devices that store confidential information
- Clear guidelines for reporting loss of equipment and repercussions for failure to do so in a timely manner
- Regular scanning for viruses and spyware, using programs such as Norton™ AntiVirus

IMAGE MEDIA

micrographics: the technology by which recorded information can be quickly reduced to a microform, stored conveniently, and then easily retrieved for reference and use

As you have already learned, records or documents may be stored in physical or electronic formats. Records may also be stored in photographic format. The primary reason for micrographics media is the tremendous reduction in storage space requirements. With microforms, storage space requirements can be reduced by almost 98 percent compared to the storage of paper documents.[3]

Micrographics is the technology by which recorded information can be quickly reduced to a microform, stored conveniently, and then easily retrieved

[3]Adapted from ARMA online "Essentials of RIM Micrographics Course," http://www.arma.org/r1/professional-development/certificate-programs/essentials-of-rim-certificate, accessed November 2011.

for reference and use. Micrographics technology miniaturizes images of recorded information. Other advantages to using image media include added security to ensure that vital information is protected and longer life expectancy for long-term preservation.[4]

microforms: photographic document storage media. Microform is the collective term for all microimages such as microfilm, microfiche, aperture cards, and microfilm jackets

Microforms are photographic document storage media. Microform is the collective term for all microimages such as microfilm, microfiche, aperture cards, and microfilm jackets. Microfilm contains photographic reproductions of documents that are greatly reduced in size from the original on fine-grain, high-resolution film that requires a reader for viewing. Because the photographic image is greatly reduced in size, it is called a *microimage*, and it cannot be read without magnification. The miniaturized image of a document is called a *microrecord. Microfilming* is the process of photographing documents to reduce their size. Microforms offer compact storage for active and inactive phases of the records life cycle.

What makes a microform a unitized microform?

All microforms originate from roll microfilm, which is the most popular type. Microforms can be produced from physical documents, called *source documents*, or from computer-generated information. The most common microforms are roll film (open reels and cartridges) and unitized or flat microforms (microfiche, microfilm jackets, and aperture cards). These flat forms contain one unit of information such as one report or one document. Because roll film can hold a large number of images, unrelated documents may be stored on one roll. Microforms also are very stable and are excellent for retention periods exceeding 10 years.

resolution: a measure of the sharpness or fine detail of an image

Important considerations for using microfilm include size and quality, which is determined by the resolution, density, reduction ratio, and magnification ratio of the microfilm. **Resolution** is a measure of the sharpness or fine detail of an image. Good resolution requires high-quality film and a camera with a good lens. High resolution means that a microimage is clear and easily readable when magnified on a reader with a viewing screen and a light source, or when printed from the reader.

density: the degree of optical opacity of a material that determines the amount of light that will pass through it or reflect from it

Density is the degree of optical opacity of a material that determines the amount of light that will pass through it or reflect from it. A densitometer is used to measure the contrast between the dark and light areas of microfilm. A high-quality microimage has a wide variation in the dark and light areas of the microfilm. *Line density* indicates the opacity of characters, lines, or other information in a microimage. *Background density* refers to the opacity of noninformation areas. The higher the contrast, the easier the images are to read. Uniform densities are important for microforms used in automated duplicators, enlarger/printers, and scanners. Contrast sharpness depends on the quality of the source document as well as the proper lighting during filming.

reduction ratio: the relationship between the dimensions of the original or master and the corresponding dimensions of the photographed image

The **reduction ratio** is the relationship between the dimensions of the original or master and the corresponding dimensions of the photographed image. The ratio also is a measure of the number of times a dimension of a document is reduced when photographed. For example, a reduction ratio expressed as 1:24 means that the image is 1/24th the size of the original record, both horizontally and vertically.

---

[4]Adapted from ARMA online "Essentials of RIM Micrographics Course," http://www.arma.org/r1/professional-development/certificate-programs/essentials-of-rim-certificate, accessed November 2011.

Reduction ratios range from 53 to 2400×, with 24× being the most commonly used reduction. Higher reduction ratios result in smaller images; consequently, a greater number of images can be photographed on one square inch of microfilm. For example, 8100 regular-size bank checks can be photographed on 100 feet of microfilm at 24× reduction; 16,600 checks at 50×. Some banks use microfilm in 2000-foot lengths. For easy retrieval, however, the film is cut into 100-foot or 215-foot lengths after developing.

A microimage must be enlarged or magnified for reading. Magnification is the opposite of reduction. It measures the relationship between a given linear dimension of an enlarged microimage as displayed on a screen or on a printed copy and the corresponding dimensions of the microimage itself. Magnification is expressed as 24×, 48×, and so on. Magnification can also be expressed as a ratio—1:24, 1:48, and so on. The **magnification ratio**, also called the *enlargement ratio*, is a method of describing the relationship between the size of an image and the original record when viewed on a microfilm reader screen. For example, a one-inch square microrecord that is magnified 10 times (10×) appears in its enlarged form as 10 square inches. An image filmed at 24× reduction must be magnified at 24× to produce an original size copy.

magnification ratio: a method of describing the relationship between the size of an image and the original record when viewed on a microfilm reader screen

Microfilming Procedures

The three stages of an image records system include the following records procedures: preparation, processing, and use of records. The procedures used in an image system are described in the next section.

Document Preparation

Preparing source documents for microfilming is one of the most time-consuming and labor-intensive aspects of microfilming or scanning. Document preparation is entirely manual work necessary for preparing documents and placing them into proper sequence for filming. Correspondence and other documents must be removed from file cabinets or other containers and folders and stacked neatly in correct sequence. Documents must be checked carefully; all paper clips and staples removed; torn pages mended; and attachments to records, such as envelopes, routing slips, and sticky notes, removed. Source documents are usually prepared for microfilming in batches so that an entire 100- or 215-foot roll can be filmed at one time.

Indexing Procedures

Recording information to serve as a location directory for microforms or electronic records is referred to as *indexing*. An index attaches identification data, called an *address*, to microrecords or electronic records. The term *index* refers to a list of microrecords on roll film, microfiche, microfilm jackets, or aperture cards. An index may be handwritten or created with a computer. Microrecord indexing may be prepared manually during filming or after filming.

Processing, Duplicating, and Production Equipment

After records are microfilmed, the film is processed. A microfilm processor applies heat and chemical treatments to make microimages visible for display, printing, or other purposes. Because a cover on the processor protects exposed film, a darkroom is not required. A master microform may be a camera-original microform produced directly from source documents or a copy that is one or more generations removed from the original. The term *generation* is used to indicate the relationship of a copy to the original source document. Camera-original microforms are first-generation microforms. Copies made from camera-original microforms are second-generation microforms. Copies of those copies are third-generation microforms, and so on. The master microform is the storage copy, and it is not circulated for use. Duplicates are used as working copies. Working copies may be distributed for use or serve as intermediate copies from which more copies will be produced. A duplicate may also be made by simultaneously exposing two rolls of film in the film unit of the camera.

Why are copies of microforms referred to as generations?

Because equipment costs necessary for in-house microfilming and processing can be quite high, commercial imaging services can provide a practical alternative for businesses and other organizations. Such a service may offer microfilming, processing, duplicating, inspecting and testing, cartridge loading and labeling, and producing microfilm jackets and aperture cards.

Microform Storage and Retrieval

Microform storage copies are intended for retention purposes, and they are seldom referenced. Working copies are prepared for reference and use.

Why is creating working copies of microforms important?

Because working copies are used to conduct normal work activities, they are subjected to dust, skin oils, fingerprints, liquid spills, contamination by foreign materials, and exposure to excessive light and temperatures. Microfiche may be folded or torn. Microfilm in jackets or aperture cards may become separated from their carriers. Microfilm cartridges can crack or come apart. All microforms may be damaged by readers or display devices, printing equipment, duplicators, scanners, or storage equipment. Additionally, environmental conditions can affect the long-term storage of microfilm and microforms.

Why is special equipment needed to read and print microforms?

Microforms are duplicated so that one or more working copies are created for viewing, printing, or scanning. Because images are reduced in size, special equipment is necessary for performing these operations. Microforms must be removed from their storage containers before they can be viewed, printed, or scanned. For manual location of microforms on reels and cartridges, extra equipment is not required. Human-readable headers on flat microforms—microfiche, microfilm jackets, and aperture cards—make retrieval easy, and no special equipment is necessary for manual retrieval.

Some reader/printers are capable of scanning microfilm or microfiche to a CD or USB flash drive. Other digital scanners can scan microfilm directly to a PC and a LAN printer. Combined with software, users can access stored microfilm from any location with an Internet connection.

Image Records Retention

Microfilm records in a carefully controlled environment can be protected and preserved for decades. To ensure their protection, master copies of microfilm or electronic records are not circulated for use. Working copies are made for everyday use or for loan. In some organizations, optical disc records are transferred to new storage media every 10 years to ensure their continued high-quality condition. The process of making new copies of a master record is called *remastering*, and it helps extend the life span of electronic records.

Why is microfilm often used for vital records?

Additional retention guidelines include the following:

- Records kept for three years or less may be kept as physical records or on digital or optical disc storage.
- Records kept from 7 to 15 years should be considered for optical disc storage, solid state storage, or microfilming. These records can be kept accessible and stored in less space than physical records.
- Vital and archival records are often kept on microfilm because of its established durability.

Microfilm records remain in original text format—just reduced in size. Reading the text requires only projection and magnification. The standardized format of microfilm protects records from technological obsolescence that could occur over long periods with electronic records. In addition, long-standing federal law permits acceptance of microfilmed records as legal documents, admissible as evidence in a court of law. Multimedia storage containers are used to store electronic and image media.

Microforms usage has diminished in recent years with the proliferation of computer databases and electronic records storage. However, microforms offer superior stability and ease of use. With their long life expectancy, microforms should continue to have a place in long-term retention and archival preservation programs.[5]

---

[5]Adapted from ARMA online "Essentials of RIM Micrographics Course," http://www.arma.org/r1/professional-development/certificate-programs/essentials-of-rim-certificate, accessed November 2011.

CHAPTER REVIEW AND APPLICATIONS

KEY POINTS

- An electronic record is a record stored on electronic storage media that can be easily accessed or changed.
- Electronic media include magnetic, optical, and solid state media.
- Mobile devices, such as smartphones, tablet PCs, and personal digital assistants, are becoming increasingly popular for workplace and personal usage.
- An image record is a digital or photographic representation of a record on any medium such as microfilm or optical disc.
- Electronic records must be included on an organization's records retention schedule and destroyed according to the schedule.
- Safeguarding records against intentional or unintentional destruction or damage and protecting records confidentiality are known as *records protection*.
- Microforms are photographic document storage media and can be used for long-term storage.

TERMS

Bring Your Own Device (BYOD)
data warehouse
density
digital signature or e-signature
electronic record
encryption
firewall
flash drive
image record
magnetic media
magnification ratio
media compatibility
media stability
microform
micrographics
migration
optical character recognition (OCR)
optical media
password
personal digital assistant (PDA)
reduction ratio
resolution
scanner
smartphone
solid state drive (SSD)
tablet computer
virus

REVIEW AND DISCUSS

1. Define *electronic record* and *image record* and describe the relationship between the two records media. (Obj. 1)

2. Define *magnetic, optical,* and *solid state media* and list two types of each media. (Obj. 2)

3. List two advantages of using removable data storage devices. (Obj. 2)

4. List two records protective measures and two methods of ensuring records security. (Obj. 3)

5. What are some of the security steps an organization can take to limit losing confidential information on mobile devices? (Obj. 4)

6. What is BYOD, and what are the advantages and disadvantages of such a policy? (Obj. 5)

7. List and describe four factors related to microfilm quality. (Obj. 6)

8. How are documents prepared for microfilming? (Obj. 7)

9. List two retention guidelines for long-term retention of image records. (Obj. 8)

APPLICATIONS

12-1 Research Electronic and Image Records Topics (Obj. 1)

Use the search engine of your choice to search the Internet for information on RAID and microforms.

1. Look for new information about RAID (redundant array of independent disks) that is not provided in this chapter. Write a brief paragraph about what you find.
2. Search for information about county government agencies for property documentation, power companies, or companies that use microforms. Write a brief paragraph about what these organizations store on microforms.

12-2 Research Mobile Devices (Obj. 4)

You've just been given a $500 scholarship for purchasing a smartphone, a tablet PC, or PDA mobile device. Your benefactor will give you the money when you have justified your choice.

1. Make a list of the features or programs that you want on your device.
2. Access a search engine on the Internet. Conduct three searches using the key words *smartphones, tablets,* and *personal digital assistants.*
3. Choose three devices that match your list of features. Compare and contrast the brands and models. Then, recommend a device to purchase.
4. Send the summary of your findings in an e-mail to your instructor.

12-3 Research Bring Your Own Device Policies (Obj. 4)

Your employer has decided to allow employees to use their own mobile devices to access the organization's information. As a records specialist, you have been assigned to develop a BYOD policy that limits the type of information that can be accessed by employees and ensures that the information remains secure.

1. Review the information on BYOD security concerns and measures in your textbook.
2. Search the Internet to learn more about BYOD security concerns and measures. Look for sample BYOD policies used at companies or organizations.
3. In a Word document, draft a policy statement indicating the BYOD security concerns and include a list of security measures in order to limit employee access and prevent unauthorized disclosure of confidential corporate information.
4. Submit your work as your instructor directs.

ADDITIONAL RESOURCES

For data files, Microsoft® Access tutorials and more, go to www.cengagebrain.com.

CHAPTER 13

Electronic Records Management Tools and Processes

LEARNING OBJECTIVES

1. Determine whether a document is a business record.
2. Define *electronic content* and types of *repositories*.
3. Describe the advantages of using cloud computing.
4. Discuss the advantages and disadvantages of using Microsoft SharePoint.
5. Describe how ECM tools must meet business wants and RIM requirements.
6. Describe business processes for electronic and physical records.
7. Simulate the use of an ECM system, using metadata and a file plan.

Courtesy of Bruce Miller

ON THE JOB

Bruce Miller is the president of RIM TECH, Inc., a records management software consulting firm located in Ottawa, Ontario, Canada. Bruce consults with many organizations on software issues, problems, and implementation.

Bruce is an expert on SharePoint software and is the ARMA SharePoint Certification instructor. Bruce indicates that SharePoint 2013 can be a viable ECM solution for organizations only with supplemental software add-ons. The core set of records management applications has not changed from SharePoint 2010 to SharePoint 2013.

Many large and small organizations will be changing or are planning to change to SharePoint in the next few years. Bruce sees this trend occurring within his own client base as more are now using SharePoint to manage records.

Bruce's advice for records managers or students just starting to learn about electronic records management is to get "technical" and learn SharePoint and other records management software. An employee with this knowledge and expertise will be an asset to an organization. Less than 5 percent of the records managers with which Bruce now consults are truly comfortable with the technology.

Also, students and records managers need to focus on learning document management. Document management includes unstructured data such as e-mail, social media, messaging, and tweets. Unstructured data presents risks involving security, metadata, and proper categorization. Knowledge of SharePoint and complimentary software is important when working with unstructured data.

As for the future, Bruce sees SharePoint as becoming the dominant records management platform within the next three to five years. In the meantime, software companies will continue to invest talent, energy, time, and money into SharePoint add-on programs.

ELECTRONIC RECORDS MANAGEMENT TOOLS

As you learned in Chapter 2, enterprise content management (ECM) or electronic document records management systems (EDRMS) are the technologies, tools, and methods used to capture, manage, store, preserve, and deliver content across an enterprise. The value of ECM is not only in technology, but also in the activities that involve people and processes. Organizations need a solution that enables their users to share documents and provides collaborative features (such as discussion threads, calendar items, team managed documents, and additional project information) in a secure manner.

This chapter describes the possible sources of electronic records and where the information may be stored. The chapter then addresses the role cloud computing plays in managing content. Records management software systems are discussed next. The last topic in the chapter delves into business processes used by organizations to manage all records.

First, you will look at how business records are determined and why businesses want to cut down on physical records.

Is it a Record?

When managing information, the records manager must identify what information is a record, regardless of the repository in which it resides. You were introduced to records types and values in Chapter 1; see Figures 1.1–1.3 on pages 6–8 to refresh your memory. Here's another way to help identify records.[1]

If you answer "yes" to any of the following questions, the information is a record.

1. Was the information created or received in the conduct or transaction of official business?
2. Is the information required for the operation of the department or company?
3. Does the document support a financial or legal claim or obligation?
4. Is the material necessary for legal concerns?
5. Does the material have administrative or fiscal value?
6. Does the material have historical, informational, or evidential value?
7. Does the material have value to the organization as a whole?

Once the information has been determined to be a record and the repository located, business processes must be in place to manage the records life cycle.

Reducing Physical Records

Many businesses are attempting to develop business processes that reduce or eliminate the amount of physical records that are generated. As a result, business processes are changing when business transactions occur. According to a 2013 AIIM survey, the top four issues with physical-based records were as follows:

[1]"Is It a Record," Rebecca Perry, ARMA 2012 Conference TU02-3311_2012, accessed March 1, 2014.

1. Time spent re-keying data, searching for paper copies, and filing
2. Storage volume and outsource paper storage costs
3. Inability to monitor workflow progress
4. "Lost" paperwork or case files.[2]

What are two advantages of using electronic records?

Two of the major customer service advantages for electronic records are faster response time and the capture of more accurate customer data.

Sources and Storage of Electronic Content

What are some sources of unstructured information?

unstructured information: include text files generated from word processing documents, e-mails, PDF files, blogs, social media posts, tweets, and web pages

As mentioned in earlier chapters, information can come from many sources. This information can be structured or unstructured and may or may not be considered a record.

Sources for **unstructured information** can include text files generated from word processing documents, e-mails, PDF files, blogs, social media posts, tweets, and web pages. Unstructured data represents 80 percent of all electronic content. Ninety percent of unstructured data is considered unmanaged, and 70 percent of organizations have six or more document repositories within which this type of data resides.[3]

What are examples of structured data?

structured data: information that resides in fixed fields within a record or file, such as databases and spreadsheets

On the other hand, **structured data**, like spreadsheets and databases that reside in fixed fields within a record or file, represent a significantly lower percentage of all organizational electronic information. If an organization does not address unstructured data using solid records management practices, disciplines, and principles, the organization's risk in decision making and litigation is increased.[4]

In a large corporation, information may be stored on magnetic tapes, optical discs, solid state drives, TIFFs (tagged image file formats), and microforms. Documents may be created with software applications (such as Microsoft® Word, Excel, and Access), e-mail applications (such as Microsoft® Outlook and G-mail), documents in shared drives, company intranet, company websites, other websites, social media, text messages, videos, and more. One challenge to RIM professionals is to know where the content originates from and how it should be managed. Figure 13.1 shows various electronic records sources and where they may be stored.

Where can you look to find files?

As shown in Figure 13.1, systems or repositories are available for the various media: document management system (DMS), electronic mail system (EMS), and financial systems. Sometimes these individual systems can be separate silos of data. The repositories may or may not talk to each other; consequently, the information is not managed as a resource. When organizations implement ECM systems, one of the needs of the system is to utilize all repositories of information. In other words, make the information sharable and more valuable.

---

[2]Doug Miles, AIIM White Paper, "Winning The Paper Wars," July 30, 2013, http://www.aiim.org/Research-and-Publications/Research/Industry-Watch/Paper-Wars-2013

[3]Gartner Portals, Content & Collaboration Summit, 2012.

[4]Electronic Records Online Course from ARMA, http:/www.arma.org, handouts and notes accessed 17 January, 2014.

FIGURE 13.1 **Sources of Electronic Content and Storage**

SOURCES OF ELECTRONIC CONTENT
• Electronic Documents (Word, Excel, PowerPoint, Visio, PDF) • Instant Messages • Voice Messages • Text Messages • E-mails • Social Networking posts and messages (LinkedIn, Blogs, Twitter, Facebook) • Photos/Images/Drawings/TIFFs/JPEG's • Databases • Cache/Browser history
WHERE THE CONTENT COULD BE STORED
• DMS (Document Management System) • EMS (E-mail Management System) • RMS (Records Management System—where documents can reside) • Servers (Shared and local) • Local Drives • External Hard Drives • Smartphones and PDAs • Tablets • Flash drives/CDs/DVDs • Notebook PCs • Private PCs Databases • Cloud Systems/Repositories

The Cloud

cloud computing: a model for enabling convenient, on-demand network access to a shared pool of configurable computing resources (e.g., networks, servers, storage, applications, and services) that can be rapidly provisioned and released with minimal management effort or service provider interaction

Have you used cloud storage for your personal data?

XaaS (Delivered as a Service): cloud service on demand with a minimum contract

IaaS (Infrastructure as a Service): cloud service provides infrastructure meaning no hardware costs and can be private or public cloud

PaaS (Platform as a Service): a hardware and software platform that is RIM ready

SaaS (Software as a Service): provides software as a service to the organization's infrastructure

The simplest definition of the cloud refers to the Internet (or a network of servers). According to the National Institute of Standards and Technology (NIST), **cloud computing** is a model for enabling convenient, on-demand network access to a shared pool of configurable computing resources (e.g., networks, servers, storage, applications, and services) that can be rapidly provisioned and released with minimal management effort or service provider interaction.[5]

As a cell phone customer, you may have space in your provider's cloud. As a student, you may have space in Microsoft's One Drive.

One main advantage of cloud computing is that you can access your information from any of your devices: smartphone, tablet, or laptop. Organizations gain the same advantage by obtaining the information from any device with a connection to the Internet.

Four major cloud computing service options are available. Each service option provides solutions for individuals and organizations. **XaaS (Delivered as a Service)** is service on demand with a minimum contract such as Google, Amazon, and others. **IaaS (Infrastructure as a Service)** provides infrastructure as a service, meaning no hardware costs, and can be a private or public cloud service such as iApple, Google, Amazon, Microsoft OneDrive, and others. **PaaS (Platform as a Service)** provides a platform that is ready for your company to meet RIM needs such as Microsoft SharePoint and other ECM companies. **SaaS (Software as a Service)** provides software as a service to the organization's infrastructure. The organization owns the hardware, and a vendor, such as cell phone carriers Verizon, AT&T, T-Mobile, and others, provides the software.

[5]http://www.nist.gov/itl/cloud/index.cfm, accessed January 1, 2014.

Many organizations use cloud storage, whether managed by their own information technology (IT) departments, commercial vendors, or a platform. Cloud technology has evolved and makes possible more efficient ECM software.

ENTERPRISE CONTENT MANAGEMENT (ECM) SOFTWARE

As mentioned in Chapter 2, records and information managers are challenged by the massive amount of information and unstructured data, the different ways of storing all the information, and the decision on the best way to utilize the latest technology. ECM tools and processes are about managing not just records but also all unstructured content throughout the information life cycle, from creation through disposition.

As ECM software and processes have developed, all facets of the organization need to be part of the changes: people, workflow, business processes, automatic metadata, and executive level management. An ECM tool must meet the business wants for a lean, profit-generating enterprise, as well as the RIM requirements for all legal and business obligations, as shown in Figure 13.2.[6]

FIGURE 13.2 **Development of an ECM Tool**

WHAT BUSINESS WANTS	RIM REQUIREMENTS

• Repositories (or a place to store records)	• Retention Schedule
	  • Determine what to delete and when
	  • Apply retention rules to all documents

• Search and Retrieval	• Legal holds (applied as required)

• Version Management (tracking production or versions)	• Record declaration
	  • Declare as an official record
	  • Delete only via the retention policy

• Collaboration (Who does what to the document?)	• Classification (metadata and retention rules applied to records)

• Workflow (Defined process for document creation/approval)	• Disposition
	  • Delete records per approved retention schedule
	  • Maintain a supporting audit trail

What is the end goal of ECM?

The end goal of ECM is to organize the company into business activities or processes. The company must assign official retention policies to business processes or records series, as you learned in Chapter 7. Last, the company must match documents to business processes correctly. By adhering to these principles, the software is truly a tool for the entire enterprise.

Many vendors (such as Laserfiche, Tab, Collabware, and Iron Mountain) offer RIM systems with proprietary software that allow organizations to combine electronic and physical records with digital tracking. These vendors offer solutions to organizations for managing both physical and electronic records.

[6]"SharePoint® Records Management Certificate: Solutions for EDRMS Success," Bruce Miller, presenter, Los Angeles, March 2012.

Microsoft® SharePoint and SharePoint Partners

For RIM purposes, does Microsoft® SharePoint out-of-the-box provide ECM?

Microsoft® SharePoint is a "platform as a service" (PaaS) cloud application. SharePoint "out of the box" is not an enterprise content management system. SharePoint's strengths are in how the content is organized, how the websites are available to users, how easily users can search for a particular document, how the user can integrate this accessibility into the work environment (e.g., integration with Microsoft® Word and other software programs), and how the user's workflow is enhanced.

However, SharePoint has limitations as an ECM tool. SharePoint functionality does *not* include the RIM processes of auditing, retention updates, legal discovery, and the retaining/storing, migrating, retrieving records, and finally destruction or permanent archiving. Many vendors are partners with Microsoft® SharePoint to add RIM requirements so that the goals of ECM are met. Gimmal®, KnowledgeLake®, and many other systems add value to SharePoint. According to AIIM in a survey of companies who use SharePoint, 44 percent are using some form of ECM/DM alongside SharePoint.[7]

As with any business dealing with records management, the records life cycle is followed from creation to disposition. Gimmal®, KnowledgeLake®, and other systems have comparable suites of products that interface with SharePoint and deliver a true ECM product. The following example explains how the records life cycle is used with SharePoint and a partner add-on.

Creation, Capture, Distribution, and Use

born digital: digital materials which are the originating source of content

A document that is **born digital** is often produced with Microsoft® Office applications. Digital materials which are the originating source of content are called "born digital." The metadata is added with each new document when the records series is identified. To classify a document, the question "Is it a record?" must be answered. In SharePoint, three categories are defined: Nonrecord—known *not* to be a record; Record—known to be a record; and Unknown—not known whether it is a record or a nonrecord. Bruce Miller, SharePoint expert, uses a third category called work in progress (WIP). If the user thinks that the document may be used as a reference or draft, the document can be classified as a work in progress.

If the document is physical, it must be scanned and metadata added, before it is sent to the appropriate file plan folder. The metadata rules are applied to common records series (contract drafts, purchase orders, invoices, and accounts payable). The metadata fields are decided in advance by the members of IT, legal, RIM, and business departments who are implementing this software as discussed in Chapter 11.

The metadata goes into a database that is accessible by the appropriate departmental users and by the RIM department. As you have learned, the metadata makes finding the record or the WIP document easy. Users can then look up information for distribution and use.

Disposition

The RIM department keeps track of the disposition dates from the metadata. After the disposition date, the appropriate department is notified and an approval procedure is followed before the records disposal process is completed.

[7] Association for Image and Information Management (AIIM), The SharePoint Puzzle (2012), www.aiim.org, accessed January 17, 2014. © AIIM 2013 www.aiim.org © EMC 2013 www.emc.com.

Applications 13.2 through 13.12 at the end of Chapter 13 simulate the XML databases generated by SharePoint. The electronic folders simulate the file plan folders for Electronic Slates, a fictional company introduced in Chapter 11.

BUSINESS PROCESS EXAMPLES

How are records management tools used in business processes of organizations? Here are four examples of the business processes used by organizations of various size and type. In each example, business needs and RIM requirements are met.

Example 1: Card, Gift, and Flower Shop

For a small business that sells cards, gifts, and flowers, business processes are transacted with both physical and electronic records. The owner uses a hybrid system that combines a point of sale (POS) system, financial software program (QuickBooks®), and a paper filing system to conduct business.

What does a point of sale system do?

The POS system is tied to the cash register, an inventory program, and a report system. When a customer purchases a gift and pays for it, the transaction is recorded electronically. At the end of the day, the POS reports on the sales of the day. If any quantities of inventory appear to be running low or are depleted and need to be ordered, an inventory report can be manually generated.

When the owner orders items to be added to the inventory, a purchase order form is filed in one of two physical folders: one for Christmas items and one for all other items. The purchase orders are filed chronologically by the month when the items are to be shipped to the store. Figure 13.3 shows the information flow of the business processes for this small company.

FIGURE 13.3 **Records Information Flow—Card, Gift, and Flower Shop**

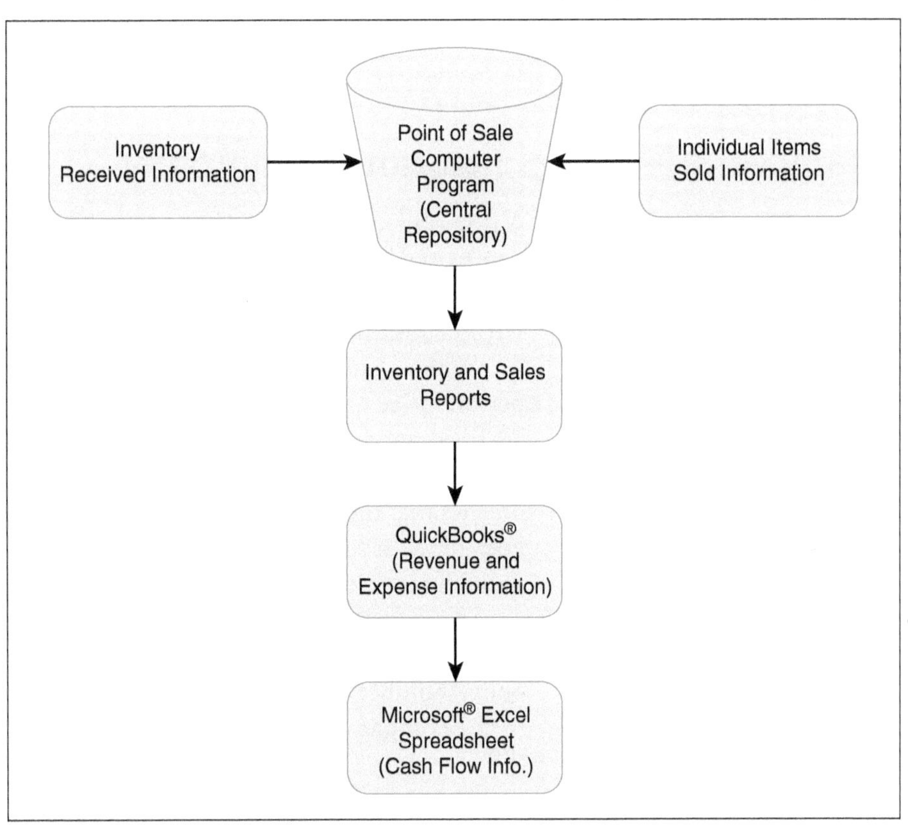

Shipments of new items are scanned using a barcode or manually assigned a six-digit number and added to the inventory. Items are then priced and stored until the appropriate holiday or event such as Christmas, Mother's Day, and graduation. The owner uses a ticket gun to affix the prices to all items. The price label also contains the date that the item was placed on display. The item can then be monitored and put on clearance sale if it does not sell in a reasonable period of time.

The POS system monitors inventory item by item and identifies the supplier's name and address, cost of the item, date entered into the inventory, price of the item, date of sale, and other information for tax purposes. The POS system will also track special sales and clearance sales by including beginning and ending dates of the sale, and it will automatically adjust prices during and after the sale.

The POS system can generate daily, weekly, monthly, and annual sales and inventory reports by department, item category, and supplier. Information from these reports, along with other costs of doing business, such as lease payments, utility bills, office supplies, and so on, are entered into the QuickBooks® system along with payroll information for the two other employees. To summarize important information generated by the POS system, the owner uses a Microsoft® Excel spreadsheet to track overall cash flow. Total monthly sales, available credit, and business expenses are listed on the spreadsheet.

The combination of point-of-sale software, QuickBooks® software, and physical records meet the records needs for this small business. Sales and inventory records are tracked in one system and can be retrieved immediately. Business expenses and payroll information are also available immediately in a separate system. Physical records act as a backup and ensure that inventory is replenished adequately. Even though the systems are not connected and require manual data entry into QuickBooks® and physical filing, the small business owner has the appropriate records management tools to operate the store and pay taxes.

Example 2: National Insurance Company

Automobile, life, and home insurance policies are available from this large company. Automobile insurance policies contain three major provisions: (1) vehicle coverage, (2) personal liability, and (3) personal injury protection. Each provision has claim adjustors.

When a customer contacts an agent's office by e-mail, text, phone, or in person, price quotes, and applications are created electronically. Applications are filled out on the computer and are automatically put into the ECM system. The local agent uses electronic records to keep track of the customer and the policies that the customer has purchased in his or her office. Some agents may keep physical records as backups. Applicant signatures are electronic when the individual agrees to terms and services of whatever policy is purchased.

Identifying information in policy files includes policy number, name, address, contact information, and coverage. The metadata includes policy type, policy number, the date insurance coverage begins, the location of the record in the company's repositories, and the local agent's name and identification number. The database of customers is available to workers throughout the company if the worker has the correct security access. These databases make finding customers and policies easy. Figure 13.4 describes the records information flow in the business processes.

When an auto accident claim is filed by the insured or insured's agent, an electronic record is created in the document center. Metadata is assigned, and the claim is routed to the appropriate claims adjustor(s). Depending upon the severity of the accident, three separate adjustors may be needed.

- If the vehicle was damaged, a vehicle claims adjustor is notified.
- If the policy holder was at fault in the accident, a bodily injury liability claims adjustor is notified.
- If someone was injured, the personal injury protection claims adjustor is notified.

FIGURE 13.4 **Records Information Flow—Large Insurance Company**

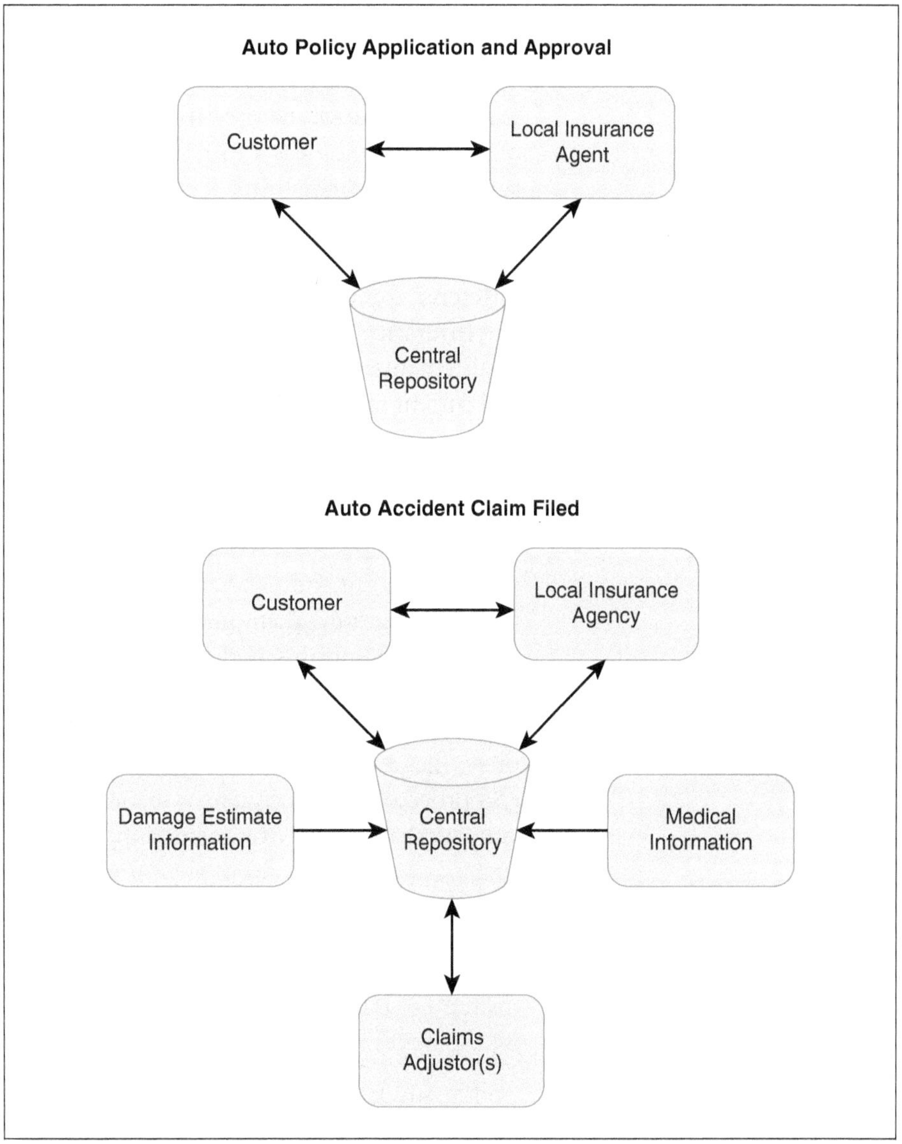

Why do vehicle and personal liability claims adjusters not have access to personal injury medical information?

Claims adjustors have access to the electronic claim files, based on the coverage provision that they are assigned. Vehicle and personal liability claims adjustors do not have access to personal injury medical information because of the Health Insurance Portability and Accountability Act (HIPAA) law. While processing the claim, the adjustor can access the information through searching by claim number, date of loss, or exact name spelling.

The software program has a diary or log feature where the adjustor makes notes and takes action. When a claims adjustor accesses a claim file, the diary is tagged with the adjustor's user identification, date of access, and actions taken. The metadata and content are provided as part of the claim's case file and as an audit trail. All supporting records are stored in the case file in the document center. Documents may include damage estimates to the vehicle, medical bills, payments made to providers, and any written correspondence incoming or outgoing.

Time lines include the number of days that the insurance company has to respond, and it may be mandated by state or federal law. Most claims (65 percent) are usually closed by three months. The recently closed claim files are held in the archive zone for approximately 90 days; then the claim case files are moved to the archives.

Claim files are time sensitive because auto damage claims have a six-year statute of limitations. Bodily injury liability claims have a two-year statute of limitations, unless a minor is involved, which then ends when the minor turns 18. Personal injury claims are closed within one year or when medical benefits are exhausted or discontinued. Auto claim files are archived in Oregon for seven years from the date of the accident. Other states may have different retention schedules.

Insurance businesses must adhere to federal and state legal and regulatory requirements in managing their records. The company must maintain accurate and current records to meet customer legal rights to fair claim damage settlements.

In this example, the business processes and software tools meet the requirements for an effective RIM program. Metadata is assigned when the policy or claim record is created. A retention schedule is created based on the date and type of loss. Exceptions will apply for legal holds and litigation processes. An audit trail is attached to each record so that an outside auditor can review any action taken on a claim. Records are disposed according to a legally defensible retention schedule.

The business processes also meet the business wants for the insurance company. The company has a central repository for policy and claim records. From there, files are routed and assigned to the appropriate claims adjustor for review and processing. Subsequently, records are tracked, updated with both internal and external sources of information, and maintained in the central repository.

Example 3: Governmental Department

The Oregon Employment Department processed 173,220 new unemployment insurance (UI) claims in 2013.[8] Unemployment insurance benefits are based on the wages that an individual earned while working in covered employment.

---

[8]State of Oregon, "Regular Yearly Local Office Claims Activities Report," 2013, http://www.oregon.gov/EMPLOY/BUDGET/UI/reports/948/2013/UIPub948-YTD_Summary.pdf, accessed March 6, 2014.

All employers with employees performing covered work in Oregon are required to pay UI taxes. In addition to paying the taxes, these employers report the total wages paid and the hours worked for each employee for each calendar quarter. The wages and hours of work are reported under the employee's Social Security number.

New UI claims are filed electronically or via telephone. As of March 2014, claimants filed 71 percent of initial claims online, whereas they filed only 29 percent over the telephone. If the claimant files online, eligibility information is collected electronically. If the claimant is filing by telephone, some eligibility information may be obtained via physical document forms mailed to the claimant and to employer(s). Employers have the option to provide eligibility information electronically if they choose to enroll in a national database. Any physical claim forms returned to a central repository are scanned into TIF formats with metadata manually added. The TIFF file becomes the official record, and the physical documents are then destroyed within a prescribed period of time.

When do employers have the option to provide eligibility information electronically?

If an eligibility issue arises, the claim record is assigned to a claims adjudicator (the person who makes the decision regarding the claim) in the UI center near where the claimant resides. The claims adjudicator then has electronic access to all claim records. The claim records are accessed by Social Security number, the date the claim expires, or category.

Any action taken on the claim is annotated with the date, the person who accessed the record, and documentation of the action taken. If the individual is disqualified from receiving benefits, a written decision is generated and electronically entered into the claim record. A copy of the decision is printed and mailed to the claimant along with appeals information. Figure 13.5 shows the records and information flow of the UI business processes.

FIGURE 13.5 **UI Claim Records Information Flow—Oregon Employment Department**

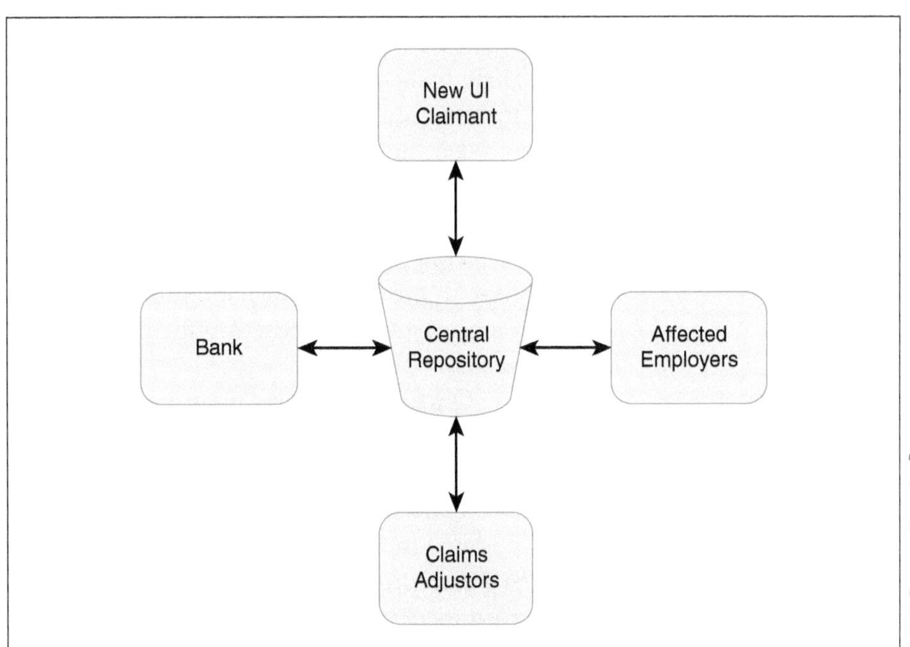

Benefits are claimed weekly via telephone or online. Benefit payments are made by direct deposit or through crediting a bank debit card that is provided to the claimant when the first payment is made. Weeks claimed and benefit payment information is added to claim records as they occur.

The minimum retention period for regular UI claim records is five years from the filing date; UI wage records are kept for seven years from the end-of-calendar quarter in which they were reported. At the end of the retention period, a review process takes place prior to destruction of the claim and wage records.

With the massive amount of claim records that are processed annually, the Oregon Employment Department has maintained "born digital" records and reduced the amount of physical document handling within the claim process.

In this example, the business processes and software tools meet the requirements for an effective RIM program. These processes also allow for unemployment insurance claims to be processed in a timely and efficient manner. The department has established a central repository for claim records. Records are tracked and updated with both internal and external sources of information. A legally defensible retention schedule is in effect, and an audit trail is attached to each claim record so that any action taken can be reviewed by management or outside auditors.

Example 4: Major Utility Company

A major utility company uses a sophisticated, automated electronic records system when power outages occur. The company has relational databases that are updated as events unfold.

When an outage occurs, technicians become immediately aware of the affected geographic areas by power outage alerts shown on their power grid monitors. This information is relayed to dispatch operators who immediately send out work crews. The dispatcher then updates the automated phone system with information regarding the work crew status and the approximate length of time that power is expected to be out.

When customers call to report the outage, they are asked to provide their name and address. At that point the automated system will provide information about the number of customers who have already reported the outage, the length of time that they can expect the outage to last, and that a work crew has been dispatched. As each additional customer calls in, the number of calls received is updated. If customers call on the phone number of record, their address is accessed automatically. If not, the customer will have to provide his or her address to be given the latest outage information. Figure 13.6 charts the outage information flow when an electrical outage occurs.

Once power has been restored, a historical record of the outage is kept and eventually permanently archived.

The automated phone message is updated based on power grid records, dispatcher records, and customer names and addresses records. Information updated in one database revises information in another database. The result is a current, seamless communication of the outage situation to the impacted customers.

FIGURE 13.6 **Outage Information Flow for a Major Utility Company**

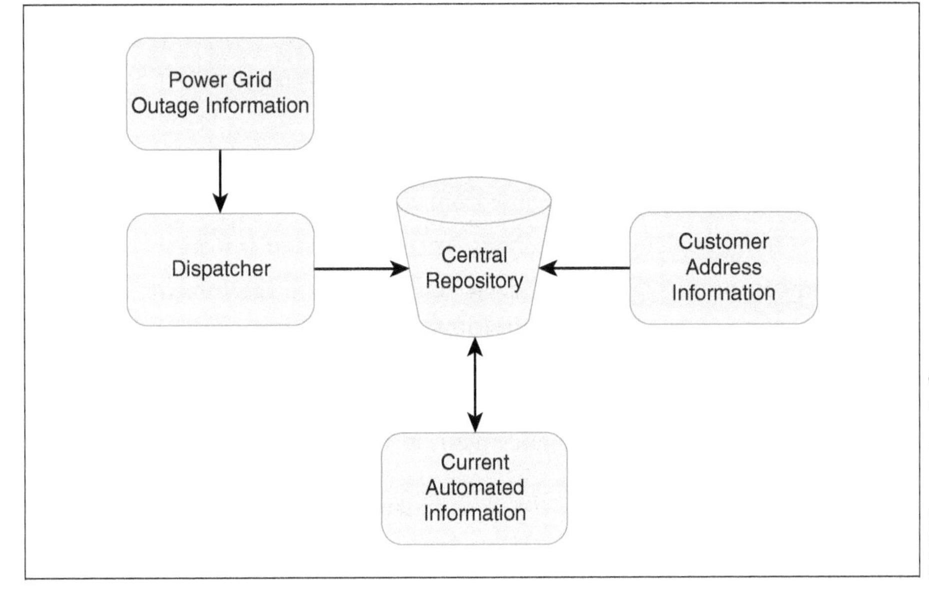

In all of the four of process examples, the business needs are met through capture, access, and retrieval of information from a central data repository. The RIM requirements of legal and business obligations are also met for each organization.

RIM TOOLS SUMMARY

One answer to the RIM challenges of pace of technological changes, new laws and regulations, new records formats, and new risks, is to use a cloud-based enterprise content management (ECM) system. Microsoft® SharePoint, in conjunction with other vendors providing RIM requirements, is a market leader.

What ECM features does Microsoft® SharePoint offer out of the box; and what do other vendors add?

SharePoint offers the following features:

- Search and retrieval
- Repositories
- Version management
- Collaboration with other knowledge workers
- Efficient business process design

Other vendors add RIM requirements:

- Retention schedules
- Legal holds
- Records declaration
- Classification using metadata and retention rules applied to records
- Disposition

ECM systems help organizations manage records and information for all repositories and all content. Total records and information management is the number one issue for ARMA International and AIIM professional organizations.

CHAPTER REVIEW AND APPLICATIONS

KEY POINTS

- Electronic information can come from many sources and may be structured or unstructured.
- The primary question to ask about any document or information: "Is It a Record?"
- Cloud computing offers multidevice connection to the Internet and software applications as well as a variety of solutions to an organization's enterprise content management.
- Microsoft SharePoint's strengths are in content organization, availability of websites to users, ease of searching capability for a particular document, ability of the user to integrate this accessibility into the work environment, and enhancement of the user's workflow.
- Microsoft SharePoint is not a true enterprise content management system. SharePoint partners add RIM requirements.
- The development of ECM software must meet business wants and RIM requirements.
- Small businesses may use a combination of physical and electronic records to track inventory and sales.
- Businesses and organizations use central repositories to capture, retrieve, and process electronic records.
- A large utility company uses relational databases to revise repositories in real time.

TERMS

born digital
cloud computing
IaaS (Infrastructure as a Service)
PaaS (Platform as a Service)
SaaS (Software as a Service)
structured data
unstructured information
XaaS (cloud service on demand)

REVIEW AND DISCUSS

1. List at least five questions to ask to determine whether information is a record. (Obj. 1)

2. Name at least six sources of electronic content. (Obj. 2)

3. Name at least eight places where electronic content could be stored. (Obj. 2)

4. What are the advantages of using cloud computing? (Obj. 3)

5. List at least five strengths of using Microsoft SharePoint. (Obj. 4)

6. What is the main disadvantage of using Microsoft SharePoint as a RIM tool? (Obj. 4)

7. Name at least three business wants in an ECM tool. (Obj. 5)

8. Name at least three RIM requirements in an ECM tool. (Obj. 5)

9. Describe the business processes in place for a small business. (Obj. 6)

10. Summarize the business processes for a large insurance company. (Obj. 6)

APPLICATIONS

13-1 Classifying Documents

The following table shows documents that need to be determined if they are records, nonrecords, or works in progress. Place a checkmark in the appropriate column for each record.

Description of Document	Record	Nonrecord	Work in Progress
Remittance notice for an invoice			
Second past-due letter for an invoice			
Invitation to a retirement party for your boss			
First draft of contract for Allen Gates Foundation			
First past-due letter for an invoice			
Official transcript for a newly hired employee			
Second draft of contract for Allen Gates Foundation			
E-mail on keeping the break room clean			
Final draft of contract for Allen Gates Foundation			
E-mail notice of system maintenance for Friday			

13-2 Determine the Correct File Plan Folder

Data File

1. Download the data files in the folder 13-2 *Invoices* to a computer or a removable storage device. You will open these files with Microsoft® Excel.
2. Open the 13.2 *Invoices* data folder which contains 15 invoices created by Electronic Slates.

3. Use the customer ID to determine into which file plan folder the following invoices should be filed. Example: In Figure 13.7 (Invoice 1116), the Customer ID gives the file plan number.

Invoice No.	File Plan Folder
1116	
1112	
1117	
1115	
1120	
1119	
1114	
1121	
1122	
1123	
1125	
1126	
1124	
1118	
1113	

FIGURE 13.7 **Invoice 1116**

Electronic Slates, Inc.
4889 E. Julian St.
San Jose, CA 95112-4125
Ph: 408-555-0100
FAX: 408-555-0102
Invoices@electronic_slates.com

INVOICE

Invoice No: 1116
Customer ID: 06-10-102
Date: 2/10/2016

To: Albany Baptist Seminary
778 N. Main St.
Albany, New York 12201-1502

Ship to: Same

Sales Agent	P. O. Number	Date Shipped	Shipped Via	Terms
Jill Napen		2/6/2016	UPS Ground	

Quantity	Description	Unit Price	Amount
25	Blue 10" 16 GB Tablet	$ 275.00	$ 6,875.00
25	Optional Keyboards	$ 75.00	$ 1,875.00
		Subtotal	$ 8,750.00
		Shipping and Handling	$ 25.00
		TOTAL DUE	$ 8,775.00

Thank you for your business!

13-3 Create a Query for Employees

Read through the Electronic Slates file plan (Figure 13.8). You will be working with four of the Electronic Slates (ES) database tables.

Data File

Download the data file *13-3 EX metadata.accdb* to a computer or a removable storage device, and then open it with Microsoft® Access.

Four tables are included:

- Employee
- Invoice_metadata
- Remittance_Advice
- Wholesalers

FIGURE 13.8 **File Plan for Electronic Slates**

TITLE			DESCRIPTION	FILE NO.
PRIMARY	**SECONDARY**	**TERTIARY**		
02 Administration	10 Travel		Travel applications forms, approvals, policies	02-10
	20 Insurance		Insurance coverage, policies, renewals	02-20
	30 Records Management	101 Information Governance	Policies for the records life cycle	02-30-101
		201 Records Inventory	Current and historical records inventory	02-30-201
		301 Archives	Archive policies, current and historical inventory	02-30-301
		401 Disposition	Disposition policies current inventory	02-30-401
		501 File Plan	Current file plan documents and agreements	02-30-501
03 Assembly	10 Components	250 IM Chips	Drafts and master contracts, negotiations, cancellations, and terminations to all contracts	03-10-250
		175 Byte, Inc.		03-10-175
	20 Process	370 Chip Control, Inc.	Engineering reports and contracts	03-20-370
04 Sales and Distribution	10 Contracts		Draft and master contracts for distributors of the tablets	04-10
	20 Reporting		Reports to regulating government entities	04-20
	30 Sales	100 Gene Vershum	Sales receipts, contracts	04-30-100
		150 Tyler Young		04-30-150
		300 Jill Napen		04-30-300
05 Human Resources	10 Employees	307 Able, Albert	Employee files including offer letters, contracts, disciplinary records, promotions	05-10-307
		601 Flint, Errol		05-10-601
		310 Tudor, Henry		05-10-310
	20 Policies	100 Workplace Safety	General policies on employment and workplace safety, business, conduct, etc. Drafts and approved copies	05-20-100
06 Finance	10 Accounts Receivable	102 Albany Baptist Seminary	Accounts Receivable: Invoices	06-10-102
		175 Big Box Store		06-10-175
		225 Explorer Energy		06-10-225
		280 Georgia Labor Dept.		06-10-280
		420 Meridian Hospital		06-10-420

continues on next page

FIGURE 13.8 ***(continued)***

		720 Simmons Insurance		06-10-720
		840 Tualatin School District		06-10-840
		324 Health Care HMO		06-10-324
		375 East Coast Electric & Gas Co.		06-10-375
		462 Mississippi Wholesalers		06-10-462
		512 Buyers Warehouse		06-10-512
		583 Technical & Career College		06-10-583
		636 Salem Brooms Base-ball Club		06-10-636
		691 Finest Office Products		06-10-691
		704 Allen Gates Foundation		06-10-702
	20 Accounts Payable		Accounts Payable	06-20
	60 Tax	Return 2010	Tax Return including challenges, supporting documents, notices of assessments, etc.	06-60-2010
		Return 2011		06-60-2011
		Return 2012		06-50-2012
		Return 2013		06-50-2013
		Return 2014		06-50-2014

You are working as a records coordinator for the Finance Department. To help you become familiar with other employees and their departments, you will create a Staff Directory query.

1. Create a simple query using the Query Wizard.
2. Use the Employee table, and choose the fields: ID, Last Name, First Name, Office Extension, and Business Function.
3. Name and save the query as Staff Directory.
4. Choose Modify Query Design and click Finish.
5. In the design view, sort the Last Name field in ascending order.
6. Then sort by the First Name field in ascending order.
7. Run the query.
8. Save and close the query.
9. Save and close the Employee table.

13-4 Create a Query for Wholesalers

You will be working with Accounts Receivable. Your task is to create a report that shows the Company ID, the Company Name, and the File Plan Number. You will be using the Wholesalers table.

Data File

Download the data file *13-4 ES metadata.accdb* to a computer or a removable storage device, and then open it with Microsoft® Access.

1. Create a simple query using the Query Wizard.
2. Use the Wholesalers table.
3. Select the following fields: Company ID, Company Name and the File Plan Number.
4. Name the query "Wholesalers Directory."
5. Choose Modify Query Design and then click Finish.
6. Sort in ascending order by the Company Name.
7. Save and close the query.
8. Close the Wholesalers table.
9. Follow your instructor's directions to show your work.

13-5 Change Records Status

Today is September 13, 2012. You have been transported back in time to change the status of remittance advices from Work in Progress to Nonrecord. You will be working with the Remittance_Advice table. The remittance notices tell ES that funds are being paid electronically. These notices are Work in Progress for five days to make sure that the amounts are credited to ES.

Data File

1. Download the data file *13-5 ES metadata.accdb* to a computer or a removable storage device, and then open it with Microsoft® Access.

2. Open the Remittance_Advice table. Notice the Status Date field. Today is after the date listed in this field.
3. Change the field named Status, captioned "Rec/NR/WIP" from WIP to NR for nonrecord for each record in the table.
4. Save and close the table.

13-6 Create a Report for Scheduled Dispositions

Create a report showing which remittance notices are scheduled for disposition.

Data File

Download the data file *13-6 ES metadata.accdb* to a computer or a removable storage device, and then open it with Microsoft® Access.

1. Open the Remittance_Advice table. Create a report using the Report Wizard.
2. Choose Remittance_Advice table.
3. Choose the following fields: ID, Status, Status Changed, and File Name
4. Save the report as Permission to Delete Remittance Notices.
5. Save and close the report.
6. Follow your instructor's directions to show your work.

13-7 Filling in the Metadata

You just received an e-mail from Judy Ginn, Records Manager. She gave permission to destroy these expired remittance notices.

Data File

Download the data file *13-7 ES metadata.accdb* to a computer or a removable storage device, and then open it with Microsoft® Access.

1. Open the Remittance_Advice table.
2. Click on the Add a field after the File_Name field.
3. Right-click and choose Text or Short Text.
4. Key Authorization as the first new field.
5. On the new Add a field, right-click and choose Date and Time.
6. Key Date_dest. The table with the metadata is kept to show what happens to the records.
7. The authorization is from the Records Manager, Judy Ginn. Her name would be filled in "J Ginn, RIM" for each invoice.
8. Key 9/15/2012 in the Date_dest field for each record.
9. Create a report using the Report Wizard.
10. Use the Remittance_Advice table.
11. Select the following fields: ID, Status, File Name, Autorization, and Date_dest.
12. Sort by the ID field in ascending order.
13. Name the report Permission to Delete Remittance Notices.
14. Save and close the report.
15. Follow your instructor's directions to show your work.

13-8 Delete Expired Remittance Notices

Data File

Download the data files in the 13-8 File Plan Folders directory to a computer or a removable storage device. These files can be opened with Microsoft® Word or Microsoft® Excel.

1. Go into the file plan folders and delete the Payment Notices for Invoices 501-515.
2. Follow your instructor's directions for showing your work.

13-9 Create a Query for Amounts Paid for September 2012

Data File

In this activity, you will create a query that shows data from three tables. Download the data file *13-9 ES metadata.accdb* to a computer or a removable storage device, and then open it with Microsoft® Access.

1. The database has relationships between the Invoice_metadata, Wholesalers, and the Remittance_Advice tables.
2. Click Database Tools, and then click Relationships. Because you have already created some relationships, check to see whether the following steps were followed:
   a. Drag the Invoice_metadata table to the relationship screen.
   b. Drag the Remittance_Advice table to the relationship screen.
   c. Drag the Wholesalers table to the relationship screen.
   d. Use the Invoice ID as the relationship between Invoice_metadata and Remittance_Advice tables.
   e. Make a relationship between the Invoice_metadata and Wholesalers tables using the File Name to the Plan Number.
3. Save and close the relationship.
4. Create a query using the Query Wizard:
   a. Choose Simple, click Next.
   b. Choose Table: Invoice_metadata.
   c. From the listed fields send "Invoice No." to the Selected Fields box.
   d. Choose Table: Remittance_Advice.
   e. From the listed fields send "Amount Paid" and "File Name" to the Selected Fields box.
   f. Choose Table: Wholesalers.
   g. From the listed fields send "Company Name" to the Selected Fields box.
   h. Click Next and save the report as "September 2012 Invoices Paid"
   i. Click Finish.
   j. Change the view to Design.
   k. Sort in ascending order on InvoiceNo field.
5. Save and close the query Invoices Paid September 2012.
6. Save and close the Remittance_Advice table.

13-10 Create a Report for the Amounts Paid for September 2012

Tim Read, your supervisor, wants a report showing the Invoice No., Company Name, Amount Paid, and File Plan No. for the month of September 2012. The Amount Paid field should have a total.

Data File

Download the data file *13-10 ES metadata.accdb* to a computer or a removable storage device, and then open it with Microsoft® Access.

1. Open the September 2012 Invoices Paid query.
2. Use the Report Wizard.

3. Use the Invoices Paid September 2012 query.
4. Send all fields to the Selected Fields box.
5. Sort the report by the Invoice No. in ascending order.
6. Name the report "Invoices Paid September 2012"
7. Choose Modify Report Design. Click Finish.
   a. The title is "Invoices Paid September 2012."
   b. Change the Page Header to Invoice No., Amount Paid, File Plan Number, and Company Name. You will need to widen the Amount Paid field.
   c. Change the size of the fields so that the data fit comfortably on the report.
   d. Click Group & Sort. You will see that the ID field is sorted in ascending order.
   e. Add a group on the field Amount Paid, from smallest to largest, by entire value.
   f. Click More.
   g. On the second line, pull down No Totals and change Total On field to the field Amount Paid. Select "Show grand total."
   h. Change the header section to "without a header section."
   i. Change "do not keep whole group together on one page" to "keep whole group together on one page."
   j. Save the report.
   k. Change view to Layout Report view.
11. Save and close the report.
12. Save and close the Remittance_Advice table.
13. Follow your instructor's directions to show your work.

13-11 Create a Query for Invoice Disposition for October 2015

It is now October 3, 2015. In this activity, you will prepare a query.

Data File

Download the data file *13-11 ES metadata.accdb* to a computer or a removable storage device, and then open it with Microsoft® Access.

1. Open the Invoice_metadata table.
2. Create a query using the Query Wizard.
3. Choose the Invoice_metadata table.
4. Select the following fields: Invoice No., Category, and Dis-Date.
5. Name the query "Expired Invoices."
6. Select Modify the query design and click Finish.
7. The Dis-Date field needs to have criteria added so that only 10/1/2015 dates will show. Click the criteria row for Dis-Date.
8. Right-click Criteria and choose Build.
9. Choose Operators in the Expression Elements column.
10. Double-click on = (equals sign) in the Expression Values.

11. In the Expression box, key "10/1/2015" one space after the = sign.
12. Run the Query.
13. Save and close the Expired Invoices query.
14. Follow your instructor's directions to show your work.

13-12 Add an Audit Trail to the Metadata Table and Delete Expired Invoices

You've received permission to destroy the expired invoices.

Data File

Download the data file *13-12 ES metadata.accdb* to a computer or a removable storage device, and then open it with Microsoft® Access. Also download the 13-12 File Plan Folders from the data files.

1. Open the Invoice_metadata table.
2. Add two new fields:
   a. Use Short Text or Text for a field named Authorization.
   b. Use Date and Time for a field named Date-Dest.
3. For invoices 501 through 515, fill in "J Ginn, RIM" for each record on the Authorization field.
4. For the same invoices, in "10/5/2015" for each record on the Date_Dest field.
5. Save and close the Invoice_metadata table.
6. Go into the appropriate file number folder and delete the expired invoices:
   a. Open the File Plan Folders.
   b. Open the Finance folder.
   c. Open Accounts Receivable.
   d. Open each folder and delete the appropriate invoice.
7. Follow your instructor's directions to show your work.

ADDITIONAL RESOURCES

For data files, Microsoft® Access tutorials and more, go to www.cengagebrain.com.

PART 3 RIM Program Administration

CHAPTER 14

Managing a RIM Program

LEARNING OBJECTIVES

1. Discuss information governance.
2. List five duties and responsibilities of a RIM manager.
3. Discuss goals and objectives of the RIM program.
4. List four components of a records and information management (RIM) program.
5. List actions taken to implement a retention schedule.
6. Define and describe the purpose of a records audit.
7. Describe two ways in which to create a form.
8. Explain the phases of a disaster recovery plan.
9. Discuss social media use in organizations.

Courtesy of Marc Kosciejew

ON THE JOB

As a lecturer in Library and Information Science (LIS) at the University of Malta, Dr. Marc Kosciejew's academic and administrative duties and responsibilities include developing LIS course curricula, delivering lectures, researching, publishing in journals, and presenting at conferences.

The contemporary information environment is experiencing rapid evolution and radical expansion; it is a data deluge. Gartner® warns of an impending information crisis because of the absence of comprehensive, coordinated, and/or mature RIM programs in many organizations, challenging the governance, trust, use, and valuation of their information assets.

In Dr. Kosciejew's opinion, RIM will consequently move to the forefront of institutional structures and business and managerial decision making in order to (1) determine, maximize, and extract the value of information assets through such practices as content analyses; and (2) ensure alignments in enterprise-wide information practices to help reduce operational and financial costs, eliminate data duplication and rot (redundant, obsolete, or trivial), prevent compliance violations, and mitigate security and privacy risks. This shift will necessitate deeper integration between RIM and other relevant areas that handle information, including IT, legal, and accounting; indeed, RIM serves as the foundation for the design, implementation, and maintenance of this integration.

Although continuous changes occur in technology, systems, and services, and amounts and kinds of information are ever growing, RIM's conceptual foundations and professional principles remain constant and sound. RIM students and professionals need to remember that a solid understanding of and appreciation for these foundations and principles will help them adapt to, align with, and successfully manage whatever informational changes—technological, size and scope, and content-wise—that they may confront.

RIM WITHIN THE INFORMATION GOVERNANCE PROGRAM

"RIM—with its focus on developing and implementing policies, systems, and procedures to manage information throughout its life cycle—is the foundation that supports information governance."[1] Organization-wide governance is usually executed by upper-level management who can delegate lower-level managers to establish governance for their specific areas. Continued growth in the volume of information and electronic data, the search for more storage repositories, the need to understand more complex compliance issues, the need to evaluate risks, and the need to be litigation-ready have resulted in new initiatives for organization-wide information management and governance. RIM managers have the experience and knowledge to establish new programs to determine the value of the organization's information, and are involved at the center of these initiatives. RIM managers are capable of developing and implementing strategies to eliminate information no longer of value to the organization. Organizations must implement comprehensive information governance programs to meet these needs. They must find ways to inventory, organize, control, and discover the data stored throughout the organization. Beyond legal and compliance, information governance will affect all departments and lines of business within an organization. Records managers' expertise will drive the shifts of organizational records and information programs to enterprise-wide initiatives for information governance.[2]

Information Governance

As you learned in Chapter 2, information governance is the overarching framework within which the records and information management (RIM) program resides. Governance is about providing leadership, setting goals and strategies, obtaining and allocating resources, protecting resources and assets, and monitoring results and trends.[3] Management is about implementing programs, achieving goals, using allocated resources, directing operations, and reporting results.[4] Information governance is a strategic framework that includes standards, processes, roles, and metrics that motivate and hold people accountable to create, organize, secure, maintain, use, and dispose of information in ways that effectively support the organization's goals.[5]

---

[1]Vicki Wiler, "Making the Leap to an Information Governance Role," *Information Management*, January/February 2014 (Lenexa, KS: ARMA International), pp. 38–40.
[2]"Information Governance Takes Center Stage in 2013: Spotlight Shines on IG Pros," *Information Management*, November/December 2012 (Lenexa, KS: ARMA International), p. 23.
[3]ARMA International, *Using Social Media in Organizations* (Lenexa, KS: ARMA International, 2012), p. 3.
[4]Ibid., *Using Social Media*, p. 3.
[5]Paula F. Lederman, "Getting Buy-in for Your Information Governance Program," *Information Management*, July/August 2012 (Lenexa, KS: ARMA International), pp. 34–37.

ARMA International's Generally Accepted Recordkeeping Principles®

A RIM program encompasses a variety of responsibilities. By using the ARMA International's Generally Accepted Recordkeeping Principles® (The Principles), as discussed in Chapter 2, organizations can review and evaluate their information governance practices and identify areas that do not meet the desired level for each principle, evaluate the risks to the organization, and determine how to further develop their program.

Accountability

The senior executive, such as the records and information manager, as part of the duties and responsibilities of the position, should develop policies and procedures for RIM audits that focus on user behaviors and ensure that audits are conducted on a regular basis.

Integrity

An organization's RIM program policies should clearly state to employees the expectations for honest and ethical behavior at all times. The organization's policies should also include requirements for the integrity of content in all company communications via physical documents, e-mail, or social media.

Protection

The organization's records and information policies and procedures should specifically address the protection procedures that must be followed for official records and confidential and vital records and information. (See Chapters 3–5, 6–7, and 11–12.)

Compliance

The organization must assume responsibility for all records created, received, stored, and transmitted via postal mail, fax, e-mail, or social media by employees as they conduct the business of the organization, and it must have policies and procedures for documenting compliance with applicable laws, regulations, and requirements.

Many organizations have also made adjustments to their policies and procedures to adhere to ISO 15489, the international records management standard. If an organization is involved in international trade, it must adhere to ISO 9000 guidelines. These guidelines specify how product development procedures are documented and how the records are maintained. Emphasis is placed on quality. (See Chapters 2, 11, and 13.)

Availability

What tools can organizations use to ensure that information is available?

Organizations should ensure that information is indexed and retrievable through the use of taxonomies (indexes) with policies and procedures to maintain efficient access and retrieval of information that the organization creates, receives, and stores in accordance with established retention periods. (See Chapters 3–5, 7–10, and 11–13.)

Retention

Organizations should apply their records retention schedules to all records created, received, and transmitted via postal mail, fax, e-mail, or social media that are deemed to be records in a format that preserves the integrity of the original record and is easily accessible. (See Chapters 7, 11, and 12.)

Disposition

The organization's records management, information technology, and legal departments should be aware of the disposition requirements for all records, including any records residing on social media sites. (See Chapters 7, 11, and 12.)

Transparency

Organizations should develop policies for conducting the organization's business through physical and electronic letters, e-mail messages, or social media postings in terms of what information is prohibited and to require employees who conduct business through any of these forms of communication on behalf of the organization to identify their roles in the organization.[6] (See Chapters 11–13.)

RECORDS AND INFORMATION MANAGER'S DUTIES AND RESPONSIBILITIES

The principal employee responsible for records and information management in many organizations is often a records manager. Although job titles may vary among organizations, as you have seen in the Career Corner features throughout this book, they usually have the word *records* in them. As the primary individual responsible for developing and maintaining RIM governance policies and procedures, the records manager needs to have a variety of skills in order to fulfill the following responsibilities:[7]

1. Establish goals and objectives for the RIM program to support the organization's strategic plan.
2. Evaluate potential options for facilities based on short- and long-term resource and space requirements.
3. Manage the purchase of RIM supplies and equipment.
4. Establish and monitor records retention policies and schedules in compliance with RIM program policies, legal and regulatory requirements, and organizational needs.
5. Manage RIM storage facilities as well as security and protection of the organization's information assets.
6. Establish policies and practices for preserving and maintaining vital records.
7. Collect and preserve archival records according to organizational policy and practice.
8. Control the forms management program.

---

[6]ARMA International, "Principles for Managing Web-based Information," *Information Management*, September/October 2012 (Lenexa, KS: ARMA International), pp. 30–36.
[7]ARMA International, *Job Descriptions for Records and Information Management* (Lenexa, KS: ARMA International, 2008), pp. 72–81.

RIM PROGRAM GOALS AND OBJECTIVES

strategic plan: a document used to communicate with the organization the organization's goals, actions needed to achieve those goals, and all other critical elements developed during the planning exercise

strategic planning: a systematic process of envisioning a desired future and translating this vision into broadly defined goals or objectives and a sequence of steps to achieve them

The records manager needs to understand how to develop a plan for running the business of the RIM program, including finances, personnel, and equipment; records storage facilities, supplies, and equipment; records audits; records retention policies, procedures, and compliance; image and electronic records management; vital records management; records security and protection; forms management; and legal and regulatory requirements. The RIM manager needs to have knowledge of and contribute to the organization's strategic plan. A **strategic plan** is a document used to communicate with the organization's goals, actions needed to achieve those goals, and all other critical elements developed during the planning exercise.[8] **Strategic planning** is a systematic process of envisioning a desired future and translating this vision into broadly defined goals or objectives and a sequence of steps to achieve them.[9] These goals and objectives for the organization may be created for the next 10 years, for example—typically broken down by 1st year, 2nd year, 3rd year, and so on through the 10th year. How does the RIM program fit into the organizations plans for the next 10 years? What changes or improvements in policies, procedures, or compliance will be needed in the coming 10 years? Will additional records storage equipment or facilities be needed before the end of the next 10 years? The records manager will be involved in all these decisions and will lead the formulation of the RIM portion of the strategic plan through a committee selected by senior management or the records manager, depending on organizational practice. The records manager must analyze the organization's goals for supporting RIM functions and to prioritize goals to achieve the objectives.

RIM PROGRAM COMPONENTS

A comprehensive RIM program includes responsibility for storing records in a variety of formats; records retention and destruction; compliance with all applicable laws and regulations; managing active and inactive records; and protecting vital records.[10] Other responsibilities may include micrographics technology (discussed in Chapter 12); the records audit; forms management; disaster prevention, preparation, and recovery; RIM software selection, implementation, and management; and RIM policy implementation and enforcement.

Why is a records and information manual needed?

The most important reference for a RIM staff is a records and information manual. Especially useful in conducting the records audit, this manual is the official handbook of approved policies and procedures for operating the RIM program. Responsibility for various phases of the program, standard operating procedures, and aids for training employees are included in the manual.

---

[8]Business.Dictionary.com, http://businessdictionary.com/definition/strategic-plan.html, accessed May 13, 2014.

[9]Ibid.

[10]William Saffady, *Records and Information Management: Fundamentals of Professional Practice* (Lenexa, KS: ARMA International, 2011), p. 9.

This manual contains all information necessary for managing a RIM program (e.g., policy statements; records retention schedules; indexing, coding, and filing procedures; vital records storage and access procedures; records inventory procedures; general policies and procedures; records and information manual distribution and use; administrative responsibilities; disaster prevention and recovery plan; and so on).

Records Storage

What is the basis for records storage?

The records storage component of the RIM program is based on the records and information life cycle presented in Chapters 1 and 11. The storage method—alphabetic, subject, numeric, or geographic—is determined after a records inventory is completed and the records manager has determined the types and formats of the organization's records and how and where they are currently stored. (See Chapter 7 for more on the records inventory.) Managing records storage includes not only making decisions about storage supplies and equipment for storing active and inactive records but also managing the safety, security, and environment for all stored records.

Records Storage Facilities

Active records are consulted frequently soon after they are created and need to be stored near filers and users. As records age and become inactive, they are accessed less frequently and do not need to be near users. The concern for inactive records becomes records preservation, space conservation, and reducing storage costs. Off-site storage, conversion of physical records to electronic/digital media, and microfilming provide solutions that address these concerns.

Where may inactive records be stored?

As you studied in Chapter 7, inactive records are not accessed frequently. Consequently, they do not need to be stored near filers and users. They may be stored in a records center—either in-house, off-site, or in a commercial records storage facility. By implementing and adhering to established retention and destruction schedules, inactive records that need to be available for long periods are maintained for the time periods dictated by the schedules.

Records managers need to have knowledge of space planning procedures, records storage design and best practices, safety and fire protection standards, cost/benefit analysis methodologies, construction estimating and scheduling, and equipment for storage and information handling. The records manager will also need to be able to evaluate costs associated with in-house operations as compared to off-site or commercial storage costs, review safety and file protection plans, estimate space allocation and potential growth, and oversee construction and installation projects.[11]

Storage Supplies and Equipment

Records managers manage the process for obtaining RIM goods and services and need a variety of knowledge and skills to make those purchases, including budgeting, evaluating vendors and bids, and negotiating contracts.[12]

---

[11]ARMA International. *Job Descriptions for Records and Information Management* (Lenexa, KS: ARMA International, 2008), p. 74.
[12]Ibid.

Records Retention and Destruction

Why is having a records retention schedule important?

Determining which records should be kept, how long they should be kept, and how they are disposed of (destroyed or stored permanently) are critical activities that are governed by approved policies and procedures. Through these procedures and policies, an organization can ensure that records are available for recommended periods. A basic records control tool is the records retention schedule, which is illustrated and discussed in Chapter 7.

The records manager needs to know the organizational legal and regulatory environment, the long-term value of the organization's information, and the organization's level of risk tolerance. The records manager needs the ability to conduct legal research, to develop training for retention schedule users, and to develop the RIM audit component.[13]

Records Retention Schedule Development and Implementation

After records inventory surveys completed by each department are collected, a tentative organizational records retention schedule is prepared. Members of each department, members of the legal staff, and other staff members involved with regulatory requirements review the schedule and verify suggested retention periods. When all parties agree, the records retention schedule is finalized and approved by senior management.

To ensure that all employees are aware of and adhere to the records retention schedule, the schedule is distributed to each department along with detailed instructions for its use. Special meetings or training sessions may be held to explain the schedule further if necessary. The records manager will select the disposal and destruction methods used by the organization as well as document disposals and the destruction process according to RIM procedures.

Records Retention and Migration

Why should electronic records be migrated to new media?

Retention periods established during preparation of the records retention schedule still apply when physical records are converted to electronic/digital records. Stored digital records should still be maintained in accordance with the retention schedule and disposed of as part of a compliant RIM program. Storage media are most often hard drives and optical disks. Some electronic/digital records can be refreshed by copying records on an older CD onto a new CD. Media stability and life expectancy limits require migration to new media to ensure that records can be accessed throughout the full term of their retention periods. Obsolescence is a part of technology, and organizations need to keep up-to-date with changes and improvements in records storage technology. New applications should be backward compatible with existing applications.

Policy Implementation and Enforcement

A records retention program includes not only retention and destruction schedules but also policies for implementing those schedules. In organizations in which records retention policies have been established, the RIM manager is responsible for implementing the policies and ensuring that all employees are

[13]Ibid., p. 80.

complying with them. In order to achieve organization-wide implementation, each department may appoint RIM coordinators to assume responsibility for organizing and supervising retention activities in that department. Possible retention actions are listed in Figure 14.1.

FIGURE 14.1 **Retention Implementation Actions**

RETENTION SCHEDULE IMPLEMENTATION
• Identify records series eligible for retention actions.
• Destroy records with elapsed retention periods.
• Transfer inactive physical or photographic records to off-site storage.
• Transfer inactive electronic/digital records from hard drives to removable media for off-line or off-site storage.
• Destroy physical copies after records are microfilmed or scanned.

Source: Adapted from William Saffady, *Records and Information Management: Fundamentals of Professional Practice* (Lenexa, KS: ARMA International, 2004), pp. 6–7.

Records coordinators locate records eligible for retention actions and remove them from cabinets, shelves, and other containers. They locate electronic records in hard drive directories and subdirectories. These manual activities are time consuming and labor intensive. To comply with specified retention periods, records in some records series need to be subdivided by dates such as the end of a calendar or fiscal year.[14]

Information Security and Protection

The records manager manages the security and protection of the organization's information assets in its RIM facilities. Consequently, the records manager needs to have knowledge of records storage and preservation methods for physical, micrographic, and electronic/digital records, and of records center standards and guidelines. The records manager also determines the processes that authorize individual access to RIM facilities and repositories by evaluating users in accordance with organizational policies. To accomplish these responsibilities, the records manager needs to be familiar with the organization's privacy policy, emergency operating procedures and policies, information security methods and best practices, and how to evaluate risks and potential impacts. The records manager applies legal security requirements and determines the level of security required and to whom they should be applied by analyzing the requestor's need to access the information, the requestor's credibility, and the right to access certain information.

What information is analyzed to determine a requestor's level of security?

Records Audit

records audit: a periodic inspection to verify that an operation is in compliance with a records and information management program

A **records audit** is a periodic inspection to verify that an operation is in compliance with a RIM program. "Audits can be viewed as one way to measure a component or components of an organization's managerial well-being. Audits can be internal or external to an organization."[15] An organization can

[14]David O. Stephens and Roderick C. Wallace, *Electronic Records Retention: New Strategies for Data Life Cycle Management* (Lenexa, KS: ARMA International, 2003), pp. 48–49.

RECORDS MANAGEMENT IN ACTION

National Archives and Records Administration (NARA) Records Management Manual and Records Retention Schedule

Some topics included in the National Archives and Records Administration (http://www.archives.gov) records and information manual (http://www.archives.gov/records-mgmt/handbook) are listed below:

- E-mail management
- Records management frequently asked questions (FAQs)
- Guidance and policy for accessioning (Accessioning is the process of transferring physical and legal custody of permanent records from federal agencies to NARA in the Washington, DC, area.)
- Electronic records management (ERM)
- Records management policy and guidance
- Electronic records archives

NARA's records retention schedule http://www.archives.gov/about/records-schedule is organized in chapters according to functions and operations of the agency. For example, Chapter 1, Mission and Organization, provides the information on the topic of program direction for regional NARA records services facilities in the first illustration below. Each category of records that fits into this section of the schedule and disposition of those records is clearly described. Chapter 2, General Administration, includes clear descriptions of administrative function records and their disposition for the regional records services facilities as shown in the second illustration below. Users may need to access several chapters to find retention and disposition information on specific records for which they are responsible. The National Archives is a large federal government agency, and its records and information manual and retention schedule are extensive. The National Archives provides a good example of records and information management.

Program Direction - Regional Records Services Facilities

File #	Description	Disposition
147	**Program Direction**	
	Involves planning, managing, and evaluating all activities at NARA Regional Records Services facilities.	
147-1	Region-Wide (Regional Administrator). Records related to directing and coordinating the performance of all NARA programs and activities assigned to Regional Records Services facilities.	PERMANENT. Cut off at the close of the fiscal year. Transfer to the National Archives in 5-year blocks when the newest records are 5 years old. (N1-64-07-5, item 1)
147-2	Operational unit. Records created in operational units which are related to planning, managing, and evaluating activities and programs created in operational units.	Cut off at the close of the fiscal year in which the project/activity/transaction was completed OR superseded. Destroy 5 years after cutoff. (N1-64-07-5, item 2)

Source: http://www.archives.gov/about/records-schedule/chapter-0.1/html

Administrative Functions - Regional Records Services Facilities

File #	Description	Disposition
266	**Administrative Functions**	
	Records documenting most administrative functions as performed by staff at Regional Records Services facilities. EXCLUDES records of other administrative functions specifically described under items 267, 268, and 269.	Cut off at the end of the fiscal year in which the project/activity/transaction was completed OR superseded. Destroy when 3 years old. (N1-64-07-5, item 5)

Source: http://www.archives.gov/about/records-schedule/chapter-0.2/html

use an internal audit to self-monitor its process-related effectiveness and to isolate specific organizational functions or systems. "For example, a RIM professional may engage in an internal audit to assess the RIM function, as a system or as a series of processes with the organization."[16] The RIM manager conducts regular reviews and assessments of the RIM program and therefore, needs knowledge of auditing principles and techniques. From the audit, managers look for ways to improve the program's performance. Large organizations may use their own trained staff to undertake such an audit, or they may hire outside consultants that have more experience and are likely more objective. Small firms often use outside auditors because they usually do not have a qualified records auditor on staff.

What information does a records audit provide?

A records audit provides three kinds of information about a RIM program:

1. **Information about current operations**. This information includes how well the objectives are being achieved, whether written policies and procedures are available and followed by all personnel, whether policies and procedures reflect the way documents are processed, and the scope of RIM activities and any problems associated with them.
2. **Analysis of the current system**. This analysis includes the layout of files, effectiveness and validity of policies and procedures, staff qualifications, uses of available equipment, active and inactive storage systems, system operating costs versus projected costs, and security measures for preserving and protecting records. Customer satisfaction with the RIM program is also evaluated.
3. **Recommended solutions for improving the RIM program**. These solutions also include cost estimates for implementing the recommendations.

RIM software can be used to provide audit trails for tracking document use and staff productivity. A system administrator can monitor electronic image and electronic records use by determining who has been viewing which documents, where, and when. Monitoring sensitive documents that need to be kept secure, tracking staff productivity, and tracking search activity among public records can be done using audit logs generated by the software.

Vital Records Protection

What are mission-critical records?

First mentioned in Chapter 1 and discussed again in Chapter 7, vital records are sometimes described as *mission-critical records* because their existence is critical for the continued operations and purposes of an organization. As a consequence of their importance, organizations implement special procedures for protecting their vital records. Vital records stored on microfilm or electronic media are subjected to specific environmental, security, and safety controls to ensure their continued usefulness for as long as they are needed—permanently for some documents and records. The records manager needs to

[15]Nancy Dupre Barnes, Ph.D., CRM, CA, and Nicholas R. Barnes, CPA, "Driving Quality Improvement Through Audits," *Information Management*, January/February 2012 (Lenexa, KS: ARMA International), p. 40.
[16]Ibid., "Driving Quality Improvement Through Audits," p. 40.

understand best practices for preservation of physical and digital materials and the ability to communicate the benefits of preserving and having access to legacy information assets. As discussed later in this chapter, developing and implementing a disaster preparedness and prevention program are part of the protection plans for all stored records.

Archival Records Preservation

Developing an organizational policy and practice for collecting and preserving archival records is often the RIM manager's responsibility. To accomplish this task, the records manager needs to have knowledge of the organization's culture, goals, priorities, and the history of the organization and of the surrounding community. Examples of items that may be important to the organization and would be recommended for the archives include historical documents, photos, and newspaper articles about the groundbreaking ceremony for the construction of the headquarters building; news releases and articles about the purchase of another company; news releases, photos, and articles about the release of a new product; or news articles about an important anniversary such as the 50th anniversary of the founding of the company/organization. Other important items stored in the company's archives would include blueprints for all company buildings.

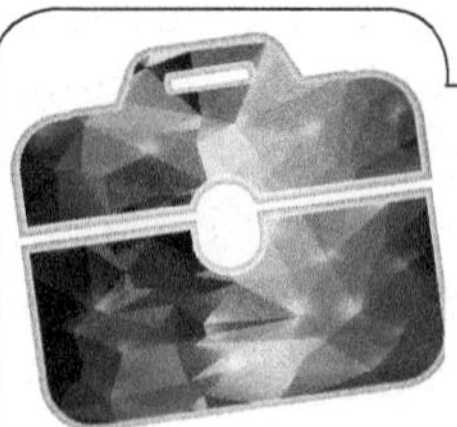

CAREER CORNER

Job Description for Archivist and Records Manager

The following job description is an example of a career opportunity in records and information management at a university.

GENERAL INFORMATION

The archivist and records manager's duties will be evenly split between the archives and records management. The archivist and records manager is responsible for developing and implementing systems and procedures for the proper management of the university's records.

RESPONSIBILITIES

- Catalog and index the archives to comply with national standards.
- Acquire new documents, photographs, and artifacts.
- Conduct records surveys and establish retention and destruction schedules.
- Maintain a university-wide records management system.
- Ensure that storage facilities and environments meet long-term preservation needs for historical and current records, literary papers, architectural drawings, board of trustee minutes.

EXPERIENCE AND EDUCATION

- Graduate degree in library science or business management with coursework in records management
- Experience in an academic archives and/or library environment desirable
- Experience working with wide-ranging records management systems, including with born-digital and digitized records
- Excellent oral and written communication skills
- Knowledge of cataloguing software

Forms Management

form: a physical or electronic document with a fixed arrangement of predetermined spaces designed for entering and extracting prescribed information or variable data

What are a RIM manager's responsibilities for forms management?

A **form** is a physical or electronic document with a fixed arrangement of predetermined spaces designed for entering and extracting prescribed information or variable data. Forms are efficient data-collection instruments when properly designed. A large amount of information can be collected from a one-page form. In large corporations, schools, universities, and other organizations that use a large number of forms, this responsibility may be delegated to a forms manager and staff who are part of the RIM program. A RIM manager's responsibilities regarding forms management are to identify all forms that the organization is currently using to collect information it needs to conduct various business processes. The manager needs also to identify duplicate forms that collect the same information, any forms no longer being used, and any forms that do not collect the correct information needed. Forms management includes version control to ensure that the latest revised form for a specific purpose is the one available for users. When the majority of forms are available on an organization's website or its intranet, someone in information management (IT) may be responsible for form number assignment and for posting the forms to the Web or the intranet. Ideally, each department designs its own forms to meet its data-collection needs.

Often, forms are created using office productivity software, such as *Microsoft® Word* or *Microsoft® Access*, and are easily revised or updated as data collection needs or procedures change. With the variety of form templates available in word processing software, users can simply select a form that meets their needs and customize it with the company name, address, telephone numbers, logo, and so on. See a sample invoice template in Figure 14.2. Users can also create a table in word processing software, label the fields for the information to collect on the form and move or insert new columns and/or lines as needed to create a highly functional form. Well-designed forms assist in maintaining an efficient and productive forms management program.

Organizations that use online forms are able to reduce paper and printing. Users can sign forms with an electronic signature or just type their names on provided signature lines, according to the Electronic Signature in Global and National Commerce Act (E-Sign) of 2000. Unlike paper forms, electronic forms are not printed and stocked. Instead, they may be completed online and either transmitted via e-mail to another location or printed. Interactive web-based forms are created, edited, and stored in databases in the cloud.

Standardized forms are used in large numbers because they are capable of handling large quantities of information in the least amount of time, effort, and space. As forms continue to be an efficient way of gathering and transmitting information, their design, use, cost, and storage require managerial approval and periodic evaluation.

Disaster Prevention, Preparedness, and Recovery

Organizations all over the world adopt plans for dealing with emergencies caused by weather disasters or other events as well as internal emergencies such as broken water pipes and small electrical fires. Some organizations have developed plans for terrorist attacks. Other organizations have developed business continuity/disaster management plans. Disaster recovery plans may also

FIGURE 14.2 **Sample Microsoft® Excel Invoice Template**

Your Company Name **INVOICE**

Your Company Slogan

Street Address
City, ST ZIP Code
Phone (509) 555-0190 Fax (509) 555-0191

DATE: December 30, 2009
INVOICE # 100

Bill To: Name
Company Name
Street Address
City, ST ZIP Code
Phone

Ship To: Name
Company Name
Street Address
City, ST ZIP Code
Phone

Comments or Special Instructions:

SALESPERSON	P.O. NUMBER	SHIP DATE	SHIP VIA	F.O.B. POINT	TERMS
					Due on receipt

QUANTITY	DESCRIPTION	UNIT PRICE	AMOUNT
			$ -
		SUBTOTAL	$ -
		TAX RATE	8.60%
		SALES TAX	-
		SHIPPING & HANDLING	
		TOTAL	$ -

Make all checks payable to **Your Company Name**
If you have any questions concerning this invoice, contact Name, Phone Number, E-mail Address

THANK YOU FOR YOUR BUSINESS!

be referred to as *contingency plans, emergency plans,* or *disaster plans.* Whatever their title, these plans are developed and implemented to provide guidance for protecting records and information and continuing business operations when emergencies and disasters occur.

What is the difference between an emergency and a disaster?

An emergency is an unforeseen event that calls for immediate action. Examples of an emergency include a broken water pipe, a bomb threat, or a sudden storm that requires actions but does not usually result in major loss or disruption of operations for an organization. A disaster is a sudden emergency event that results in major loss of resources or disruption of operations for an organization. Disasters can result in significant financial damage. Examples of disasters include a destructive fire, a flood causing major facility or product loss, or a tornado that causes major damage to one or more facilities.

Disaster prevention is the first phase of the disaster plan in which measures are taken to reduce the probability of loss resulting from an emergency.

If an emergency occurs, these measures can reduce the severity of the disaster and limit the loss.[17]

Preparedness, the second phase, is simply being prepared to respond when an emergency occurs. Once an emergency is recognized, personnel know what to do and whom to call. Preparedness activities include developing a response team, developing and updating the plan, testing emergency systems, training employees, stocking emergency supplies, arranging for recovery vendors, and establishing hot sites (locations where a complete computer operation is set up and ready). Responding to an emergency event means activating resources necessary to protect the organization from loss. These activities occur before, during, or directly after an emergency and include contacting the response team, notifying appropriate authorities, securing facilities, and notifying RIM recovery vendors.

What activities take place in the recovery phase?

disaster recovery plan: a plan developed and implemented to provide guidance for protecting records and information and continuing business operations when emergencies and disasters occur

Recovery, the third phase, involves necessary activities to restore operations quickly, especially vital systems and processes that will keep producing products and services as well as retaining customers. These activities include dehumidifying records, restoring data onto computers, and returning vital records from off-site storage.[18] A **disaster recovery plan** is a written and approved course of action to take when disaster strikes, ensuring an organization's ability to respond to an interruption in services by restoring critical business functions. The plan also details how records will be handled before and during a disaster and after in the recovery stage. Procedures for the immediate resumption of business operations after a disaster are included as well. How an organization prepares for a disruption to its business determines how well, or whether, it survives. Flooding from leaking roofs, leaking air conditioners, overflowing toilets, broken water mains, broken water pipes, overflowing sewer systems, and other water sources is a commonly occurring type of business interruption. Equipment outages and power outages are also common causes of interruption to business activity. Fire or explosion, earthquake, hurricane, and building outage resulting from construction or environmental problems are more serious causes of business interruption. Hurricanes, earthquakes, bombings in major cities, and terrorist attacks have alerted all businesses to the critical importance of a disaster recovery plan.

A disaster recovery plan is the basis for the following activities:

- Identifying preventive measures against records and information loss.
- Initiating a company-wide response to disasters that threaten records and information.
- Identifying response personnel and their roles.
- Estimating cost of and various types and lengths of business disruptions.
- Providing off-site storage for vital records and back-up computer data storage.
- Designating alternative sites for mission-critical tasks, including computer-related operations.
- Establishing recovery procedures for damaged records and information.
- Establishing recovery priorities.

---

[17]Virginia A. Jones, CRM, and Darlene Barber, *Emergency Management for Records and Information Programs*, 2nd Ed. (Lenexa, KS: ARMA International, 2011), p. 5.
[18]Ibid., *Emergency Management*, p. 6.

- Identifying sources of supplies, equipment, and services for recovery and restoration of damaged records and media.
- Testing the plan through mock disasters and making appropriate changes.

How can electronic records be protected?

Records can be lost and/or damaged when necessary precautions are not taken to protect them. Routine precautions are taken to protect electronic data such as controlling extremes in temperature and humidity, backing up valuable data, installing antivirus programs that detect and remove computer viruses, installing firewall programs to prevent unauthorized network intrusions, installing surge protectors to minimize damage caused by electrical variances, and removing magnetic items from around hard drives and removable drives. Discussions in Chapter 12 include procedures for controlling and protecting records from physical hazards, controlling environmental conditions necessary to ensure safe storage of all records, and protecting records from unauthorized access. The test of a sound disaster recovery plan—and any other precautionary procedures and safety measures taken to protect records and business operations—is whether it allows business activity to resume within a few days after a disaster. Such a plan includes not only a recovery of records but also a recovery of the work site, essential equipment, and the work force.

Business Processes

The records manager needs the knowledge and skills necessary to administer, implement, or maintain the non-RIM functions an organization performs, or needs to perform, to achieve its objectives. These business processes include the supervision of RIM staff, budgeting, providing customer service, mapping work processes, providing input to management, and strategic management.

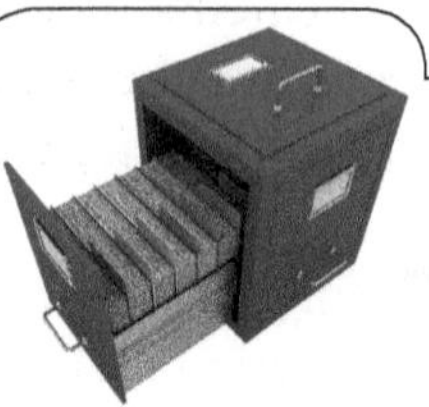

MY RECORDS

Records Safety in an Emergency

If the smoke alarm went off in your home, which records would you decide to save? If you must be evacuated from your home, what records should you take with you?

The most important task in any emergency is for the personal safety of you and your family. The American Red Cross website contains many suggestions for coping with emergencies, including how to prepare for them.

Throughout this text, the My Records sections have given tips about managing your personal records. These tips are helpful to you in case of an emergency. The next step in safeguarding your records is to act on the tips.

- Identify your vital records and make certified copies (see Chapter 1, My Records).
- Document the original vital records (and you may have many) with addresses, phone numbers, contact people, and the location where you have stored these records off-site.
- Store the originals in a safety deposit box or similarly safe off-site location (see Chapter 6, My Records).
- Store the certified copies in a weatherproof container that you can take with you as you leave your house.
- Store the container that holds the copies with your personal survival kits stocked with food, water, medical supplies, and a change of clothing.
- Store the most recent computer backup in the same weatherproof container.
- Update the records in the storage container at least once a month.

Be prepared: Plan and then implement the plan.

The records manager must also have knowledge of the daily routine and task assignments in the RIM department, basic RIM principles, and basic written communication in order to identify, document, and provide input to management related to RIM business processes to improve the quality of the RIM program.

Managing the volume of physical and electronic/digital records, as pointed out in Chapter 7, carries with it tremendous costs. These costs include salaries, storage space, equipment, and supplies.

What cost factors are included in RIM labor costs?

Labor costs represent the largest percentage of total RIM costs. This cost factor includes managerial, supervisory, and operating personnel salaries along with employee benefits such as retirement plans, vacation days, sick days/leave, Social Security contributions, and various types of insurance. Installing automated RIM systems can help reduce long-term labor costs. A clearly defined and implemented records retention policy prevents an organization from retaining unnecessary data that keeps storage costs high.

Steps commonly taken to reduce costs include:

1. Identify and assign cost figures to the four main cost categories—salaries, space, equipment, and supplies. Include hourly rates for all records personnel, cost of equipment, and cost of the space that the equipment occupies. Then, calculate the costs of maintaining typical files (such as five-drawer vertical file cabinets) and use this information in cost-reduction studies.
2. Compare labor costs for storing and retrieving records in-house and using off-site or commercial storage facilities. Evaluate the cost of picking up records, storing records, using a pick list to retrieve records, delivering records to the company, and destroying records. Include costs incurred by emergency records requests and fast delivery.

   Costs of equipment, space, salaries, and supplies can be controlled by (1) eliminating unnecessary records, (2) carefully supervising the use of equipment and supplies, and (3) selecting equipment and media that require less space and less time to operate.

Taxonomies

What is a taxonomy?

As you learned in Chapter 11, a taxonomy is a structure used for classifying materials into a hierarchy of categories and subcategories. In RIM, a file plan or classification/taxonomy is essential for efficient filing and retrieval of stored physical documents and electronic data. A list of file titles, whether in a text document, spreadsheet, or database file, is a basic file classification/taxonomy that can be used for future physical file system development and electronic repositories.

Social Media

social media: forms of electronic communication (as websites for social networking and microblogging) through which users create online communities to share information, ideas, personal messages, and other content (such as videos)

Social media are forms of electronic communication (as websites for social networking and microblogging) through which users create online communities to share information, ideas, personal messages, and other content (as videos).[19] Organizations are using social media for a variety of purposes,

[19]Merriam Webster, http://www.merriam-webster.com/dictionary/social%20media, accessed May 14, 2014.

including conducting sweepstakes, marketing, sales transactions, and customer relations. Social media implementation requires coordinated integration with both RIM and IT personnel.[20] All organizations—large and small—that use social media should have a policy for using it in terms of acceptable usage to achieve the organization's goals, guidelines for official versus personal use, ways for monitoring social media utilization, types of information available on social media that may be relevant to the organization, security of the information, and whether information should be collected. See Figure 14.3 for some suggested elements of a social media policy. Social media information may be discoverable during litigation because the information originates with users, and it is arranged according to interactions between users.[21]

FIGURE 14.3 **Social Media Policy Suggestions**

Before any business or organization employs social media, company executives need to develop a policy for the use of any social media platform—Internet environment. Important areas to cover in this policy include the following:

1. *Code of Conduct.* Employees who engage in business-related social media interactions need to know about and follow the organization's code of conduct.
2. *Consistency.* Ensure that postings are consistent with the organization's reputation and business practices.
3. *Confidentiality.* Avoid naming clients, suppliers, or any other business associates without their approval.
4. *Ownership.* Employees must identify themselves and make clear that the postings are their own and do not necessarily represent the opinions of the company.
5. *Responsibility.* Employees may be held personally responsible for everything that they post. They should make sure that their online activities do not interfere with their ability to fulfill their job requirements or their commitments to their managers, co-workers, or customers.
6. *Language.* Avoid derogatory or discriminatory remarks, ethnic slurs, personal insults, or any similar conduct that would not be acceptable in the workplace or would violate the code of conduct.
7. *Terms of Service.* Follow the terms of service for all social media sites.
8. *Applicable Laws.* Respect copyright and fair use laws.
9. *Security.* Ensure that social media records are as secure as other organization records formats.
10. *Logo and Trademark Abuse.* The company logo and trademarks should not be used for personal postings or in such a manner as to have a negative impact on the company's business.
11. *Designated Employees.* Only those employees officially designated can use social media to speak on behalf of the company in an official capacity; employees may use social media to speak for themselves individually or to exercise their legal rights under the National Labor Relations Act.
12. *Confidential and Proprietary Information.* Employees may not share any confidential and proprietary information, such as financial information, new product releases, sales, number of employees, or any other information that has not been publicly released by the company.

[20]ARMA International, *Using Social Media in Organizations* (Lenexa, KS: ARMA International, 2012), p. 3.

[21]A. Allen, J.D., PMP, and Michael C. Wylie, J.D., "Managing and Collecting Social Media for E discovery," *Information Management*, May/June 2013 (Lenexa, KS: ARMA International), p. 24.

Organizations that incorporate social media to address complaints about products, executive comments, or manufacturing processes, may delegate that responsibility to one department, one team, or one person, depending on the size of the business. Using a consistent message and getting the message out quickly is important for the public perception of the organization. Smaller organizations may outsource Facebook management to a media services company when they find that the designated employee no longer has the time to read and respond to posts or to post new messages. **Social media posts** are the interactions among people on a social media website, such as Facebook, including photos. Posts are usually arranged in reverse chronological order.

social media posts: the interactions among people on a social media website, such as Facebook, including photos

Social Media Legal Issues

Laws and regulations have not kept up with the numerous legal issues surrounding the use of social media in the workplace. Some employers have and continue to request social media or Facebook passwords when interviewing potential employees. Although some employers have made the release of social media passwords optional, applicants still find the requests disturbing. Some schools require student athletes to friend a coach so that the coach can monitor the athletes' social media interactions. Although several states have passed laws prohibiting such practices, no federal laws have been passed, and schools and businesses continue to make such requests.[22]

The Kroger Co. dropped its online communication policy after a National Labor Relations Board administrative law judge determined that four provisions of the policy would interfere with employees' ability to exercise their rights to discuss issues such as wages, transfers, potential shutdowns, closures, and layoffs.[23]

Social Media Records Management

Before an organization takes steps to develop a social media policy, executives need to develop the records and information management component of social media. Some difficulties associated with capturing and managing social media records or data are that they might never pass through the corporate network; communications can be deleted instantly; content exists in a variety of formats; and capturing old content is impossible. Social media interactions are dynamic in that one person posts a comment or personal news, and a friend responds immediately. The interactions are happening in real time, and they may be subject to e-discovery.

RIM employees who have studied and gained experience in all topics discussed in *Records Management*, Tenth Edition, can look forward to long, successful careers in the records and information management profession.

---

[22]Jonathan Dame, "Will Employers Still Ask for Facebook Passwords in 2014?" *USA Today College*, January 10, 2014, www.usatoday.com/story/money/busisness/2014/01/10/facebook-passwords-employers/4327739/.

[23]Greiner, Jack, "Strictly Legal: Employers' Social Media Rules Limited." Cincinnati.com, May 10, 2014, www.cincinnati.com/story/money/2014/05/10/strickly-legal-employers-social-media-rules-limited/8936843/.

CHAPTER REVIEW AND APPLICATIONS

KEY POINTS

- RIM is the foundation that supports information governance.
- A records manager's duties and responsibilities encompass all components of the RIM program.
- The records manager is responsible for meeting goals identified in the organization's strategic plan.
- The records retention schedule is a basic records control tool.
- RIM program components include records storage facilities; storage supplies and equipment; records retention and destruction; security and protection of an organization's information assets, including vital and archival records; and forms management.
- The RIM program is responsible for conducting the records audit; developing records retention schedules and enforcing them; and developing a disaster prevention, preparation, and recovery plan.
- A records manager needs to understand business processes such as supervising, budgeting, providing customer services, and managing costs.
- A taxonomy is a structure used for classifying materials into a hierarchy of categories and subcategories.
- A social media policy is necessary for effective use of social networking services and to monitor and collect information for business and legal purposes from social media services.

TERMS

disaster recovery plan
form
records audit
social media
social media posts
strategic plan
strategic planning

REVIEW AND DISCUSS

1. Explain the differences between governance and management. (Obj. 1)

2. List five responsibilities of the records and information manager. (Obj. 2)

3. List three areas that are included in the goals and objectives of the RIM program. (Obj. 3)

4. List four components of the RIM program. (Obj. 4)

5. List three actions taken to implement a retention schedule. (Obj. 5)

6. Define *records audit* and describe its purpose. (Obj. 6)

7. Describe two ways to create a form. (Obj. 7)

8. What are the phases in a disaster recovery plan? Explain what occurs during each phase. (Obj. 8)

9. List four purposes for having a social media policy. (Obj. 9)

APPLICATIONS

14-1 Design an Information Form (Obj. 6)

Assume that you are a property manager for the Green Gables condominium complex. You need to collect information about the automobiles owned by condo residents. Your goal is to keep track of all automobiles that regularly park in the condo parking lot by issuing preprinted parking stickers for each vehicle. Use the software program of your choice to create a table for the form. If using word processing software, press the Tab key to add more rows as needed.

1. Design a form that will be printed and given to residents to complete by hand. Include the complex name and the form title "Automobile Registration" at the top of the page.
2. Provide brief instructions for completing the form, and indicate that the completed form should be returned to the management office. Indicate that residents should complete and submit a form for each vehicle that will be parked in the condo complex parking lot. Remind residents to submit new forms if they change vehicles.
3. Provide space on the form for residents to write the following information:
    - Current Date
    - Owner Name
    - Unit No.
    - Telephone No.
    - Automobile Make
    - Automobile Model
    - Automobile Color
    - License Plate No.
    - State of Registration
4. Include a space for the parking sticker number to be recorded, and indicate that the manager will assign the number.
5. At the bottom of the form, key the form identification code "AUTO" and the current month and year as the revision date. For example: AUTO Rev. 06/14.
6. Save the form as "14-1 Auto Form." Print the form.

14-2 Enter Data Using a Database Form (Obj. 6)

In Application 14-1, you created a form to collect data for the Green Gables condo complex. Now you will create an Access database to store and organize the automobile information.

1. Create a new database file named "14-2 Automobile Registration."
2. Create a new database table named "Automobile Registration." Include the following fields in the table:
    - Form Date
    - Owner Name
    - Unit No.
    - Telephone No.
    - Make
    - Model
    - Color

- Plate No.
- State
- Sticker No.

3. Select **Number** as the field type for the Unit No. and Sticker No. fields. Select **Text** or **Short Text** as the field type for all other fields. Select **Sticker** No. as the primary key.
4. Create an AutoForm based on the Automobile Registration table. Enter the data shown in Figure 14.4 for six residents, using the AutoForm. Enter the current year in dates.

FIGURE 14.4 **Data for Six Residents**

Form Date: 05/06/--	Form Date: 05/04/--
Owner Name: Jose Rodriguez	Owner Name: Andrea Phillips
Unit #: 907	Unit #: 312
Telephone #: 513.555.0198	Telephone #: 513.555.0120
Make: Toyota	Make: Jeep
Model: Camry	Model: Cherokee
Color: White	Color: White
Plate #: CRL 5534	Plate #: DDM 6589
State: OH	State: KY
Sticker #: 153	Sticker #: 155
Form Date: 05/05/--	Form Date: 05/06/--
Owner Name: Joshua Gibson	Owner Name: Sarah Fields
Unit #: 401	Unit #: 611
Telephone #: 513.555.0156	Telephone #: 513.555.0134
Make: Ford	Make: Chevrolet
Model: Focus	Model: Impala
Color: Silver	Color: Black
Plate #: 23 DV 56	Plate #: ORK 3448
State: IN	State: OH
Sticker #: 154	Sticker #: 152
Form Date: 05/07/--	Form Date: 05/05/--
Owner Name: C. J. Andrews	Owner Name: Frank Patruso
Unit #: 205	Unit #: 710
Telephone #: 513.555.0167	Telephone #: 513.555.0123
Make: Ford	Make: Lexus
Model: 500	Model: ES300
Color: Navy Blue	Color: Pearl White
Plate #: RCT 1562	Plate #: XMV 2198
State: KY	State: OH
Sticker #: 156	Sticker #: 157

5. Add two more records, using the AutoForm. Assume that two of your classmates live in Units 403 and 708. Interview your classmates, and enter their auto information using the form. Assign sticker numbers 158 and 159 to their autos. Close the form without saving it.
6. Create a report based on the Automobile Registration table using the Report Wizard. Include all fields in the report except the Form Date field. Sort by the Unit No. field in ascending order. Choose **Landscape** orientation, if needed, to have all fields show on one page.
7. Name the report "Automobile Registration." Print the report.

ADDITIONAL RESOURCES

For data files, Microsoft® Access tutorials and more, go to www.cengagebrain.com.

APPENDIX A

How Computers Sort Data

A computer performs sorting operations quickly and can store a great amount of data in a small space. It pays great attention to detail and can retrieve information faster and more accurately than humans *if* the input is accurate. You should be aware, however, that computers sort data differently than you would sort records manually. When you sort records manually, you look at each letter, number, or symbol to determine the indexing units. You understand each one to have a different meaning. When sorting, for example, you know that key indexing units that begin with numbers are placed before key indexing units that begin with letters. You know that the letter *A* comes before *E*. Computers understand only numbers. Computer programs use character codes to represent the symbols, numbers, and letters in the data you enter.

CHARACTER SETS STANDARDS

In Chapter 1, you learned about the International Organization for Standardization (ISO). The American National Standards Institute (ANSI) is a member of the ISO. Standards help all computers interpret data in the same way. Data standards work on the computer so that it is readable on all machines using the English language. Each country has a standard for their language. As more information is displayed on the Internet, standardization is even more important to global communication. On html pages, the document is encoded with a particular character set. UTF-8 is often used on html pages originating in the United States.

ANSI uses the American Standard Code for Information Interchange (ASCII, pronounced "Ask E") for compliance to the ISO standard. ASCII is a character code that was developed as a standard and logical way to recognize character data on computers. ASCII assigns specific numeric values to the first 128 characters of the 256 possible character combinations. ANSI, an expanded version of the code, is used for other characters. Most operating systems compensate for ASCII values, and sorting is transparent to the user on newer laptops and tablets.

Each character you enter into an electronic record is represented by a unique number in that character code. For example, in ASCII, the code number for letter *C* is 67. The code number for letter *W* is 87. When a computer program sorts data, it uses the character code numbers assigned to the symbols, numbers, and letters you have entered. The resulting sort order may be quite different from the way you would sort the same records manually.

SORT ORDER

When you manually sort a list of names, you look at the letters to determine the order. When a computer sorts data, it reads each character as a value in the character code. Because these values are numbers, the computer places the lowest value, or number, first. The sort order depends on the character code used by the computer and possibly on other settings that have been selected in the software application. For example, some computer applications ignore the case of letters when sorting. With Microsoft® Word and Microsoft® Excel, the user can set options to determine whether the sort is case sensitive. The default setting is no checkmark in the case sensitive box. Figure A.1 shows the options for selecting Case Sensitive for sorting in Word and in Excel. Access ignores the case when sorting on a particular field. If Access encounters two identical values, for example, one uppercase and the other lowercase, Access lists them in the order in which they were entered. For example, if a record with the value **jones** in the Last Name field was entered before a record with the value **Jones** in the same field, the record containing **jones** will be displayed before the record containing **Jones**.

FIGURE A.1 **Microsoft® Word and Excel Sort Options**

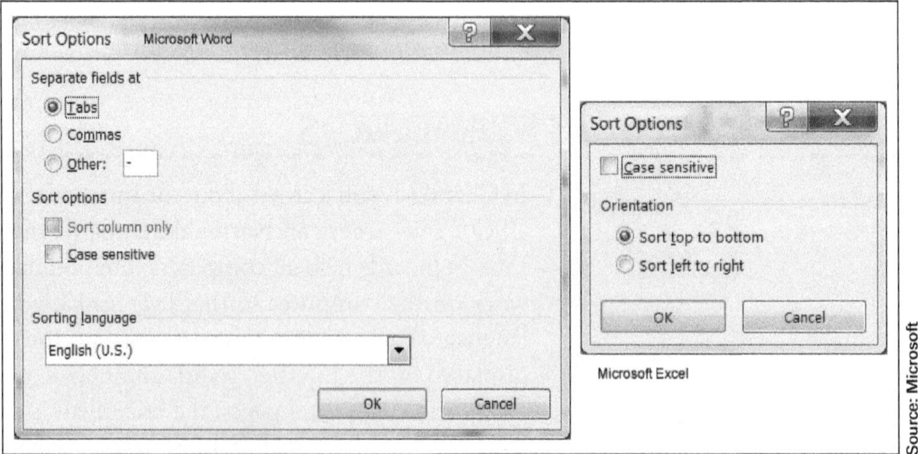

Source: Microsoft

In Microsoft® Access, the user can select a default sort order for a new database. The option selected affects how data is sorted. The General option, shown in Figure A.2, is appropriate for a variety of languages, including English.

The sort order of electronic data can be affected by general settings selected for the computer. For example, for computers that use the Microsoft Windows operating system, settings can be selected on the Region and Language Option in the Control Panel, as shown in Figure A.3.

FIGURE A.2 **General Category for Microsoft® Access 2013**

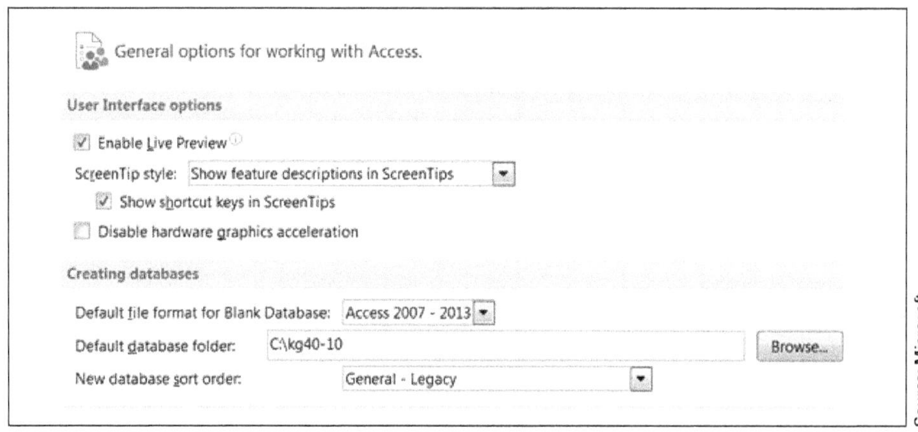

Source: Microsoft

FIGURE A.3 **Region and Language Options for Windows**

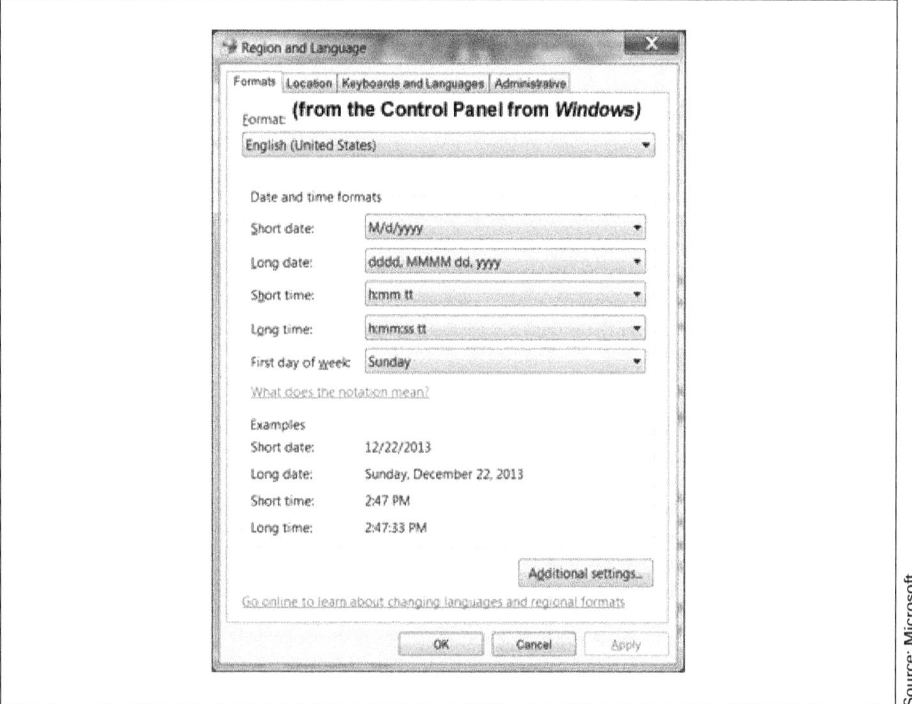

Source: Microsoft

The Company Name Computer Sort column of Figure A.4 shows a computer sort of example names. The names were keyed into the computer as they were written. The Indexing Order Manual Sort column shows the same list of names (with no punctuation) keyed in indexing order (as would be used for manual filing) and sorted. Notice the difference in the order of the examples. What causes the difference? Part of the difference is due to placing the names in indexing order, and part of the difference is due to the way computers sort data.

FIGURE A.4 **Comparison of Sort Orders**

Company Name Computer Sort	Indexing Order Manual Sort
# Off Diet Center	3 Rs Nursery School
$ Value Store	26 Highway Service
"A-OK" Smart Shop	405 Shopping Center
26 Highway Service	AOK Smart Shop
3 Rs Nursery School	Dollar Value Store
405 Shopping Center	Labelle Fashion Boutique
LaBelle Fashion Boutique	Larrys Restaurant
Larry's Restaurant	Pounds Off Diet Center

OTHER SORTING DIFFERENCES

When you are entering records for computerized storage, careful attention to detail and knowledge of how a computer processes data are important points to remember. You have learned that computers sort records in a particular way depending on the character code used and other settings specified by the user. This section points out some other specific differences you may find between how a computer sorts records and how the records would be sorted for manual filing.

Titles and Suffixes

Names with titles and suffixes are indexed for physical records according to Rule 5, Chapter 3. Numeric suffixes (I, II) are filed before alphabetic suffixes (CPA, Jr., Sr.). The computer reads Roman numerals as letters and sorts them after numbers. Figure A.5 shows examples of names with suffixes sorted by a computer and sorted for manual filing. Note the differences in the sort order. In Example 1, CPA is filed before Roman numeral II.

FIGURE A.5 **Comparison of Sort Order for Suffixes**

Example 1 Computer Order			Example 2 Manual Order		
Last	**First**	**Title/**	**Last**	**First**	**Title/**
Jones	Allen	CPA	Jones	Allen	II
Jones	Allen	II	Jones	Allen	III
Jones	Allen	III	Jones	Allen	CPA
Jones	Allen	Jr	Jones	Allen	Jr
Jones	Allen	Mayor	Jones	Allen	Mayor
Jones	Allen	Mr	Jones	Allen	Mr
Jones	Allen	Sr	Jones	Allen	Sr

Numbers in Business Names

As mentioned earlier, a computer program may not sort numbers in a text field in consecutive order. Most people know that 2 comes before 10 in a listing of numbers. To a computer, which reads from left to right, 1 comes first, then 10 through 19, then 2, followed by 20 through 29, continuing to 99. Be aware that numbers in text fields may not sort in consecutive order. However, numbers in a database number field can be sorted in consecutive order.

Numbers in a database, such as customer IDs, invoice numbers, or product numbers, are sometimes keyed with leading zeroes so that all numbers have the same number of digits and can be sorted consecutively even in a text field. Adding leading zeroes works well with numbers a company can control or assign. Figure A.6 shows examples of numbers with and without leading zeroes.

FIGURE A.6 **Comparison of Sorted Numbers With and Without Leading Zeroes**

Example 1 without Leading Zeroes		Example 2 with Leading Zeroes	
Customer ID	**Last Name**	**Customer ID**	**Last Name**
1	Allen	001	Allen
11	Jones	002	Thomas
111	Perez	011	Jones
2	Thomas	022	Leon
22	Leon	111	Perez
222	Chin	222	Chin

Spacing and Punctuation

When filing physical records, spaces are disregarded in some situations. For example, in last names such as *De La Torres* or *Van de Hoef*, the spaces are disregarded when filing physical records. When keying these names into electronic records, the spaces will be considered and the filing order will be different than it would be for physical records.

When filing physical records, punctuation is disregarded in determining filing order. When records are keyed in a database, punctuation is not ignored. Therefore, the same names will sort in a different order from the sort order used for manual filing of physical records.

When filing physical records, the word *The* at the beginning of a business name is considered the last indexing unit. When keying a name into a computer database, the name stays in its original order that begins with *The* as the first word. Therefore, the same names will sort in a different order from the sort order used for manual filing of physical records.

In some cases, you may want to change the way you enter records into a computer application to achieve the same sorted order as when related physical records are sorted. For example, you might have an index of company names in an electronic database that corresponds to records. In this case, you might want the electronic index to show the same sort order as the sort order used for the physical records. An easy way to achieve the same sort order would be to add an Indexing Order field to the database table. The company name would be entered into the Company Name field as it is written. This field would be used for tasks such as creating mailing labels where the name should appear as written. In the Indexing Order field, the name would be keyed in indexing order according to manual filing rules. When sorted electronic records are needed to match sorted physical records, the Indexing Order field can be used for the sort.

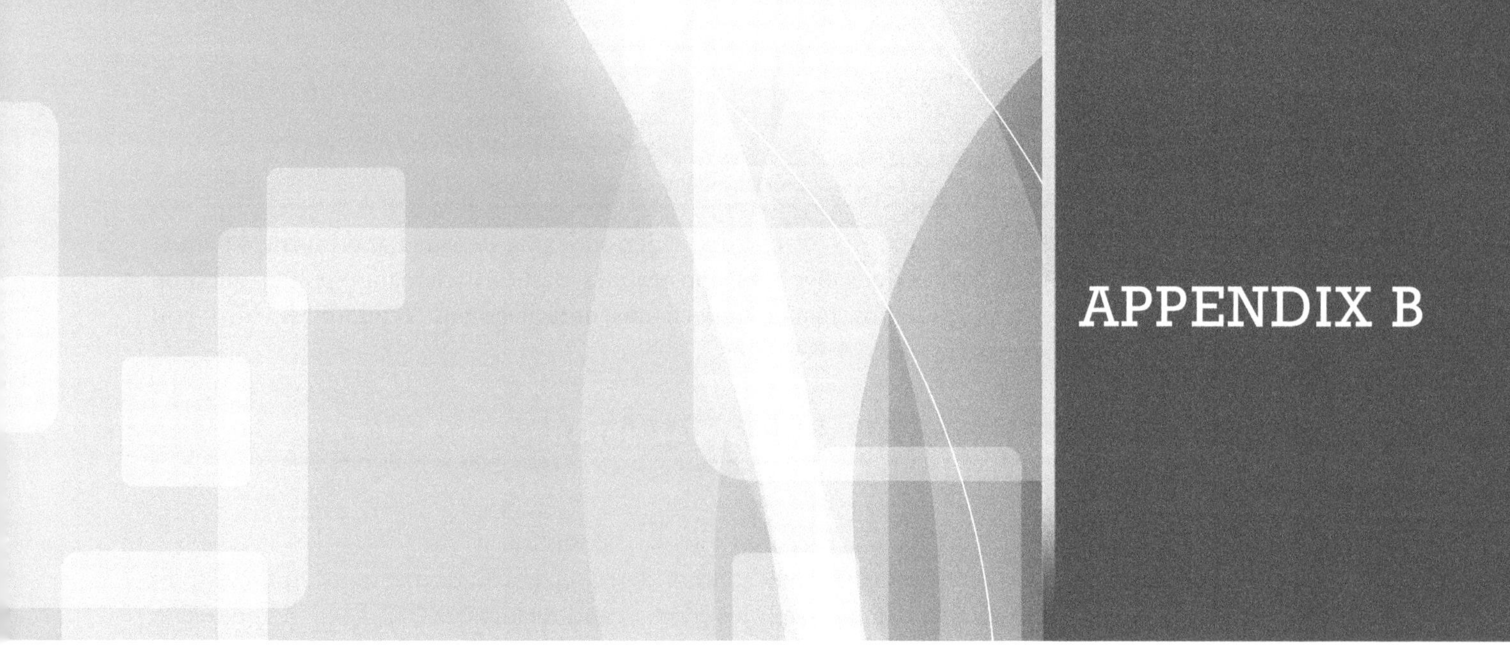

APPENDIX B

Alphabetic Indexing Rules

RULE 1: INDEXING ORDER OF UNITS

A. Personal Names

A personal name is indexed in this manner: (1) the surname (last name) is the key unit; (2) the given name (first name) or initial is the second unit; and (3) the middle name or initial is the third unit. If determining the surname is difficult, consider the last name written as the surname. (You will learn how to handle titles that appear with names in a later rule.)

A unit consisting of just an initial precedes a unit that consists of a complete name beginning with the same letter—*nothing before something*. Punctuation is omitted.

B. Business Names

Business names are indexed *as written* using letterheads or trademarks as guides. Each word in a business name is a separate unit. Business names containing personal names are indexed as written.

RULE 2: MINOR WORDS AND SYMBOLS IN BUSINESS NAMES

Articles, prepositions, conjunctions, and symbols are considered separate indexing units. Symbols are considered as spelled in full. When the word *The* appears as the first word of a business name, it is considered the last indexing unit.

Articles:	a, an, the
Prepositions:	at, in, out, on, off, by, to, with, for, of, over
Conjunctions:	and, but, or, nor
Symbols:	&, ¢, $, #, % (and, cent *or* cents, dollar *or* dollars, number *or* pound, percent)

RULE 3: PUNCTUATION AND POSSESSIVES

All punctuation is disregarded when indexing personal and business names. Commas, periods, hyphens, apostrophes, dashes, exclamation points, question marks, quotation marks, underscores, and diagonals (/) are disregarded, and names are indexed as written.

RULE 4: SINGLE LETTERS AND ABBREVIATIONS

A. Personal Names

Initials in personal names are considered separate indexing units. Abbreviations of personal names (Wm., Jos., Thos.) and nicknames (Liz, Bill) are indexed as they are written.

B. Business Names

Single letters in business and organization names are indexed as written. If single letters are separated by spaces, index each letter as a separate unit. An acronym (a word formed from the first, or first few, letters of several words, such as NASDAQ and ARCO) is indexed as one unit regardless of punctuation or spacing. Abbreviated words (Mfg., Corp., Inc.) and names (IBM, GE) are indexed as one unit regardless of punctuation or spacing. Radio and television station call letters (KDKA,WNBC) are indexed as one unit.

RULE 5: TITLES AND SUFFIXES

A. Personal Names

A title before a name (Dr., Miss, Mr., Mrs., Ms., Professor, Sir, Sister), a seniority suffix (II, III, Jr., Sr.), or a professional suffix (CRM, DDS, Mayor, MD, PhD, Senator) after a name is the last indexing unit.

Numeric suffixes (II, III) are filed before alphabetic suffixes (Jr., Mayor, Senator, Sr.). If a name contains a title and a suffix (Ms. Lucy Wheeler, DVM), the title *Ms* is the last unit.

Royal and religious titles followed by either a given name or a surname only (Princess Anne, Father Leo) are indexed and filed as written.

B. Business Names

Titles in business names (Capt. Hook's Bait Shop) are indexed as written. Remember, the word *The* is considered the last indexing unit when it appears as the first word "of a business name."

RULE 6: PREFIXES, ARTICLES, AND PARTICLES

A foreign article or particle in a personal or business name is combined with the part of the name following it to form a single indexing unit. The indexing order is not affected by a space between a prefix and the rest of the name (Alexander La Guardia), and the space is disregarded when indexing.

Examples of articles and particles are: a la, D', Da, De, Del, De La, Della, Den, Des, Di, Dos, Du, E', El, Fitz, Il, L', La, Las, Le, Les, Lo, Los, M', Mac, Mc, O', Per, Saint, San, Santa, Santo, St., Ste., Te, Ten, Ter, Van, Van de, Van der, Von, Von der.

RULE 7: NUMBERS IN BUSINESS NAMES

Numbers spelled out (Seven Lakes Nursery) in business names are filed alphabetically. Numbers written in digits in business names are filed before business names with alphabetic letters or words (B4 Photographers comes before Beleau Building and Loan).

Names with numbers written in digits in the first units are filed in ascending order (lowest to highest number) before alphabetic names (229 Club, 534 Shop, First National Bank of Chicago). Arabic numerals are filed before Roman numerals (2 Brothers Deli, 5 Cities Transit, XII Knights Inn). Names containing Roman numerals are filed in ascending order according to their Arabic number equivalencies. VIII-Ball Club, XL Days & XL Nights Motel, C-Note Lounge (8, 40, 100); Lucky VII Casino, Lucky X Car Wash, Lucky LX Drive-In (7, 10, 60). A chart of Roman numerals is shown in Figure B.1.

FIGURE B.1 **Table of Roman Numerals**

I	1	XX	20
II	2	XXX	30
III	3	XL	40
IV	4	L	50
V	5	LX	60
VI	6	LXX	70
VII	7	LXXX	80
VIII	8	XC	90
IX	9	C	100
X	10	D	500
		M	1000

Names with inclusive numbers (20–39 Singles Club) are arranged by the first digit(s) only (20). Names with numbers appearing in other than the first position (Pier 36 Cafe) are filed alphabetically and immediately before a similar name without a number (Pier 36 Cafe comes before Pier and Port Cafe).

When indexing names with numbers written in digit form that contain *st, d,* and *th* (1st Mortgage Co., 2d Avenue Cinemas, 3d Street Pest Control), ignore the letter endings and consider only the digits (1, 2, 3).

When indexing names with a number (in figures or words) linked by a hyphen to a letter or word (A-1 Laundry, Fifty-Eight Auto Body, 10-Minute Photo), ignore the hyphen and treat it as a single unit (A1, FiftyEight, 10Minute).

When indexing names with a number plus a symbol (55+ Social Center), treat it as a single unit and change the symbol to a word (55Plus).

RULE 8: ORGANIZATIONS AND INSTITUTIONS

Banks and other financial institutions, clubs, colleges, hospitals, hotels, lodges, magazines, motels, museums, newspapers, religious institutions, schools, unions, universities, and other organizations and institutions are indexed and filed according to the names written on their letterheads.

RULE 9: IDENTICAL NAMES

Retrieving the correct record is easy when using a computer database containing identical names of people or businesses. A records management database typically contains a unique field with information specific to a particular person or business name–often a phone number, a special identification number, or an assigned number generated by the database software. Because each person or business has a unique identifier, filers do not need to look for other information to determine which person is which.

Determining which person or business is the correct one when correspondence files contain other identical names can be a challenge. When personal names and names of businesses, institutions, and organizations are identical (including titles as explained in Rule 5), the filing order is determined by the addresses. Compare addresses in the following order:

1. City names.
2. State or province names (if city names are identical).
3. Street names, including *Avenue, Boulevard, Drive,* and *Street* (if city and state names are identical).
   - **a.** When the first units of street names are written in digits (18th Street), the names are considered in ascending numeric order (1, 2, 3) and placed together before alphabetic street names (18th Street, 24th Avenue, Academy Circle).
   - **b.** Street names written as digits are filed before street names written as words (22nd Street, 34th Avenue, First Street, Second Avenue).
   - **c.** Street names with compass directions (North, South, East, and West) are considered as written (SE Park Avenue, South Park Avenue).
   - **d.** Street names with numbers written as digits after compass directions are considered before alphabetic street names (East 8th Street, East Main Street, Sandusky Drive, South Eighth Avenue).
4. House or building numbers (if city, state, and street names are identical).
   - **a.** House and building numbers written as digits are considered in ascending numeric order (8 Riverside Terrace, 912 Riverside Terrace) and placed together before spelled-out building names (The Riverside Terrace).
   - **b.** House and building numbers written as words are filed after house and building numbers written as digits (11 Park Avenue South, One Park Avenue).
   - **c.** If a street address and a building name are included in an address, disregard the building name.
   - **d.** ZIP Codes are not considered in determining filing order.

RULE 10: GOVERNMENT NAMES

Government names are indexed first by the name of the governmental unit—city, county, state, or country. Next, index the distinctive name of the department, bureau, office, or board. A discussion of local and regional, state, federal, and foreign government names follows.

A. Local and Regional Government Names

The first indexing unit is the name of the county, city, town, township, or village. *Charlotte Sanitation Department* is an example. *Charlotte* (a city) would be the first indexing unit. Next, index the most distinctive name of the department, board, bureau, office, or government/political division. In this case, *Sanitation* would be the most distinctive name of the department. The words *County of, City of, Department of, Office of,* etc., are retained for clarity and are considered separate indexing units. If *of* is not a part of the official name as written, it is not added as an indexing unit.

B. State Government Names

Similar to local and regional political/governmental agencies, the first indexing unit is the name of the state or province. Then index the most distinctive name of the department, board, bureau, office, or government/ political division. The words *State of, Province of, Department of,* etc., are retained for clarity and are considered separate indexing units. If *of* is not a part of the official name as written, it is not added as an indexing unit.

C. Federal Government Names

Use three indexing "levels" (rather than units) for the United States federal government. Consider *United States Government* as the first level. The second level is the name of a department or top-level agency that is rearranged to show the most distinctive part first; for example, *Agriculture Department (of).* Level three is the next most distinctive name; for example, *Forest Service.* The words *of* and *of the* are extraneous and should not be considered when indexing.

D. Foreign Government Names

The name of a foreign government and its agencies is often written in a foreign language. When indexing foreign names, begin by writing the English translation of the government name on the document. The English name is the first indexing unit. Then index the balance of the formal name of the government, if needed, or if it is in the official name (China Republic of). Branches, departments, and divisions follow in order by their distinctive names. States, colonies, provinces, cities, and other divisions of foreign governments are followed by their distinctive or official names as spelled in English.

CROSS-REFERENCING

Some records of persons and businesses may be requested by a name that is different from the one by which it was stored. Such requests may occur often if the key unit is difficult to determine. When a record is likely to be requested by more than one name, an aid called a *cross-reference* is prepared. A cross-reference shows the name in a form other than the one used on the original record, and it indicates the storage location of the original record. The filer can then find requested records regardless of the name used in the request for those records.

Cross-references for data stored in an electronic database are often not needed. Because the search features of database software are extensive, a record can usually be found easily using any part of the filing segment. Also, entire records are often visible when a search result shows on the screen. In some instances, however, a cross-reference may be needed under an entirely different name. In these instances, a cross-reference database record can be created.

Four types of personal names should be cross-referenced:

1. Unusual names
2. Hyphenated surnames
3. Alternate names
4. Similar names

Also, nine types of business names should be cross-referenced.

1. Compound names
2. Names with abbreviations and acronyms
3. Popular and coined names
4. Hyphenated names
5. Divisions and subsidiaries
6. Changed names
7. Similar names
8. Foreign business names
9. Foreign government names

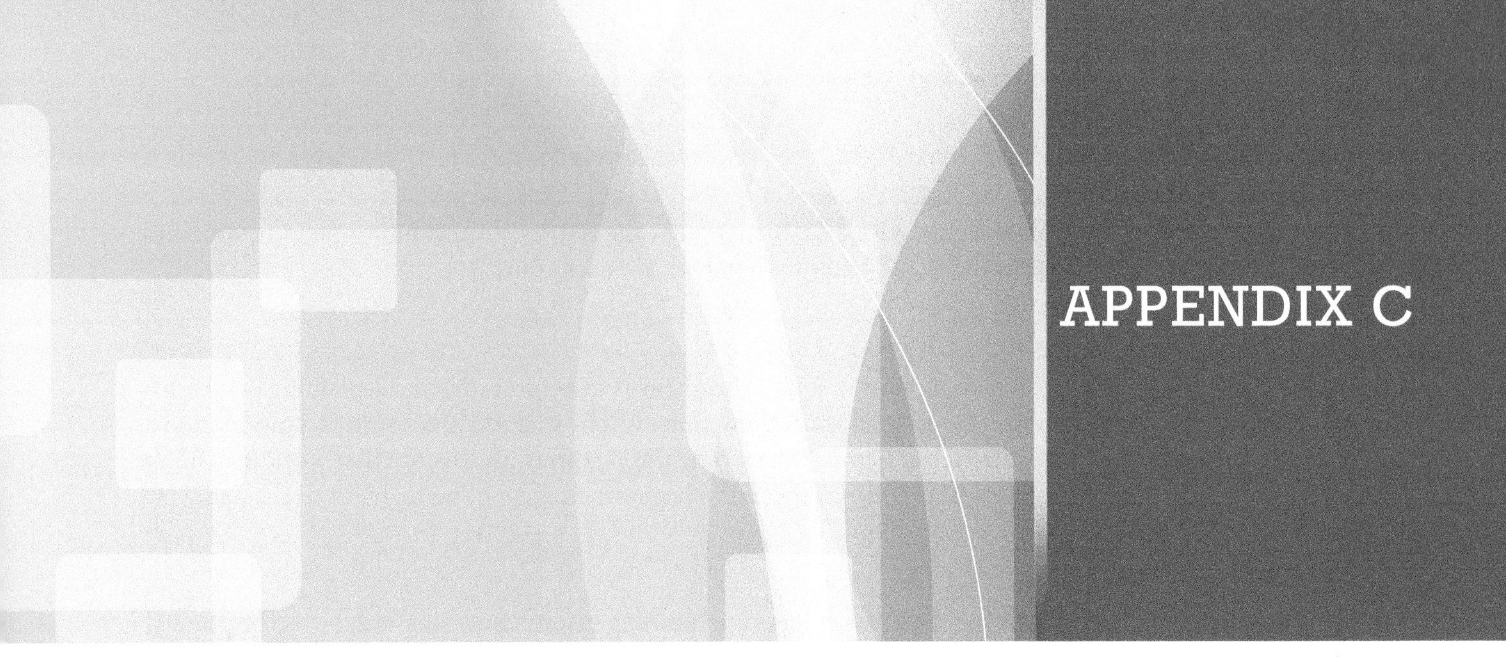

ARMA International's Alphabetic Indexing Rules

OVERVIEW OF ALPHABETIC INDEXING

Alphabetic indexing rules are followed in arranging alphabetic sequences in subject, alphabetic, and alpha-numeric systems. This chapter contains general and specific rules from which to select in the development of a filing system. General rules can be applied to all systems, without hesitation, because of their widespread acceptance and use. They are the fundamental standards that ensure consistency in filing and are the first step toward automated filing and retrieval.

The standard rules use the "unit-by-unit" filing method and define a unit as a number, letter, word, or any combination of them. Refer to the individual rule to determine the specific delineation of a filing unit. An entire personal, organizational, or governmental name is generally comprised of two or more filing units that together are considered a filing segment.

Different offices have different needs for information storage and retrieval. Examine and analyze those needs before developing a new filing system or changing the existing one. Efficiency and effectiveness are the primary aims when designing a filing solution. Document the solutions being implemented and their application to the organization's filing needs.

Everyone using the filing system must be thoroughly instructed in its design. Individuals responsible for filing and retrieving documents and information should receive periodic refresher training in proper system operation. Consistency in filing and retrieving documents and information is the goal.

GENERAL ALPHABETIC INDEXING RULES

When consistently applied, the following general rules will help ensure the development of an effective and efficient filing system.

1. Filing Segments

Alphabetize filing segments (e.g., file names) by arranging them in unit-by-unit order and letter-by-letter within each unit.

2. Filing Units

Each filing unit in a filing segment is to be considered. Depending on the filing system developed, these units might include prepositions, conjunctions, and articles. Because the word "the" is often used as the first word in a filing segment, it is moved from the beginning of the filing segment to the end.

3. Nothing before Something

The standard rule of indexing "nothing before something" might also be phrased "the least before the most." For example, the filing segment for a document about proposed changes to the design of a ship is "New Ark Ship Company." It would be filed immediately preceding a document with "Newark Produce Company" as the filing segment, even though the same letters in the same order are used in the first units of both filing segments. That is, the filing segment starting with a word using only three letters (New) would be filed before a filing segment starting with the same three letters but in a longer word (Newark).

4. Punctuation, Special Characters, Diacritical Marks

Ignore all punctuation, special characters, and diacritical marks when alphabetizing. Punctuation marks include periods, commas, dashes, hyphens, apostrophes, etc. Special characters include®, ™, etc. Diacritical marks include any marks used for pronunciation purposes. Hyphenated words might be considered one unit depending on the filing system developed.

5. Numbers (Arabic and Roman)

Arabic (e.g., 1, 2, 3) and Roman (e.g., I, II, III) numbers are filed sequentially before alphabetic characters. All Arabic numerals precede all Roman numerals. (This sequencing might not be possible in an automated system without a separate field for the numeric data because the characters used for Roman numerals are alphabetic characters and will sort as such in an automated system.)

6. Acronyms, Abbreviations, Call Letters

Acronyms, abbreviations, and broadcast station call letters are filed as one unit.

7. Common Usage vs. Legal Form

Index the most commonly used name or title, and cross-reference the other names or titles by which the indexed name might be known or requested. (This rule can be reversed if the name indexed in an automated system is also used for labels or reports, and the organization requires the legal form of the name on the labels and reports.)

For ARMA's publication "Establishing Alphabetic, Numeric, Subject Filing Systems," visit www.arma.org/go/prod/v4726.

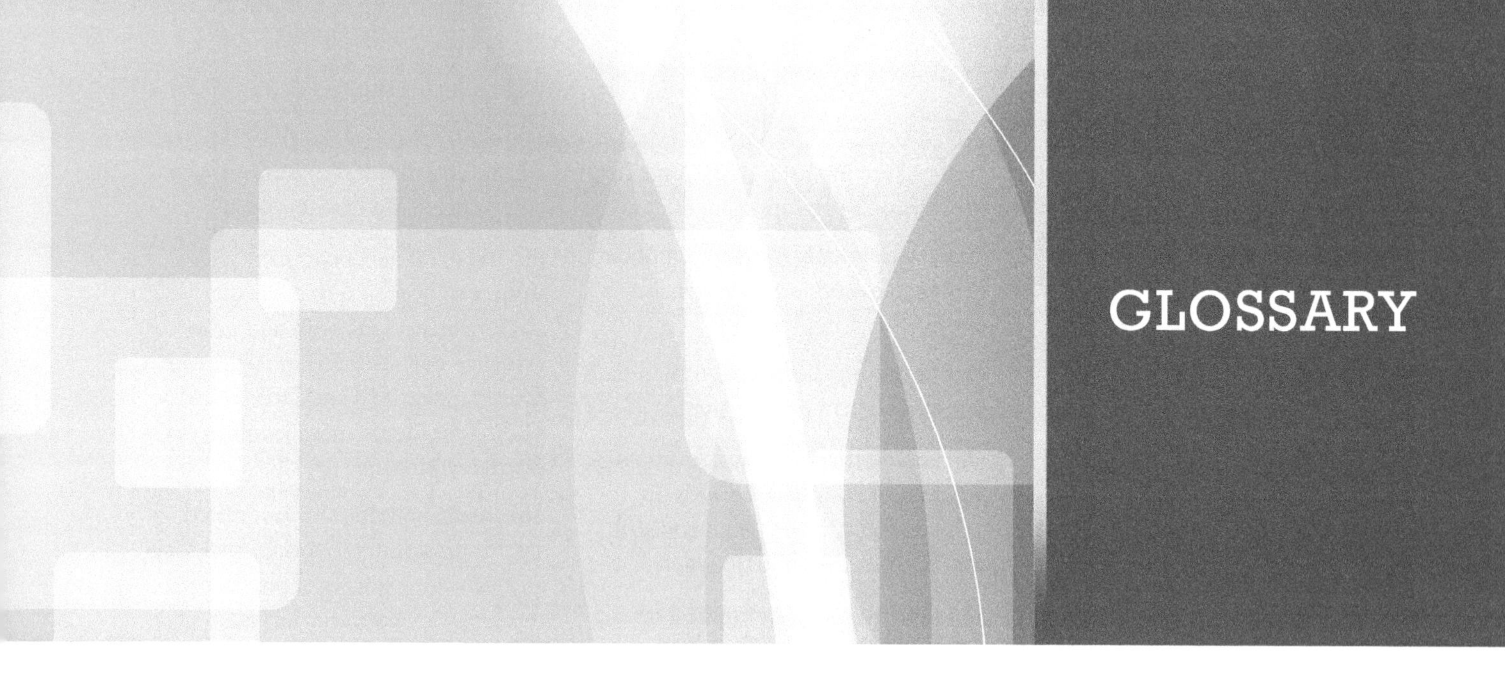

GLOSSARY

A

accession log A serial list of numbers assigned to records in a numeric storage system, also called an *accession book* or *numeric filelist*.

active records Frequently used records needed to perform current operations.

AIIM (Association for Information and Image Management) A global, nonprofit organization that provides independent research, education, and certification programs to information professionals.

alphabetic index A reference to a numeric file, organized alphabetically, that is used when the name or subject is known, but not the assigned number.

alphabetic records management A method of storing and arranging records according to the letters of the alphabet.

alphanumeric coding A coding system that combines letters and numbers, in combination with punctuation marks, to develop codes for classifying and retrieving information.

archive records Records that have continuing or historical value and are preserved permanently by an organization.

archives Records that are preserved because of their historical or continuing value; also the building or area where archival materials are stored.

ARMA International An association for information management professionals.

ARMA's Generally Accepted Recordkeeping Principles® ("The Principles") Form the foundation for which an effective information governance program can be built.

B

backup A copy of electronic files and/or folders as a precaution against the loss or damage of the original data.

block-numeric coding A coding system based on the assignment of number ranges to subjects.

blog A shared online journal.

bring your own device (BYOD) The policy to allow employees to use their own smartphones, tablets, and laptops to access corporate information.

born digital Information in which the original source of content is digital.

C

caption A title, heading, short explanation, or description of a document or records.

charge-out A control procedure to establish the current location of a record when it is not in the records center or central file, which can be a manual or automated system.

charge-out and follow-up file A tickler file that contains requisition forms filed by dates that records are due back in the inactive records center.

charge-out log A written or electronic form filed by dates that records are due back in the inactive records center.

chronologic storage A method by which records are filed in date sequence, either in reverse sequence (with the most recent date on top) or forward sequence (with the oldest record first).

cloud Internet or a network of servers.

cloud computing A model for enabling convenient, on-demand network access to a shared pool of configurable computing resources (e.g., networks, servers, storage, applications, and services) that can be rapidly provisioned and released with minimal management effort or service provider interaction.

coding The act of assigning a file designation to records as they are classified.

color accenting The consistent use of different colors for different supplies in the storage system—one color for guides, various colors for folders, one color for OUT indicators, and specific colors of labels or stripes on labels.

color coding Using color as an identifying aid in a filing system to divide the alphabetic sections in the storage system.

compass point Any of 32 horizontal directions indicated on the card of a compass.

compass term A compass point used as part of a company name or subject.

consecutive numbering method A method in which consecutively numbered records are arranged in *ascending* number order—from the lowest number to the highest number.

cross-reference Shows the name in a form other than that used on the original record, and it indicates the storage location of the original record.

cross-reference guide A special guide that serves as a permanent marker in storage indicating that all records pertaining to a correspondent are stored elsewhere.

cross-reference sheet A sheet placed in an alternative location in the file that directs the filer to a specific record stored in a different location other than where the filer is searching.

D

data migration The process of moving data from one electronic system to another, usually in upgrading hardware or software, without having to undergo a major conversion or re-inputting of data.

data warehouse A collection of data designed to support management decision making.

database A collection of related data stored on a computer system.

decimal-numeric coding A numeric method of classifying records by subject, in units of 10 and coded for arrangement in numeric order.

density The degree of optical opacity of a material that determines the amount of light that will pass through it or reflect from it.

destruction date file A tickler file containing copies of forms completed when records are received in a records center.

destruction file A file that contains information on the actual destruction of inactive records.

destruction notice A notification of the scheduled destruction of records.

destruction suspension A hold placed on the scheduled destruction of records.

dictionary arrangement A single alphabetic filing arrangement in which all types of entries (names, subjects, titles, etc.) are interfiled in alphabetic order.

digital signature Electronic signature, or *e-signature*, consists of a string of characters and numbers added as a code on electronic documents being transmitted by computer.

direct access A method of accessing records by going directly to the file without first referring to an index or a list of names to find a document or folder.

disaster recovery plan A plan developed and implemented to provide guidance for protecting records and information and continuing business operations when emergencies and disasters occur.

discovery When a company is subject to litigation or a lawsuit, all information, records, and other evidence that are relevant to the case must be identified and retrieved. These procedures are called the discovery process.

document imaging An automated system for scanning, storing, retrieving, and managing images of physical records in an electronic format.

duplex-numeric coding A coding system using numbers (or sometimes letters) with two or more parts separated by a dash, space, or comma.

E

e-commerce An electronic method to communicate and to transact business over networks and through computers.

e-discovery The process of identifying and providing all electronically stored information and records relevant to the case.

electronic data interchange (EDI) A communication procedure between two companies that allows the exchange of standardized documents (most commonly invoices or purchase orders) through computers.

electronic fund transfer (EFT) Electronic payments and collections.

electronic mail (e-mail) A system that enables users to compose, transmit, receive, and manage electronic documents and images across networks.

electronic record A record that can be readily accessed or changed and is stored on electronic storage media.

electronic records life cycle Consists of five phases: creation, classification, use and distribution, retention and maintenance, and disposition.

encryption The process of converting meaningful information into a numeric code that is only understood by the intended recipient of the information.

encyclopedic arrangement A subject filing arrangement in which records are filed under the specific subtitle to which they relate.

encyclopedic arrangement The alphabetic arrangement of major geographic divisions plus one or more geographic subdivisions also arranged in alphabetic order.

enterprise content management (ECM) The strategies, methods, and tools used to capture, manage, store, preserve, and deliver content and documents related to organizational processes.

external record A record created for use outside of the organization. It may be created inside or outside of the organization.

F

field A set of one or more characters treated as a unit of information.

file name A unique name given to a file stored for computer use that must follow the computer's operating system rules.

file plan A classification scheme that defines and identifies all files, including indexing and storage of the files, and referencing the disposition schedule of each file.

filing method The way in which records are stored in a container, such as a filing cabinet or a folder on a hard disk, on a removable storage device, or in the cloud.

filing segment The name by which a record is stored and requested.

firewall A combination hardware and software buffer that many organizations place between their internal networks and the Internet.

flash drive A read/write device that attaches to a computer and is usable as a standard hard drive.

folder (or directory): A subdivision of storage space created by the operating system of a computer.

follow-up A system for ensuring the timely and proper return of materials charged out from a file.

follower block (compressor) A device at the back of a file drawer that can be moved to allow contraction or expansion of the drawer contents.

form A physical or electronic document with a fixed arrangement of predetermined spaces designed for entering and extracting prescribed information or variable data.

G

general folder A folder for records to and from correspondents, that has a small volume of records that does not require an individual folder.

geographic filing system The classification of records by geographic location usually arranged by numeric code or in alphabetic order.

geographic information system (GIS) A computer system designed to allow users to collect, manage, and analyze large volumes of data referenced to a geographic location by some type of geographic coordinates such as longitude and latitude.

geographic records management A method of storing and retrieving records by location using a geographic filing system.

guide A rigid divider used to identify a section in a file and to facilitate reference to a particular record location.

H

HTML (Hyper Text Markup Language) The language the Internet browsers such as Internet Explorer, Google Chrome, or Mozilla Firefox interpret and display.

I

IaaS (Infrastructure as a Service): Cloud service that provides infrastructure, such as computers (physical or servers) and other resources.

image record Digital or photographic representation of a record on any medium such as microfilm, optical disk, or solid state devices.

inactive records Records that do not have to be readily available but which must be kept for legal, fiscal, or historical purposes.

inactive records index An index of all records in the inactive records storage center.

index A systematic guide that allows access to specific items contained within a larger body of information.

indexing The mental process of determining the filing segment (or name) by which a physical record is to be stored and the placing or listing of items in an order that follows a particular system.

indexing order The order in which units of the filing segment are considered.

indexing rules Written procedures that describe how the filing segments are ordered.

indexing units The various words that make up the filing segment for the physical record.

indirect access A method of access to records that requires prior use of an external index.

individual folder A folder used to store the records of an individual correspondent, with enough records to warrant a separate folder.

information governance (IG) The overarching framework within which the records and information management (RIM) program resides.

inspecting Checking a record to determine whether it is ready to be filed.

internal record A record that contains information needed to operate an organization.

Internet A worldwide network of computers that allows public access to send, store, and receive electronic information over public networks.

ISO 15489 A standard for records management policies and procedures.

K

key unit The first unit of a filing segment.

L

label A device that contains the name of the person, subject, or number assigned to the file folder or section contents.

lettered guide plan An arrangement of geographic records with primary guides labeled with alphabetic letters.

location name guide plan An arrangement of geographic records with primary guides labeled with location names.

M

magnetic media A variety of magnetically coated materials used by computers for data storage.

magnification ratio A method of describing the relationship between the size of an image and the original record when viewed on a microfilm reader screen.

master index A printed alphabetic listing in file order of all subjects used as subject titles in the filing system.

media compatibility Refers to how well the media and the equipment needed to access information stored on the media work together.

media stability Refers to the length of time the media will maintain its original quality so that it can continue to be used.

metadata Structured information that describes, explains, locates, or otherwise makes it easier to retrieve, use, or manage an information resource.

microforms Photographic document storage media. Microform is the collective term for all microimages such as microfilm, microfiche, aperture cards, and microfilm jackets.

micrographics The technology by which recorded information can be quickly reduced to a microform, stored conveniently, and then easily retrieved for reference and use.

middle-digit storage A numeric storage method in which the middle digits are used as the primary division for organizing the filing system.

N

name index A listing of correspondents' names stored in a subject file.

nonconsecutive numbering A system of numbers that has blocks of numbers omitted.

nonrecord An item that is not usually included within the scope of official records such as a day file, reference materials, and drafts.

numeric index A current list of all files by the file numbers.

numeric records management Any classification system for arranging records that is based on numbers.

O

office of record An office designated to maintain the *record* or *official copy* of a particular record.

official record A significant, vital, or important record of continuing value to be protected, managed, and retained according to established retention schedules.

on-call form A written request for a record that is out of the file.

one-period transfer method A method of transferring records from active storage at the end of one period of time, usually once or twice a year, to inactive storage.

operating system An organized collection of software that controls the overall operations of a computer.

optical character recognition (OCR) Machine reading of printed or written characters through the use of light-sensitive materials or devices.

optical media A high-density information storage medium where digitally encoded information is both written and read by means of a laser.

OUT indicator A control device, such as a guide, sheet, or folder, that shows the location of borrowed records.

P

PaaS (Platform as a Service): A category of cloud computing services that provides hardware and an operating system that is RIM ready.

password A string of characters known to the computer system and a user, who must specify it to gain access to the system.

periodic transfer method A method of transferring active records at the end of a stated period of time—usually 1 year—to inactive storage.

perpetual transfer method A method of transferring records continuously from active to inactive storage areas whenever they are no longer needed for reference.

personal digital assistant (PDA) A handheld computer that is portable, easy to use, and capable of sharing information with a desktop or notebook computer.

pick list A list containing specific records needed for a given program or project.

podcast A broadcast sent over the Internet to receivers who hear and/or view the information via computers or other electronic devices.

portable document format (pdf) Users can easily save a file as a pdf and set the properties so that the document cannot be altered.

position The location of the tab across the top or down one side of a guide or folder.

primary guide A divider that identifies a main division or section of a file and always precedes all other material in a section.

pull technology Occurs when the user initiates the request for the data each time.

push technology Allows a central server to notify a computer or cell phone when an event occurs.

Q

query A database object used to instruct the program to find specific information.

R

radio frequency identification (RFID) A technology that incorporates the use of an electromagnetic or electrostatic radio frequency to identify an object, animal, or person.

record (computer record) All the fields related to one person or organization make up a record.

record Stored information, regardless of media or characteristics, made or received by an organization that is evidence of its operations and has value requiring its retention for a specific period of time.

record copy The official copy of a record that is retained for legal, operational, or historical purposes.

records and information life cycle The life span of a record as expressed in the five phases of creation, distribution, use, maintenance, and final disposition.

records audit A periodic inspection to verify that an operation is in compliance with a records and information management program.

records center box A box designed to hold approximately one cubic foot of records, either legal or letter size.

records center A low-cost centralized area for housing and servicing inactive records whose reference rates do not warrant their retention in a prime office space.

records destruction The disposal of records of no further value beyond any possible reconstruction.

records disposition The final destination of records after they have reached the end of their retention period.

records inventory A detailed listing that could include the types, locations, dates, volume, equipment, classification systems, and usage date of an organization's records.

records management The systematic control of all records from their creation or receipt, through their processing, distribution, organization, storage, and retrieval, to their ultimate disposition.

records retention program A program established and maintained to provide retention periods for records in an organization.

records retention schedule (RRS) A comprehensive list of records series titles, indicating for each the length of time it is to be maintained.

records series A group of related records filed and used together as a unit and evaluated as a unit for retention purposes.

records system A group of interrelated resources—people, equipment and supplies, space, procedures, and information—acting together according to a plan to accomplish the goals of the records and information management program.

records transfer The act of changing the physical custody of records with or without change of legal title or moving them from one storage area to another.

reduction ratio The relationship between the dimensions of the original or master and the corresponding dimensions of the photographed image.

reference record A record that contains information needed to carry on the operations of an organization over long periods.

relative index A dictionary-type listing of all possible words and combinations of words by which records may be requested.

release mark An agreed-upon mark such as initials or a symbol placed onto a record to show that the record is ready for storage.

requisition A written request for a record or information from a record.

resolution A measure of the sharpness or fine detail of an image.

retention period The time that records must be kept according to operational, legal, regulatory, and fiscal requirements.

retrieval The process of locating and removing a record or file from storage or accessing information from stored data on a computer system.

S

SaaS (Software as a Service): Cloud service that provides software licensing and a delivery model where software is licensed on a subscription basis.

scanner A device that converts an image (text, graphic, or photograph) of a document into electronic form for processing and storage.

SEE ALSO cross-reference A notation on a folder tab or cross-reference sheet that directs the filer to multiple locations for related information.

smartphone A cell phone with software applications and access to the Internet.

social media Forms of electronic communication (as websites for social networking and microblogging) through which users create online communities to share information, ideas, personal messages, and other content (such as videos).

social media posts The interactions among people on a social media website, such as Facebook, including photos.

solid state drives (SSDs) Provide data storage on interconnected flash memory chips. The data are retained even when the device is not plugged into a power source.

sorting Arranging records in the sequence in which they are to be filed or stored.

special (auxiliary) guide A divider used to lead the eye quickly to a specific place in a file.

special folder A folder that follows a special guide in an alphabetic arrangement.

storage The placement of records, according to a plan, on a shelf or in a file drawer or saving an electronic record.

storage method A systematic way of storing records according to an alphabetic, subject, numeric, geographic, or chronologic plan.

storing Placing records into storage containers.

strategic plan A document used to communicate with the organization the organization's goals, actions needed to achieve those goals, and all other critical elements developed during the planning exercise.

strategic planning A systematic process of envisioning a desired future and translating this vision into broadly defined goals or objectives and a sequence of steps to achieve them.

structured data Information that resides in fixed fields within a record or file, such as databases and spreadsheets.

subject records management An alphabetic system of storing and retrieving records by their subject or topic.

suspension (hanging) folder A folder with built-in hooks on each side that hang from parallel metal rails on each side of a file drawer or other storage equipment.

T

tab A projection for a caption on a folder or guide that extends above the regular height or beyond the regular width of the folder or guide.

tables Data in a table are organized in fields and records.

tablet computer A mobile computer that has a touchscreen on which you can directly input data and navigate using your fingers or a stylus.

taxonomy A high-level, hierarchical classification system for documents and records that facilitates the management of recorded information throughout its life cycle.

terminal-digit storage A numeric storage method in which the last two or three digits of each number are used as the primary division under which a record is filed, and groups of numbers are read from right to left.

tickler file A date-sequenced file by which matters pending are flagged for attention on the proper date.

transaction record A document used in an organization's day-to-day operations.

tweet A short message posted on the Twitter® social network website.

U

unstructured information Include text files generated from word processing documents, e-mails, PDF files, blogs, social media posts, tweets, and web pages.

V

virus A computer program that replicates itself into other programs that are shared among systems with the intention of causing damage.

W

wanted form A written request for a record that is out of the file.

webinar A video presentation given over the World Wide Web.

wiki A page or collection of web pages that allows people who access the site to contribute or modify content.

X

XaaS (Delivered as a Service) Cloud service on demand with a minimum contract.

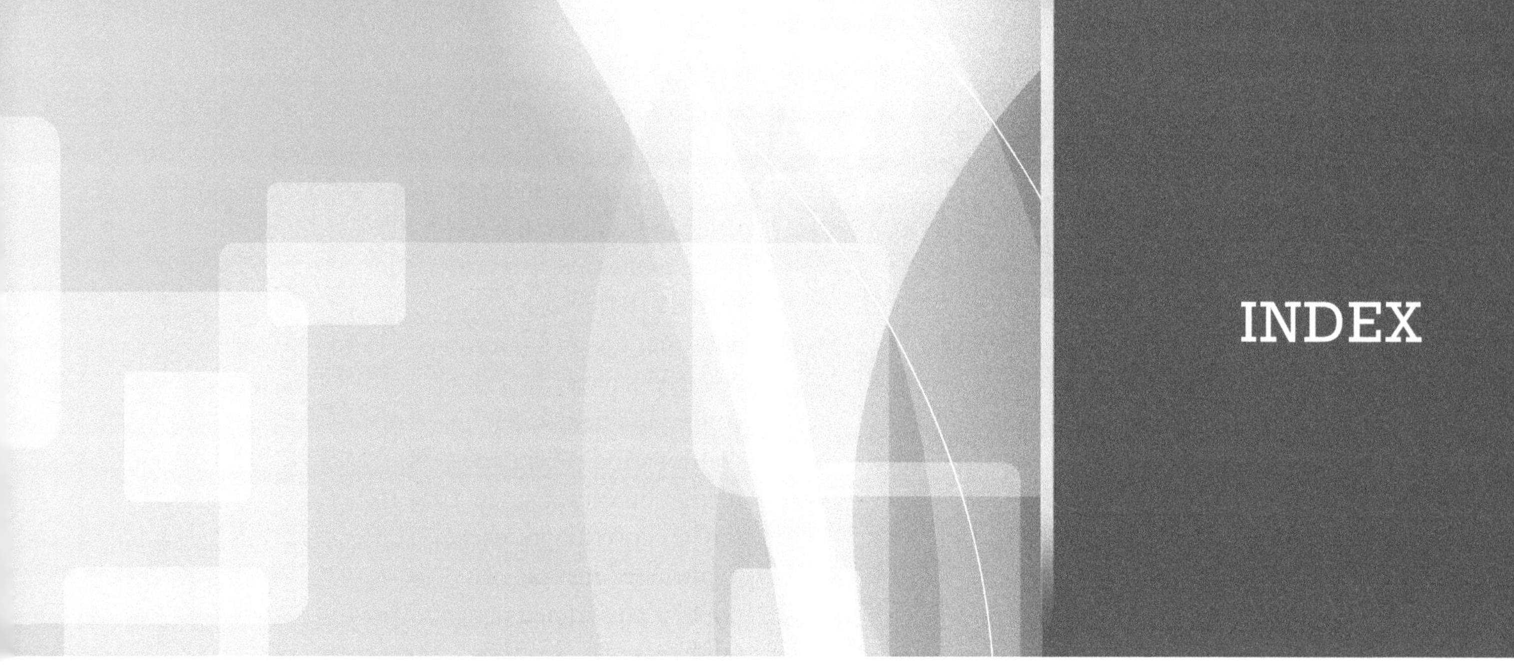

INDEX

A

F

G

N

O

T

U